CRIME, INSTITUTIONAL KNOWLEDGE AND POWER

PIONEERS IN CONTEMPORARY CRIMINOLOGY

Series Editor: David Nelken

The titles in this series bring together the best published and unpublished work by the leading authorities in contemporary criminological theory. By drawing together articles from a wide range of journals, conference proceedings and books, each title makes readily available the authors' most important writings on specific themes. Each volume in this series includes a lengthy introduction, written by the editor and a significant piece of scholarship in its own right, which outlines the context of the work and comments on its significance and potential. The collected essays complement each other to give a retrospective view of the authors' achievements and a picture of the development of criminology as a whole.

Titles in the series

A Criminological Imagination
Pat Carlen

Working Out of Crime
David Downes

Building Modern Criminology: Forays and Skirmishes
David F. Greenberg

Crime, Institutional Knowledge and Power:
The Rich Criminological Legacy of Richard Ericson
Kevin D. Haggerty, Aaron Doyle and Janet Chan (eds)

Policing, Popular Culture and Political Economy
Robert Reiner

Victims, Policy-making and Criminological Theory
Paul Rock

Transnational Crime and Policing
James Sheptycki

Thinking about Punishment
Michael Tonry

Crime, Institutional Knowledge and Power

The Rich Criminological Legacy of Richard Ericson

KEVIN D. HAGGERTY,
University of Alberta, Canada

AARON DOYLE
Carleton University, Canada

JANET CHAN
University of New South Wales, Australia

PIONEERS IN CONTEMPORARY CRIMINOLOGY SERIES

Routledge
Taylor & Francis Group
LONDON AND NEW YORK

First published 2011 by Ashgate Publishing

2 Park Square, Milton Park, Abingdon, Oxfordshire OX14 4RN
711 Third Avenue, New York, NY 10017

Routledge is an imprint of the Taylor & Francis Group, an informa business

First issued in paperback 2018

British Library Cataloguing in Publication Data
Ericson, Richard Victor.
Crime, institutional knowledge and power : the rich criminological legacy of Richard Ericson. – (Pioneers in contemporary criminology)
1. Criminology.
I. Title II. Series III. Haggerty, Kevin D. IV. Doyle, Aaron. V. Chan, Janet B. L.
364-dc22

Library of Congress Control Number: 2011925715

ISBN 978-0-7546-2983-2 (hbk)
ISBN 978-1-138-37869-8 (pbk)

Contents

Acknowledgements *vii*

Introduction *ix*

1 Being Free
Young Offenders and Their Social Work, 1975, pp. 167–204. 1

2 Social Distance and Reaction to Criminality
British Journal of Criminology, **17**, 1977, pp. 16–29. 41

3 The Occupational Environment of Detective Work
Making Crime: A Study of Detective Work, 1981, pp. 41–67. 55

4 Dealing with Victim-Complainants
Reproducing Order: A Study of Police Patrol Work, 1982, pp. 100–36. 83

5 Order out of Court II: The Position of the Accused and the Plea Decision
(with Patricia M. Baranek) *The Ordering of Justice*, 1982, pp. 152–78. 125

6 Patrolling the Facts: Secrecy and Publicity in Police Work
British Journal of Sociology, **40**, 1989, pp. 205–26. 155

7 Media and Markets
(with Patricia M. Baranek and Janet B.L. Chan) *Representing Order: Crime, Law and Justice in the News Media*, 1991, pp. 20–46. 177

8 How Journalists Visualize Fact
Annals of the American Academy of Political and Social Science, **560**, 1998, pp. 83–95. 207

9 The Moral Hazards of Neo-Liberalism: Lessons from the Private Insurance Industry
(with Dean Barry and Aaron Doyle) *Economy and Society*, **29**, 2000, pp. 532–58. 221

10 The Policing of Risk
(with Kevin D. Haggerty) *Embracing Risk: The Changing Culture of Insurance and Responsibility*, 2002, pp. 238–72. 249

11 Uncertainties of Earthquakes: Absorbing Risk, Mitigation, and Infrastructure (with Aaron Doyle) *Uncertain Business: Risk, Insurance and the Limits of Knowledge*, 2004, pp. 180–211. 285

12 National Security *Crime in an Insecure World*, 2007, pp. 36–71. 319

Name Index *359*

Acknowledgements

The chapters in this volume are taken from the sources listed below. The editors and publishers wish to thank the authors, original publishers or other copyright holders for permission to use their material as follows:

Chapter 1: 'Being Free', in *Young Offenders and Their Social Work*, Farnborough: Saxon House, 1975, pp. 167–204.

Chapter 2: 'Social Distance and Reaction to Criminality', *British Journal of Criminology*, **17**, 1977, pp. 16–29.

Chapter 3: 'The Occupational Environment of Detective Work', in *Making Crime: A Study of Detective Work*, Toronto: Butterworths, 1981, pp. 41–67. Copyright © 1981 Richard V. Ericson.

Chapter 4: 'Dealing with Victim-Complainants', in *Reproducing Order: A Study of Police Patrol Work*, Toronto: University of Toronto Press, 1982, pp. 100–36. Copyright © 1982 University of Toronto Press.

Chapter 5: 'Order out of Court II: The Position of the Accused and the Plea Decision', with Patricia Baranek, *The Ordering of Justice*, Toronto: Toronto University Press, 1982, pp. 152–78. Copyright © 1982 University of Toronto Press.

Chapter 6: 'Patrolling the Facts: Secrecy and Publicity in Police Work', *British Journal of Sociology*, **40**, 1989, pp. 205–26.

Chapter 7: 'Media and Markets', with Patricia M. Baranek and Janet B.L. Chan, *Representing Order: Crime, Law, and Justice in the News Media*, Milton Keynes: Open University Press, 1991, pp. 20–46. Copyright © 1991 Richard V. Ericson, Patricia M. Baranek and Janet B.L. Chan.

Chapter 8: 'How Journalists Visualize Fact', *Annals of the American Academy of Political and Social Science*, **560**, 1998, pp. 83–95.

Chapter 9: 'The Moral Hazards of Neo-Liberalism: Lessons from the Private Insurance Industry', with Dean Barry and Aaron Doyle, *Economy and Society*, **29**, 2000, pp. 532–58. Copyright © 2000 Taylor & Francis Ltd.

Chapter 10: 'The Policing of Risk', with Kevin Haggerty, in *Embracing Risk: The Changing Culture of Insurance and Responsibility*, Chicago: University of Chicago Press, 2002, pp. 238–72. Copyright © 2002 The University of Chicago Press.

Chapter 11: 'Uncertainties of Earthquakes: Absorbing Risk, Mitigation, and Infrastructure', with Aaron Doyle, in *Uncertain Business: Risk Insurance and the Limits of Knowledge*, Toronto: University of Toronto Press, 2004, pp. 180–211.

Chapter 12: 'National Security', in *Crime in an Insecure World*, Cambridge: Polity Press, 2007, pp. 36–71. Copyright © 2007 Richard Ericson.

Every effort has been made to trace all the copyright holders, but if any have been inadvertently overlooked the publishers will be pleased to make the necessary arrangement at the first opportunity.

Introduction

Criminology lost a world leader with the death of Richard V. Ericson at age 59 on 2 October 2007. Richard was one of the pre-eminent criminologists of the last 40 years and one of the most cited (see, for example, Cohn and Farrington, 2007). This volume has been produced by three of his former graduate students,[1] all of whom were involved for lengthy periods with Richard in collaborative research and writing. Those readers who are already familiar with a range of his work will appreciate the challenge of trying to select highlights from his extraordinarily productive and creative career. In this relatively brief Introduction, the three of us have also taken on another challenge: while we record for posterity some memories of Richard as a working criminologist, we also attempt to draw out some key aspects of what might be considered an Ericsonian approach to doing criminology – an approach illustrated by the 12 essays selected for this book. The latter aim offers a particular challenge because Richard himself never portrayed his work as constituting a unified perspective nor did he attempt to outline the tenets of such a perspective. Nevertheless, we argue that key elements of an Ericsonian approach to criminology can be identified, drawing both on his body of research and on our first-hand observations and reminiscences of him at work. In the first half of this Introduction, we draw out a number of key themes in Richard's research as illustrated by the essays in this volume, and show how each is representative of broader currents in his work. In the second half of this Introduction, we situate Richard's essays in the context of the various major studies from which they have been taken.

Doing Criminology the Ericson Way

From 1972 to 2007 Richard Ericson published 12 book-length research studies, plus five shorter research monographs, eight edited volumes and over 100 journal articles and book chapters, covering a range of topics from more conventional criminological areas such as law, justice, policing and crime control to broader social, cultural and economic issues pertaining to, for example, the news media, risk, security or insurance. We have identified, and represented in this volume, five central properties running through Richard's impressive body of work: a focus on institutions, knowledge and power; an examination of a broader range of institutions than are traditionally studied by criminologists; a deep connection with social theory; a strong commitment to interdisciplinarity; and a solid foundation in rich and diverse empirical data.

---

1 Richard Ericson successfully supervised over 40 Master's and more than a dozen PhD theses; a large number of his former doctoral students are professors of criminology, mostly at Canadian universities. Richard's generosity towards his students was legendary – this is perhaps the most enduring legacy of all.

A Focus on Institutions, Knowledge and Power

As demonstrated by the 12 selected essays, Richard Ericson's criminology focused on institutions, on the institutional production of knowledge and on how this is imbued with power relations. It did not focus on etiological questions about why people might or might not commit crime. Throughout his research career, Richard steered away from such questions, because, to him, they missed the point. For Richard, crime was not a naturally given phenomenon; instead, certain acts *become* crimes through highly variable institutional practices of categorization, monitoring and processing. Consequently, to understand crime, one must understand the various institutions that lay claim to the crime issue. Richard therefore dedicated his career to developing an 'institutional' approach to criminology, something that involves studying not only the institutions that help establish and process certain phenomena as crimes, but also some of the distinctive governmental techniques used by these institutions, such as surveillance, risk management and mobilizing accounts in the news media.

At one level, Richard was a social constructionist in that the focus of his work was the institutional production of knowledge. In all of his studies, Richard continually returned to questions about the power and paradoxes of official knowledge. This involved scrutiny of the production of official accounts, of shifts in the types of knowledges that institutions use to govern populations, of divergent institutional logics and structures for communicating knowledge, and of institutional decision-making in contexts of imperfect knowledge.

Indeed, Richard had a highly developed sense of irony, often focused on paradoxes in official knowledge and behaviour, and on the hypocrisy of official accounts. He searched for moments of irony as sociologically revealing: 'Irony provides critical understanding of what is taken for granted in institutions, which in turn reveals the limits of those institutions' (Ericson, Doyle and Barry, 2003, p. 94). Richard also loved language and used word-play to illustrate such ironies: for example, accountability became instead 'account ability' (Ericson, 1995), meaning the ability of institutions, when called to account, to produce self-serving official narratives and to have them accepted by others as legitimate. Thus, a sly shift in wording inverted the original meaning of the term.

The Criminological Study of a Broader Range of Institutions

As Ian Loader wrote recently, 'Ericson will, I suspect, long be remembered, read and hugely influential as a gifted and astute sociologist of institutions' (Loader, 2008, p. 409). A major Ericson-headed research project typically culminated in several large volumes dedicated to different facets of a particular institution. The law, as a regulatory and symbolic institution that cross-cuts others, features strongly in Richard's work. His criminology also expanded the range of institutions normally studied by criminologists, in order to examine some new institutions that produce crime and justice. Richard's work crossed many boundaries; the diversity of his research areas and theoretical avenues is a consequence of both his intellectual curiosity and his conscious desire to avoid intellectual stagnation, something he did by reinventing himself academically approximately every decade. He shifted his research focus first in the 1980s from policing and the justice system (see Chapters 1–6 and 10) to the news media as another key institution that produces crime and deviance (see Chapters 7 and 8). Then, starting in the 1990s, he moved on to examine the hidden world of insurance (see Chapters 9 and 11) and to the array of public and private justice measures that insurers dispense through risk management. In this way Richard progressively broadened the scope of criminological research by pushing the criminological study of institutions beyond the traditional triumvirate of policing, courts and corrections.

A Deep Connection with Social Theory

Richard frequently moved beyond criminology to look at major social theoretical developments to inform his work. He was neither a strict constructionist nor a structuralist; instead, he combined detailed studies of interactions with an analysis of the structural constraints under which people operate. His intellectual trajectory began with labelling theory (see Chapters 1 and 2) and symbolic interactionism and expanded to include many influences drawn from, for example, media studies, Beck's sweeping risk-society theorizing, and post-Foucauldian analysis of governmentality. Indeed, *Policing the Risk Society* (Ericson and Haggerty, 1997) is not only a book about policing, but also, in the broader theoretical literature on risk, the most noteworthy and sustained effort to synthesize the perspectives of Beckian and Foucauldian scholars. Richard's books are situated in macro-level analyses of, for example, the knowledge society (Ericson, Baranek and Chan, 1987, 1989, 1991), the risk society (Ericson and Haggerty, 1997; Ericson and Doyle, 2004a, 2004b), and neo-liberal governance (see especially Ericson, Doyle and Barry, 2003) but they move skilfully between micro, institutional, and macro levels of analysis. In *Negotiating Control* (Ericson, Baranek and Chan, 1989), for instance, Richard brilliantly made use of Goffman's (1959) and Giddens' (1984) refinement of the notion of 'front' and 'back' regions and extended this social–psychological framework for analysing individuals' 'presentation of self' to the 'sociological level of how organizations protect and present their activities by policing spatial regions and knowledge' (Ericson, Baranek and Chan, 1989, p. 9). Richard resisted following fashionable trends in theory; he challenged conventional wisdoms (but never resorted to adversarial or simplistic positions that exaggerate differences) and always picked out the best in those he did not agree with, rather than simply demolishing them. *Policing the Risk Society* (Ericson and Haggerty, 1997 – see Chapter 10 for a summary of some key findings) is an excellent demonstration of how Richard's innovative approach not only revitalized policing research and the sociology of deviance and control, but also made significant contributions to the sociology of organizations and institutions, the sociology of occupations and professions, and the sociology of science and technology. By venturing into new territories and putting his own stamp on to contemporary debates, Richard reshaped both criminology and social theory.

A Strong Commitment to Interdisciplinarity

Beyond connecting with broader social theory, Richard was a leader in defining criminology as interdisciplinary. He linked criminology with many other disciplines and subfields, such as media studies, in which he made important contributions (some of the particular contributions of his work to mid-range theories of the news media are discussed below). Chapters 7 and 9 represent a body of work that played a key role in creating the emerging interdisciplinary field of insurance studies; his theoretical work on surveillance (Haggerty and Ericson, 2001) has been characterized as a seminal piece in the emergence of surveillance studies (Wood, 2002).

Richard served as a professor of criminology and sociology, of sociology and law and of criminology and law at different stages in his career. He shared and fostered the interdisciplinary vision of the Centre of Criminology at the University of Toronto, where he was based for more than 20 years, eventually serving multiple terms as director. The Centre brought together faculty and graduate students who were substantively interested in criminal justice from a range of other disciplines, including sociology, law, history, psychology and political science. Later, as the founding principal at Green College, an interdisciplinary residential graduate student college at the University of British Columbia, Richard attended and hosted hundreds of talks across numerous disciplines, never failing to contribute to, and draw from, the discussion. These scholarly exchanges frequently informed his work. Indeed, there seems to be a clear link between Richard's critical sociology of institutions and his skill at institution-building. This was most evident in his role, as principal for its first ten years (1993–2003), in building the wonderful interdisciplinary environment at Green College. Richard felt that this was perhaps his most meaningful and important achievement; indeed, David Garland (2007) called Green College Richard's 'individual masterpiece'. Under Richard's leadership, Green College was born as an almost utopian intellectual environment and was home for dozens of talented graduate students across many disciplines, along with a number of visiting scholars, including more than a handful of criminologists from around the world. While scholars living at Green College worked on their individual research projects, all residents enjoyed lively exchanges over communal breakfasts and dinners daily in the Great Hall, attended countless academic talks and other events almost every day, and generally shared a vibrant intellectual life in a stunning setting among the British Columbian West Coast pines and firs.

Richard's commitment to interdisciplinary research is evident in the diverse backgrounds of scholars who contributed chapters to Richard's edited books such *as Governing Modern Societies* (Ericson and Stehr, 2000), *Risk and Morality* (Ericson and Doyle, 2003) and *The New Politics of Surveillance and Visibility* (Haggerty and Ericson, 2006). His books are important in a variety of disciplines: each of the books has been reviewed in more than a dozen journals by scholars from criminology, sociology, political science, law, and (for the media books) journalism, communication and cultural studies.

A Solid Foundation in Rich and Diverse Empirical Data

Another key to Richard Ericson's scholarship, illustrated throughout the essays in this volume, was that he was an extraordinarily committed and productive empirical researcher. Richard undertook a progression of large empirical projects that were theory-driven and cross-cut different disciplines. While many academics shy away from the rigours of the field later in their careers, Richard was an unrelenting field researcher throughout his working life. His methodological orientation was largely qualitative, and typically involved face-to-face interviews with people representing different roles within the institutions he was studying. Richard's major projects also often featured a great deal of direct ethnographic observation of the operations of such institutions. This volume spans a massive body of his first-hand empirical research. It begins with the work on offenders he conducted as a junior scholar, but also demonstrates how his work in the field continued even in the last years of his career. The empirical material in the 2004 article 'Catastrophe Risk, Insurance and Terrorism' (Ericson and Doyle, 2004a) was gathered first-hand by Richard alone as he sat through a high-level insurance industry conference on managing catastrophic terrorist risks, taking along his tape recorder and interviewing many of the participants. Likewise, the interview and documentary material on earthquake insurance analysed in Chapter 11 was gathered entirely first-hand by Richard, at a time when he was at the peak of his seniority, and despite his administrative duties as principal of Green College and a massive array of other responsibilities. We recall the meticulous attention and sharp ethnographic eye that, even late in his career, Richard brought to the quotidian, to what others might find mundane and not worthy of remark: interviewing a police bureaucrat about changes in official forms, or observing how an insurance adjuster examined a damaged car and then negotiated the claim. Richard had many theoretical insights during the interviews or observations he conducted and loved debriefing, perhaps over a beer, after a day in the field. When he was unable to accompany us on interviews or field research due to his numerous other academic and administrative responsibilities, he was always eager for an account from us immediately after our fieldwork experiences, asking if there were 'Any nuggets?' or 'Any gems?'. There is a quote by Lord Chesterfield to his son at the beginning of the first chapter of *Uncertain Business*, 'The knowledge of the world is only acquired in the world and not in a closet'(Ericson and Doyle, 2004b, p. 3), which captures Richard's view of the importance of grounding theorizing in empirical research. Richard was also an award-winning teacher and mentor to graduate students, and excelled at using the first-hand involvement of his doctoral students in his empirical research as an opportunity to teach all of us and his other students.

In many of his published works Richard argued for the importance of trying to understand the lived experience of people within particular institutions – something that cannot be achieved by studying statistics (or by focusing only on the official documents that currently receive much attention as the empirical target of governmentality researchers). That said, Richard would quantify things if appropriate, including measures of police patrol practices (see Chapters 4 and 6) or media content (Ericson, Baranek and Chan, 1991). This is how his empirical research was grounded: ethnographic data about people's values, intentions, behaviours and interactions only told one side of the story; the use of quantitative data was not to appease sceptics of qualitative research. Instead, it was often tied to a conscious attempt to demonstrate some of the patterns of structural constraints under which people operate.

It is his attention to blending social theory with rich and very thorough qualitative and quantitative empirical detail that gives Richard's books their distinctive flavour and importance. In his excellent 'appreciation' of Richard and his scholarship, David Garland (2007) linked this combination of theoretical and empirical to a blend in Richard's work of traditions from different continents. As Garland put it:

> Richard's scholarship was grounded in the intellectual traditions of North America and those of the UK and Europe and he had the best qualities of both: the conceptual depth and critical edge of European social theory, but also the professionalism, methodological rigour and empirical focus of American work. (Garland, 2007, p. xv)

As Richard sometimes joked while patting one of his sizable books, their vast troves of painstakingly gathered and theorized ethnographic data constituted the 'weight of the evidence'. We were constantly impressed by Richard's encyclopaedic knowledge of criminological and social theoretical literatures and of a vast range of other works, and by the meticulous way he kept notes of his readings and analysis of qualitative data. He had a set of filing cabinets filled with transcripts, institutional documents and photocopied academic articles, along with his large library. All of this was organized through thousands of index cards that went back at least to the early 1970s. Without the benefit of search engines, Richard could retrieve every quote or note he had ever recorded from his readings. He often lent us his books, and every page was underlined and marked up with observations and responses. So the 'weight of the evidence' was not just in the printed pages, but in the gravity of Richard's overall approach to scholarship.

The Politics of Ericsonian Criminology

Richard's politics were broadly progressive, and he was certainly not afraid to take a strong normative position: for example, he challenged police repression of protest at the APEC international summit at the University of British Columbia in 1997 during his time as principal of Green College (Ericson and Doyle, 1999). Generally, though, Richard did not approach his research overtly as a vehicle for advocacy. He did, nonetheless, believe that sound empirical scholarship could serve as a critical political force, although the impact of academic knowledge on policy was often more oblique and unpredictable than academic activists might prefer. One of his last published articles addresses the topic of 'public sociology' and points out that sociology is always critical to the extent that '[i]t refuses to accept social structures, institutions, organizations, processes and relations in the terms in which they are conventionally presented' (Ericson, 2006, p. 366). That statement stands as a testament to his more than 30 years of research that recurrently accentuates power imbalances and institutional inequities.

Ericson's Major Criminological Studies

Having outlined these general themes, we now shift the focus to putting each of the 12 essays in this volume into context as part of the broader major studies led by Richard.

Young Offenders

The first two chapters in this volume are taken from Richard's research on young offenders and the labelling process for his doctoral dissertation at Cambridge. This research was an early demonstration of his intensive ethnographic approach; it is based on a study Richard conducted in 1972, while he was still in his early 20s, at a British youth detention centre; he then continued to spend time with 15 young offenders after they had been released from their first-time imprisonment and returned to their community. Noteworthy already was Richard's characteristic play with language. The title of the book he wrote on the basis of this research, *Young Offenders and Their Social Work* (Ericson, 1975), referred not to conventional social work practice, but instead to the work that offenders themselves must do socially in identity management post-imprisonment in an attempt to regain acceptance. Richard's data highlighted how the ex-inmates were able to convince family and close friends that they were simply normal people with criminal problems, but remained criminal people with only 'residual normalcy' in the eyes of the more socially distant, such as employers and agents of the justice system in particular. Richard's career-long concern with the ironies and paradoxes of control processes was already evident in this quote from Chapter 2:

> ... part of the probation officer's officially defined role is to minimise the ex-inmate's criminal identity and maximise conventional commitments in the domestic and occupational spheres. However, this ideal cannot be accomplished because of the probation officer's own identity as someone whose primary function is defined in terms of his clients' criminal tendencies. He is a law-enforcement officer who helps to conceive, use and perpetuate society's common-sense categories of the criminal; for this reason he remains distant, and a source of stigmatisation. (p. 51)

Policing

As a junior faculty member at the University of Toronto, Richard oversaw a team of researchers examining the operation of the criminal justice system in Canada. Two of the books they produced studied the police, but even at this early stage Richard recognized the police as one instance of policing more generally, understood as governmental efforts to control, develop, shape and refine the population. *Making Crime* (1981) is a study of detectives, represented by Chapter 3; *Reproducing Order* (1982) focuses on police patrol work and is represented by Chapters 4 and 6. While the books detail differences between these types of policing, the image that emerges from these studies is one of policing that involves little of what might be called 'crime work'. Instead, police are called upon to deal with a plethora of different forms of disorder. Officers use their low occupational visibility and vague laws as enabling resources to help them transform troublesome situations into a normal and efficient state, and, in the process, reproduce the existing social order. Rather than being governed by rules, the police use rules and their control over the production of knowledge as major resources to transform a world of complexity into a simple authoritative account on which other players in the criminal justice system ultimately must depend.

In a famous incident in the annals of policing research, the Board of Commissioners of Police for the organization studied in *Making Crime* (from which Chapter 3 is an excerpt) objected to the book's representation of police discretion, 'rule breaking' and other forms of deviance, and tried to stop the book from being published. With the support of the university, and following extensive negotiations, the monograph was published despite these official censorship efforts, and consequently contains a fascinating (if often confusing) 12-page response by the Board of Commissioners of Police and Richard's reply. That exchange, together with the book's extended section on the realities of actually conducting police research – difficulties that Richard attributes to the fact that the presence of researchers threatened the police's control over producing authoritative accounts – constitute a captivating resource and cautionary account for researchers studying any institution. This episode also demonstrated the strength of Richard's integrity as a researcher: he stood firm when his work and his commitment to research ethics was threatened by powerful forces.

Chapter 10 summarizes some key findings in Richard's later book, *Policing the Risk Society* (co-authored with Kevin Haggerty and published in 1997). Here, Richard returned to the issue of policing, although now employing a substantially different orientation from his earlier volumes. This book situates the police in the context of the rise of risk-based forms of governance. The emphasis is on how the police, through their increasingly regimented, formatted and controlled information work, serve the risk management needs of a host of institutions external to the police. In order to represent the police in this way, the authors move away from the usual focus on police frontline work to study the large volume of mid-level managers in policing, whose role is dominated by structuring, processing, categorizing and conveying risk-relevant information.

The Courts

Richard also produced one of the most important studies ever of the day-to-day operations of the criminal courts. In *The Ordering of Justice* (Ericson and Baranek, 1982), from which Chapter 5 of this volume is taken, the authors examined the position of the accused person as he or she moves through the criminal justice process. In conjunction with Richard's policing books, *The Ordering of Justice* still stands as a refutation of populist claims that the criminal justice system is skewed to the advantage of defendants. Instead, the authors present a disturbing image in which '… once the mould is set by law enforcement agents there are few resources available to the accused to shape his destiny within the criminal process' (Ericson and Baranek, 1982, p. 28). Defendants are actually 'dependants', disadvantaged by virtue of being 'one-shot' players who lack the all-important relationships and experience or 'recipe knowledge' available to repeat players such as police, lawyers and judges. Consequently, the role of the defendant is institutionally and interactionally structured towards passivity and cooperation. The defendant as dependant is subject to rules and processes designed to enable law-enforcement personnel to control him or her, and the total picture that emerges has Kafkaesque overtones of disempowered defendants being processed through an alien and alienating process.

The News Media

Richard's next major research initiative culminated in three volumes on the news media (Ericson, Baranek and Chan, 1987, 1989, 1991), which became some of the most important and most cited ethnographies of news production more generally. Chapter 7 in this volume is taken from the third book of that trilogy, *Representing Order*, while Chapter 8 is an article that summarizes key ethnographic findings about journalistic work from this study. The three books are set against the larger backdrop of a theory of the knowledge society, in which power-knowledge represents the key dimension of hierarchy. They are based on ethnographies of six major urban print and broadcast news organizations, as well as qualitative and quantitative analysis of their content. The research included extended direct observation of the news-making process, numerous interviews with news personnel at various organizational levels and with 93 key news sources in four institutional arenas: the police, courts, legislature and private sector. It examined the news process from assigning stories and reporting to editing, even devoting a chapter in *Negotiating Control* to the decision-making process by which letters to the editors are published. Richard and his co-authors also made a key theoretical turn in audience research, shifting the focus from researching influence on individual audience members to understanding media influence on institutional audiences such as the police or government.

The first book in the trilogy, *Visualizing Deviance* (1987), broadened our understanding of 'crime in the media' by making the original argument that the primary element of news is the social construction of deviance (broadly defined) and control – particularly deviance from procedural propriety, although also including deviance from common sense. Journalists are crucial workers in a knowledge society, helping to transform specialized bureaucratic knowledge into common sense. Yet their legitimacy often depends on that of the powerful 'authorized knowers' whom they quote. As Chapter 8 shows, journalists 'visualize' events for audiences in ways that are inherently political, drawing on implicit understandings of social order. The media are crucial to contemporary politics in establishing a discourse of failure and reform among 'deviance-defining elites', in which non-elite players are merely spectators. Journalists know little about their audience beyond direct contact with their regular circle of authorized knowers. Investigative journalism that penetrates beyond source accounts is rare in deed, but not in myth. Journalism offers a closed circle in which reporters often draw on other outlets for information but do not overtly criticize the claims made by other news organizations. However, while other accounts portray the media as monolithic, in fact, conflict within news organizations over what stories to cover and how is also rife – conflict not only with interpersonal bases and over resources, but also for ideological reasons.

The second media book, *Negotiating Control* (1989), is the definitive study of the central place of official news sources in journalism, and of how the media are thus intertwined with other institutions in an ongoing dialectical struggle of power and knowledge. The book explores the politics of this knowledge through an analysis of both enclosure and disclosure in front- and back-regions of these institutions. The detailed ethnographies allow a much more nuanced account of source–journalist relations, one that reveals the previous influential model of official sources as 'primary definers' in Hall *et al.* (1978) to be quite simplistic. For example, 'inner circle' police reporters tend to be very close to police sources and reflect police ideology to a large extent, self-censoring to maintain those close ties. In the outer circle there is a much less cosy relationship with the police and much more emphasis on police and organizational deviance. Studying the courts, the researchers found that journalists seldom watch trials for any length of time and tend to portray only fragments of the proceedings. The legislature was the most open institution in the justice system, with politicians seeking coverage at every opportunity, while for corporations, power may derive partly from the ability to stay out of the media.

The final book in the media trilogy, *Representing Order* (1991), contains rich data on how news of crime, law and justice varies by media and market (see Chapter 7, this volume), and focuses on the quantitative and qualitative study of media content, both longitudinally and cross-sectionally. This varies considerably – for example, in the choice of topics or type and number of sources used, and in the degree of personalization, by market (quality, popular) and by medium (television, newspapers, radio). Yet, as the authors demonstrate, accounts of crime and deviance dominate all news media, with items about crime, law and justice making up roughly one-half of all the news. Considering the question of 'balance', all media outlets provided only one side in most stories. 'Journalists and their sources are too concerned about making moral judgements, and effecting social control on the basis of those judgements, to avoid taking sides'(Ericson, Baranek and Chan, 1991, p. 179). Another common facet across all media outlets – a very important one for criminologists – is that structural causal explanations of deviance are given almost no play.

Insurance

During the mid-1990s Richard's research interest turned to the governance of risk. Following *Policing the Risk Society*, Richard made a bold and challenging move by turning his focus to insurance, an institution of comparable scope and importance to the criminal justice system and the news media, but one much less in the public and academic spotlight and much less 'sexy' in academic terms, as well as one that had never been the subject of such a research project. This stage in Richard's research is represented by Chapters 9 and 11. His two books *Insurance as Governance* (Ericson, Doyle and Barry, 2003) and *Uncertain Business* (Ericson and Doyle, 2004a), from which Chapter 11 is taken, provide a painstakingly detailed analysis of insurance as a vital institution of modern governance. Richard and his co-authors drew upon 224 interviews with individuals in private and government insurance institutions, and with insurance consumers, to demonstrate that insurance has long been overlooked as a key institution of governance, and that private insurance becomes particularly prominent as the state progressively withdraws from direct service provision. Again, these developments are set in the context of a 'risk society', composed of intersecting institutions that organize in relation to the production and distribution of knowledge of risk. Because of the hidden importance of insurance there has in fact long been a 'risk society', but today the influence of insurance organizations is particularly profound and multifaceted. Insurers involve themselves in governance through producing knowledge about risks and making them calculable, using actuarialism to create risk pools that bind populations together legally, protect against loss of capital, manage risks through surveillance, and serve as a social technology of justice.

Although the façade of actuarial science provides insurance with a very scientific public face, the second major insurance study, *Uncertain Business*, reveals and accentuates the limits of such knowledge, even in a context that is ostensibly all about rational calculation. While much influential previous writing on risk emphasized the modern capacity to assess and calculate risk, in contrast this new study revealed the extent to which this capacity is elusive and illusory. Companies insure many things for which they do not have good knowledge of risk, as *Uncertain Business* demonstrates with studies of life, disability, earthquakes (as Chapter 11 of this volume details) and terrorism insurance. In the absence of such knowledge, insurers move away from governance through risk and towards governance in conditions of uncertainty. Although this presents difficulties for insurers, it also provides a context for ingenious solutions about how to proceed in a context of imperfect knowledge, as the book reveals in its demonstration of how each kind of risk entails its own logic of governance.

For anyone looking for an entrée into Ericson's oeuvre, we would recommend his final, shorter book, *Crime in an Insecure World* (2007), represented by the final essay in this volume, 'National Security' (Chapter 12). Richard's final book was a departure from his usual approach in that it is not based on new empirical research, featured a more overt sense of moral urgency, and, as he told us, represented a deliberate attempt to reach out to a broader audience. *Crime in an Insecure World* offers an extensive narrative that cross-cuts institutions and nation-states (especially the UK, the USA and Canada). It traces the history of liberalism and of risk and uncertainty, and argues not only that the problem of uncertainty has now replaced the problem of order and is central to neo-liberal governance, but also that criminalization has become the leading response to such uncertainty and becomes mobilized through what Richard calls 'counter-law'. Richard examines this process across the realms of national, social, corporate and domestic security. This short book can be taken as a briefer capstone statement that draws upon a lifetime of research and thinking.

A Final Word

Anyone familiar with Richard Ericson's scholarship will be aware that our brief summary in this Introduction, and the essays in this volume, must necessarily feature some important omissions. One example is his thought-provoking observations on the disciplines of criminology and sociology (see Ericson and Carriere, 1994; Ericson, 2003, 2006). Such oversights are inevitable when trying to encapsulate the work of a scholar who, in his authored or co-authored books, published several thousand pages, a number that does not include his many other articles and book chapters. The chapters that follow represent 12 key moments in Richard's work, and, we hope, a useful introduction to, and overview of, his rich criminological legacy.

References

Cohn, Ellen G. and David P. Farrington (2007), 'Changes in Scholarly Influence in Major International Criminology Journals', *Australian and New Zealand Journal of Criminology*, **40**(3), pp. 335–59.

Ericson, Richard V. (1975), *Young Offenders and Their Social Work*, Farnborough: Saxon House.

Ericson, Richard V. (1981), *Making Crime: A Study of Detective Work*, Toronto: Butterworths.

Ericson, Richard V. (1982), *Reproducing Order: A Study of Police Patrol Work*, Toronto: University of Toronto Press.

Ericson, Richard V. (1995), 'The News Media and Account Ability in Criminal Justice', in P. Stenning (ed.), *Accountability for Criminal Justice*, Toronto: University of Toronto Press.

Ericson, Richard V. (2003), 'The Culture and Power of Criminological Research', in L. Zedner and A. Ashworth (eds), *The Criminological Foundations of Penal Policy: Essays in Honour of Roger Hood*, London: Oxford University Press.

Ericson, Richard V. (2006), 'Publicizing Sociology', *British Journal of Sociology*, **56**(3), pp. 365–72.

Ericson, Richard V. (2007), *Crime in an Insecure World*, Cambridge: Polity Press.

Ericson, Richard V. and Baranek, Patricia (1982), *The Ordering of Justice: A Study of Accused Persons as Dependants in the Criminal Process*, Toronto: University of Toronto Press.

Ericson, Richard V., Baranek, Patricia and Chan, Janet (1987), *Visualizing Deviance: A Study of News Organization*, Toronto: University of Toronto Press.

Ericson, Richard V., Baranek, Patricia and Chan, Janet (1989), *Negotiating Control: A Study of News Sources*, Toronto: University of Toronto Press.

Ericson, Richard V., Baranek, Patricia and Chan, Janet (1991), *Representing Order: Crime, Law, and Justice in the News Media*, Toronto: University of Toronto Press.

Ericson, Richard V. and Carriere, Kevin (1994), 'The Fragmentation of Criminology', in D. Nelken (ed.), *The Futures of Criminology*, London: Sage.

Ericson, Richard V. and Doyle, Aaron (1999), 'Globalization and the Policing of Protest: The Case of APEC 1997', *British Journal of Sociology*, **50**(4), pp. 589–608.

Ericson, Richard V. and Doyle, Aaron (eds) (2003), *Risk and Morality*, Toronto: University of Toronto Press.

Ericson, Richard V. and Doyle, Aaron (2004a), 'Catastrophe Risk, Insurance, and Terrorism', *Economy and Society*, **33**, pp. 135–73.

Ericson, Richard V. and Doyle, Aaron (2004b), *Uncertain Business: Risk, Insurance, and the Limits of Knowledge*, Toronto: University of Toronto Press.

Ericson, Richard V., Doyle, Aaron and Barry, Dean (2003), *Insurance as Governance*, Toronto: University of Toronto Press.

Ericson, Richard V. and Haggerty, Kevin D. (1997), *Policing the Risk Society*, Toronto: University of Toronto Press and Oxford: Oxford University Press.

Ericson, Richard V. and Stehr, Nico (eds) (2000), *Governing Modern Societies*, Toronto: University of Toronto Press.

Garland, David (2007), 'Richard Ericson: An Appreciation', *Canadian Journal of Sociology*, **32**(4), pp. xi–xviii.

Giddens, Anthony (1984), *The Constitution of Society: Outline of the Theory of Structuration*, Cambridge: Polity Press.

Goffman, Ervin (1959), *The Presentation of Self in Everyday Life*, Garden City, NY: Doubleday Anchor Books.

Haggerty, Kevin and Ericson, Richard V. (2000), 'The Surveillant Assembalge', *British Journal of Sociology*, **51**(4), pp. 605–22.

Haggerty, Kevin and Ericson, Richard V. (eds) (2006), *The New Politics of Surveillance and Visibility*, Toronto: University of Toronto Press.

Hall, S., Critcher, C., Jefferson, T., Clarke, J. and Roberts, B. (1978), *Policing the Crisis*, London: Macmillan.

Loader, Ian (2008), 'Review Symposium: The Anti-Politics of Crime. Richard V. Ericson, Crime in an Insecure World. Jonathan Simon. Governing Through Crime', *Theoretical Criminology*, **12**(3), pp. 399–410.

Wood, David (2002), 'Foucault and Panopticism Revisited', *Surveillance and Society*, **1**(3), pp. 234–39.

[1]
Being Free

> Freedom only exists in a world where what is possible is defined at the same time as what is not possible.[1]

Many elements of the social work which the ex-inmate engages in to re-establish himself in the community are also employed on a routine basis once he is settled there. This is simply recognition of the fact that being established is only a matter of degree, still open to incursions from without and conversions from within. In brief, the work done socially to present an acceptable identity does not suddenly stop when the person realises what he has become, but continues on in a perpetual process of negotiating his being. While the task may be less arduous at this stage because it has become routine, it must still be engaged in on a continuous basis.

For the person who is deemed to have a high potential for crime, and who carries the label 'criminal' as one social fact about him, there may be continuing problems which threaten his freedom. Being free may still be limited to the extent that the crime and criminal facts are routine and expected in the spheres of life which are important to him.

This chapter is concerned with the continuing role of crime and the criminal social fact in the life of the ex-inmate. The potential for further criminal activity is considered, as well as the use of techniques to avoid crime that were developed at the point of entry into the community. The contexts in which the invitational edge to 'crime' is traversed completes the discussion on the persistent impact of the crime fact.

The criminal fact, which lingers on as one part of the ex-inmate's social identity, is considered as it affects the ex-inmate personally in the first few months after his release. The continuing reactions of police, probation officers, employers, neighbours and intimate others are discussed. Consideration is given to a decline in the initial pattern of negative reaction from the most socially distant others. The basic theme is that being free allows considerable choice, within limits.

Dealing with the 'crime' fact

The potential for trouble

Every person in the Birmingham follow-up group revealed that in each of their communities, crime is a fact of life. This is not the same as saying it is a way of life, for no one claimed or displayed a preoccupation with crime that was even remotely as important as many other aspects of life. Crime is a fact of life because it is there as a possible consequence of one's normal activities. The ex-inmate has certainly experienced it, as have many others with whom he has daily contact. While crime as a social fact is known as part of social reality, it is not an obsession.

For every individual studied, his own neighbourhood was full of people with crime potential. It is part of existence; everybody knows somebody who has 'done a job', been arrested, appeared in court, been 'sent away'. To be an ex-inmate is neither abnormal nor extraordinary. Out of fifteen subjects, six had extended-family members who had been inside or were still inside at the time of the Birmingham fieldwork. With all fifteen, acquaintances who were ex-inmates were talked about or actually met during fieldwork activities.

For example, part of a normal pub conversation would include some transmission of information about persons known inside.

> (In a pub with Dave, Rob and one of their mates)
> Dave: Bob and Ross come out next week. Tuesday is it?
> Rob: Yea.
> Mate: Is that them who went in as a gang?
> Rob: There was three of them.
> Dave: (Addressing himself to the researcher) They all go in off our estate. It's only a small estate but everyone gets in trouble. Whatton's full of them. Not many we know who haven't been inside somewhere.

Crime arises as a subject of normal conversation because it is part of the taken for granted reality. It always seems that somebody known is in trouble, and his case arises in general conversation about the community.

> (In Ed's home, with Ed, his brother – also an ex-inmate from detention centre – his mother and a mate. During a general conversation about Handsworth and the fact that the houses they were living in had been scheduled for demolition four years ago)
> Ed: Did you read in the papers the other night where a kid, a sixteen-year-old kid, got life for attempted murder? There's a kid around the corner . . .
> R: Was it someone from around here?
> Ed: No, I say a kid I know around the corner is up on the same charges. I wonder if they'll give him the same.[2]

(Turning to mate) What's this I hear about you passing dud cheques down at the Oasis?

Mate: Weren't me man!

Ed: Well, somebody with the same description and the same name.

Mother: (Addressing the researcher) You see, they're all bad around here.

Invariably, the reality of crime for the ex-inmate and his contemporaries involves situational or occasional acts rather than a systematic attempt at personal gain through crime. There is no intention of establishing a criminal career in occupational ('professional') terms, nor is there much contact with older persons who appear to have selected this life style. Occasionally some affiliation with 'real criminals' is *talked of.* For example, while he was still inside, Paul promised me that he would introduce me to 'some real cons who're always thieving and doing time – that'll get you some better stuff for your book than with these lot'. However, the closest I came to this during meetings with Paul after his release was Paul's request that I ship him guns from North America – 'Not for me, like, but I know where I can get thirty apiece for them' – and his claim to have visited his best mate in Winson Green Prison.

(In a pub with several of Paul's mates. A side conversation with the researcher)

Paul: I was down to Winson Green last Saturday. My best mate went in just as I came out (of Whatton). He was serving five years in Gartree for robbery, but he escaped after two and a half. He got picked up for drugs then, and got another year for that plus a hundred days' loss of remission for escaping. Not like doing a runner from Whatton! Still, I guess he might get some parole. Sure hope he does anyway. He's a good lad!

R: How old is he?

Paul: Twenty-four or twenty-five. He was the one I used to do thieving with a lot.

There is no evidence of criminal organisation and no tendency to seek membership in such an organisation. There is no more systematic organisation to their criminal activity than there is to efforts at getting a group of mates together to kick a football around on Sunday afternoon. The first division may be dreamed about; the individual may even fancy that he is in the big time while actually playing the game. But in reality the big leagues are out of the question for someone whose style and competence is at this level.

Crime potential for the ex-inmate among his contemporaries seems to arise out of the normal activities he engages in once he has found his bearings. That is, he soon gets back into the same routines which require the same adaptations as he made before. The word 'routine' is important: while he longs to order his relations when he first returns to the community, the ex-inmate paradoxically finds that when this is accomplished his life is unpleasantly mundane.

> (After spending Saturday afternoon watching television and losing Ed's last ten pence in an effort to win fifty pence in a café pinball machine)
>
> Ed: That's all you do around here, fill in time. You just find little things to fill in your day. It's stupid really, meaningless.

This is one source of Steve's statement, already quoted in the last chapter, that when in detention, 'You think everything is out here, outside, but when you get out it ain't. There ain't anything here, is there? What is there to do?' Meaningfulness is rarely created by work, for it too is part of the routine. As Paul explained, 'Any job is just to get enough money to go out at the week-ends.' The search for something meaningful occurs outside necessary or utilitarian routines such as work. This is a major reason why the detention experience is viewed as meaningless. It is also the major reason why meaningfulness outside in fact centres on activities which the person himself can institute: going to football matches, picking up girls, drinking beer, driving cars. It is in these situations where there is a potential for meaningfulness that there is also potential for crime.[3]

One of the greatest sources of meaningfulness is the active support of a football team. This does not simply entail going to a match for two hours on Saturday afternoon; it involves football and related activities as a way of life. There is a culture of football supporters who organise their life around their team's symbol, making it their focal concern.

The football team represents a source of affinity among several thousand youths. While there are only a few persons on one's street or in the local area who are members of this group, they have the feeling that it is easy to call upon the support of thousands in a conflict situation. Hence, one important aspect in the organisation of each small group in a neighbourhood is identification on the basis of one of the city's football teams. This identification is symbolically expressed in terms of scarves bearing team colours and badges with the team name. These publicly identify the individual as a member of a 'mob': for example, in the Birmingham conurbation people would talk about the 'Blues mob' (Birmingham City), the 'Villa mob' (Aston Villa), and the 'Albion mob' (West Bromwich Albion).

Much of the dealing is in images, but these are as important or perhaps more important than the reality. Some of the images concern football itself. The week is spent discussing last Saturday's game and the game next Saturday in every situation: over the workbench, in a pub at night, in front of the television, and so on. But more significant is what the individual and his mob themselves did before, at, and after the match. They met the opposing mob at the train station and chased them up the platform; they 'pinched' some team badges from a souvenir stand; they grabbed a member of the opposing mob and stole his scarf; they knocked off a copper's hat with a roll of toilet paper; one of them got arrested. Small stuff, but it can be told and retold throughout the week to the many who are only too eager to be excited by others' excitement. The story tellers gain recognition. They are helping to make a mundane existence somewhat exciting. A 'good time' is defined in terms of its suitability for verbal reconstruction in the mass of time which is defined as not so good. The appeal is not only the excitement of the moment, but the excitement that moment can re-create in the countless dull moments at work, in front of the television and in pub conversation.

Another set of images revealed by observation among those subjects who returned to participation in this sphere concerns the nature of the mob itself. The individual maintains a social identity in this mob, which makes him feel a part of the organisation he himself helps to construct. He and members of his neighbourhood group feel powerful because in a conflict situation they can claim to have the backing of thousands of supporters. The image of the core members is not dissimilar to that which Yablonsky described among violent gang members in New York City.[4]

In a small skirmish they can claim that all their supporters will be out in force the next time. There is at least some evidence for this belief, because every Saturday they stand shoulder to shoulder with thousands of similar identified comrades. Losing a sense of personal identity, they sway as an aggressive force on the terraces. A sense of power is created when several thousand point and yell at the opposing mob such phrases as 'You're going to get your fucking heads kicked in'. This power is rarely exercised, although the publicity of 'football hooliganism' and the numbers in detention for affrays at football matches attest to the fact that the feeling of power is sometimes turned into the exercise of power. In face of limited opportunities for other forms of meaningfulness, meaningfulness is sought in the form of aggression and violence.[5]

The sense of power instilled by this scene was described by Paul and his mate as we returned from a match.

Mate: We had the second biggest crowd in the league today, next to Man. United. That shows we have one of the best mobs in the whole division. There would have been some real trouble today if it weren't for all those coppers between the fences (separating Birmingham and Derby supporters).

R: Weren't many Derby supporters, were there?

Paul: (Offended by my statement) What do you mean!? That whole fucking end was full of them! I'll bet there was five thousand, at least four thousand. You just don't see them up where we was because the coppers direct them into the stand. They can go anywhere they want but they'd never come up to our end 'cause they'd just get smashed up, wouldn't stand a chance against all of us. The Blues are a tough mob; they would have murdered any fucking Derby fans who came near our end.

Mate: Fucking right. Today you saw how fucking strong the Blues mob really is.[6]

Only some of the persons followed up renewed an active interest in the football culture. Others had been active supporters in the past, but were afraid of the potential for trouble involved and stayed away. Terry was among those who used this justification.

(In the sitting room of Terry's house, in private conversation)

Terry: I won't go to Albion matches anymore because of the trouble. I got a police assault stuck on me once there. Someone pushed me into a copper. I couldn't help it, it was the crowd. I'd just come from work you see. I hadn't no time to change, so I had my work boots on – with the steel toes, you know. As soon as the coppers saw them, that was it. A hundred and fifteen pound fine. Next time it'll be Borstal.

For most of the others, participation in activities with football supporters is for 'younger lads'. They simply feel what Rob expressed as he and the researcher watched from a distance while Paul taunted some opposing fans and the police: 'I think I'm a bit past this stage. It's childish really.'

For persons like Rob, *the* meaningful part of life is a night out at a pub where there is opportunity for 'bird' watching and catching. *The* major source of myth creation, *the* thing talked about when not involved in this setting, *the* definition of a good time in times that are not so good, is the pursuit of women; they gain self-esteem and the recognition of others by describing their exploits with women.

On an off-night – which invariably happened when the researcher was present – the following explanation was typical.

(After driving two girls home from a pub)

Rob: It was all your fault Dave. They just wanted a lift. Like I said to Dick, they're all right if that's the sort of thing you're after.

Dave: You've got to try, don't you?

Rob: This was a bad night, this night. Not many nights we go without some fanny.

Dave: Yea, we've been doin' great lately. A different one every night.

In this sphere, as with football, it does not essentially matter if it comes off in reality or not. That is, the enjoyable part is the activity associated with the game rather than the results in the end. The pub or disco are *the* places to present yourself socially, in public. In this context, you can forget about your own status and the status of others by presenting acceptable attire – proper hair and clothes. You are not then a factory labourer, a pipe-fitter, unemployed, or a plasterer. You are male and ready for the game of bird watching with the occasional pay-off of bird catching. Little is lost if this latter pay-off does not ensue – you have the option of drinking yourself into an equally oblivious and insatiable existence. Status relatively equalised, personal style the only contestable point, a world is created which is really social play, games people play. As Rob commented after one of the seven occasions we went through this routine together, 'I don't care if I get a wench or not. But I enjoy the game of trying. That's the best fun.'

It is in the course of pursuits of this nature where behaviour deemed criminal can naturally occur. It is not a matter of being wilfully committed to crime as a fundamental part of membership and participation in these activities. It is not a matter of choosing crime because other meaningful activity has been foreclosed by a 'criminal' label lingering on from the past. It is because crime occurs as a by-product of these meaningful situations for anyone who chooses to participate. Because these activities provide the major source of significance in life, they are not likely to be given up because they also include a potential for crime.

Obviously the persons themselves are aware that places of meaningful action are also signified as trouble spots by the public and their agents of social control. Most still engage in at least one type of activity where crime potential is magnified. To do otherwise is to deny a meaningful existence at all; if everything is meaningless, then it does not matter where you do your time. Hence, there is little sense of risk involved.[7]

To illustrate, we can consider the case of Dave. He was incarcerated for wounding a person whom he had quarrelled with in a pub and later met on the street. Dave explained his action by saying that earlier the same night he had a fight with his girl friend, got drunk and just had to take out his anger on someone. After his release, we were in a pub with Dave, Rob and a mate. They started to tease their mate about his girl friend, and the mate picked up his beer mug and threatened to hit Dave with it. After this incident, Rob and Dave commented on this and crime in general.

> Rob: You see! Ninety per cent of all British violence is over women.
> R: What about the other ten per cent?
> Dave/Rob: (Simultaneously) This (pointing to beer).
> R: So how can you stop it?
> Dave: You can't. Ain't nothing better than booze and women. If you give them up you might as well be in the nick.

Avoiding trouble

The potential for trouble in the spheres of life the ex-inmate wishes to participate in makes him initially wary. In the first few weeks many avoid places where trouble is prevalent, mainly because the memory of incarceration compares unfavourably with their freedom outside, even if that freedom is minus what they enjoy most. Although Dave eventually returned to his usual activities for the reasons cited above, it was not a sudden decision. At first, both Dave and Rob would travel several miles to a different area rather than frequent the places they knew spelt trouble.

> (On our first meeting outside, Dave and Rob suggested that we go for a drink in a village about ten miles away. As we passed their local pub the following comments were made)
> Rob: That's the local bottle there, Dick. That's the local boozer.
> Dave: The only thing to do is to keep out of there, that's a trouble spot.

(Later, in Dave's house)

Father: Where did you go, up to the (local pub) . . .

Dave: (Interjecting sharply) Couldn't very well go in there, could we?

(On our next meeting)

R: Why don't we go into town?

Rob: We stick to the village pubs now. You can't go anywhere in town without there being a fight. They fight everywhere down there.

Dave: We haven't been to town at all. Too much trouble down there.

Mate: Do you know Walsall has the highest rate of violence in Britain?

Dave: You see why we can't go to town. That's out. Go down there and you're sure to get in a fight, so we just stay clear.

Similar statements were common among most others when they first came out of detention, the only variation being the activity they considered to be the greatest source of vulnerability. For Terry, it was football matches. For Bill, it was the discos:

> (On our first meeting, Bill having turned down a suggestion by his mates that we go to a dance)
> I go to dances on Saturday mornings. They're only a bunch of teenies there, but at least you can dance any way you want to. I go to the discos sometimes but they laugh at me there. They don't appreciate good dancing. They just look for a reason to fight; call you flash and bang, that's it.

At this stage there is no rationale given to mates other than the fact that the ex-inmate fears trouble. Many even amplify the threat of trouble as a justifiable excuse for not engaging in an activity which others try to coax them into, and which ex-inmates themselves desire. They deny themselves participation in some meaningful activity on the justification that to do otherwise may lead to trouble and ultimately to official others again denying them participation in any meaningful activity.

Within a few weeks, after other spheres become routine and mundane, the ex-inmate realises that he can only attain enjoyment from involvement in those activities where trouble is predictable. He begins to participate, although always wary that trouble will ensue. The activity is enjoyable, but partially spoilt by the threat of trouble. For example, two mates of

Rob finally convinced him to go to a night club that stayed open to 3 am. Once there, he seemed to shift from a state of enjoyment to one of apprehension. At one stage he remarked, 'I feel comfortable in a place like this; at least you have something (women) to look at.' Minutes later, he said, 'These places are all right but you have to watch yourself. There's always trouble. I'd never bring a bird in here and expect to walk out with her.'

Occasionally there is trouble, which is interpreted by the ex-inmate as potentially implicating him. He may be with a group of mates when one of them becomes involved in a fight. He may discover himself riding in a stolen car. He may be challenged to a fight by others who enter an objection to his demeanour or some specific thing he has done. He may be caught up in a football mob and be associated with an illegal act effected by one of his comrades. Troublesome events are infrequent, but they are bound to occur for those who participate regularly in these spheres of life. The ex-inmate must prepare himself for the likelihood of trouble, and effect a course of action which allows him to save himself both in the immediate situation and from the long term effects of being officially in trouble.

For a considerable time, the worry of official trouble predominates over face-saving in a situation with high crime potential. The ex-inmate forgets about his detention experience in most aspects of everyday life, but his memory is quickly sparked if he senses any incident which recalls the events which led to his incarceration. A favoured response if trouble is imminent is to forgo face-saving activities and simply leave the scene of trouble. In other words, he runs.

Rob proposed this course of action as we sat in a pub with Dave and discussed some of the incidents that frequently occur there: 'If there was a fight in here now, I'd run the other way. I'd be through that door so fast!' Later that night, we moved to a disco where a fight did develop. As soon as the initial blows were struck, and in spite of the fact we were not directly involved, the response was to leave. To Rob, the reason was obvious: 'We're the first ones to get blamed if the coppers come. They know our faces.' On another occasion, after a steady diet of football and beer from noon to midnight, Rob was involved in another conflict situation. This was the incident where Paul became involved in a fight over a scarf; again, Rob decided to flee from the scene as the safest alternative: 'I just come out for wounding. With a record like mine I would have been done for sure.'

Face-saving for those who choose to run is done verbally. Feeling that he may be defined as 'chicken' by those who stayed on while he ran, the individual tries to compensate by describing past trouble situations in which he performed as expected. For example, after the incident with Paul just described, Rob used every opportunity to insert his past illegal exploits into the conversation. Feeling lowered by his actions, Rob tried to raise himself by relating past behaviour which showed others (especially Paul) that he was not always law-abiding. This was not limited to previous fights, but to all types of offences. For instance, as we sat in a restaurant, the following comment by Rob was typical:

Paul: If we had a tie on and some shirts we could go to the Locarno.

Rob: I used to get all the shirts I wanted when Stumpy – Dick, you know Stumpy – when Stumpy worked in the boutique in town. Under the counter. We walked out with bundles, we did.

When Rob gave his reasons for resolving a conflict situation by leaving it, he mentioned the fact that his record would signify him as especially culpable if the 'law' became involved. This is another common justification for backing down from the challenge of others. It carries more weight because others also firmly believe in the causal relationship between past record and severity of treatment if caught. This was the argument Bill used when his prediction about trouble at a disco came true. Employing a mediator known to members of the opposing factions and who had just come out of prison himself, Bill made the following appeal:

> I just came out of detention and if I get in a fight I'm the one who gets picked up. It's the one who's been inside who gets it, not the others. Even if they started it I'd be the one who'd get nicked. Can't you tell them that I've just come out and don't want to go back again?

There is a third source of justification which involves a claim of greater loyalty and significance outside those under examination. The ex-inmate can claim that his job is too meaningful to risk by future trouble, or that his girl is trying to keep him out of trouble and will leave him if anything happens. Because these arguments are thought to be methods of opting out by one's mates, they are rarely invoked for longer than the first month after release. When they are employed, it is more to avoid specific incidents than as a general excuse for non-involvement. For example, Bill usually took his girl friend with him to any of the numerous 'night spots' he frequented. However, there were certain occasions when he wished to avoid these spots or other places that mates suggested because of suspected trouble. On these occasions he would say that his girl friend wished to do something else or that she would not allow him to go even though he was willing. One night, more than two months after his release, a mate wanted him to go to a pub for a disco. Bill declined, simply stating, 'Ann doesn't like me to go up there 'cause of the Mecca Mafia (a group of youths whose headquarters was in the pub). She's still trying to keep me straight.'

During the period of getting back to meaningful activities with one's contemporaries, options are left open for exit in trouble situations. Similar situations in the past, often involving only a few minutes or even seconds, resulted in the person spending four months away from his normal meaningful existence. This clears the mind when incidents resembling those fateful situations recur after release. It is in these situations that deterrence exists as a powerful force and appropriate exits are taken.

Engaging in trouble

For a time, abstinence is in order. While the ex-inmate gets back to normal fairly quickly in his everyday situations with others, it takes him a little longer to establish the normality of situations with crime potential. However, this is eventually done because these same situations, and sometimes illegal activity itself, are a most important part of normal existence. With time, at least minor offences are normalised as part of meaningful activity.

It should again be noted that the subject is not in search of a deviant role at this point. He does not seek personal worth in a 'criminal' identity, mainly because he sees himself as conventional, but also because there is no real career structure of crime open to him in any case. There is no supportive environment for a criminal role, although there is support for crimes as part of activities involved in other roles which are available.

Crime exists as a part of normal activity in those spheres of life to which these youths attribute greatest significance. Hence, to be back to normal, to be free, requires the decision to traverse the invitational edge and become immersed in all aspects of meaningful activities, even if this includes crime. One cannot very well go to a party where pot is available without smoking it; one cannot very well go for a joyride in a stolen car without having a go at it; one cannot very well be abused by others without having a go at them. The role of observer is most unpleasant, and the lure of participation is too great for those seeking meaningful experiences. Hence, the initial wariness because of sensitivity to the criminal fact gives way to the desire to be normal.

(Sitting in a pub with Paul, two months after his release)

R: Dave and Rob don't go into town much any more, into Walsall. There's always fights down there. One night I was with them and we went to a place where there was a big fight. We took off . . .

Paul: That's what it's like at first, when you first come out. But after awhile, you just say, 'Oh the hell with it' and join in for a laugh. I'll bet when you see them the next time they'll be back to normal, joining in the fights instead of running.

Getting back to acts which could be deemed illegal if detected is a final move towards normality. These acts can be engaged in willingly, part of the excitement which goes with participation in the particular activity which interests them. Petty crimes are frequent as part of the enjoyment of a good 'night out'. There is an awareness of the illegality of the acts, but this causes little reservation because the night would not be as complete or meaningful without them. The development of crime amid other social activities can be depicted by describing a week-end enjoyed by Paul.[8]

Paul went to work on Friday afternoon. 'I went between one and two, to get my pay. That's the only part (of work) I like.' After work, it was straight to the local pub, where he met nine of his mates and drank until closing time. As closing time approached, they considered where they might go.

Mate: The Meridan Club is O.K.

Paul: I can't go to the Meridan Club. I got banned from there for fighting.

Mate: How 'bout the Florida Club then?

Paul: No, wait, that's the one I got banned from. That's the place where you go upstairs isn't it?

Mate: Yea.

Paul: Why don't we go to the Locarno? I don't think we're banned from there. I'm banned from so many places – about ten places – I don't know . . .

After a few dances and drinks in the Locarno, the group started to shout and stamp their feet in unison. Failing to heed the warning of 'bouncers', they were bounced. Paul and a mate described this to a mutual friend they later met in a restaurant.

Paul: It was great. There were about ten of us, and we all got up and started stamping our feet. It was great until the fucking bouncers told us to stop.

Mate: Yea, there's more bleedin' bouncers in there than customers.

Paul: We've been kicked out of there four times now. It's getting so that there's no place we can go any more.

Another source of ban is the many Pakistani restaurants which are invaded by Paul and his mates most Friday nights. Wishing to conserve their funds for the remainder of the week-end, they often decide not to pay the bill. On this particular night, everyone enjoyed a steak dinner and was having coffee when someone sensed that the waiters could speak more English than expected. One of the waiters was on the phone, apparently telling the police that there was a gang of youths plotting to leave without paying. As the police station was just around the corner this signalled a quick exit, with Paul throwing aside the lone waiter trying to bar the way. The police approached as everyone scattered. This was the end of a night out, but only the beginning of the week-end.

At noon the next day the group gathered in the pub, this time with the intention of going to the Birmingham City football match. During the course of consuming four pints of beer, football 'aggro' developed. While singing their football songs, Paul and a mate went outside the pub and started a snowball, stone and brick fight with three young boys. This did not end until Paul put a rock through the pub window and his mate chased one of the boys down the street with a brick. Soon after, they proceeded up the road to the football match, only to learn that it was cancelled because of weather conditions. The 'aggro' was not immediately suspended, as passers-by were jeered and attacked with both rocks and snowballs. There were also a few proverbial milk bottle thefts, with Paul remarking, 'A pint a day the healthy way'. Paul, two mates and I eventually ended up in the billiard hall where we played snooker for the remainder of the afternoon.

After supper at Paul's house it was back to the meeting place, the smoke room (public bar) in the local pub. From there, a group of thirteen moved around the corner to another pub because it stayed open until two in the morning behind closed doors. There Paul passed the word about a party at a girl's home in a 'posh district'. They decided some pot was needed, and sent the only West Indian in the group because he could find a supply most readily. Everyone contributed fifty pence, and the messenger soon delivered the goods. Paul explained this in the same way that every other activity was explained.

Paul: We always have a little grass, just for kicks, you know. It's mostly booze, but you can have a good time with grass as well.

Mate: Smoking only has an effect when you expect it to. Smoking doesn't do anything for me. You have to make it do something, you have to make yourself aware.

Paul: Yea, you're right, it only affects you when you want it to, but it's good for a laugh.

At one in the morning, the group set off for a party, some in a taxi and some in a stolen car which had been acquired by one of the participants the night before. The party lasted until the morning, with no further incidents to note other than the consumption of the pot and the following account given to me later of what I had missed by going home 'early':

Paul: Ted was a real laugh, Dick. Well, a nut. He does stupid things for a laugh. He's at the party and he goes up to this bird and says, 'Will you go to bed with me?' When she says 'No' he says, 'Do you want this glass in your face?' And she goes to bed with him! The girl started crying. He went upstairs and shagged the ass off her, and she went home crying as well. What a laugh man. He's mad! But what a laugh at a party. He'll do anything!

Another source of offence occurs when the opportunity crops up to drive a car during a night out. Many have a passion to drive; a car is their vehicle to a meaningful existence. It is not that a car is a source of status gain, a convenience, or something craved for only because it is denied. It is simply a passion, a joy, a joyride. As Steve's mother explained:

> (In Steve's home, a private conversation)
> His whole trouble is that he loves the car. He just can't resist it. If he sees a car, any car, outside there, he has got to get it.

One of Steve's mates offered an additional explanation to the researcher:

> (In a pub, private conversation while Steve was at the bar)
> I think car thefts – or Steve's case anyhow – is just an escape. A car is an escape for these kids. They want to get away from everything, and the car is one way that they can escape. It's exciting, challenging, different. Even being chased or caught isn't always bad, it just adds to the excitement.

Steve's relationship with me was bridged by my car. Whenever it was available, Steve literally begged to drive it, even to simply turn it around once we had arrived at his house. When he did drive it, he was totally unaware of any offence he might be committing. For example, one evening he smoked pot, drank six pints of beer, and then climbed into the driver's seat and drove to his house. Technically, in addition to possession of pot and drinking under age charges, he could have been arrested for driving under the influence of alcohol, driving while disqualified, and driving with no insurance. Yet he assured me on this occasion and on many subsequent occasions that he had not committed even one offence since his release from detention.

(Private conversation in a pub)

Steve: Paul is screwin' ain't he? He's taken some cars.

R: I don't know. How do you know that?

Steve: Well, last week I asked him if he'd taken any more cars, and he said, 'Just a couple'.

R: I didn't know about that. He's been doing minor things, petty stuff . . .

Steve: I ain't. I ain't even done that. I haven't broken one law since I come out.

Only one month after being put on probation for taking and driving offences, Steve was caught again and sent to detention on similar charges. Within one month of leaving detention, he was driving illegally. At the end of the follow-up research period, he intimated that he was driving stolen cars. This latter choice may have been a function of the decreased opportunities I provided. Steve's only means of fulfilling his lust was to illegally drive a car belonging to someone he knew, or even more illegally, to take and drive the car of someone he did not know. The question became whether he would eventually reach a climax or whether he would again be temporarily castrated by the penal system.

Passions of another sort lead to engagement in trouble which is not sought or participated in willingly. A major source of fighting is over girls, arising from challenges in specific situations. Such encounters were observed during the course of fieldwork. For example, one night during a party at Paul's house, someone grabbed his girl saying, 'Come here you fucking wench'. Incensed by this, Paul hit the offender and a few blows were thrown before order was restored by others present. Later Paul, who had by all definitions lost the fight and lost face, recounted the incident with a mate.

Paul: The trouble is he's a big bastard. I was going to smash him with a bottle. He was really getting me mad.

Mate: The thing with him is that even a bottle wouldn't put him down.

Paul: I know, but I was so mad at the fucker I was going to do it anyway. The trouble is there weren't enough birds here. Things went wrong. People were coming up to the bed(room)s and everything.

Occasionally, fights over girls arise because the subject's girl friend continues a relationship with someone else which developed while the subject was in detention. Steve renewed his former friendship with a girl, but within two months after release he could no longer tolerate her dual loyalty. The method of conflict resolution was obvious to Steve: a fight. I did not observe the actual encounter, although the fight publicity and retrospective accounts were prolific among those who were associated with the combatants. Steve lost the fight and his girl friend. Steve's accounts centred on the fight rather than on his former girl.

(In a pub, with a mate and the researcher)

The fight finished it. It was a fair battle though, no weapons. I cut him over the eye and he ripped my brand new coat up the arms and all down the side. It cost me ten quid.

The fight game is also part of the scene in football activities, in pubs, and at discos, as we have already discussed in separate incidents involving Paul, Rob, Dave and Bill. The prediction that fighting is the most probable source of trouble holds true because it is part of normal activity and is a normal means of conflict resolution. Fighting is a fact of life, although a possibility rather than a probability. It is a natural means of asserting oneself, of gaining freedom in spite of the risk that outsiders will deem it unnatural and cause a further loss of freedom.

All of these troublesome activities are not seen in terms of a commitment to anything but enjoyment of the moment. They may be a part of a way of life, but only one part in the definition of a good night out. This suggests 'the episodic rather than constant character of moral release. [It] is episodic release from moral constraint'.[9]

Even after four months in detention and a further period of dealing with that fact in the community, the subjects are not bound to a deviant role. Nevertheless, the nature of their meaningful leisure activities does mean that they are sometimes bound to become involved in crime.

Dealing with the 'criminal' fact

The crime fact is of greatest significance in the spheres of life which the individual chooses to participate in as a way of seeking meaningful experience. The criminal fact can be more pervasive, for it cuts across spheres of life where it is socially known and/or privately felt. The fact of criminal conviction, and particularly the detention experience, must be put in place along with other social facts in each sphere of life.

The influence of the detention experience is summed up. The role of official agents in the community – the after-care officer and the police – is realised. A resolution is reached on the issue of employment and respectability. Further consideration is also given to the reactions of intimates. In combination, these others outline the structure within which the ex-inmate must operate; they define the nature of, and limits to, his freedom. He is of course free to traverse the boundaries, the effect being either greater freedom in the different structure he helps to create, or a loss of freedom if others choose to remove him forcefully to their own idea of the appropriate structure for persons of his type.

The continuing personal influence of the detention experience

While others may deem the fact of detention relevant, there are also ways in which the ex-inmate himself can realise the continuing influence of the detention experience. The impact of incarceration may affect the ex-inmate's general outlook and approach to life. In addition, the ex-inmate may himself refer to the detention experience and use it in specific situations with certain types of audiences. Also relevant is the extent to which he maintains the identity he held within the inmate structure, including his contacts with other ex-inmates.

In terms of a lasting effect on everyday life, the detention experience is of little significance. It can only be repeated that after the person gets back to normal outside, detention seems a remote and distant interlude in everyday life. This of course varies according to specific situations and depends on the reactions of others.

Amidst the usual surroundings and acquaintances outside, the only spontaneous comments about detention in general were about its remoteness. For instance, Paul suddenly stepped out of his involvement with mates in his local pub to remark to me: 'It seems like ages since I was there (in detention); as if it didn't happen at all; as if each week-end I was here at The Railroad with my mates rather than in that place.'

Caught up in everyday life, the individual does not often reflect on the past or the future. In contrast, the period of detention is viewed as a time for stock-taking, a time when the course of his life is reflected upon, charted, and predictions are made on this basis.

(Sitting in a pub with Rob, Dave and a mate, discussing women)

Rob: Inside you have lots of time to think of women and you come to know how you feel about ones (them). It's the same with everything, you come to know about how you feel about all kinds of things. You sort of take stock I guess.

An explanation of why stock-taking is characteristic of life in detention, but not outside, centres on the fact that existence inside is not like normal everyday life. In a different environment, the inmate can stand outside his normal everyday affairs and assess them from inside. As we have seen, this is particularly prevalent in the first two weeks of incarceration, but it continues later because there is ample time for reflection and still later because the person is about to return to the reality outside. The inmate takes stock, and while doing so starts to imagine things in his world outside which his circumstances prevent him from dealing with in reality. Consequently, he re-enters the community worried that he has changed, others have changed, and thus that the structure of their relationship will not be the same. Everything will be abnormal; most frightening, he will be abnormal. But when these images are compared with the reality once outside, his fears are soon allayed and he gets back to normal. Detention has little impact after all. For this the ex-inmate is thankful; because of this the prominence of detention quickly fades.

(In a pub with Terry and two mates, a month after his release)

Terry: (In a side conversation with the researcher) Be four weeks, a month next Friday since I come out.

R: Yea, it goes quickly.

Terry: Seems like two months.

R: Does it seem remote?

Terry: What do you mean?

R: Uh, let me see. Does it seem like it almost didn't happen?

Terry: Yea, it seems long ago. You know when you asked me about the last few weeks (inside) and I said it really drags?

R: Yea.

Terry: Well it drags, and you worry what people will be like when you get out. But everyone has been great to me. You can see here (pointing to mates) my mates have helped me, got on with me. We go out, buy each other pints, just as before. Everybody in here, they just accepted me on the first night. They were just glad to see me.

R: Is there anyone who treated you in the way you were worrying about?

Terry: No one really. All me mates at work talked to me and just said they were glad to see me back. Just them who don't know you very well, they're always a little suspicious.

Once the feeling of acceptance and normalcy is established, the ex-inmate is no longer suspended in a reflexive mood. He goes about everyday activities much as he always did, his reflexive capacities only sparked when others bring up the detention fact. He no longer dwells upon a map of past, present and future; he lives for the moment, enjoying a present that does not consider the detention experience to be very relevant.

The detention experience is simply not considered relevant while engaging in everyday activities where reminders from others are absent. Its only entrance into everyday conversation is via the ex-inmate's wish to offer anecdotes about the world inside to those audiences entertained by such stories. In this context, he dwells upon the informal system, discussing the formal system only in terms of negative aspects, of how abnormal the place is. Mainly, he recounts stories about the 'underside' of the institution by describing activities, mostly illegal, within the inmate system. The accounts are often amplified; distortion is not deemed relevant because these are merely stories for amusement. The ex-inmate's audience cannot confirm his description in any case, and this is conducive to amplification for effect. He thereby achieves a little recognition, a touch of status, not in the sense of gaining reputation (as in a delinquent gang) but simply as an entertainer to enliven an otherwise dull situation.

The official regime of the institution is rarely talked about, and when it is, the depiction is of an unpleasant place which had little effect on the individual. Stories centre on the deprivations, such as no television, insufficient food, unsanitary conditions, poor medical facilities, no smoking, officers' rule by the 'knuckle', and so on. Most often, these stories are exaggerated to conform with the outside world's mythology about the decadence of prisons. For instance, Ken told his relatives about the cockroaches in the dorms; Pete described in detail to his mates an alleged case of a mousetail being found in somebody's soup. In most cases, the point which the ex-inmate wishes to make is that the institution is no more than a bad place. That is, he did his time, met the deprivations, but came out unscathed. Apart from being 'lowered' at the time of the experience because of the deprivations and degradations, he was not essentially changed.

(Bill, with his girl friend and the researcher in a pub, broke a lull in the conversation by talking about detention)

Bill: Inside you're nothing, they take everything away from you. That's why everybody acts so childish. When they take everything away from you, it turns you into a little boy. The biggest treat they give you in there is shampoo. That's right! They were trying to get toothpaste when I left.

Girl: I don't like them places.

Bill: They're all right. They made me a bit more dependent at the time. But they didn't change me. I'm just the same now as when I went in; nothing's changed.

The predominant accounts of the detention experience centre on the illicit activities developed and sustained within the inmate structure. Steve would tell others about his activities as a tobacco dealer whenever the opportunity arose.

(Steve, his girl friend, and a mate, in a pub)

Girl: Don't tell me you're having another one (cigarette).

Steve: I'm still making up for when I was inside.

Mate: I thought you used to smoke in there as well.

Steve: Never went a night without one. I used to get everything in there 'cause I was the tobacco daddy. Sometimes I'd have forty toffee bars, three of those duffs [cake, in exchange for tobacco].

Rob's favourite story concerned his thefts from the kitchens while he was doing a painting job there. Talking about the perks of his job to a mate, Rob said, 'I used to steal buns out of the kitchen and take them down to the boys. I'd stuff them down my socks every time I came back from the kitchen.' Most had a story about an actual fight or a near fight while inside. Pete enjoyed telling his two younger sisters about 'sitting on a fat kid (Blake) and rubbing his face into the floor'. Everyone had similar incidents to recount; if they did not have personal experiences they created them or described the activities of others.

Descriptions of the inmate system itself would also be offered. Usually the person outlining the system would place himself at the top – 'I (or we) used to rule' – and give instances where others were subjugated. Hence Bill, who by self-definition and social definition inside was on the verge of div status, placed himself in a different position when describing the system to an outsider.

(On the street, talking to his girl friend and four mates)

Bill: When we (referring to some fellow kitchen workers) was inside we used to rule. There was a queer in the kitchen . . . The kitchen lads would always go up last for grub. Well, we had a signal that when he went up last everyone would shout 'Queer!' They did, and he was so shocked that his tray flew up in the air! All the screws laughed too! We'd always get down on somebody who was different at all really. (Pause) D.C. was a good laugh, at least for the daddies.

The ex-inmate uses the detention experience to gain a flutter of significance among those who are impressed by such affairs. The extent to which these stories are used to gain a snippet of recognition varies according to the individual himself, other resources for status gain, the possibility of being discredited, and the availability of a receptive audience. Bill, a noted teller of stories about detention and a host of other experiences, was relied upon by his mates to supply entertainment along these lines. On one occasion, while Bill and another ex-inmate (from Winson Green) took turns at relating inside stories, a mate said to the researcher, 'You'd better get in close and listen to this. I've heard it a hundred times before, but it's still a laugh. He's always on about the nick.'

The subjects themselves are often sensitive to the function of such stories. One evening in a pub, we met two friends of Dave and Rob. Dave stood talking to them for fifteen minutes about his experiences inside, while Rob and I sat chatting. At one stage Rob said, 'Look at Dave, look at him, he's telling them all about being inside. He likes to talk about it you know. (Gesturing with his shoulders) It makes him look bigger.' Both Rob and I gave a faint 'Ahh', which caused Dave to remark, 'Isn't that right, that warden was a nut case?' When we did not reply, Dave sought my help in backing him up. 'Hey Richard, wasn't that warden off?' I replied, 'Yes, I guess he was a bit different.' Rob then said to me, 'He's just trying to be big.'

As Dave would readily agree, it is much easier to present these stories and an identity based on them without the presence of others who have first-hand knowledge of the world inside. When knowledgeable others are present, the description of what happened and who one happened to be must be negotiated with these others, rather than simply presented to fit one's personal needs.

Rob and Dave were the only two persons studied in the Birmingham area who remained as mates after the detention experience or who even bothered to initiate contact.[10] This may be because of their friendship before incarceration, the feeling that they were 'in it together' on the same charges, and the fact that they were residing within close proximity. However, in the case of Terry and Andy, the same elements were involved but they made no effort at contact after release. None of the other eleven made contact with any ex-inmate, except if by a chance meeting or at the instigation of the researcher. Explanation of this lack of persistence in social relationships created within the detention structure after release revolves around the question of discrepant identities inside and out.

We have already seen how each individual constructs and maintains his identity within the detention centre. In an effort at self-preservation, he employs images of himself which make him out to be more than he knows he is, tries to minimise a similar presentation by others, and aligns with those who will aid his cause. Naturally concerned about his self, he is essentially selfish in his relations with other inmates and tries to use them to his own advantage. Friendships are a marriage of convenience, forced by the nature of the reality inside and likely to alter drastically in another reality.

To illustrate, we can consider what happened when I brought Rob and Paul together for the first and only time after their release. Rob experienced a marked sense of distance from Paul's everyday sphere of life, and frequently commented to me about his estrangement. On the environment, Rob had several observations.

> (Approaching Paul's house with the researcher)
> 'It's pretty grotty, ain't it? Look at the homes, all falling apart. Wouldn't fancy living 'round here.' Later, passing a shop with an 'Anything bought or sold' sign, Rob was reminded of Paul's incessant talk inside about his antique business. Rob said with sarcasm, 'I'll bet that's the "antique" business Paul used to work at.' Sitting in a pub with Paul and some of Paul's mates, Rob commented to the researcher, 'This place is even worse than the local bottle (pub on his housing estate at home). Don't like boozin' in these places.'

Rob also commented on the nature of his relationship with Paul.

> (In a pub, an aside with the researcher apart from the general conversation with Paul and his mates)

Rob: It's funny, even though we were the best of mates inside – really close – we still had our squabbles. It's hard to get on with anybody in there; you could have a scrap even with your best mate. You're only mates 'cause you're inside, but outside is completely different.

R: Why is that?

Rob: You have to protect yourself and each other, but outside you have your own mates, your own life.

As mentioned before, part of the reason why meetings after release are rare and why strain is induced when they do occur relates to the problem of presenting a consistent self. If as an inmate he described his home community in a way which is impossible to confirm in reality, then he may decide it is better to preserve the image by not exposing the reality.

What happens when this is not done was displayed when Steve and Paul got together about three months after their release, again at my instigation. Inside, Steve had presented his area as a centre of excitement, describing the pubs and discos on his estate and presenting his life, if not his area, in 'crime-paranoid' fashion, that is, crime was a common part of the generally exciting community. With each story Paul told about similar escapades, Steve had one better. The one and only night they met after release, on Steve's territory, there was a mutual definition of disaster. Paul defined the entire scene as a bore, and did not reserve his comments for himself or me. He attacked what Steve valued: regarding the pub we were in, at best, thus 'It's all right for bringing a really good bird in for a quiet drink'; at worst, 'Is this your local? I'd rather be inside!' None of Steve's mates were around, causing Paul to remark, 'Where's all your big mates Steve, inside (pause) the house?' Paul suggested going to Steve's house for coffee after the pub closed, but Steve had to recommend the chip shop because his parents would not let him bring his friends into the house. Paul referred to him as 'homeless'.

This was their first and last meeting. When I suggested getting together the following week, Paul interjected, 'I'm not coming all the way up here just for this. I can pop into town for a better time than this.' In response to this as to Paul's other comments during the night, Steve was forced by the circumstances to opt for little more than silence.

When Paul was faced with bringing an ex-inmate from inside into *his* world outside, he chose a different means of resolving the discrepancy between images created inside and the reality outside. When I brought Rob to have a 'day out' as defined by Paul, Paul decided to effect a convergence between inside myths and outside reality. That is, he acted as if his world was really full of excitement, including exciting forms of 'crime', as he had described inside. Rob was introduced to all of Paul's 'criminal' friends. The day was highlighted by Paul engaging in a fight, and challenging opposing fans and police at a football match. While these activities were in a sense normal for Paul, they seemed to be amplified for Rob's benefit. Faced with the image of himself he had created inside, Paul tried to make it as real as the circumstances would allow. Rob remained unimpressed. Inside he went along with Paul or at least acknowledged that his outside world seemed exciting. Faced with this world, Rob neither joined in the 'crimes' nor felt part of the scene created by Paul.

(Near the end of the day, in a pub with Paul and several of Paul's mates, Rob spoke in an aside to the researcher)

Rob: I don't like places like this. This ain't my idea of, well (Pause) I feel like that chap on TV who always fights with his manager.

R: What, er, what's that?

Rob: You know that programme. He's always in a fight with his manager at work and nobody talks to him.

R: How does that fit into this situation?

Rob: You, well, you and Paul are the only ones I know here. I just feel out of it, as if this isn't my kind of place.

Rob and Paul did not meet again.

If relationships inside are not continued outside, there is not likely to be much persistence of the inmate structure created by the inmates inside. The social types of the inmate system seem to be created for the world inside, then rejected and forgotten about in dealing with the reality outside. The individual's social category inside – as a daddy, div or somewhere in between – is largely irrelevant in the very different reality back home. The desire to be rid of the inmate structure along with other aspects of the detention experience may be a further reason why relationships are not continued. The structure does not persist because contacts are not made; conversely contact is not made out of fear that the structure may persist.

This fear was most evident in considering the continuing power which daddies might hold if we met outside. Leaving detention is not only being freed from the hold of the official system, but also from the intimidation of powerful inmates. Above all else, the ex-inmate wishes to avoid those who might continue their demands, carry out threats, or whatever else can be imagined. Many of the persons studied in Birmingham were especially sensitive to Fred, the biggest daddy of them all. They would mention in retrospect his activities inside, speculate on his activities upon release, and actually avoid places which he was thought to frequent. Typical was Pete's reaction when I mentioned some ex-inmates at a night club.

(In Pete's home, with Pete and his two younger sisters)

R: I was down at The Rainbow with Tony the other night.

Pete: Oh yea?

R: Errol and Chico (two friends of Fred inside) were there too.

Pete: What about Fred, was he there? (Changing tone, almost alarmed)

R: No.

Pete: Oh (as if relieved). I'd never go anywhere that bastard might be.

Former mates from inside, like the detention establishment itself, are kept out of everyday life as much as possible. They are a source of reflection, discussion, and even personal significance when the detention experience arises as a topic in everyday discourse. However, the reality they are believed to represent is avoided by the ex-inmate, cast aside in the quest for normal existence within his own community, within his own definition of that community. Hopefully other people in the community see it that way as well.

The continuing public influence of the detention experience

While the ex-inmate can personally relegate the detention experience to a minimal level of concern, he still must take into account how various publics continue to view this aspect of his identity. Since he learnt on release that the greater the social distance the greater the potential for negative reaction, the ex-inmate may be particularly wary of those official and officious others who might limit his freedom.

We have already discussed how the released subjects were particularly sensitive to the police. Nearly everyone predicted some degree of police suspicion based on their 'ex-convict' identity. This belief was not met by personal reality; as weeks, then months passed by, not one of the Birmingham subjects was picked up or even stopped by the police.

This is not to say that some special sensitivity to police presence does not persist. If the police are present, they usually become the focal point of concern. The ex-inmate feels self-conscious, and his comments reflect those feelings. Hence, two months after release, Rob and Dave were still jittery about even seeing a police car.

(While driving my car, with Rob and Dave as passengers. At a roundabout, we saw a police car. Dave immediately became 'jumpy' when we spotted a car behind us as we came off the roundabout.)

Dave: Is that the coppers behind us?

Rob: I don't know. It looks like a Mini. I think the police car was a Triumph. No, it was an Escort, a Ford Escort.

Dave: I hope it's not the coppers. I feel funny every time I see those bastards.

The police would occasionally come into a pub frequented by a subject and his mates. Although glances would be cast in the direction of the ex-inmate and his associates, there was rarely an attempt even to engage in conversation. In fact, on one occasion Steve spotted the policeman who had arrested him, and tried to initiate an encounter himself. Steve went up beside the policeman, stared at him, even nodded, apparently attempting to impress mates assembled in the pub. The policeman acted with ignorance, simply drinking and chatting with his two colleagues.

In Paul's local pub, a policeman would occasionally come off duty and join Paul and his mates for drinks and games. He was in no way a hindrance to the normal course of events. On the first occasion Paul informed me: 'See that bloke there? He's a copper. You'd never think so would you, in here amongst all this lot?' The policeman did not come in until eleven at night, and he was still there when we departed at one in the morning. He played chess and darts with Paul's mates, and shared in the purchase of drinks with them. [11] The group smoked pot in his presence, and he could easily tune into conversations about crime, including the fact that there was a stolen car in front of the pub. This did not act as a restraint, and the policeman seemed to be viewed more as a mate than as a possible informer.

In sum, one of the most unanimous predictions about negative reaction does not hold true in the subjects' eyes. When I asked about this approximately two months after the subjects' release, they generally shifted their perspective by saying that only if the police had some proof that the individual had actually done something would they act on suspicion. Thus Terry commented, 'The coppers don't care unless they know you done a job. They ain't going to bother you if you're just sittin' in a pub with your mates, minding your own business.'

A similar degree of unconcern evolves with respect to the other arm of the 'law' in the community, the probation officers. Usually after the first month, the weekly meetings are cut back to once a fortnight and eventually to once a month. This is seen strictly in terms of a reduction in official harassment, as a further move away from identification with the 'law'. At this stage, the main discussion about after-care centres on dispensing with the formal requirements and feeling relieved that the demands are minimal. Dave offered a typical comment in saying, 'I see the probation officer once a month now. *He's really laid off* . . . He's going to see about getting me off it in six months.'

The feeling that the probation officer has 'laid off' implies that the ex-inmate previously felt some pressure exerted over him by the after-care requirement. The source of this pressure is usually the law enforcement function; specifically, the belief that the after-care officer may order a return to detention or prolong the supervision period if one does not appear to be conforming with the requirements of the licence. The ex-inmate feels in a bind, for his preoccupation in face of the after-care requirement is to present a favourable image to the officer above all else. For example, the ex-inmate will not even use the probation officer in a search for another job if he feels that the officer would view his job change as an indication of his tainted identity. In other words, he will not always use the service for what he defines as its major purpose because of the law enforcement powers of the officer. Ken was one person who experienced this bind.

(In Ken's home, with Ken, his grandfather and grandmother)

Grandfather: Ken has had three jobs now.

R: Three? What happened to the painting job?

Ken: They wanted me to go on a high ladder with no support. I said 'No' and they said, 'You're no use to us', and dismissed me.

Grandfather: The next week he got a job at a discount shop down the street from here. He and his sister both got a job there. He just left that today, both of them left that and got another job in the city centre at another shop.

R: Have you asked the probation officer about a job?

Grandmother: Oh, no, no. We haven't told him anything about Ken changing jobs.

R: (To Ken) He still thinks you're in the painting job?

Ken: Yea, because he told me you have to lead an industrial life. If you don't they can send you back. Two months, I could still do two more months at that place, so I don't say anything to the probation officer.

Even when the officer is used for apparently utilitarian purposes, his actions may be defined as stifling by the ex-inmate. Helping to obtain a job is seen as a very important function of the probation officer. However, as will be discussed shortly in relation to the employment question, with time many ex-inmates are not interested in the types of jobs which probation officers are able to procure. Many decide that the dole is as good as a job which pays little more in wages or status. In these cases, the probation officer's 'help' may be defined as a hindrance. Rob was one who experienced this.

(In a pub almost three months after Rob's release, Rob talking with two mates and the researcher)

Rob:	My probation officer went down with me to get my old job back, the bastard. We went straight down and got it. But I'd rather be on the box than that, so I quit (work) when I came out of the hospital (after an appendicitis operation). Probation officers can't get you decent jobs.[12]

In the end, the probation officer is used for very little. There is rarely a close personal relationship. As in Ken's case, this may partially be due to the law enforcement element. A related reason is that the subjects cannot see any purpose in such a relationship other than as a check on themselves. The officer just seems to fill up time with the same incessant questions which evoke only the answers the subjects want them to hear. They are both doing their duty, nothing more. By the time the probation officer 'lays off' – in other words, when he invokes the ritual at less frequent intervals – the ex-inmate is ready to lay off as well.

(Two and a half months after his release, during a night out with his mates, Steve engaged in a brief side conversation with the researcher)

Steve:	I was supposed to see my probation officer today but I didn't go. I didn't get home until 6.30 and I thought, 'Oh, bugger it.'
R:	What time were you supposed to go?
Steve:	6.30.
R:	Does he say anything when you don't turn up?
Steve:	I'll go tomorrow. It's my day off tomorrow. I'll go see him then. Just think, a bloody year of that. I thought when I was sent down that I had got rid of probation. I thought, 'Great, I won't have to see that bugger.' But then they gave me a year of it anyway. I hate going

> down there. You have to wait around for half an hour while he's seeing other kids, then you're only in there five bleedin' minutes. 'How's your job? How's your family? Have you got a bird? Ta Ta! See you in three weeks.'

Another problematic area is employment. As we have already discussed, part of becoming free is to gain respectability through having a job. Everyone in the follow-up group obtained a job soon after release in an initial quest for respectability. Opportunities were not blocked in terms of obtaining *a* job, although the jobs available were near the bottom of society's scheme of things.

It is not long before the individual begins to realise that he is at the bottom, that it is not very rewarding in respectability or financially to be a labourer and earning twelve pounds a week. He searches for alternatives. Some stay in their original job and try to be content with it. Others cannot resign themselves to this position, and begin changing jobs in the search for something better. The many who realise that 'job hopping' gets one no further eventually conclude that the dole is a preferred alternative.

Within two months after their release, only half the subjects held the same job as when they first came out. Most of those who maintain their job are not content with their work, but neither are they intent on getting another position. Past experience informs them that mobility can only be horizontal, not vertical, and geographical, not social. They may occasionally take a shot at another job, but usually one out of their class. For instance, Paul applied for a job in a car factory.

> (In a pub, private conversation)
> You start at forty-two quid a week. But they found out I was lying when I said I'd been at the firm (he is presently at) three years and never been in trouble.

Paul resigned himself to making one-third of the car factory wage in a local machine shop, and sought meaning elsewhere.

The only thing these people can do is to give appearances of significance by making their job out to be more than they know it is. Bill said his job involved travelling – to London and Scotland – when the only travelling he did was on the bus to and from the factory. Steve said he earned more than he did; Ken designated himself as a 'mechanic' rather than a 'garage boy'. They may try to appear respectable and successful while personally resigning themselves to a lowly occupation.[13]

The other half refuse to resign themselves, and start a process of moving from one job to another. The move is usually a search for something better, and it is at this stage that those who have done trade training inside attempt to gain employment in a related field outside. Only in one case was success struck. Dave doubled his wage from ten to twenty pounds a week when he moved from the labouring job he had held since he had left school to a job with a plastering firm. Aided by a sympathetic employer – 'He likes ex-cons, says he wanted to be a prison warden, that's what he wanted to do' – Dave used his trade training to obtain respectability. His new job became and remained a focal concern.

This is the exception. The other people who had trade training did not attempt to get a job in their field or quickly gave it up if they did do so. The explanation for this is that most employers willing to take ex-inmates on in a type of work related to their trade training are seen as exploitive as other types of employers. Both Rob and Ken left their painting jobs because the benefits of the job were no greater than others they had in different fields. In other words, they discovered that to be a painter or bricklayer or plasterer was no more enhancing than to be a factory labourer or shop assistant, that their trade training would not free them from the problem of unrespectable employment.

Some fail to grasp the power of this bind and continue their search by taking one job after another. In his first three months after release, Ken was a painter, a shop assistant in two different places, a hospital porter, and an assistant in a car repair garage. Ken left the painting job because of low wages and because he was asked to climb heights under what he considered to be dangerous conditions. He quit the job at one shop because he did not get paid for overtime, and in the other job he was not paid fourteen pounds owing to him, and the fight to get this became a preoccupation of the family. He left the porter's job because, 'I felt like everybody's bleedin' servant', and took a job in a garage. The primary fact about himself was always his job. Whenever he met anyone, including me, he would mention his latest job and what a fortunate position he was now in.

(Going to call on Ken, the researcher spotted him on the street)

Ken: (As he approached) Hi Rich. I'm working as a mechanic at a garage on Bristol Street.

R: A mechanic?

Ken: (Smiling) Sixty pence an hour!

R: When did you start there?

Ken: Thursday. I've just been there two days.

Unfortunately, the reality of the situation was not as respectable as it sounded.

(Later on the same day, in Ken's home with his grandparents)

Grand-mother: The job he has isn't no good you know.

Grand-father: Nah. You know what he earns?

R: Sixty pence an hour, isn't it?

Grand-father: Fifty pence an hour, and that's if he gets the job done in time.

Ken: (Looking dejected) They say how long the job should take, and if you take longer than they say, you don't get paid for it.

R: How have you been making out then? Have you been finishing in time?

Grand-father: He's earned four pounds fifty in the last two days. That's five bob an hour, twenty-five pence an hour! That's no good! A top mechanic earns one thirty-five an hour, at least judging by what the garage charges you.

Grand-mother: It must be a training then, Ken. They must be teaching you the job to only pay you that much.

Many begin to realise that changing jobs provides little solution to the problem. Unemployment becomes equally attractive, and within two months of leaving detention, some had chosen this alternative. Among these was Rob, who offered his reasons for going on the dole.

(In a pub with the researcher and a mate)

Rob: If I went back to work I wouldn't last for another week.

R: Why is that?

Rob: Just can't take it in there.

R: What were you doing anyway?

Rob: Welding, repetition. Just the same thing.

R: Did you get paid while you were off?

Rob: No.

R: No union?

Rob: Never heard of it in that place. (Pause) I'm staying on the box. I felt great this week but I don't think I'll go back to work at that place. I think I may go on the dole. If others can get away with it I don't see why I can't.

Mate: (Overhearing our conversation) That's no good.

Rob: It's as good as a dead-end job.

Ed, who chose the unemployment option after three weeks of work, offered the economic side of the argument:

> (In a café, with several of Ed's acquaintances)
> I get six pounds a week from youth employment plus thirteen pounds a month from social security. The last place I worked at I took home fourteen pounds (a week). It's not worth working in a place like that, man. Social security gave me twenty pounds when I came out of the nick too.

During the two to four-month period after release, nearly everyone settles on one of the three alternatives described. They accept their lot by staying in one job and trying to make it appear respectable; they do not accept their lot and continue their search for something better; or, they throw in their lot and become unemployed. Whatever stage the individual is involved in, he eventually realises that he can expect little more although he always desires a lot more. The ex-inmate usually reconciles the discrepancy between what he desires and what he has come to expect, by seeing it as part of the order of things – as something he has no power to change. This is implied in a statement by Pete:

> (In Pete's home, private conversation)
> I'd be made up if I had a motor. But some of them who aren't even ex-cons don't get ahead. It's just the way life is around here.

Little change occurs in relationships with intimate others. The initial act of bringing the ex-inmate back gives way to the normal patterns which existed before the incarcerated period. Even Cliff, the only subject to leave home during the Birmingham research period, continued to return home for meals every Sunday and to call his mother at work daily. The fact of detention has only a minimal lasting effect on relationships with family and friends.

Under the condition of continuing agreeable relationships, there is a subtle effect of detention which is experienced by all. This involves both the ex-inmate and his intimates in remaining wary of possible trouble and the repetition of the agony this brings. Even three months after the person's release, his parents still offer him words of caution as he departs for a night out. Although the individual is simply going to a pub with some mates, he is subject to warnings about trouble. Typical were comments by Dave's mother on one such occasion. Dave was leaving the house, and his mother offered him a reminder of who he was by simply saying, 'Be careful'. She then reminded him of what effect he has because of who he is by pleading, 'Now don't you stay out too late David, *please*'.

That such pleas are never-ending in fact denotes the main lasting effect of the detention experience among intimate others. If the ex-inmate does not keep to a routine – for example, if he does not appear at the usual or expected time – the fear of trouble is the first thing which comes to mind. Thus, the ex-inmate feels slightly constrained by the knowledge that anything he does which is unpredictable will lead to anguish for intimates. Of course, the unpredictable elements can be reduced by keepings others informed, as Rob did when he decided to spend the night at a friend's house. While in a pub, Rob left to call someone to give a message to his parents about his intention to spend the night at his friend's house. He felt the need to comment on this to the group at the table:

> You know, I never used to do this, but since . . . (Pause) Uh, I used to stop out for days and never let them know. But since I've been in trouble I always give them a call. Otherwise, they'd worry that I'd been picked up or something. I think it's best to let them know anyway.

To illustrate what happens when uncertainty remains, we can consider an evening when Bill did not meet his girl friend, a mate and the researcher at the expected time. We were scheduled to meet Bill at 6.30 on the street corner nearest his house. He was due home from work at that time, and had planned to change immediately and go out with us. When Bill had still not appeared by 7.30 his girl friend became visibly upset. At first she said, 'He usually calls if he's late.' Then, three separate times, 'He's only been this late before when he's been in trouble' and 'The last time he was this late was when he was put away'. By 8 o'clock her talk along these lines had become incessant:

> I'll bet he's got in trouble. What could he have done? I've only known him to be this late when he's been in trouble. I'm not going out with him tomorrow night. And I'm going to the Top Rank (without him) on Saturday.

Bill appeared shortly after 8 o'clock with the simple explanation that he had had to work overtime. Prolonged arguing ensued, reminding Bill of his special character. He later said to me, 'I can't move without upsetting somebody. They always think I'm in trouble.'

To the extent that intimate others remain wary, the detention fact does not recede in its influence. However, this is usually no more than a gnawing annoyance and is rarely a bar to normal actions.

In stating that relationships continue much as before, this does not mean that they are all defined as good. Although most exist amid tolerant relations with their family, a few find that old troubles are renewed. Bill's social world can again be used as an illustration.

Bill never felt that his house was a home. He was never allowed to bring friends into his house. Given the conditions, which he viewed as unrespectable, he did not wish to in any case. In addition, Bill was not allowed into his mates' homes, mainly because each of them was also taboo to their parents. Typical was a scene where we stood talking in front of a mate's house for forty-five minutes, until he finally said, 'My parents will be home from the club any minute,' to which Bill replied, 'Oh no, we'd better be off before they get back.'

The source of exclusion was much deeper than the simple fact that Bill had been in detention. In an area full of trouble, each parent was trying to protect their offspring from other people's children. However, in Bill's case this was probably amplified because he came from a 'problem family'. His father had been in prison and his brother was in Borstal. The house was always a scene of disarray and commotion in the eyes of neighbours. One of Bill's mates described the family as 'the worst of a bad lot'; this seemed to depict the community reaction. Believing in contamination, parents did not wish to encourage friendships by providing a place for their children to associate.

This exclusion was most crucial for Bill in his relationship with his girl friend. Her parents would not let him near the house or even near her. Bill could only explain it by saying, 'Her parents don't want me around because I've been in trouble – inside and all.' However, this exclusion occurred long before his present trouble. Part of the lore of the neighbourhood concerned the only snippet of interaction that ever occurred between Bill and his girl's father. The one and only time Bill called at her house, the father chased him onto the street with an axe. This story was repeated constantly by Bill and his mates. The essence of it is given in the following pub conversation between me, Bill and Bill's girl friend.

Bill: You'd think after eighteen months they'd (girl friend's parents) give up and realise that we're not going to split up, that they can't break us up.

Girl: He'll (father) never give up.

Bill: I suppose it's because of my age (four years older). But he doesn't know my age does he?

Girl: It's not that.

Bill: It may be because I've been inside, been in trouble all along. I don't know. The first time I ever went with her, her old man chased me down the street with an axe. (Smiling, turning to his girl friend) Didn't he?

Girl: Yea.

R: What happened?

Bill: He just went mad! He came out of the house yelling; had an axe in his hand and he chased me with it. I just ran.

This exclusion had the effect of forcing Bill, his girl friend and their mates to meet in public. They were forced to go to public entertainment spots – the places where trouble occurs – rather than enjoying the sanctity of their own homes. Apart from causing strained relations with parents, this had the effect of creating trouble, the very thing the parents were trying to prevent through their policy of exclusion. One of the many examples occurred on the night of the fight at the dance hall, described earlier. The original plan was to have a party at a mate's house in his parent's absence, but this was foiled when the parents heard of the plan and decided to stay home. The alternative was the dance hall, and trouble. Of course, this trouble might well be interpreted by the parents as further evidence that it really is his peers who lead their son into deviance. Further exclusion is likely, and so on.

With time, the greatest area of sensitivity concerning one's criminality may occur with intimates. Law enforcers, contrary to initial expectations, keep their distance and do not appear specially concerned with the ex-detention inmate. Employment expectations, being near the bottom of society's scheme of things, lead most to consider their lot as normal given their place in society. With intimates, the fact of detention is also not very important, although it is always there, ready to upset those whom one had hoped would most easily forget about it.

For the first few weeks after release, more distant persons were thought to be the source of negative reaction. With time, this relationship begins to disappear and there is an indication of the opposite: that intimates become the most regular reminder of one's tainted character. This change in the overall pattern of reaction, however, is not usually powerful enough to alter the feeling that one is essentially free.

The ex-inmate negotiates his essential freedom within the confines of the community which he has always known. He joins his fellows in their collective dilemma of perpetually trying to become free. The individual is freed when he can ascertain the structure of social reaction to him, when he can make things predictable.

> Freedom is not unpredictability. As Weber has shown, if this were the case, the madman would be the freest human being. The individual who is conscious of his own freedom does not stand outside the world of causality, but rather perceives his own volition as a very special category of cause, different from the other causes that he must reckon with.[14]

Paradoxically, the very act of making things predictable allows others to control him. 'The less uncertain his life, the more society can make use of him.'[15] Being free, the choice is there, within limits.

Notes

[1] A. Camus, *The Rebel,* p. 63.

[2] What later became nationally known as the Paul Storey case; cf. *The Times,* 20 March 1973, p. 1.

[3] Lofland develops the idea that, 'It might accurately be observed that the typical and mundane features of human societies themselves are the most fundamental facilitants of deviant acts.' (J. Lofland, *Deviance and Identity,* p. 116)

[4] L. Yablonsky, *The Violent Gang.*

[5] Cf. R. Cloward and L. Ohlin, *Delinquency and Opportunity,* esp. pp. 171–2.

[6] In these situations, petty crime is prevalent. However, this is not the stuff of which criminals are made, for the special context of trouble at football matches exempts the individual from a criminal identity. As Rock states, 'Special deviant contexts permit a moral escape from the everyday self; in them, the situational deviant can respectably claim exemption from the obligations and rights pertaining to his normal self. He becomes "not himself". . . .' (P. Rock, *Deviant Behaviour*)

On another level, it may also be functional for the society to provide such outlets for aggression. Containing aggression within special contexts such as football matches may minimise it in other contexts. This may be one reason why 'street violence' in isolated acts is much less prevalent in Britain compared with, say, America.

[7] As one parolee has expressed it, 'I'm not suppos'ta drink, drive, or screw. What else is there?' (F. Elli, *The Riot,* pp. 171–2; quoted by J. Irwin, *The Felon,* p. 89)

[8] The following description is not meant to overdramatise criminality or to portray it as a central fact of existence. As reiterated through this chapter, crime is at most a situational release. This description of Paul's

actions is intended to illustrate the types of situations in which trouble does ensue, and its quality as a 'moral release' rather than as an indication of commitment.

[9] D. Matza, *Delinquency and Drift,* p. 69.

[10] Even this was influenced by the researcher; see detailed discussion on this relationship in R. Ericson, *The Labeling Perspective and the Study of Criminality,* Chapter 16.

[11] The only indication of suspicion was the several glances he threw in the researcher's direction, a reminder that the researcher was the only odd one out.

[12] A similar situation is noted by Irwin: 'Some [parole] agents have contacts with industries or small businesses which use parolees as a source of cheap labor. . . . . These jobs usually have extremely low pay and/or undesirable working conditions. The agent cultivates these contacts because they serve as a last resort. He is able to place his least employable parolees through them. Often the agent receives other types of cooperation from such employers. They will keep him informed of the activities of the parolee and in this way the agent is able to increase his surveillance over him. The employers are served by having a source of cheap labor over which they have extra controls. The parolee is in the disadvantageous position of having few or no job resources, and often he is required to stay on the job by the agent.' (J. Irwin, *The Felon,* p. 122)

[13] The meaning of respectable employment, and the special need for it by the ex-inmate, is perceptively analysed by Lofland: 'Type of work (or lack thereof) is very frequently the pivotal category of other-imputed and self-imputed normality (or lack thereof). Being in a presumptively normal work place, of course, exposes Actor to Others who may be making unanimous imputations of him as a pivotally normal worker; but more to the point here, this kind of *place* frequently is itself a saleable commodity to yet Others at other times and in other places. The mere mention of the place where Actor works gives rise to presumptions as to his pivotal character, apart, even, from the particular job he performs. So it is perhaps understandable that keypunch operators traffic in saying only that they "work for IBM" and file clerks traffic in reporting only that they "work for General Motors downtown in the Fisher Building".' (J. Lofland, *Deviance and Identity,* p. 240)

[14] P. Berger, *Invitation to Sociology,* p. 143.

[15] E. Goffman, *Interaction Ritual,* p. 174.

Bibliography

Berger, P. and Luckmann, T. (1971). *The Social Construction of Reality,* Penguin, Harmondsworth.

Camus, A. (1962). *The Rebel,* Penguin, Harmondsworth.

Cloward, R. and Ohlin, L. (1960). *Delinquency and Opportunity,* Free Press, Glencoe.

Elli, F. (1966). *The Riot,* Coward-McCann, New York.

Ericson, R. (1974). *The Labelling Perspective and the Study of Criminality,* Ph.D. thesis, University of Cambridge.

Goffman, E. (1972). *Interaction Ritual,* Penguin, Harmondsworth.

Irwin, J. (1970). *The Felon,* Prentice-Hall, Englewood Cliffs.

Lofland, J. (1969). *Deviance and Identity,* Prentice-Hall, Englewood Cliffs.

Matza, D. (1964). *Delinquency and Drift,* Wiley, New York.

Rock, P. (1973). *Deviant Behaviour,* Hutchinson, London.

Yablonsky, L. (1967). *The Violent Gang,* Pelican, Harmondsworth.

[2]
Social Distance and Reaction to Criminality

A BASIC assumption of the labelling or social reactions approach to the study of criminality is that various " conventional others " attach a stigma to the person whose behaviour is in question, so that he is " disqualified from full social acceptance " (Goffman, 1968, p. 9). The stigmatised individual begins to experience difficulty in continuing relationships with conventional persons in conventional social organisations. One possible consequence is that this societal reaction leads the " criminal " into more and more illegal activities and organisations, as he gradually comes to accept his social identity (*cf.* Becker, 1963, p. 34). Thus, one of the favourite topics of theorists working in this area concerns the irony of how criminal control efforts may not have the intended effect of straightening out the slightly crooked subject, but may actually make him even more bent.

One problem with this approach is that many theorists are not specific about the persons and places involved in the social reaction. There is frequent reference to how " the members of the community seem reluctant to accept the returning individual on an entirely equal footing " (Erikson, 1964, p. 16), but little attempt to specify who are the persons and groups stigmatising the individual, in what circumstances this takes place, the methods used, and the place of the " criminal " fact *vis-à-vis* other social facts about the individual.

The primary condition under which a person is likely to be fundamentally stigmatised is where there is unanimous opinion among all relevant social groups that he is essentially criminal (*cf.* Lofland, 1969, p. 155). It is doubtful if such unanimity is often achieved given the variance in reaction from such different parties as family, friends, neighbourhood acquaintances, employers, probation officers and police. Unless the researcher considers how the same individual experiences different stigmatic reaction from each of these parties, he will do no more than reaffirm in the broadest terms the mythical beliefs about how " criminals " and especially " ex-convicts " have a difficult time returning to conventional existence. He will deal in societal images rather than the reality of stigmatic processes as experienced by those imputing the attribute and those subject to such imputations.

One potentially fruitful way of examining the differential reactions of all relevant others as experienced by the criminal subject is to consider the degree of social distance between the offender and those reacting to him. That is, one way to explain differential reaction and hence the differential impact of the criminal label is in terms of the degree of intimacy, and all this entails, between the criminal and the various social reactors.

This is a topic which has been the subject of theorising by many writers,

This article is partially based on Ericson (1974a). The author is grateful to Professor F. H. McClintock for his comments on this work.

but it has been accompanied by little supporting evidence. In fact, two conflicting arguments have been made in this connection. Some, most notably Goffman (1968), argue that familiarity may breed contempt, so that intimates as opposed to more distant others are more likely to exclude the criminal from full social acceptance. Intimates are often unable to reconcile what the individual is now—a person with a tainted identity—with what he was before he acquired that identity. " Post-stigma acquaintances ", on the other hand, have known him only as a tainted person and therefore are not faced with the problem of reconciling previous experiences with the present reality (*cf.* Goffman, 1968, p. 49). A further reason for exclusion by intimates is " the tendency for a stigma to spread from the stigmatised individual to his close connexions . . ." (Goffman, 1968, p. 43). Contaminated by their close association with a condemned person, intimates also face the possibility that they themselves will be condemned; consequently, they are likely to sever the relationship.

The conflicting view has been put forward by several writers, including Rubington and Weinberg (1973, esp. p. 8) and Rock (1973, esp. pp. 25 *et seq.*), who argue that the greater the degree of intimacy between the criminal and another, the less the likelihood that the criminal will be labelled as such and fundamentally stigmatised. This is explained in terms of the fact that intimates have more social information about the individual than do more distant persons, information which allows them to assess the individual according to many aspects of his social identity involving many social roles. Among intimates, as compared with more socially distant persons, he is not first defined as criminal and then evaluated, but is evaluated according to all aspects of his identity before he is defined.

This is an introduction to a set of ideas that are in need of expansion and clarification if one is to achieve systematic study of social reactions to criminality. In this article there is an attempt to outline the way in which the relationship between social distance and social reaction to criminality has been treated in the literature. This literature is then examined in light of observational evidence from a theoretical sample of individuals who were incarcerated for the first time and subsequently experienced the reactions of various others upon return to their home communities. We examine how these individuals accomplish the necessary " social work ", the work they must do socially in order to regain social acceptance. This will lay the groundwork for further investigation into how labelling effects vary according to the degree of social distance between the offender and those who find him offensive.

Social Distance and Social Reaction

Theoretical ideas developed by several writers (*cf.* Lofland, 1969, p. 204; Rock, 1973, pp. 25, 29; Rubington and Weinberg, 1973, p. 8) can be linked to provide the following hypothesis:

> The greater the social distance between the person whose behaviour is in question and those reacting to it, the more likely deviant identity will be imputed;

the broader (less specific) the category of deviant that can be effectively used;
the greater the ease with which it can be effectively applied;
the quicker it can be effectively applied;
the greater the stigma experienced by the person whose behaviour is in question, leading him to see himself as essentially deviant in the eyes of the reactors.

There have been some attempts to explain why the more socially distant, as compared with intimates, are more likely to label the criminal in this way. With the aid of writers who have discussed these relationships, we shall outline the reasoning that has been employed to date.

It is possible to argue that the main purpose of categorising someone is to reduce uncertainty about him. The development of typical beliefs about persons who engage in certain forms of threatening behaviour can help to reduce fear when one is forced to deal with one of these persons. These beliefs are even more likely to be used as a justification for avoiding contact altogether; as Schur (1971, p. 51) notes, " To the extent that this avoidance tendency is present, the likelihood of reliance on stereotypes is heightened, for it offers a relatively comfortable way of dealing with threatening behaviour."

Fear based on unpredictability is particularly acute if there is a lack of information about the person being reacted to (*cf.* Rock, p. 29n.). As Lofland (1969, p. 152n.) observes, no one has a random sampling of events by which to judge a person. We impute identities on the basis of a biased sample. The point is that this tendency towards bias is more likely among socially distant others because they have a smaller number of events on which to base their judgment. Very often, theirs is a sample of one: knowing that the person has a criminal record, they can rely on typical conceptions of what constitutes a criminal without checking the applicability of this typology to the specific person in question. Equipped with this highly selective typical knowledge, they do not wish to know any more; they know enough to get by, enough to order their relationships with this person to the extent that they know he knows his place. " Social typing has the effect of reducing uncertainty about persons. Social order is then re-established when a person is retyped." (Rubington and Weinberg, 1973, p. 7.)

This is the process which leads to the creation of a " master status " (*cf.* Becker, 1963, pp. 31–34), where the individual's criminal identity overshadows all other aspects of his identity. Known primarily as a criminal, every action taken by the individual is indexed by others according to this over-riding status. The knowledge of socially distant others about his criminality " overwhelms what other knowledge of him we may have and dampens our desire to obtain such knowledge." (Schur, 1971, p. 30.)

This leads to what Matza (1969, pp. 159–162) terms " gross " exclusion as opposed to " reasonable " exclusion. In Matza's terms, it is reasonable to exclude the homosexual from one's shower, but gross to exclude him from a job in one's office. Similarly, it may be reasonable to exclude a thief from a job as a night-watchman, but gross to exclude him from any job at all. Gross exclusion means that the relationship is finished before it starts, for it rules out the possibility of others even considering any competing evidence. In short, " Gross exclusion withers the possibility of ancillary identities." (Matza, 1969, p. 160.)

This process can be summed up by comparing it with people who refuse to enter a cinema because they object to the single frame of the film displayed as advertising out in front. They think that this frame tells them all they need to know about a film of this type, and they categorise the film as essentially " violent " or " pornographic ". They feel that they do not have to watch the picture in motion from start to finish to understand the meaning it attempts to convey. By missing the action they do not have to confront alternative meanings, thereby avoiding questions which might challenge their own conception of the order of things.

The stigmatised individual may collaborate in this enterprise. To the extent that he worries what more distant others might find out about him, he might try to sustain distance from them (*cf.* Goffman, 1968, p. 122). To close the distance gap is to become involved; involvement means that the others will have increased access to information which may only serve to strengthen their preconceived view of him as essentially criminal, without giving him a chance to accentuate other features of his identity. To avoid this possibility, he avoids them. Lacking more intimate information, these others who have been kept at a distance are forced to rely on stereotypical conceptions and all this entails.

Another group of collaborators is the agents of criminal control. They help to perpetuate the prevailing stereotypes by the very fact that they are organised on behalf of society to categorise individuals so as to reinforce a sense of order. As Rubington and Weinberg (1973, p. 122) point out, "The ironic results of a person's contact with formal control agencies are that laymen have a ready-made perspective for dealing with persons who have just left the agency."

This collaboration is also inevitable because formal controllers are themselves forced to remain at a distance from the persons they deal with. Even the probation and after-care officer, who has ideally to befriend his clients is unable to do so because of his fundamental role as a controller acting on behalf of the interests of the wider society. While he may provide practical aid, he does not have frequent contact, peership, understanding and warmth, conditions which Lofland (1969, p. 275) suggests are facilitative of more intimate relationships. As a professional controller he remains at a distance, doing little more for the offender than continuing to " foster and sustain a conception of him as a pivotal deviant " (Lofland, 1969, p. 276).

These conceptions have informed the writing of theorists concerned with the nature of labelling processes among deviant individuals and various social reactors. What is now required is an attempt to see how these conceptions coincide with the experiences of individuals subject to stigmatising processes. A small study of young offenders experiencing incarceration and subsequent return to their home communities provides some pertinent information in this connection.

Research Design

Based on the common view among labelling theorists that " penalisation confirms the belief that the main part of the process of becoming deviant has been concluded " (Matza, 1969, p. 154n.), and that it is the incarcerated who are fundamentally stigmatised, the researcher decided to take a group of persons experiencing incarceration for the first time and to follow them up upon their return to the community.[1]

The theoretical sample was initially based on all admissions over a two-month period to a senior detention centre, (1) who were serving four months (a six-month sentence minus one-third remission), (2) who had no previous institutional experience, and (3) who were willing to co-operate. This yielded a sample of 45, who were followed through their entire period of incarceration on the basis of interviews and participant observation.

The 15 who returned to Birmingham upon their release were followed up there on a participant observation basis over a two to four-month period, depending upon their time of release. The field work in Birmingham involved the researcher in everyday activities in pubs, clubs, discos, home visits, parties, football matches, and just " hanging " on the street. In all cases the researcher was dependent on the invitation of the subject to open up access in his own sphere of life, on his own territory, in marked contrast to his previous " openness " in the detention centre.

The analysis to follow is based on the final interview just before the subjects' release from the detention centre, on the fifty direct contacts the researcher had with the fifteen subjects in Birmingham after their release, and on the few additional contacts he had with the family or friends of the subjects who often welcomed the researcher even though the subject himself was not present.

Observational Evidence

The observational evidence to follow is generally supportive of the relationship outlined earlier: the more socially distant a person is, the greater the likelihood that he will treat the ex-inmate as fundamentally stigmatised. Presentation of this evidence serves to describe the way in which the process operates, and to elucidate further the reasons why it might operate in this manner. In the following discussion, we shall begin with those who are most intimate and proceed to contrast them with persons and groups who are more socially distant.

Among members of the ex-inmate's family, including the individual himself, there is an initial mood of optimism that all—particularly the ex-inmate—is not lost. During the period of detention and the first few weeks back in the community, old conflicts within the family are suspended in the hope that they will go away. With time these conflicts become more pronounced, but they do not lead to the point of exclusion.

All 15 subjects returned to their family fold upon release from detention.

[1] The research discussed here is part of a larger research project which is reported elsewhere (Ericson, 1974a; 1975b). For purposes of the present discussion, only that part of the research design relevant to the information used here will be discussed. For a detailed account of the methods used, and methodological issues involved, see Ericson (1974a, Chapters 7, 15, 16).

Only one left home during the follow-up period, and even he continued to visit home. Under such conditions of physical intimacy it is not difficult to understand why there is also social intimacy. Parents become familiar with the behaviour of their sons, and often collaborate with them in their efforts to present a favourable image.

Family members, along with close friends, are already the persons who have intimate information about the individual. The ex-inmate most often co-opts them into his presentation of a conventional image to outsiders by keeping intimates up-to-date on what he is doing, particularly things they will view in positive terms. Consequently intimates are enjoined in the collective effort to make things appear conventional to outsiders. Of course, in this effort it is possible that intimates may engage in self-deception (*cf.* Lemert, 1972, p. 80) as well as induce the ex-inmate to think that he is more accepted than he actually is (*cf.* Goffman, 1968, p. 120).

This collaborative effort was frequently evidenced through the observational period. For instance, one individual started to engage in what his grandparents (his guardians) defined as erratic behaviour, changing jobs frequently and staying out late at night either with his friends or with a woman twice his age. In spite of his frequently expressed annoyance, the grandfather did no more than say, " I could tell him that if he goes out any more that I'd have to put him out of the house, but I couldn't do that because I know he'd be wandering the streets and I couldn't have him doing that."

This largely contradicts Goffman's (1968, esp. pp. 43, 49) view that " pre-stigma acquaintances ", such as family members, will sever relationships with the individual, perhaps because they are contaminated by him. If anything, the contamination serves as a further reason for family members to collaborate with the stigmatised individual in trying to help him achieve a conventional social identity. The family has a stake in the status of each individual within and without its unit, for each individual's social identity is taken by others as an indicator of the entire family's moral character, the family's identity. If one member is socially defined as deviant the entire family is somewhat tainted, for the common social conceptions of cause usually hold them at least partly to blame. Thus, it is not only the deviant member who undertakes self-analysis because of social reactions to his behaviour, but his family as well. The family's social control system is brought into question, they become sensitised to this, and they try to articulate an effective response.

The ex-inmate also realises that the fact of his criminality cannot be isolated to his own identity, but also affects the identity of his family. As one person expressed it: " My family took it pretty well, better than I thought. All the neighbours talk, but my parents have tried to ignore this, you know. You've seen them when they're standing on the doorsteps. ' Oh, did you know their son has been sent away? It was in the paper. It just shows what control they have over him.' My folks have suffered too. . . ."

In a sense, then, family members are involved in the same stigmatic processes as their errant member. One subject's mother wrote to him while he was still in detention to say that she was giving up her part-time employment because she could no longer tolerate the reactions of her fellow-workers. One line of this letter read: " I'm going to leave my job, it's only £3.90 a week and they're always gossiping about me." By the time this person was released his mother had quit and was looking for a job in another area. When the researcher asked the subject about this in our first meeting outside, he replied: " It's been in the papers and that, you know. They talk as if it's her fault." The point is that, contrary to what Goffman suggests, rather than removing the contamination by disassociating themselves from their son, parents are likely at this stage to join the stigmatised individual in a collective effort at seeking a conventional identity.

The danger in this approach is, of course, that parents tend to become too helpful and too sensitive, thereby communicating a belief in their son's basic tainted identity (*cf.* Lofland, 1969, p. 276). Within a short time at home, " nagging " expectations of parents about whom the individual should be with and places he should not go can lead to a loss in intimacy. The more negative consequences of this process will be considered later. For now it is sufficient to say that parents, and the family as a group, offer only minor stigmatising reactions. As one inmate described it just before release: " Me parents and people around me don't think I'm criminal. I reckon the police might. Me parents and that know me, they know I'm not a hardened criminal. If it's a first glance, people tend to judge the book by its cover. You always think the worst of a person, and until they get to know you the criminal part is always there."

Goffman's ideas about the tendency of pre-stigma acquaintances to exclude are also refuted when the reactions of close friends are considered. It is among close friends that the ex-inmate status is of greatest insignificance. The returning person anticipates and receives extraordinary treatment from his friends only in the first few days. Friends lend him money, and he is treated to as much beer as he can consume after four months without any. This is customary, expected. The ex-inmate has offered similar hospitality to others before, whether they were returning from the army, prison, or working away in another town. What one person envisaged in interview just before release generally came true after release: " My mates will be happy. They'll treat me differently for the first few days, buying me drinks, but then it will just slacken off. They won't think I'm different though, they won't think I'm big."

The returned person is a mild celebrity for this brief period, for he has tales to tell which are interesting and different from the normal discussion about women and football which prevails in the pub. He thereby achieves a little recognition, a touch of status, not in the sense of gaining reputation (as in a delinquent gang) but simply as an entertainer to tell a few inside stories. Outside this flutter of significance brought about by the entertainment function, there is no different treatment by mates; among them, status is neither lost nor won by the fact of detention.

Referring to his friends, one person stated: " They don't think I'm bloody hard because I've been away, just take it with a pinch of salt." The fact of having " been away " is extraordinary only in the sense that a minority do it; only in this sense are they deviant. When they come home they have stories to tell based on a different experience, and that is the end of it. Again, an ex-inmate makes the comparison with more distant others: " Me mates know what I'm really like. They know many sides of me, whereas others just think of the criminal side first, sort of thing."

Among those who only " know of " rather than know the individual—more distant neighbourhood acquaintances who rely on popular images of criminality—there is a dramatic difference in the reaction. As one subject described it: " The ones that know you, they don't see you as criminal. But with others, it will be a big cross on your back. It made the front page of the papers. If it hadn't been in the papers, only my mates and relations would know. But being in the papers, you get it from the neighbours, busy-bodies, your work-mates—everybody else."

" At a time when the individual can get almost everything else off his back, there remains the cross of personal character—the one he bears, albeit lightly, when he is in the presence of others." (Goffman, 1971, p. 187). As the present discussion implies, the weight of the cross depends on whom the others happen to be. If they are friends or family members, the cross can be borne much more lightly than is the case with neighbours. The point made over and over again by persons under study is that the less well-known one is to another, the more predominant the " criminal " aspect of one's self becomes, and the likelihood of negative reaction is increased. These are the persons who rely on the " master status " of " criminal ", who react on public images of what " criminals " or " convicts " are like, rather than putting it in perspective by learning about other aspects. This is the tendency summed up by a subject, who stated: " People who don't know me think I am a big-time gangster, not to be trusted. When they don't know the details they think of the first thing that comes to their head."

This points again to the question of information. When little is known, the first thing that comes to mind is the more negative aspect of the person's identity. Others ". . . squeeze from meagre amounts of available information a large amount of ' indicativeness ' . . . When some doubt is raised as to the standing of a given Actor under conditions of anonymity and, therefore, under conditions of a measure of distrust and fear, the safest course is quickly to presume the worst, that is to code for pivotal deviance . . ." (Lofland, 1969, p. 142). Or, as one ex-inmate put it, " When they don't know you, people are always ready to criticize and condemn, always talk of the worst points of a person, not the good points."

These reactions are not of great personal consequence except to the extent that they are related to specific actions by neighbours directed at the ex-inmate's tainted identity. Such actions are most frequently related to the belief that the ex-inmate will contaminate those with whom he associates. Consequently, parents of the ex-inmate's friends often encourage their sons and daughters not to associate with him. This is frequently carried to the stage of banning the ex-inmate from the neighbours' homes. This practice has the effect of forcing the youths involved to meet in public places—including places of public entertainment where trouble is likely to occur—rather than allowing them to enjoy the sanctity of private space.[2] If the individuals involved do get into trouble, this only serves to reconfirm parental images that it really is the ex-inmate who is to blame.

This type of amplification spiral was frequently observed during the Birmingham field-work period. One case involved an ex-inmate and seven friends who planned to have a party at a friend's house in his parents' absence, but this was foiled when the parents heard of the plan and decided to stay home. The alternative was a dance hall, and trouble. A group of youths objected to the "flash" dancing and football loyalties of the ex-inmate's group, and a fight followed.

New employers are the most important example of distant others who impute a " master status " on the basis of little information about the ex-inmate. New employers usually have no other facts to go on and are predominantly concerned with signs of trust and reliability. These signs come up negative if " crime " and " prison " are part of the personal data of the prospective employee. This poses a dilemma for the ex-inmate seeking employment, for to obtain a job he must appear respectable, but to appear respectable he must obtain steady employment. Faced with social distance, the discrediting facts predominate because other signs of respectability are lacking. In relations with potential employers, barriers are created which last long after one has left the prison walls, as the following protest indicates: " I have trouble (getting a job) because I've been inside. The forms for jobs ask if you have a record. The instant you say " Yes " it scars you right away. It puts up a mental block for the person who interviews you, that you must be a bad one."

The potency of this reaction means that the subject is treated as generally untrustworthy because of the criminal fact, and *in terms of seeking employment* many subjects come to accept this definition. A self-fulfilling prophecy results, which means that the individual lowers his expectations concerning job opportunities. He no longer seeks what is desirable, only what seems possible.

Because the youth leaving detention has accepted the fact that employment is *the* indication of respectability (*cf.* Ericson, 1974, esp. pp. 268–269), he remains determined to gain employment upon release. His employment opportunities may be limited but not foreclosed. The option is to approach the market with limited aspirations, obtaining any job at first but hoping for better things in the long run. Firms are sought and employment is obtained with employers who are least likely to be concerned about criminality. Almost invariably these are firms which pay low wages, are without a union, and have high staff turnover. They are tolerant because the conditions of employment do not allow them to make many demands on their workers. Among persons who sought jobs on this basis when they returned to Birmingham, wages were as low as £12 a week, and never more than £20 for a full work week. These employers do not ask for much and they do not give much in return.

[2] The implications of this private-public distinction for the nature of criminality have been lucidly outlined by Stinchcombe (1963).

The ex-inmates accepting employment on this basis are fully aware of the nature of the enterprise. They realise that being inside is, as one ex-inmate described it, " Like being branded a troublemaker; therefore it depends on what kind of job you want".These employers have a record of taking people with a record. They know that ex-inmates are anxious for a job, and they treat them accordingly. This is at the bottom rung of respectability in the occupational hierarchy; however, in the initial quest for respectability, it is slightly above the status of being unemployed.

It is not long before the individual begins to realise what it means to be at the bottom end of society's scheme of things, that it is not very rewarding in respectability or financially to be a labourer and earning £12 a week. Within two months after leaving detention, only one-half of the subjects held the same job they had when they were first released. Most of those who maintained their jobs were not content with their work, but neither were they intent on obtaining another position. Past experience informed them that mobility is only horizontal, not vertical, and geographical, not social. The only effort they made towards mobility was to give appearances of significance by making their job out to be more than they knew it was. One person said his job involved travelling to London and Scotland, when the only travelling he did was on the bus to and from the factory. Another said he earned more than he did, while a third designated himself as a " mechanic " rather than a " garage boy ". They tried to appear socially respectable and successful while personally resigning themselves to a lowly occupation.

The other half refused to resign themselves, and started a process of moving from one job to another. With one exception—a person who doubled his wages when he moved from a labouring job to a position with a plastering firm—they had no success. Some of this group eventually realised that changing jobs provided little solution to the problem. Unemployment became equally attractive, as the following conversation illustrates:

Ex-inmate: If I went back to work I wouldn't last another week.
RE: Why is that?
Ex-inmate: Just can't take it there.
RE: What were you doing anyway?
Ex-inmate: Welding, repetition.
RE: Did you get paid while you were off?
Ex-inmate: No.
RE: No union?
Ex-inmate: Never heard of it in that place. (Pause) I'm staying on the box. I felt great this week but I don't think I'll go back to work at that place. I think I may go on the dole. If others can get away with it I don't see why I can't.
Mate: (Overhearing conversation) That's no good.
Ex-inmate: It's as good as a dead-end job.

Those who reach this conclusion may be the ones who are also the most likely candidates for involvement in behaviour which is commonly known as theft. Through contacts with some subjects over a year after the field-work ended, the researcher learned that at least one person had chosen this option: he was serving time in prison for a series of break-ins.

Formal agents of criminal control specialise in all the properties of labelling included in the social distance—social reaction hypothesis. In particular, the police are the masters at employing a "master status"; they are only interested in other facts about a person as they pertain to the criminal fact, rather than as a means of minimising the criminal fact.

Ex-detention inmates are fully aware that police prediction techniques sensitise them to persons with criminal records. The greatest predictor of future crime is the number of previous convictions; the greatest predictor of a future specific type of crime is past conviction for that type of crime. They know they fall into a group of potential offenders and they know the police are going to view them with this fact in mind. If one has been deemed bad enough to have been sent away, then one is a prime candidate for signification. The police do a more intensive analysis of the criminality fact than of any others; an ex-convict is in a high risk category.

Everyone expresses a sensitivity to this type of police suspicion. One subject commented: "I shall have that feeling [of police suspicion]. Same as when you get banned, when you start driving you're all eyes to see if there are any coppers. You feel a bit cautious about them, cringe a bit when you see them."

With time, these feelings begin to diminish, remaining more subtle and latent. However, until the ex-inmate realises through time that constant suspicion does not occur, he remains wary, aware of the possibility that police efforts might exacerbate his problems: "The police will bug me, but when they finally get used to me they'll leave me alone. They'll be at the door every night at first. It makes you feel bad and you eventually say, 'Blow it, I'm going to do something'. Then you start doing one, then another, and that's it then. I'll have to carry a little diary and show it to the police when they stop me."

These beliefs remained largely unsubstantiated by concrete instances during the field-work period. It is the other formal control agent, the probation officer, who has a much more direct impact on the ex-inmate.

The information about the ex-inmate which the probation officer has at his disposal might lead one to assume that he achieves a degree of intimacy which allows him to diminish the "criminal" fact. In fact, part of the probation officer's officially defined role is to minimise the ex-inmate's criminal identity and maximise conventional commitments in the domestic and occupational spheres. However, this ideal cannot be accomplished because of the probation officer's own identity as someone whose primary function is defined in terms of his clients' criminal tendencies. He is a law-enforcement officer who helps to conceive, use and perpetuate society's common-sense categories of the criminal; for this reason he remains distant, and a source of stigmatisation.

The image constructed by ex-inmates is that, at very best, a probation officer can help one immediately upon release with respect to basic necessities. That is, the probation officer can be *used* to find a job, clothes and money.

They not only get one used to the outside world, but can be used to further one's own ends. One ex-inmate stated: "Probation officers can be a help if they are *used* right."

With this function of the probation service predominant, the one-year licence is seen as much too long. Since one can be given these commodities very quickly upon release, there seems to be little use in extending the after-care period beyond a few weeks. The extended period only reminds the ex-inmate of the more over-riding control function of the relationship. Thus, one person commented: "You've done your time, you don't need a reminder of it. They should find out about a job, see how you're getting on. The licence should be for a month, not a whole year."

It is in this connection that the after-care requirement is viewed as punitive, a reminder that because he requires a community agent to watch over him he is still not accepted by the community. One ex-inmate referred to the after-care requirement as "like two sentences in one", while another stated: "If you go out on probation you're still being punished really. If you have nothing to do with the law it gives you a fresh start."

As the routine proceeds over the weeks after release, the ex-inmate continues to validate his feelings that the probation officer is essentially a control agent, a check on the ex-inmate to remind him of his status in circumstances where he might forget it. This hold is annoying but not powerful. The brief meetings held at infrequent intervals do nothing to change this conception. As one ex-inmate told some friends: "He asks the same questions every time. How's your mum? How's your dad? How's your job? Keeping out of trouble? See you next week. That's it! . . . You can give him a load of lies and he believes you. You can go screwin' every night, and tell him it was women, not houses!"

Even the utilitarian function of providing a job—the only readily available means at the disposal of the probation officer to close the distance gap (*cf.* Lofland, 1969, p. 275)—can be negated because of the officer's status as a control agent. The ex-inmate's preoccupation in face of the after-care licence is to present a favourable image to the officer above all else. The ex-inmate will not even use the probation officer in his search for another job if he feels that the officer would view his job change as an indication of his tainted identity. In other words, he will not always use the service for what he defines as its major purpose because of the law-enforcement powers of the officer. The following conversation indicates the experiences of one person in this situation:

Grandfather: [Ex-inmate] has had three jobs now.

RE: Three?

Ex-inmate: They wanted me to go on a high ladder with no support. I said, "No" and they said, "You're no use to us", and dismissed me.

Grandfather: The next week he got a job at a discount shop down the street from here. He and his sister both got a job there. He just left that today, both of them left that and got another job in the city centre at another shop.

RE:	Have you asked the probation officer about a job?
Grandmother:	Oh, no no. We haven't told him anything about [ex-inmate] changing jobs.
RE:	He still thinks you're in the painting job?
Ex-inmate:	Yea, because he told me you have to lead an industrial [industrious] life. If you don't they can send you back. Two months, I could still do two more months at that place, so I don't say anything to the probation officer.

In this respect, the ex-inmate himself collaborates in keeping the probation officer at a distance. Because of his position, the probation officer can be a source of further stigma if he is allowed to obtain certain information. This is of course paradoxical in relation to the social distance conceptions discussed earlier. The more intimate the probation officer becomes through his knowledge, the greater the likelihood that he will discover and reveal information that will further stigmatise the ex-inmate and thus reconfirm the probation officer's socially distant official role. The ex-inmate's solution, similar to that of distant others reacting to him, is that social distance yields safety, and that it is better to be safe than sorry.

Conclusions and Implications

The evidence produced in support of the social distance—social reaction hypothesis, based as it is on a theoretical sample, does no more than raise the issues in an ideal-typical fashion. What has been shown is the way in which the ex-inmate is able to accomplish the necessary social work to convince those who are more intimate that he is simply a normal person with a criminal problem. Conversely, with the more socially distant he remains a criminal person with only residual normalcy.

This article has attempted to convey the sense in which the stigmatised individual himself plays a significant part in shaping his social identity. He is not simply subject to the reaction of others who have set roles with fixed degrees of social distance. It is not only a matter of " all societal response and no deviant stimulus " (Bordua, 1970, p. 458), and not a simple determinism based on the belief that " social control leads to deviance " (Lemert, 1967, p. v.). Shattered by the publicity of his fall from respectability, it takes more than all the Queen's resources and all the Queen's men to put the ex-inmate back together again. The ex-inmate also makes corrections himself; he assesses what others make of him so that he can be on the make with them. The dynamics of this process in relation to conceptions of social distance held by ex-inmates themselves has been the subject of this article.

A final " practical " note is in order. It seems inevitable that the tendency for the more socially distant to rely on " ready-made ", " easy on " labels with " super adhesive qualities " [3] will continue as long as society itself tends towards greater structural differentiation (*cf.* Rock, 1973, p. 25). Moreover, as Lemert (1972, p. 92) observes, " a high energy society mediated

[3] That these terms have a contemporary commercial character should not be surprising.

by a delicately integrated technology can ill afford to risk granting unqualified statuses to persons of doubtful integrity or competence ".

Short of a major overhaul of society aimed at immediately decreasing structural differentiation, it seems that one must rely on intimate others as the major sources of assistance to the stigmatised. In this connection, it may be worthwhile to stop the wishful thinking that official agents of criminal control can also achieve intimacy and thus be helpful, and to start thinking of mobilising community resources in a way which eventually decreases official involvement (*cf.* Ericson, 1974b, 1975a, b, c,). Over the long run this will serve to decrease fundamental stigmatisation, which in turn may be a step towards a decrease in structural differentiation.

References

Becker, H. (1963). *Oursiders.* Glencoe: Free Press.

Bordua, D. (1970). " Recent Trends: Deviant Behaviour and Social Control,' in C. Bersani, *Crime and Delinquency: A Reader.* Toronto: Collier-MacMillan.

Ericson, R. (1974a). *The Labeling Perspective and the Study of Criminality.* Ph.D. dissertation, University of Cambridge.

Ericson, R. (1974b). " Turning the Inside Out: On Limiting the Use of Imprisonment." *Community Education Series* 1, *No.* 3. Toronto: John Howard Society of Ontario.

Ericson, R. (1975a). " Responsibility, Moral Relativity and Response Ability: Some Implications of Deviance Theory for Criminal Justice." *University of Toronto Law Journal* **25,** 23–41.

Ericson, R. (1975b) *Young Offenders and their Social Work.* Farnborough, Hants: Saxon House.

Ericson, R. (1975c) *Criminal Reactions: The Labelling Perspective.* Farnborough, Hants: Saxon House.

Erikson, K. (1964). " Notes on the Sociology of Deviance," in H. Becker, *The Other Side.* Glencoe: The Free Press.

Goffman, E. (1968). *Stigma: Notes on the Management of Spoiled Identity.* Middlesex: Pelican.

Goffman, E. (1971). *Relations in Public.* London: Allen Lane.

Lemert, E. (1967, 1972). *Human Deviance, Social Problems and Social Control.* New Jersey: Prentice Hall.

Lofland, J. (1969). *Deviance and Identity.* New Jersey: Prentice Hall.

Matza, D. (1969). *Becoming Deviant.* New Jersey: Prentice Hall.

Rock, P. (1973). *Deviant Behaviour.* London: Hutchinson.

Rubington, E. and Weinberg, M. (1968, 1973). *Deviance: The Interactionist Perspective.* New York: MacMillan.

Schur, E. (1971). *Labeling Deviant Behaviour: Its Sociological Implications.* New York: Harper and Row.

Stinchcombe, A. (1963). " Institutions of Privacy in the Determination of Police Administrative Practice." *American Journal of Sociology,* **69,** 150–160.

[3]
The Occupational Environment of Detective Work

The starting point for an analysis of detective work is the police organization. The police organization embodies the structural framework for detective work and includes the occupational culture of detectives through which the structural framework is filtered. In this chapter we stay *within* the police organization, examining what detectives produce in terms of internally established parameters. We initially describe detectives' work related shift activity. We then proceed to analyze how detectives as workers are tied into the organization. As Manning (1979a: 42) states, "[A]ny depiction of police work that overlooks the centrality of the integration of actors into the organization, and the form and content of that integration, will remain a partial picture." Our portrayal of detective work in this chapter provides us with necessary background for our analyses in subsequent chapters, where we examine detective transactions with those persons outside the police organization who provide grist for the mill of crime production.

An Overview of Detective Activity

Detective activity was primarily geared to the disposition of cases. A case involved one or more occurrence reports. One occurrence report was submitted for each incident that was deemed by a police officer to be worthy of reporting for organizational purposes. The occurrence reports were usually linked with a complainant, e.g., if in one act a person threw a can of paint over three cars owned by three different people, three occurrence reports would be produced. One case could have one or more occurrence reports. Whether or not there was more than one occurrence report for a case usually depended on whether occurrences could be linked on the basis of a similar *modus operandi* of the suspect(s) or other knowledge that the same suspect(s) was responsible for multiple occurrences.

As documented in Chapter Four, most cases that detectives worked on were initially mobilized on the basis of occurrence reports submitted by a patrol officer to his patrol sergeant, and from the patrol

Table 3:1

Detective Shift Activity Related to Case Clearance

Activity	Number 179 shifts	Mean 179 shifts	Number of shifts on which activity undertaken	% of 179 shifts	Mean for shifts on which activity undertaken
Case investigations worked	310	1.73	156	87.2	1.98
Non-suspect citizen contacts	405	2.26	140	78.2	2.89
Criminal Control Official Contacts	92	.51	62	34.6	1.48
Suspect Contacts	132	.74	88	49.2	1.50
Arrests	33	.18	28	15.6	1.18
Persons Charged	51	.29	37	20.7	1.38
Charges Laid	101	.56	37	20.7	2.73

sergeant through a staff sergeant to the detective sergeant, who either assigned the occurrence directly to a detective team or left it on a general file to be selected by any detective who chose to work on it. At this point the detective's task became one of deciding what investigations he could do to provide a legitimate written account of a particular case "clearance." He worked to "cover his ass" by producing a "clearance" with written reasons that fit within organizationally established criteria.

In Table 3:1 we provide data on detective shift activity as it related to the clearance of their cases over the 179 shifts of observation. The vast majority of these activities were connected with our research sample of 295 cases, although activities related to non-sample cases are also included in Table 3:1 in order to provide a complete picture of what was produced on the 179 shifts.

Over the 179 shifts of observation, the detectives studied undertook a total of 310 case-related investigations. This does not mean that they investigated 310 different cases; the same case investigated on separate shifts is counted each time. We learn from Table 3:1 that some case investigation was undertaken on 87 percent of the shifts, with an average of 1.73 cases per shift over all the shifts and almost two per shift on those shifts when this activity was undertaken. The 23 shifts where no investigative action was conducted primarily involved the detectives working on reports in the office. One detective team in particular spent several shifts on reports as they were trying to bring their "paper work" up to date prior to taking leave for an in-service training course.

The primary investigative activity was interviewing victims, complainants, witnesses and informants for information relevant to an investigation. This involved a telephone call, an interview with the citizen at the station, or a visit to the home or place of employment of the person. The non-suspect citizen contacts recorded in Table 3:1 include all those involving direct face-to-face contact with the citizen, and exclude telephone calls. Contacts of this sort were undertaken on 78 percent of the shifts, involving 405 separate encounters or an average of almost three per shift on those shifts when there was such activity and slightly more than two per shift overall.

One-third of the 179 shifts involved at least one contact related to case investigation with other criminal control agents. The vast majority of these contacts were with Justices of the Peace for warrant applications or the release of accused persons, and with Crown attornies for advice or to discuss charges and other case related matters. Excluded from this total are telephone conversations with other criminal control agents. These contacts averaged three for every two shifts on which they occurred, and one for every two shifts overall.

Another major form of investigative activity was contacting suspects. These were face-to-face contacts typically initiated in field settings, although they also occurred at the divisional station when the person had been arrested by other police officers or when he had been asked by detectives over the telephone to come to the station for questioning. As recorded in Table 3:1, at least one contact with a suspect occurred on one-half of the shifts. The average was two such contacts for every three shifts overall, but three for every two shifts on which suspect contacts actually occurred.

Arrests were not a dominant shift activity for general investigation detectives.[1] On average the detectives arrested someone once every five or six shifts, and on those shifts where this activity did occur, there was typically only one arrest per shift. As documented in more detail in Chapters 4 and 6, detectives often took over the interrogation and subsequent processing of suspects originally arrested by uniform officers, or in a few cases by other detectives, which in part accounts for the infrequency of arrest activity by the detectives in our study. This latter point is made obvious when we consider the fact that the detectives we observed charged a total of 51 different persons even though they arrested only 33. When we take into account that some of these arrests did not result in the person being charged, we can understand the extent to which detective production in the charge category was very much an extension of activity undertaken by their colleagues, especially members of the uniform branch.[2]

Shifts when persons were charged were not frequent. The average was approximately four persons charged for every three shifts on which this activity took place, but only slightly more than one person charged for every five shifts overall.

Finally we consider the number of charges laid, noting that multiple charging appears to be the norm. A total of 101 charges were laid in relation to the 51 persons charged, resulting in an average of two charges for every person charged. While charging only occurred once every five shifts, when it did occur there were almost three charges laid per shift. It must be noted that one case included in these totals involved a person being charged with 21 separate counts over two separate shifts. If this one statistically deviant case is removed, our totals change to 80 charges over 177 shifts, and 35 shifts on which charging took place. This reduces the mean for shifts on which the activity was undertaken to 2.28. However, it could be argued that a major case of this nature, involving a large number of multiple charges related to property offences against one suspect, is likely to occur at least once over 179 shifts for any given general investigation detective team, and in that respect it is reasonable to include this case in the totals.

The portrayal of detective activity in Table 3:1 gives no indication of the fact that only one-third of the time spent on shifts by the detectives in our study was actually devoted to active case investigation. A different portrayal of the nature of detective work comes from a consideration of how time was distributed over the variety of activities that constituted the everyday work of detectives in our sample. Table 3:2 includes data pertaining to this time distribution; these data are based on field workers' recording of time spent on each activity as contained in the research field notes.

As indicated in Table 3:2, the time spent is recorded in hours. It should be noted that while the average length of each shift was exactly eight hours, this does not mean that every shift was of this duration. Detectives worked either an 8:00 a.m. to 4:00 p.m. shift or a 4:00 p.m. to midnight shift, but they also worked overtime. Overtime typically occured when an urgent case came up during the shift which required immediate extended investigation, or when a suspect was in custody and there was a need to complete the investigation in order to release him or hold him for a bail hearing. On the other hand, detectives were able to use "credits" they had obtained in working overtime in order to take time off from their regular shift schedule. Occasionally a detective would work the first few hours of a shift and then leave early. In the present study, it happened that the balance between overtime and taking leave from the regular shift schedule resulted in an eight hour average per shift.

It is important to observe from Table 3:2 that almost one half of the detectives' time was spent in the office. This does *not* include time spent in the office interviewing citizens or dealing with suspects and accused persons. Except for one shift when the detectives drove over two hundred miles to another town to arrest and return a suspect, office activity was part of the work of every shift. By far the most common activity of detectives was to sit at a desk in an open office area to type reports, review files, call citizens connected with case investigations, and to hold both formal and informal meetings about a variety of matters relating to investigation priorities and procedures, and office routine.

Among other things, the substantial amount of time spent in the office is testimony to the organizational demand placed upon the detec-

Table 3:2

Detective Time Spent on Shift Activities

Shift Activity	Time/179 Shifts (hrs.)	% of Total Time	Mean Time/ Shift (hrs.)	# of shifts on which activity undertaken	% of 179 shifts	Mean Time for shifts on which activity undertaken
Office	664.33	46.4	3.71	178	99.4	3.73
General Patrol	31.92	2.2	.18	27	15.1	1.18
Court	34.25	2.4	.19	20	11.2	1.71
Non-Police Activity	160.92	11.2	.90	121	67.6	1.33
Miscellaneous	73.20	5.1	.41	73	40.8	1.00
Case Investigation	*315.93*	*22.1*	*1.76*	—	—	—
Non-citizen Investigation	61.58	4.3	.34	60	33.5	1.03
Travelling No investigation	42.58	3.0	.24	58	32.4	.73
Travelling Investigation	103.50	7.2	.58	137	76.5	.76
Witness Interviews	14.45	1.0	.08	22	12.3	.66
Victim-Complainant Interviews	45.10	3.2	.25	75	41.9	.60
Informant Interviews	48.72	3.4	.27	79	44.1	.62
Suspect-Accused Investigation	*151.19*	*10.6*	*.84*	—	—	—
Suspect Interviews	46.28	3.2	.26	67	37.4	.69
Suspect Interrogation	64.18	4.5	.36	40	22.3	1.60
Accused Processing	40.73	2.9	.23	32	17.9	1.27
Totals	1431.74	100.0	8.00			

tive to provide extensive written accounts of his investigative activity. More time was spent providing the accounts than actually engaging in investigative activity. This is in keeping with a statement made by an ex-FBI agent (quoted by Walters and Gillers (1973)) who considers the FBI to be a "paper police" who spend more time on paper work than on the actual detection of crime. It is also supportive of the conclusion of Greenwood *et al.* (1975: 83) that "It is . . . not appropriate to view the investigator's role as that of solving crimes. Investigators do not spend much time on activities that lead to clearances, and most of their work in this connection could be performed by clerical personnel."[3]

Activity not related to specific case or suspect investigation accounted for a further 21 percent of detective time, including 11 percent of the total time on "non-police activity." This included activities such as conducting personal business during the shift, making personal visits to friends or relatives, and shopping. One explanation of this is that supervisors allow detectives flexibility in conducting personal business during a shift in exchange for brief periods of unclaimed overtime, shortened lunches etc. when the need arises. The "miscellaneous" category includes a variety of activities usually related to criminal cases, such as travelling to and from the location of the Justice of the Peace and spending time with him, transporting prisoners, and running errands for superior officers.

Detectives did not frequently engage in general patrol acitivity, which was thus left almost entirely to the uniform patrol branch. General patrol took place on only 27 shifts, and on those shifts the average time was slightly more than one hour per shift. When general patrol did take place, it was usually taken up as a residual activity when detectives decided there was little else to do. General patrol most frequently occurred near the end of 4:00 p.m. to midnight shifts when the detectives felt it was too late in the evening to call on non-suspect citizens for interviews. Typically it involved cruising by stores that stayed open at night, especially popular "milk stores" that closed at 11:00 p.m., keeping surveillance regarding the possibility of robberies.

It should be noted that marginally more than 10 percent of *all* detective time was spent travelling to and from investigation points. The detectives were usually "on air" to the dispatcher during this time, so that one could also regard this time as involving general patrol.

Table 3:2 also indicates that detectives spent very little shift time in court. Court was attended on only 20 shifts for an average of approximately 1-3/4 hours for each of these shifts. However, the data presented here do not include time spent in court on what would normally have been time off for the detectives; as stated in Chapter 2, detectives were not observed during these periods.

The general investigation detectives in our sample spent 22 percent of their time on activity related to case investigation other than involvement with suspects, averaging approximately 1-3/4 hours per shift in this area. However, as documented in Table 3:2, this includes time spent travelling to and from investigation points (which accounted for over 10 percent of all detective time) and an additional 4.3 percent of their total time conducting non-citizen investigation (e.g., searching for physical evidence, and surveillance). Thus, between 7 and 8 percent of the total time of detectives in our study was spent on face-to-face investigative contact with citizens in the roles of victim, complainant, witness, and informant.

A slightly greater proportion of time was spent in direct contact with citizens treated as suspects or accused persons by detectives. Approximately 3 percent of all detective time was spent questioning suspects in field settings, an additional 4.5 percent of their time involved interrogation interviews, and a further 3 percent of their time was taken up with post-charge processing of accused persons prior to their release. As we noted earlier in considering the volume of detective activity related to handling suspects and accused persons, this activity did not occur at all on the majority of shifts. From Table 3:2 we learn that only fractionally more than 10 percent of all detective time was spent dealing directly with suspects and accused persons.

Detectives frequently commented about the low level of their activity and its relationship to the kind of cases they worked on. Detectives who had previously worked in other police forces, especially the Metropolitan Toronto Police Force, claimed that they investigated matters in the police force under study that would not have been investigated in their former forces. For example, a detective reflected upon the six years he had spent in the Toronto force, stating, "There was lots to do down there. Not like here. Down there they wouldn't even deal with half the stuff we investigate here, wouldn't have time."

Another detective, also with experience on the Toronto force, claimed that not only were more trivial matters investigated in the police force under study, but the investigations were more thorough and charges were more likely to be laid. During field work observation there were occasions when matters which were minor, or could only result in summary conviction charges, were pursued with vehemence. This was particularly the case in the sex offence area; for example, summary conviction "Indecent Exposure" cases were pursued vigorously. In one case, the senior detective charged a man with having sexual intercourse with a person under 16 after a reported incident between a 22 year old boarder and the 14 year old daughter of the landlady. As one detective left the house after the suspect had been charged and released on an appearance notice, the junior detective, who had waited outside asked, "Did you charge him?"

Senior Detective: Oh, yes.

Junior Detective: Its funny, a friend of mine in 23 [Division of the Toronto police] on the same Sunday had the same circumstances. A boarder and the whole thing. But they just cautioned him.

Senior Detective: Did they?

Junior Detective: Yea, they would have done that [cautioned the present accused] in Metro. They would never have charged him there.

Detectives were also involved with many minor property offences, such as "Theft Under $200" cases involving shoplifters and the use of metal "slugs" in pinball machines. The detectives sometimes claimed they were only working on these cases because there was nothing of greater consequence to pursue.

The level of work in a detective office was not constant. It is instructive to present in ideal typical fashion examples of low, medium and high activity level shifts in order to show the variation and point to some of the reasons for it.

We have already mentioned that a few shifts were spent entirely in the office. This typically occurred when the detectives were attempting to "catch up" in writing reports, or when one member of the team was serving as an Acting Detective Sergeant. There were many more shifts in which some minor investigative activity was undertaken, but which were still relatively inactive in terms of pursuing investigations. We have selected one of these shifts as an example of a low activity shift.

DS 107 involved the detectives spending the first 5-1/2 hours of the 8:00 to 4:00 p.m. period in the office, with the major task being the preparation of a court brief for the Crown attorney. At 1:30 a visit was made to the home of a victim who had previously reported a break and enter. She was shown a photograph of a possible suspect, and identified him as the person she suspected. This victim interview lasted approximately ten minutes, and was followed by a visit to the home of an informant identified by the victim as having more information about the suspect's involvement in the case. The informant was interviewed for five minutes, but refused to supply the information the victim claimed he could offer. Following this, the detective proceeded to a pre-arranged meeting with a member of the Bomb Disposal Unit regarding a bombing of a vehicle that had occurred a month earlier and was still being investigated. This meeting lasted for three-quarters of an hour after which the detective returned to the office, where he spent the last fifty minutes before departing at 4:00 p.m.

A shift with a medium level of activity typically involved the two detectives in more investigation interviews with citizens and other activity in the field, and less time in the office on reports. On DS 161, again in the 8:00 a.m. to 4:00 p.m. time period, the detectives spent the first hour in the office working on reports. They then went out "on the road," stopping in a restaurant for breakfast before proceeding to the court building. The detectives spent fifteen minutes at the court arranging for a withdrawal of a theft charge against a suspect who was due to appear on that date. From the court, the detectives returned to their divisional office and spent the following three-quarters of an hour checking through their files for occurrences for follow-up investigations.

The detectives then proceeded to contact victim-complainants associated with these follow-up occurrences. The first of these was a fifteen minute interview with the shipper at a transport company, who had reported that an ex-employee was still using the company credit card to make purchases. The detectives took the licence number from the credit card slips, stating that they would check it to find the suspect's address. From there they drove to the airport to investigate a complaint by an airline freight manager that a large quantity of recording tapes had been stolen. This interview lasted about twenty minutes.

The detectives then stopped in at a hotel restaurant that they frequented and where they had information exchange relationships with several employees. While being treated to lunch and drinks, they were asked by the manager if they could look into a case in which a convicted person was required to pay restitution to the hotel for fraudulent cheques he had written against them, but so far had failed to do so. The detectives agreed to inquire into the matter.

The detectives then proceeded to the headquarters division of the Force to check the radio call logs for information that might confirm a witnesses' account in an "obstruct justice" and "perjury" investigation. This records search lasted three-quarters of an hour, after which the detectives returned to their divisional station and spent the remaining one hour writing reports.

High activity shifts typically involved situations where the detectives initially intended to conduct some field investigative activity, and in addition were assigned a "hot pursuit" or "suspect in custody" case that added an unanticipated workload. DS 33, scheduled for the 4:00 to midnight period on a Sunday, is illustrative.

The detectives spent the first 2-1/2 hours on the shift writing reports. During this period, one of the detectives also prepared a search warrant and took it to the Justice of the Peace for his signature. The detectives then proceeded to a residential address to execute this search warrant, which pertained to a case that had been on file for over one month. The case involved an allegation by a transport company manager that six cases of liquor were missing from a shipment and that the truck driver was the likely culprit. A search was conducted at the driver's residence, and revealed nothing.

From this location the detectives proceeded to the residence of a suspect named by an accomplice as a culprit in a series of break and enters. The suspect's father told detectives that his son was out of town but would be returning later in the evening, and the father agreed to bring his son to the divisional station the following evening. The detectives returned to the station and worked on reports for slightly less than an hour when they received a call from this suspect, who asked to come to the station to discuss the matter. He arrived shortly thereafter, and the detectives proceeded to interrogate him for one hour.

During the interrogation, a uniform officer brought in two suspects he had arrested after a CPIC check had revealed one was a parolee with a narcotics record and the other had a record for break and enter, and a subsequent vehicle search revealed "weapons" and equipment deemed by the uniform officer to be intended for use in a robbery. The Acting Detective Sergeant called the detectives out of the interrogation room and asked them to take over investigation of these apprehended suspects. The break and enter suspect being interrogated refused to confess to the offences, and was released within five minutes. The detectives then proceeded to familiarize themselves with the suspect in custody case, and within an hour commenced interrogation of one suspect, alternated to the other, and continued this for over two hours. Just before 2:00 a.m. the suspects were turned over to the uniformed Staff Sergeant to be held in the cells overnight, and the detectives then spent an additional hour writing up their notebooks and reports, completing an eleven hour shift.

On the vast majority of shifts the general investigation detectives could set their own pace of work. The field workers observed a number of patterns in this connection which illuminate the considerable occupational autonomy of the detective, especially when compared with the uniform patrol officer (Ericson, 1980).

One observed pattern was the tendency of a detective to undertake a lower level of activity near the beginning and the end of a shift series. Often the first shift after rest days, and the last shift before rest days, were characterized by little investigative contact with citizens. For example, on the last shift of one five day shift series the two detectives on the team spent about 2-1/2 hours on reports in the office, made two telephone calls in connection with investigations, and attempted to interview one witness and one victim although neither of them were at home when detectives called. The rest of the time was spent over dinner; in general patrol, which largely consisted of looking at boats in a marina; and, in a two hour discussion with other detectives in the office about various aspects of the Force, after one of the two detective team members took two hours of leave time owing to him and left early. On the first day back for the subsequent series of five shifts, the first four hours were spent in the office on reports, followed by an extended lunch. Two separate interviews of victims were conducted toward the end of the shift for a total of one-half hour, after which the detectives returned to the station and went off-duty (DS 016, 017).

Another circumstance under which activity, especially activity in the field, was kept at a low level occurred when a detective was about to go on leave for a course or to be transferred. Under these circumstances, time was mostly spent completing follow-up reports for investigations previously undertaken, and preparing court briefs, with field investigation limited to serious matters requiring immediate attention or a few interviews connected with cases already on file and deemed in need of clearance (e.g., DS 165, 166).

A shift of relatively low activity was also likely if it followed one where there had been a high level of activity, overtime, and/or a major investigation. For example, following a rape investigation which involved the detectives being called on duty at 4:00 a.m. and working 16 hours to 8:00 p.m. the following evening, and then continuing at 8:00 a.m. the following morning for eight hours, the detectives decided to spend the subsequent shift in a more "quiet" manner. The first two hours were spent in the office in general conversation and on reports, followed by a visit to the court building to listen in on the bail hearing of the accused in the rape case and to talk with a Crown attorney about another matter. This was followed by lunch and a visit to the shooting range to meet the annual proficiency requirement in pistol shooting. Upon leaving the range, the detectives heard and responded to a general radio call about an "Indecent Assault" suspect reported in a specified residential area. Detectives arrested and briefly questioned a suspect, but determined he was not the person they were looking for. They then proceeded to a 10 minute interview of a witness in another case, the only investigative activity taken on the shift on their own initiative. This was followed by another 1-3/4 hours in the office before going off duty (DS 18, 19, 20).

An impression generated from observing detective shift activity was that with very few exceptions, all case investigation was a matter of routine, and largely mundane. As we document in Chapter 4, cases were often not worked on for days or even weeks after they had been taken on by a detective. As Greenwood *et al.* (1975: 55) discovered, a detective might have dozens of occurrences on his "active" investigation file, but when there was a lull in activity these cases were not worked, often because there was little or nothing that could be done on them. The prime determinant of immediate action seemed to be whether or not a suspect was known or was readily identifiable, but even in some of these cases there was considerable delay. However, once the detectives decided to work on a case it was usually pursued to the point where some conclusion was made.

During the course of a shift, there was rarely a feeling that any particular matter was pressing. Rather, the impression was that things would fall into place in due course, and investigative work was as much waiting for relevant information as it was pursuing it. If detectives were out "on the road" and blocked in an investigation—as they frequently were, for instance, when a citizen was not at home or could not otherwise be located—they were as likely to bide their time by making "social" calls, patrolling, or taking a break for food, as they were to switch to another case. Even during the course of a significant investigation, a major break would occasionally be taken for something far less significant. For example, on DS 148 the detectives were called in at 4:00 a.m. instead of the usual 8:00 a.m. starting time in order to undertake an investigation of an alleged robbery. However, later in the morning the two detective team members received an invitation to lunch from a private investigator whom they had been involved with in connection with an employee theft case. In the middle of the robbery investigation the detectives departed for a three hour session of lunch and drinks as the guest of the private investigator, and did not do any more work on the robbery case until the following day.[4]

Alteration of work activity came about as a result of a variety of situated influences. For example, on DS 51 the detectives became involved in the investigation of a suspect who was arrested by uniform officers during a series of residential break and enters in progress. The first 4-1/2 hours of the shift were spent in interviewing the victims, interrogating the suspect and searching his apartment. The detectives then returned to the divisional station and lodged the suspect in the cells while they had lunch and checked through occurrence files. Later in the afternoon they had a compulsory two hour meeting to attend with senior police administrators, and they decided to hold the culprit in for further investigation rather than release him because they did not wish to return after the meeting to continue the investigation, which would have involved considerable overtime work.

Regardless of the influences, detectives treated nearly all of their work as routine. This is a common feature of occupations that deal with peoples' troubles and troublesome people. What is dramatic and traumatic to the citizen is part of the everyday routine of the detective's work. A situation that is potentially threatening and even dangerous is treated as all part of a day's work. For example, on DS 43, the detectives responded to a radio call regarding a report of a gun shot in a closed warehouse. The detectives drove quickly to the scene, and upon their arrival saw that several patrol officers, including the canine unit, were already there and investigating the building. As one detective rolled down the car window to speak with a uniform officer, he noticed the police dog lift a leg to a tree. The detective exclaimed to the uniform officer, "If he says piss on it, so do we," reversed his car, and sped away at the same pace that marked his arrival.

Our description of the everyday routine of detective work has touched upon aspects of detective autonomy within the police organization. We now move to a more in-depth consideration of detective autonomy through an analysis of organizational controls that operated within the general investigation detective units. This analysis provides further understanding of how detective routines are organizationally produced, and of the ways in which detectives are able to establish their own routines.

Bureaucratic Organization and Detective Autonomy

Detectives were responsive to controlling elements emanating from three basic sources: adminstrative production expectations, supervision by superordinate officers, and the occupational culture of detective colleagues.

A mark of the bureaucratic organization is the effort to measure the product of its workers' labour. This has proved to be a perplexing task in the police organization. The task is not so difficult in some areas—for example, the issuance of traffic citations (Wilson, 1968: 97)—but it becomes much more difficult for tasks that require considerable time and effort to evolve information and to produce evidence. In the area of detective work, the prime evaluative criteria have been the arrest rate and the clearance rate.[5] Some (e.g., Wilson, 1962: 112) have argued that these measures allow an accurate evaluation of detective labour, while others (e.g., Skolnick, 1966: 186ff; Greenwood *et al.*, 1975) have shown the inadequacies of these measures for evaluation of detectives. Skolnick (1966) has argued that administrative evaluation of detectives by these criteria has a potent influence on detective actions; these criteria become the primary guide for detective actions, with negative consequences for the rule of law. All literature points to the ways in which bureaucratic production demands fundamentally influence how detectives make crime and criminals.

In the detective units we studied, individuals and two-person detective teams were required to submit monthly activity sheets pertaining to the case occurrences worked on and how they were cleared, as well as some indication of time spent on non-case related activity. However, contrary to the situation in the uniform branch (Ericson,

1980: Ch. 3), there was no apparent pressure on detectives to produce a specifiable monthly volume of arrests, charges and other clearances.[6] Therefore, within the Force as a whole, there existed a contradictory situation that detectives, whose primary assigned task was investigation geared toward arrest and charge, felt less sustained administrative pressure to produce in these terms than uniform patrol officers, who in all but minor offence areas had their investigative autonomy curtailed.

There were several indicators that the emphasis was upon collective cooperation among detectives rather than on individual productivity as a form of bureaucratic control. This does not mean that Force administrators were not oriented toward the production of clearance rates in order to impress various publics who might affect their organizational resources. Rather, the Force administration apparently viewed a cooperative effort with emphasis on quality as the means by which their work could be accomplished and displayed most adequately. With some exceptions to be noted later, this meant that detectives were not *primarily* oriented to the production of statistics that would aid their chances for organizational recognition.

One indicator came on DS 70 when the divisional Detective Inspector addressed all general investigation detectives in the regular monthly office meeting. He stated to the detectives that more credit would be given for signs of cooperation than for high levels of production that indicated an individualistic approach. During this address he stated, "I don't care who makes the pinch. I'm looking for quality not quantity, in investigation. You'll score no points with me for quantity."

Another indicator came from a series of memoranda circulated among administrators in the Force in reaction to a proposal to implement what was termed a "charge sheet" system. As expressed in one memorandum, this system was aimed at providing "the Deputy Chief [with] more control over the Monthly Output from each Office for which he is responsible. To do this, it would require each Officer to keep a record of the Charges he or she swears to, and in this way the Deputy Chief will have some knowledge as to what each Officer, and each Branch, is contributing to overall statistics." It is worth quoting at length two different memoranda written separately by two senior officers concerning why this "charge sheet" system was not a good idea.

Memo I

The general feeling, both from Supervisors and Investigators, is that this proposed Form would have a serious demoralizing effect on the Officers. First of all, it is felt that there would be a competitiveness formed which could, and eventually would, lead to a lack of co-operation between the Officers in their day to day investigations. This, in itself, could have a serious effect on the work output from the Branch, e.g., an officer has information on a possible arrest on Day shift; he will retain it himself until he is able to make the arrest, rather than turn it over to an afternoon shift worker. Second example, would be, that the Officer will become very concerned over the Occurrences received from the Detective Sergeant and will want only those with a possible arrest, rather than the more difficult Occurrences which require considerable investigation with no actual arrest indicated.[7] This also brings out mixed feelings from the men as they have a tendency to feel that the Detective Sergeant is favouring one team of Detectives over another, again creating morale problems.

Another problem that will arise from this proposed Form, is unnecessary work being done by Officers, e.g., on arresting a subject for Theft, a Possession Charge would also be laid, just to get the second Statistic.

A far more serious example is where an arrest has been made, where several offences have been cleared. Rather than lay one Information to cover all charges, thereby reducing the paper work considerably, the Officers will lay each Charge individually, thereby raising the Statistics.

. . . . . .

Memo II

[The "charge sheet"] does not take into account the many other various duties performed by a Detective. It could also be viewed by him as some sort of a yardstick, to compare officer to officer, or uniform vs. plainclothes.

Without having a more detailed view of the reasons behind the 'charge sheet,' I cannot support its implementation, for reasons which I will be setting out.

The introduction of a 'charge sheet,' using the basis set out by the Deputy Chief, will lead to many problem areas, all of which we have personally experienced in the past.

This unit is composed of a number of individuals, all working toward a common goal, in a collective manner. Introduction of the system, for the want of a better word, will break the "all for one and one for all" attitude. Men will become individuals and work as such, not contributing to the group, but focusing their work towards the individual. The purpose being to contribute to the sheet in an effort to attain individual recognition, not concerning themselves with the group structure of recognition. I do not suggest that individualism is not present now, but if the individual is forced to justify his performance by charges laid he will forget all else and concern himself with looking good on the sheet, by the number of informations he signs.

The "charge sheet" also leads to lack of discretion, in that duplicity of charges, such as Theft and Possession are laid, out of the same circumstance, this being to be able to fill the sheet with names, for reasons of personal recognition.

It also leads to lack of communication among the group, again the reason being, "I must look after myself first," get the charge for the sheet.

A further problem of withholding charges for the next month is also a factor. Again this being, "I must have something for the sheet, maybe next month will be slack or I am going off for a few days and when I come back I'll be in to next month." This type of attitude can and has occurred within the service.

In the area of partnerships [two person detective teams], who should get the credit on the sheet. You cannot guage the value of junior officers because they have no charge on the sheet. The junior officer may be the spark plug of the team, and should have his name on the sheet, but because he is junior doesn't get credit.

In general, the "charge sheet system" attacks the morale of the men. Gives them the feeling I must produce, when do I get an easy arrest, Joe gets all the easy arrests, etc. etc.

I also feel that Detectives should not try to be categorized in the same statistical area as that of uniform officers. It is very easy to assess statistically what a uniform officer is doing, this being based on the routine type of his work. Whereas the Detective as such, has a narrower area, but has much work that cannot be shown statistically; e.g., preparing court briefs, court itself, special investigations, major investigations, the list can go on and on. Statistical output of charges laid cannot be a justification for the making of a Detective, due to the type of job he does.

Citation of these memoranda does not confirm that administrative production demands were not salient. However, arguments of this type at various levels in the organization did apparently serve to reduce the role of quantitative production criteria in the consciousness of detectives as they went about their work. The only persons in the detective office who seemed at all "production" conscious, and who engaged in practices that reflected their concern, were those who had not attained the full detective rank. One possible explanation for this was the fact that these persons, compared with their full detective colleagues, had more recently been in the uniform branch where they would have been attuned to production requirements. In this connection, they might have seen the detective activity sheet in much the same way as the uniform branch monthly activity sheet (cf. Ericson, 1980: Ch. 3), believing it to have some impact on evaluation for promotion even if more senior officers indicated otherwise.

One example of concern over production for promotion involved a constable who was working with a full detective partner. He was due to receive an evaluation based on his performance after his first six months in the detective office. He claimed that the main criterion used in the evaluation was the number of arrests one had made, and he felt he was in a good position in this respect because of the high number of arrests he had made while serving as the Divisional Warrant Officer. It is noteworthy that this person received a poor evaluation, leading to an early transfer back into the uniform branch.

Another example concerned an Acting Detective (the position attained after one full year in the detective branch) who believed "writing off" ocurrences in large volumes was the key to giving production appearances. This person translated belief into action, including the use of a practice whereby the victim would be telephoned, and then the occurrence would be written off with statements in the follow-up report indicating that a more thorough investigation had been conducted (e.g., DS 74; DC 117).[8]

Another detective, with probationary status (the position attained after two full years in the detective branch), had a reputation as the most productive detective in the office, always willing to take on cases involving overtime, especially suspect in custody cases. One reason he attributed to his activity was the desire "to obtain my rank [full detective]."

With the exception of these individualized concerns over production for promotion, and isolated cases where the administration demanded "results," there were not sustained production expectations emanating from administrative sources. Nevertheless, one might expect that supervisory officers, especially the Detective Sergeants, would effect considerable control over production during the course of their everyday review of cases worked on by their subordinates. This, however, was not the case in any clear-cut sense.

One feature of all bureaucratic organizations is that a considerable degree of power rests with the lower ranking line members (e.g., Barnard, 1968). In the police organization, this power is strengthened by difficulties in supervision of line member activity. The difficulty of close supervision of line officers has been a favourite topic among socio-legal researchers studying the police (e.g., Wilson, 1968; Cain, 1973; Bittner, 1970, 1974; Reiss, 1974; Muir 1977; Manning, 1977, 1977a, 1980). Supervisors must allow leeway because of the nature of police work, including the ways in which the bureaucracy mobilizes officers to work as information processors. One consequence is that supervisors are involved in interdependent relationships with their subordinates. Indeed, sometimes supervisors become dependent upon subordinates to the extent that they must turn a blind eye to questionable conduct in exchange for cooperation in areas that directly reflect upon the supervisor's competence in administrative eyes.

In the general investigation detective offices, the Detective Sergeants were officially regarded as advisors, evaluators and disciplinarians. In action, they were colleagues and consultants. Their input at evaluation time for those without full detective rank had some importance and was certainly a consideration among those seeking upward mobility, but it was by no means part of the everyday consciousness of these persons. Their role as disciplinarians was virtually nonexistent; the occasions for discipline were rare and usually dealt with by the Detective Inspector.

Detective Sergeants were expected by detectives to collaborate in maintaining the considerable degree of autonomy they enjoyed in relation to how they spent their time, what they investigated, and how they went about investigating it. In routine circumstances, Detective Sergeants did not inquire into what a detective was doing when he stated that he was going out of the office, and in many circumstances they were not even informed when detectives left or returned. Detective Sergeants rarely told detectives to give priority to particular cases on their investigation files, and did not scrutinize investigative steps taken up to the point of the written follow-up report being submitted. The exception to this occurred when there was a major crime or suspect in custody case that required immediate attention in the eyes of the Detective Sergeant on duty, or when there was an administrative directive for special attention to a case. Even in these cases, however, the Detective Sergeant often asked for "volunteers" among the available detectives on the shift.

The rule that was reflected in the expectation that Detective Sergeants would be essentially non-directive was aimed at maintaining the autonomy of detectives, especially in relation to their control over their investigative role. The influence of this rule was perhaps most adequately demonstrated both by the fact that it was rarely violated, and that when it was violated there was an immediate remedial cycle engaged in to re-assert its prominence and the nature of the relationship it signified.

During the 179 shifts of detective field work there was only one occasion on which the rule was deemed to be blatantly violated in the eyes of detectives. This occurred on DS 116, a shift that involved 24 continuous hours because of major investigation into an "attempt rape" incident that occurred during the shift. The detectives initially became involved after they were asked to attend at the victim's residence by their Detective Sergeant. Subsequently, a suspect was arrested by the uniform branch and held at the divisional station until the detectives could commence interrogation of him. After the one-half hour initial interrogation period the suspect admitted to an offence and indicated his willingness to provide a written statement. During this period other officers were involved in various components of the investigation, including the Detective Sergeant and a policewoman who took a written statement from the victim, and the Detective Inspector who organized a thorough search for physical evidence at the location of the incident. These involvements by others were not seen as problematic by the detectives, but rather were seen as necessary because the detectives were engaged with the suspect.

Following a series of field investigation checks for physical evidence connected with this incident, the detectives decided to interrogate the suspect in relation to a series of "Indecent Assault (Female)" incidents that had previously been the subject of intensive investigative effort by several detectives in the office. After approximately 40 minutes of this second interrogation period, one of the two detective team members began doubting that this suspect was responsible for the indecent assaults. He withdrew from the interrogation, and the Detective Sergeant then joined the other detective team member, continuing the interrogation. After a period of time, the detective who withdrew returned and joined the Detective Sergeant in the interrogation, and the second member withdrew. This interrogation continued for one and one-half hours without a confession.

After a four hour period in which the accused was lodged in the cells, the interrogation continued on and off for a further six hours, involving various combinations, including one detective team member and another detective; one detective team member, the Detective Sergeant and a policewoman; one detective team member and the Detective Sergeant; and finally the two original detective team members. These subsequent interrogations did not produce a confession, but one hour after they were discontinued another Detective Sergeant reported for shift duty and insisted upon interrogating the suspect himself. He did so, but without results, and after a further hour the detectives took the accused to the Justice of the Peace to be held for a bail hearing.

The contentious issue in relation to our present discussion was the fact that the two Detective Sergeants actively moved into the interrogation of the suspect. When the first Detective Sergeant did so, there were a number of "rumblings" in the office among other detectives, with comments such as "What's [names Detective Sergeant] doing in there [the interrogation room]? If it was my investigation I'd tell him to to fuck right off." This was compounded when the second Detective Sergeant persisted in taking his turn. This evoked a direct negative comment from one of the original detective team members, and was seen as particularly uncalled for since the Detective Inspector had earlier informed a senior administrator that the suspect did not appear to be the culprit and had received other orders for pursuing the indecent assault investigations.

This violation of investigative autonomy became the subject of considerable discussion in the office, and at one stage the Detective Inspector was involved. The Detective Inspector attempted to placate the situation by emphasizing that every investigator had a tendency to think that he can be successful when others have failed, and that he himself is tempted to actively enter an investigation in this type of situation. In spite of this, the discussion served to establish with the Detective Inspector that this was viewed by detectives as an unacceptable encroachment, and the expectation was created that steps would be taken to prevent future incursions of this nature.

While the Detective Sergeant was kept in order as an advisor, he also functioned as an evaluator. The evaluation occurred as a matter of routine in that all follow-up investigation reports were passed to the Detective Sergeant's desk for review. All Detective Sergeants in the office also sat as a committee with the Detective Inspector in reviewing the progress of constables, Acting Detectives, and Probationary Detectives. The fact that the detective writing a report knew that it would be reviewed and judged by a Detective Sergeant, and possibly by the Detective Inspector, was something for him to keep in mind. As previously mentioned, it was of particular concern to those without full

Detective rank vis-à-vis the Detective Sergeant's input into decisions about their promotion or transfer back to the uniform branch. As discussed previously, sometimes this did influence the pattern of investigation and report writing among persons without the full detective rank, but the evaluative role of the Detective Sergeant was not an everyday focal concern as it was among members of the uniform branch in relation to the patrol sergeant (Ericson, 1980: Ch. 3).

The role of disciplinarian was not evident among Detective Sergeants, but rather was "moved up" to the Detective Inspector level. This itself seemed to be a recognition that the Detective-Detective Sergeant relationship was one of advisor and colleague, and that the requirement of enforcing disciplinary rules would interfere with this relationship. On balance, the Detective Inspector was identified with the administration, and his development and use of rules in relation to investigations, office routine, and the "appearances code" was seen as legitimate because of this identification. He was at a distance, *the* representative of the Administration within the office.

The Detective Inspector enforced disciplinary rules of two types, those relating to administrative procedures concerning the conduct of investigations (including those under the *Police Act*) and those relating to office routine. In situations where there was a violation of investigation related procedures, the divisional Detective Inspector typically reviewed the matter first and then decided whether to lay a charge against the detective concerned. If a charge was laid, a committee was formed to hear the matter; this committee was constituted by senior officers including both Divisional Detective Inspectors. In one case a detective was charged under the *Police Act* after being deemed by the Detective Inspector to have been responsible for allowing a prisoner to escape. It is interesting to note that the Detective Inspector in the other divisional office, who was required to sit on the committee hearing the case, found it necessary to address the detectives in his office on the matter. He emphasized that all assembled persons should agree that this was a major offence, and stressed that every avenue was explored before the charge was laid, thus trying to alleviate any potential conflict with his subordinates concerning the role he was required to undertake in punishing one of their colleagues (DS 130).

The Detective Inspector also functioned as an office manager who developed and enforced rules affecting the working conditions of detectives. While this was obviously not direct control over criminal production, it is important to consider because it indicates the separation of disciplinary control from the Detective Sergeants, thereby facilitating their role as advisors of, and collaborators with, detectives.

One example of this type of work routine control occurred over a period of time in one of the divisional detective offices. Detectives who wanted days off in compensation for overtime work would typically gain permission to do so when a fellow Detective was serving as an Acting Detective Sergeant; the Acting Detective Sergeant would grant the request, knowing the favour would be reciprocated when the person making the request was Acting Detective Sergeant and he himself was seeking time off. This pattern continued without interference until it was discovered by the Detective Inspector, who then created a rule that any requests of this nature must be made to himself or to a regular Detective Sergeant. Although Detective Sergeants thereby became involved in policing related to this rule, it only came about because of the Detective Inspector's interference, and enforcement could thus be legitimately displaced in the name of his authority.

The Detective Inspectors had two major sources of power in the eyes of detectives. They were experienced and knowledgeable investigators, and possessed personal authority on that basis (cf. Grosman, 1975: 35). Detective Inspectors were also key figures in the invocation of disciplinary rules that could negatively affect a detective's career, or end it. Detectives viewed these rules and their enforcement as very enabling in favour of the administration. They appreciated the irony that detective use of enabling rules against suspects was not dissimilar from the uses of internal disciplinary rules by Detective Inspectors against detectives. The Detective Inspector's power to punish was an omnipresent consideration in all detective actions (see generally Ramsay, 1972; Rubinstein, 1973; Mann and Lee, 1979).

The third internal influence on detective action were the rules and attendant practices developed within the occupational culture of detectives. Some of these rules reflected other rules emanating from the administration. For example, the administrative emphasis on cooperation in investigation was translated into rules for cooperation within the occupational culture of line officers.

In the main, general investigation detectives did not compete for cases in an effort to obtain individual credit. There were circumstances where a detective was afforded the opportunity of taking a case over from a colleague, but refused to do so. On DS 110 the Detective Sergeant re-assigned a case of theft from an airport freight warehouse involving an estimated loss of $250,000. The detective who was originally working on the case was vacationing, and there was a need to follow-up on additional information available through an informant working with an airport security officer. However, apart from talking with the airport security officer, the detective did not undertake any further follow-up even though a fence for the stolen items had been identified. He delayed any further action until the return of the vacationing detective, and did not keep the case as part of his active investigation case file.

There were some cases where one detective sought the assistance of one or more others in conducting major investigations. On DS 137, a detective investigating a series of "purse snatches," with suspects identified by an informant, requested the assistance of another detective to conduct searches and interview the suspects. It should be noted that this practice was more common when detectives were working alone rather than in two person teams.

Several other types of cooperation were observed during the field work period. On DS 171, one detective was investigating a case where drugs had been found and turned into the police; the detective later suspected that these drugs had been stolen. A suspect in this case was linked to another case of theft which was on the active investigation file of another detective. At the request of the detective investigating the "found drug" case, this detective willingly turned over the theft occurrence stating, "take as many as you like."

On DS 157, a detective became involved in a case where two suspects were apprehended shortly after a reported robbery at a milk store. The detective charged them in relation to this incident, but he did not pursue interrogation aimed at charging them for more robberies that he suspected them of. Rather, he left this interrogation for detectives coming in on the morning shift; these detectives subsequently obtained confessions to three more robberies from one of the suspects.

On DS 137, a detective used information from a suspect previously charged by another detective for "Mischief" to arrest and charge suspects wanted for "attempt robbery," "theft," and "break, enter and theft" cases. As part of the exchange for this information the detective promised the informant that he would arrange for the withdrawal of the "Mischief" charge. This detective stated to the detective involved in the earlier "Mischief" case, "I told him if this panned out we'd take care of that charge. I'm sure you and [detective team partner] wouldn't mind." The detective who had laid the "Mischief" charge agreed to the arrangement, again indicating a general rule of cooperation where it was judged reasonable. In this case it seemed reasonable both because the trade-off was for charges in relation to a more serious offence, and because it served to nurture a relationship with an informant, even if in both respects it was apparently to the advantage of one detective more than the other.

The rules of cooperation were also evidenced on occasions when detectives perceived violation. Most examples of violation came from dealings with specialized detectives outside of the general investigation units. General investigation detectives frequently complained that specialized unit detectives acted with self interest, seeking credit for all cases within their jurisdiction and ensuring that others did not encroach on their jurisdiction.[9] The homicide squad was frequently singled out in this connection, perhaps because their work represented the most haloed type of investigation in the eyes of most detectives. As an example of this, we can consider a situation where an experienced and respected investigator in the general investigation office began to use his "contacts" in developing information related to a homicide that had been difficult to solve. This officer became frustrated by what he perceived to be obstacles put up by the homicide squad, and eventually he re-directed his efforts off this case. A lunchroom conversation among three detectives about this situation is revealing:

Detective 1: He [the general investigation detective] could have the murder wrapped up now if they left him to it . . .
Detective 2: What? . . .
Detective 1: He just got pissed off with them [Homicide Squad]
Detective 3: They [Homicide Squad] want all the glory. The first thing they do in the morning when they come in is look at the papers to see if their name is there.

There were a few situations in which detectives in different units worked separately on the same case with considerable overlap of effort and little or no cooperation. This occurred in relation to DC 087, which involved Youth Bureau officers, two general investigation teams, and the sex offence team all separately seeking a person suspected of several school break-ins and one residential break-in where obscene notes were left, as well as a series of obscene telephone calls. There was no cooperation with the Youth Bureau team, even though they had previously interviewed persons the detectives later decided to interview. During one interview with a school vice principal, he said to the detectives, "You're the third or fourth group [of police officers] who have been in here" (DS 039). When detectives made a link between the break-ins and the obscene telephone calls, which had previously been investigated by the sex offence unit, they made no attempt to coordinate with this unit (DS 033). They did, however, cooperate with the other general investigation team working on the case, being kept informed about a search warrant executed in relation to one suspect and undertaking a joint interrogation of another suspect (DS 041). When the Youth Bureau finally arrested and charged a culprit, they did not involve the general investigation detectives. The general investigation detectives were extremely annoyed at this, first because they had been working on the case all along; secondly because the person was an adult; and thirdly, because the Youth Bureau officers did not charge for all offences the person admitted to and did not conduct a search of the suspect's residence for evidence of possible further offences (DS 048).

While manifest conflict of this nature existed at times between general investigation and specialized units, it was not typically evident among the general investigation detectives themselves. Occasionally some annoyance was expressed if one detective took initiative in dealing with part of an investigation which another detective clearly defined as his own. For example, in DC 078/085 one detective team charged two youths with a series of break-ins, and planned to arrest and charge a third youth who was allegedly involved in one of the break-ins. However, another detective team charged the third suspect after he had been arrested by the uniform branch on another matter, possibly because they wanted to question him about other cases they were investigating. This created some annoyance, especially because the second team did not even mention their intended actions to the first team (DS 030).

The general rule of cooperation within the general investigation detective units, where administrative production pressure was not dominant, meant that the resulting working relationships and patterns within the unit were very different from that revealed in Skolnick's (1966) analysis. On the other hand, some conflict between general investigation detectives and specialized unit detectives was evident, a phenomenon in keeping with Skolnick's analysis.

Detectives also produced their own structure of rules for use in controlling other aspects of their work, including the pace of shift activity and attendant practices. These practices were typical of those found in any large work organization. They were also in keeping with the long tradition of such activity within the police service.

The historical record documents how disciplinary control waves have always been a feature of police organizations. As noted in Chapter 1, the New Police in Metropolitan London had an annual turnover rate of one-third in the early years, due mainly to problems with drunken officers and to the fact that dismissal from the force was the only disciplinary punishment (Moylan, 1929; Cobb, 1957). Similar patterns characterized other early police forces, including the Northwest Mounted Police (Morrison, 1975: 275). The first separate detective establishment in the London police was created after an 1878 inquiry concerning the illegal gambling involvements of three senior plainclothes officers (Moylan, 1929). In Victorian times, "the popular catch-phrase, 'If you want to know the time, ask a policeman' reflected not so much the confidence of the Victorians in the reliability of the police, as their assumption that any policeman who did not quickly 'win' a watch from the pockets of a drunken reveller was unnaturally and abnormally honest, or dull" (Williams, 1961: 361). In modern times, Scotland Yard has been shaken by successive control waves against large numbers of officers involved in gambling, property offences, and pornography related graft (cf. Cox *et al.*, 1977). This has led to arguments for re-organization of Scotland Yard, based on the contention that the separation of the CID in 1878, which was in response to detective deviance, created the enabling conditions for detective deviance![10] Contemporary American examples also abound, including many accounts by socio-legal researchers (e.g., Westley, 1951; Reiss, 1971: Rubinstein, 1973; Sherman, 1974).

In comparison with these accounts, the detective operations we observed were relatively free of disciplinary control waves. This probably reflects the fact that most detective practices were viewed by superordinates as tolerable and minor, if they were viewed at all.

Many of the detective practices related to "easing" the pace of their work (cf. Cain, 1971, 1973). For example, detectives developed strategies for covering the time that they spent on personal business.

On DS 50, the detective spent 80 minutes visiting a relative. He then undertook a five minute investigative interview with a citizen, and when this was completed he informed the dispatcher that he was "clear" at the citizen's address, thus leaving the question open as to how long he had been there. Detectives leaving early but still wanting to book off at their scheduled time required the cover of their colleagues (DS 123). Similarly, detectives who took a substantial proportion of the shift for non-police activity—such as the four hours taken by the detectives on DS 124 to attend a party—were covered by colleagues who kept informed of their whereabouts in case of a serious situation or inquiries by a senior officer.

While efforts at making work more tolerable were collectively collaborated in by all detectives, they did have their limits. Detectives who "carried it too far" because they engaged in an officially deviant activity extensively or took it to extremes were subject to attempts at control, and if necessary ostracism, by their fellow detectives. As Rubinstein (1973: 119) observes:

> The collusions that men employ provide them all with the necessary cover to protect themselves from unknown ears. Revelations of laxness are almost always the consequence of some incompetence. The punishments that follow are as much payments for failures to maintain cover as they are for violations of department regulations.
> [see also Cain, 1971: esp. 90n]

The failure to be supportive is not a result of the action being seen as intrinsically wrongful, but rather because continuation of it is deemed likely to lead to a severe administrative reaction that might affect the interests of all detectives. To illustrate this point, we can consider a development in one of the detective offices. One detective started to drink to excess both on and off duty. This was affecting his work performance to the point where he was perceived as a potential threat to himself and others. At first he was subject only to negative comments by others; later other detectives refused to cooperate with him in investigations; finally some detectives actively considered the possibility of collaborating with the administration in "forcing" him to take a leave for treatment. What is noteworthy is that these reactions were apparently a result of a shared belief that the problems of this detective were causing close administrative scrutiny of the entire detective office, and this would ultimately affect everyone. A typical comment in this vein was, "He's dragging us all down." This detective was eventually pushed outside the protective ring of his colleagues, and he was dismissed from the Force.

Detective created rules concerning specific investigative tasks were in some cases also related to working conditions. Since the degree of conformity to legal and administrative expectations concerning procedural regularity will be documented in later chapters, we shall not undertake an extensive interpretation at this stage. However, it is important to point out that while there was some tolerance among colleagues for a questionable practice that might violate procedural regularity, it too was subject to peer control for the same reason as noted above, i.e., if it was taken to excess it would lead to more serious impositions from outside. Moreover, there was likely to be more of a value-based reaction in this area compared with other activities we have described. For example, a uniform officer who avoided responding to a dispatched call that involved two murders and a suicide was reported to the administration by two officers on his platoon, and was universally condemned in the detective office (DS 108). There was considerable verbal condemnation in response to a newspaper report of officers from another police force who had been charged with break and enter offences; on the other hand, detectives were much more likely to condone violent acts by policemen, especially if these acts were in response to a threat to police authority (DS 84).

While they *contribute* to the making of crime control waves, detectives are *subject* to disciplinary control waves within the Force. Detectives established rules within their occupational culture to reduce the likelihood of disciplinary control, but the arbitrary nature of the administrative rule structure and its enforcement meant that there was always an element of unpredictability. This *potential* for being proceeded against made all detectives wary. While the majority of detective labour was directed at the use of rules against others, they always kept a small reserve of energy to combat the use of disciplinary rules against themselves.

Productivity and supervisory expectations are a key part of the police Force reality as experienced by detectives; that is, they are things that must be taken into account and accounted for as detectives go about their work. However, especially in the case of detectives as compared with uniform patrol officers (Ericson, 1980), these forces are not very restrictive. The environment created within the Force is an enabling one, allowing detectives to go about their task of making crime and producing criminals in a routine manner.

Similar to the legal framework within which they operate (see Chapter One), detectives are provided with an organizational framework that is conducive to the production of the commodities most valued by the Force. An analogy can be made with the framework of rules regulating business practices in the society at large. The legal controls are loose or non-existent as they pertain to the expansion of capital. Where the law proliferates and the controls tighten is in relation to the productivity of the masses who labour for capital. A complex system of laws, enforcement, and correction exists to put back into working order those who have thrown a spanner in the works (cf. Foucault, 1977). Comparing the police Force, we can appreciate that controls are not designed to regulate the productive expansion of the crime making business itself, but only the workers who, through minor indiscretions, threaten the productivity potential of the police economy.

In this chapter we have taken the lid off the productive machinery to scrutinize how it is put together from the inside. We now turn to an examination of how the internal operations relate to the things and people that detectives work on in order to make their crime and criminal products.

NOTES

1. For a discussion on the legal definition of arrest, and the problems this definition creates for the empirical researcher, see Chapter 6.

2. As mentioned in Chapter 1 and documented elsewhere (Ericson, 1980), patrol officers are more likely to encounter suspects at the scene of complaints. However, the vast majority of occurrences reported by patrol officers are not accompanied by an apprehended suspect. Rubinstein (1973: 345) reports on a Los Angeles Police Department survey which estimates that under optimal conditions (which never actually pertain) "the chance of each patrolman capturing a burglar occurred once every three months and a robber once every fourteen years."

3. Further documentation of this point is made in Chapter 4. In a survey of police officers, Watson and Sterling (1969: 100) asked them to state the most important single problem they faced on the job. The most frequent response (27%) was "too much paper work."

4. A similar unhurried approach to investigations has been reported elsewhere. At a hearing of the Keable Commission inquiry into police activities in Quebec, a Montreal Captain of Detectives was asked why he decided to delay the arrest of an F.L.Q. suspect who was identified after his fingerprints were found on a dismantled bomb made of 31 dynamite sticks. The Captain of Detectives replied that he did not move to make the arrest because he was about to leave on vacation. (Toronto, *Globe and Mail*, 20 February 1980).

5. Other criteria may also be of importance, including the generation of information about activities that can eventually be made into crimes, and the return of stolen property.

6. Sanders (1977) likewise opposes Skolnick's (1966) findings in this area. Based upon his observations of a general investigation detective office in a small California city, Sanders (pp. 82-83) states:

> The ratio of crimes cleared to those reported and treated as actual crimes was viewed with general cynicism. The detectives pointed out that how 'stats' were defined and manipulated was far more important than the actual number of arrests made for reported crimes . . . [D]etectives are not oriented in terms of clearance rates so much as in terms of 'good rips' (arrests).

7. This is a phenomenon frequently referred to in the literature on the sociology of bureaucratic organizations (e.g., Etzioni, 1961; Silverman, 1970). There is "organizational drift" into areas that are measurable, resulting in over-production in measurable areas and neglect of the less measurable.

8. This practice is described and analyzed further in Chapter 5.

9. As Silverman (1970: 158) advises, the study of complaints made by organizational participants about each other is a useful means for understanding the expectations that guide their actions. "The role-expectations of the participants can first be established by observing the complaints that they make about each other. To complain is to imply that what one regards as a reasonable expectation of the role-obligations of another has not been fulfilled."

10. Hurd (1979: 141ff) quotes Sir Robert Mark's comments in an interview with the *Sunday Times* (13 March 1977): "Corruption within the Met is mainly the fault of the 1879 decision by the Home Office to enable the CID to become a sort of force within a force. It was disastrous, it was able to look after its own affairs. It investigated its own allegations of wrong-doing. In such circumstances corruption on a massive scale was sooner or later bound to come to light, in view of the concentration of lucrative crime and vice in central London."

Bibliography

Barnard, C. (1938) *The Functions of Executives*. Cambridge: Harvard University Press.

Bittner, E. (1970) *The Functions of the Police in Modern Society*. Rockville, Maryland: NIMH.

Bittner, E. (1974) "A Theory of the Police" in H. Jacob (ed.) *The Potential for Reform of Criminal Justice*. London: Sage.

Cain, M. (1971) "On the Beat" in S. Cohen (ed.) *Images of Deviance*. London: Tavistock.

Cain, M. (1973) *Society and the Policeman's Role*. London: Routledge

Cobb, B. (1957) *The First Detectives*. London: Faber and Faber.

Cox, S. et al. (1977) *The Fall of Scotland Yard*. London: Penguin.

Ericson, R. (1980) *Reproducing Order: A Study of Police Patrol Work* Toronto: University of Toronto Press.

Etzioni, A. (1961) *A Comparative Analysis of Complex Organizations*.

Foucault, M. (1977) *Discipline and Punish*. London: Allen Lane.

Greenwood, P. et al. (1975) *The Criminal Investigation Process: Volume III Observations and Analysis*. Santa Monica: Rand Corporation.

Grosman, B. (1975) *Police Command: Decisions and Discretion*. Toronto: MacMillan.

Hurd, G. (1979) "The Television Presentation of the Police" in S. Holdaway (ed.) *The British Police*. London: Edward Arnold.

Mann, E. and Lee, J. (1979) *R.C.M.P. vs. the People*. Don Mills: General Publishing.

Manning, P. (1977) *Police Work*. Cambridge, Mass.: MIT Press.

Manning, P. (1977a) "Rules in Organizational Context: Narcotics Law Enforcement in Two Settings." *The Sociological Quarterly* 18: 44-61.

Manning, P. (1979a) "The Social Control of Police Work" in S. Holdaway (ed.) *The British Police*. London: Edward Arnold.

Manning, P. (1980) *The Narcs' Game*. Cambridge, Mass.: M.I.T. Press.

Morrison, W. (1975) "The Northwest Mounted Police and the Klondike Gold Rush" in G. Mosse (ed.) *Police Forces in History*. London: Sage.

Moylan, J. (1929) *Scotland Yard*. London: Putnam.

Muir, W. (1977) *Police: Street Corner Politicians*. Chicago: University of Chicago Press.

Ramsay, J. (1972) "My Case Against the R.C.M.P." *MacLean's* (July): 19.

Reiss, A. (1971) *The Police and the Public*. New Haven: Yale University Press.

Reiss, A. (1974) "Discretionary Justice" in D. Glaser (ed.) *Handbook of Criminology*. Chicago: Rand McNally.

Rubinstein, J. (1973) *City Police*. New York: Farrar, Strauss and Giroux.

Sanders, W. (1977) *Detective Work*. New York: Free Press.

Sherman, L. (ed.) (1974) *Police Corruption*. New York: Anchor Books.

Silverman, D. (1970) *The Theory of Organizations*. London: Heinemann.

Skolnick, J. (1966) *Justice Without Trial*. New York: Wiley.

Watson, N. and Sterling, J. (1969) *Police and Their Opinions*. Washington: I.A.C.P.

Westley, W. (1951) "The Police: A Sociological Study of Law, Custom, and Morality." Ph.D. Dissertation, University of Chicago.

Williams, C. (1961) "The Criminal Law and Public Opinion: Some Police Reactions." *Criminal Law Review*, pp. 359-367.

Wilson, J. (1968) *Varieties of Police Behavior*. Cambridge, Mass.: Harvard University Press.

Wilson, O. (1962) *Police Administration*. New York: McGraw-Hill.

[4]
Dealing with Victim-Complainants

Citizens mobilize the police for a wide variety of purposes. In addition to reporting property-related troubles such as automobile accidents, lost property, and theft, they call the police to handle interpersonal conflicts because other forms of social control have failed, are unavailable, or are absent (Black, 1968: 117, 1972: 1099, 1976: 6; Meyer, 1974: 81–2). This failure of controls is especially frequent at particular times and places (Cumming et al, 1970: 187) and among the less powerful (Black, 1971: 1108; Bottomley, 1973: 45). The police are used as a power resource to help reproduce the order desired by the citizen.

For several reasons, the bulk of troubles complained about by the public do not result in a 'criminal' designation by the patrol officer. Citizens are about as likely to call the police for troubles they themselves define as 'non-criminal' as they are to call regarding 'criminal' troubles (Cumming et al, 1970; Punch, 1979). As we emphasize with case examples in this chapter, the types of things viewed by citizens as 'serious' enough to warrant police presence are typically not very serious at all when compared with conventional wisdom about the police and crime.

Furthermore, citizens only report to the police a small fraction of what they themselves regard as 'crimes' committed against them (Ennis, 1967; Biderman et al, 1967; Sparks et al, 1977). Moreover, as we saw in chapter 4, the communications bureau does not dispatch a substantial number of citizen calls (Jorgensen, 1979; Manning, 1979).

When they do encounter citizens, patrol officers do not routinely accept the citizens' definitions, whether 'criminal' or otherwise. Rather, they translate these requests within the framework of the police organization, employing 'recipe' rules, legal rules, and/or community rules to decide whether the matter could or should be transformed into police property (cf Christie, 1977; Ericson,

1981). In the survey by Sparks et al (1977: 156), '35 per cent of the survey-estimated crime appeared to have been reported to the police; but ... of these apparently reported incidents, only about a third appear to have been recorded in the police statistics.' Reiss (1971: 70 – 8) found that while 58 per cent of all calls for police assistance are initially defined as criminal matters by citizens, one patrol division recorded only 17 per cent of dispatches as criminal incidents.

Police officers have wide interpretive latitude in deciding what constitutes a crime and how the matter should be constituted. Ennis (1967) found that officers and lawyers agreed only slightly more than half the time on whether matters reported by respondents in a victimization survey actually constituted 'crimes.' Chappell et al (1977) found great variation between police departments in their definitions of 'forcible rape,' and this partly accounted for the difference in the incidence of forcible rape in the jurisdictions studied. The officer can transform what is initially reported as a 'service' matter into a 'criminal' incident if it appears possible or desirable to use the criminal law to handle the matter (cf Shearing and Leon, 1978).

In this chapter we examine the processes by which officers make decisions about citizen complaints. I initially describe general statistical patterns in the resolution of both minor (citizen contact) and major (incident) encounters with citizens. We then see how patrol officers construct encounters and the resulting official reports to legitimate their actions. Patrol officers may deflect complaints so that official reporting is not required, report in a way that justifies their decision not to initiate a 'criminal' occurrence, or report in a way that justifies the particular 'criminal' interpretation they give to an occurrence.

Our descriptive statistical portrayal is not an indication that we view the patrol officer as an automaton who follows unreflexively citizens' requests for action according to pre-established criteria. We look at the patrol officer *making* his judgments *within* the complexities of the encounter. He takes into account who the citizens are, their claims within the *context* in which they are made, expectations within the police organization, and the resources (legal and otherwise) available to reproduce order.

Equipped as he is with considerable authority, which routinely yields deference on the part of the public, he routinely achieves an outcome in accordance with his sense of order. His power allows him to make his definition of the situation stick; his authority usually means that the citizens involved readily accept his definition, at least to the point of not invoking an official complaint about it. As the United States National Advisory Commission on Criminal Justice Standards and Goals (1973) observed, police effectiveness depends upon 'the participant's belief that the police have more authority than they actually have.' This applies to both victim-complainants and suspects and is a key reason why the police control the reproduction of order on behalf of the state and its constituent interests.

Minor Complaints

As we saw in chapter 1, patrol officers make decisions on how to handle encounters by typing the individuals involved and using that to assess their claims. Encounters involve a 'negotiation of status claims' (Hudson, 1970: 190) which results in a situation where 'police activity is as much directed to who a person is as to what he does' (Bittner, 1970: 10). Do the citizens' characteristics indicate that they are tied into the order of things? Do their characteristics make their claims legitimate? What investigative actions might refute their claims? What final actions can citizens of this type be made to accept that will also allow police interests to be served?

One way of studying these questions is to categorize the citizens encountered according to criteria of status and role and to link these with characteristics of the encounter. We classified the 153 victim-complainants in citizen-contact encounters according to their personal characteristics, how their encounter was mobilized, the type of dispute, and the actions taken by the officer to terminate the dispute.

Age, *sex*, and *race* were categorized by the researchers. If a driver's licence was produced, or citizens gave their age, these sources were employed. Race was grouped in terms of 'white' and those from other racial backgrounds (black, East Indian, Pakistani, other Asian).

Socio-economic standing was determined by the researchers' judgments. In subsequent analysis these determinations were in turn categorized into 'lower,' 'working,' and 'middle.' This assessment proved difficult because the researchers were required to base their judgments on limited cues, such as the citizen's dress, speech, type of automobile, and/or place of residence. When they were unable to decide they omitted this item, resulting in a large proportion of 'do not know' responses.

Demeanour was judged by whether citizens were deferential to the officer and co-operative in questioning or at any point refused to afford the officer deference and did not co-operate.

Mobilization and *dispute type* were defined in the same way as described in chapter 4. Dispute type was split into 'traffic' and all 'others.' Citizen-contact disputes typically involved minor traffic accidents (damage under $200), interpersonal troubles (disputes between neighbours and domestic problems), and property-related troubles (found property, minor theft, apparent attempted theft, minor property damage).

Advice/assistance involves the officer responding to citizens' troubles by helping them in some way. Advice includes a wide range of counselling on how to obtain other remedies to rectify the trouble, e.g. informal compensation from the culprit concerning minor property damage or loss, alternative sources of help for interpersonal troubles, civil remedies available, etc. Assistance typically included speaking with the other party in a dispute, arranging transportation, providing transportation, etc. Patrol officers took this type of action in almost one-half of their dealings with victim-complainants in citizen contacts.

Official reports are general occurrence reports, property reports, or accident reports. This form of official action was undertaken for only 25 of 153 victim-complainants – on minor traffic accidents (e.g. 'failure to report an accident,' where the damage was slight), found property (e.g. 'found bikes'), minor property occurrences (e.g. 'attempt theft'), and neighbour disputes (e.g. 'barking dog').

As Table 5.1 documents, only three variables significantly differentiate those who received advice/assistance. There is a significant relationship between socio-economic status and advice/assistance. Lower-status persons were much more likely to receive advice/assistance than their higher-status counterparts. One probable reason is that persons of this type are more likely to *use* officers to help them with petty troubles because they have fewer other resources available to handle their problems.

Unco-operative people were significantly less likely to receive advice/assistance from the patrol officer. If a victim-complainant was requesting support and was subsequently not co-operative, the officer was likely to be unable and/or unwilling to offer advice/assistance. However, the 'demeanour' variable does not indicate when during the encounter the citizen became unco-operative or otherwise challenged the officer's actions. In some cases the citizen may have become unco-operative after the officer said he was unwilling to deal with a trivial trouble or something he deemed not proper police business.

Table 5.1 shows also that advice/assistance was more typically given as an alternative to official reports. Only 5 of 25 subject to offical reports also received advice/assistance, while 70 of 128 who did not have an official report taken received advice/assistance.

In Table 5.2 we consider mobilization, dispute type, and victim-complainant characteristics, as well as whether or not an official report was taken, in a stepwise discriminant analysis concerning whether advice/assistance was given.[1] The best predictor of whether or not advice/assistance was given is demeanour. Whether an official report was taken, the victim-complainant's socio-economic status, and his or her age also have influence. Victim-complainants in citizen contacts who received some form of advice/assistance were distinguishable as lower or working class, aged under 17 or over 24, co-operative, and not subject to an official report. These data, along with similar data for major complaints, support the view that in reactive work, patrol officers are often used by lower- or working-class people to handle their personal troubles (cf Downes, 1979: 12–13).

In Table 5.3 I relate mobilization, dispute type, victim-complainant characteristics, and whether advice/assistance was given to those subject to official

TABLE 5.1

Victim-complainants in citizen contact encounters: mobilization, nature of dispute, victim-complainant characteristics, and whether official report against proportion of victim-complainants given advice/assistance

		N	Percentage receiving advice/ assistance	χ^2	df
Total sample		153	49.0		
Mobilization:	Proactive	20	60.0	0.66	1
	Reactive	133	47.4		
Dispute type:	Traffic	47	42.6	0.79	1
	Other	106	51.9		
Victim-complainant characteristics					
Age:	17–24	17	58.8		
	<17 / >24	119	48.7	0.27	1
	Do not know	(17)	(58.8)		
Sex:	Male	100	50.0	0.03	1
	Female	53	47.2		
Race:	White	124	50.0		
	Non-white	28	46.4	0.02	1
	Do not know	(1)	(0.0)		
SES:	Lower	17	82.4		
	Working	55	40.0	9.38	2
	Middle	44	47.7		
	Do not know	(37)	(48.6)		
			*		
Demeanour:	Co-operative	121	56.2		
	Unco-operative	23	17.4	10.14	1
	Do not know	(9)	(33.3)		
Other patrol officer action					
Official report:	Yes	25	20.0	8.73	1
	No	128	54.7		
			*		

* $p < 0.01$
χ^2 corrected for continuity in 2 x 2 tables

reports taken on their complaints. Except for advice/assistance, none of these variables is associated with others at a statistically significant level. One reason is the small proportion subject to official reports.

In Table 5.4, a discriminant analysis employing the same variables indicates that the best predictor of whether an official report was taken is whether advice/assistance was given, followed by the additional influence of the citizen's demeanour and then type of mobilization. People receiving an official report on their complaint are grouped as being involved in reactive mobilization, being co-operative with patrol officers, and not receiving advice/assistance.

In summary, patrol officers handled most minor complaints without recording them. When advice or assistance was offered, it was usually after

TABLE 5.2

Victim-complainants in citizen contact encounters: stepwise discriminant analysis of mobilization, dispute type, victim-complainant characteristics, and whether official report taken against whether advice/assistance given

Step discriminant variables		*F* to enter	Discriminant function coefficients
Demeanour:	Unco-operative *Co-operative*	9.97	+0.683
Official report:	*No report* Report	9.62	−0.504
SES:	Middle *Lower/working*	7.55	+0.527
Age:	17–24 *<17/>24*	1.39	+0.215

Centroids: Group I – No advice/assistance ($n = 51$) −0.497
Centroids: Group II – Advice/assistance ($n = 54$) +0.469
Percentage correctly classified – 70.5%
Wilk's lambda = 0.7646; $\chi^2 = 27.11$; df = 4; $p < 0.001$

complaints by lower-status citizens about troubles with neighbours, spouses, children, or other intimates. Official reports were taken usually for property matters such as minor accidents, attempt theft under $200, or minor property damage.

Obviously our analysis is limited by what we are able to quantify. We consider the influence of the police organization in detail in 'Citizen Requests and the Production of Organizational Accounts,' later in this chapter.

Major Complaints

The greatest proportion (74 per cent) of complaints by victim-complainants are dealt with more extensively. The officers we observed undertook three general forms of action. *Advice/assistance* involved them in giving immediate help or advice (e.g. advice to stay away from the suspect for a while; calling an ambulance service for medical assistance). *Advice to take other formal action* included suggestions that the citizen seek remedies through other 'formal' channels – e.g. consult a lawyer, contact a public welfare agency, make private security arrangements – as well as advising the citizen about proceeding by private prosecution (laying a private information). *Official reports* included general occurrence reports, accident reports, found-property reports, etc. Overall, 16.9 per cent (72) of victim-complainants received advice/assistance, 14.5 per cent (62) received advice to take other formal action, and 52.0 per cent (222) had their complaints officially accepted in the form of reports. Of course, these actions were not mutually exclusive; some citizens received two or all three actions during an encounter, which is taken into account in subsequent analysis.

TABLE 5.3

Victim-complainants in citizen contact encounters: mobilization, nature of dispute, victim-complainant characteristics, and whether advice/assistance given against proportion of victim-complainants subject to official report

		N	Percentage subject to official report	χ^2	df
Total sample		153	16.3		
Mobilization:	Proactive	20	0.0	3.22	1
	Reactive	133	18.8		
Dispute type:	Traffic	47	12.8	0.31	1
		106	17.9		
Victim-complainant characteristics					
Age:	17–24	17	23.5		
	<17 / >24	119	16.0	0.19	1
		(17)	(11.8)		
Sex:	Male	100	16.0	0.01	1
	Female	53	17.0		
Race:	White	124	16.1		
	Non-white	28	14.3	0.00	1
	Do not know	(1)	(100.0)		
SES:	Lower	17	5.9		
	Working	55	20.0	2.01	2
	Middle	44	20.5		
	Do not know	(37)	(10.8)		
Demeanour:	Co-operative	121	17.4		
	Unco-operative	23	8.7	0.53	1
	Do not know	(9)	(22.2)		
Other patrol officer action					
Advice/assistance	Yes	75	6.7	8.73	1
	No	78	25.6 *		

* $p < 0.01$
χ^2 corrected for continuity in 2 x 2 tables

In Table 5.5, whether advice/assistance was given is considered according to the same mobilization and victim-complainant characteristics analysed for victim-complainants in citizen contacts. We include two features of incidents that may also have affected decisions: whether or not the victim-complainant suffered any property damage or loss of any dollar value and whether or not the victim-complainant suffered any personal injury.[2] The types of disputes considered are automobile, property, interpersonal, and others.[3]

A number of factors are related at a statistically significant level to decisions to give advice/assistance. Those involved in interpersonal disputes were more than twice as likely as those involved in any other type of dispute to receive advice/assistance. This is consistent with the fact that those not

TABLE 5.4

Victim-complainants in citizen contact encounters: stepwise discriminant analysis of mobilization, dispute type, victim-complainant characteristics, and whether advice/assistance given against whether official report taken

Step discriminant variables		*F* to enter	Discriminant function coefficients
Advice/assistance:	Advice/assistance *No advice/assistance*	6.08	+0.823
Demeanour:	Unco-operative *Co-operative*	5.48	−0.642
Mobilization:	Proactive *Reactive*	2.11	−0.390

Centroids: Group I – no official report ($n = 86$) +0.164
Centroids: Group II – official report ($n = 19$) +0.740
Percentage correctly classified – 73.3%
Wilk's lambda = 0.8777; $\chi^2 = 13.24$; df = 3; $p < 0.004$

involved in property damage or loss were also significantly more likely to receive advice/assistance. Statistically significant relationships are apparent between advice/assistance and age, sex, and race. Older persons, men, and non-whites were much more likely to receive advice/assistance.

Advice/assistance was not usually associated with any particular circumstances or characteristics. Moreover, while it often consisted of advice regarding other formal action, it was relatively rarely employed along with the taking of official reports.

In Table 5.6 a discriminant analysis is documented to sort out on a predictive basis the characteristics of the group receiving advice/assistance from those who did not.[4] The best predictor on a stepwise basis is whether or not an official report was taken, followed by the addition in order of the dispute type, mobilization, race, sex, age, advice concerning other formal action, and whether personal injury occurred. Those receiving advice/assistance characteristically are also given advice concerning other formal action but do not have a report taken. They are typically in proactive disputes, interpersonal conflicts, and conflicts that do not involve injury. In terms of citizen characteristics, they are under 16 or over 24 years old, women, and non-white.

Turning to Table 5.7 we find that those receiving advice concerning other forms of action are differentiated several ways. As with informal advice/assistance, the vast majority of victim-complainants did not receive advice regarding other types of action.

Advice to take other forms of action was overwhelmingly likely to be in interpersonal disputes and likely to be in situations that did not involve property loss or damage, but did involve a degree of personal injury. People involved were significantly more likely to come from the lowest socio-economic

TABLE 5.5

Victim-complainants in incident encounters: mobilization, dispute characteristics, victim-complainant characteristics, and other patrol officer actions against proportion given advice/assistance

		N	Percentage given advice/ assistance	χ^2	df
Total sample		427	16.9		
Mobilization:	Proactive	20	30.0	1.69	1
	Reactive	407	16.2		
Dispute type:	Auto	81	8.6	22.17	3
	Property	137	11.7		
	Interpersonal	128	29.7		
	Other	81	13.6		
			**		
Damage/loss:	Yes	217	10.6	11.45	1
	No	210	23.3		
			**		
Injury:	Yes	89	18.0	0.02	1
	No	338	16.6		
Victim-complainant characteristics					
Age:	Under 16	26	3.8	6.94	2
	16–24	96	11.5		
	25+	293	19.8		
	Do not know	(12)	(16.7)		
			*		
Sex:	Male	259	12.0	10.37	1
	Female	168	24.4		
			**		
Race:	White	314	14.0	7.28	1
	Non-white	94	26.6		
	Do not know	(19)	(15.8)		
			**		
SES:	Lower	49	24.5	2.80	2
	Working	160	18.1		
	Middle	185	14.6		
	Do not know	(33)	(12.1)		
Demeanour:	Co-operative	368	17.1	0.02	1
	Unco-operative	48	16.7		
	Do not know	(11)	(9.1)		
Other patrol officer actions					
Advice re other formal action:	Yes	62	54.8	71.49	1
	No	365	10.4		
			**		
Official report:	Yes	222	9.5	16.99	1
	No	205	24.9		
			**		

* $p < 0.05$
** $p < 0.01$
χ^2 corrected for continuity in 2 x 2 tables

TABLE 5.6

Incident victim-complainants: stepwise discriminant analysis of mobilization, dispute characteristics, victim-complainant characteristics, and other patrol officer actions against whether or not advice/assistance was given

Step discriminant variables		*F* to enter	Discriminant function coefficients
Official report:	*No report*	19.54	+0.327
	Report		
Dispute type:	Other	10.15	−0.505
	Interpersonal		
Mobilization:	*Proactive*	8.22	+0.407
	Reactive		
Race:	White	6.33	−0.357
	Non-white		
Sex:	Male	5.44	−0.320
	Female		
Age:	*<16 / >24*	2.27	+0.210
	16–24		
Advice formal action:	*Advice formal action*	2.04	+0.204
	No advice formal action		
Personal injury:	Injury	1.39	−0.164
	No injury		

Centroids: Group I – advice/assistance ($n = 64$) −0.812
Centroids: Group II – no advice/assistance ($n = 304$) +0.171
Percentage correctly classified – 70.7%
Wilk's lambda = 0.8609; $\chi^2 = 54.21$; df = 8; $p < 0.001$

status, and were somewhat more likely to be male than female. This group was particularly likely to use patrol officers in place of other agencies and/or officers were more willing to displace complaints from citizens in this category. However, as we learn from Table 5.8, the role of socio-economic status recedes when considered with other variables.

Table 5.7 also indicates that while advice concerning other formal action was often given in conjunction with other forms of advice/assistance, it was rarely combined with the taking of an official report.

From Table 5.8 we learn that on a stepwise basis, the overwhelmingly strongest predictor of advice to take other formal action was whether other informal advice was also given. The addition of dispute type to the equation is then of some importance, while the influence of the remaining variables – personal injury, official report, mobilization, and sex – is relatively less, though still statistically significant.

Those receiving advice concerning other formal action tend to receive other advice/assistance but not to have their complaints officially recorded. They are predictably more likely to be involved in interpersonal disputes, disputes that involve a degree of injury, and reactive disputes and to be men.

TABLE 5.7

Victim-complainants in incident encounters: mobilization, dispute characteristics, victim-complainant characteristics, and other patrol officer actions against proportion given advice concerning other formal action

		N	Percentage receiving advice to take other formal action	χ^2	df
Total sample		427	14.5		
Mobilization:	Proactive	20	15.0	0.07	1
	Reactive	407	14.5		
Dispute type:	Auto	81	8.6	45.38	3
	Property	137	6.6		
	Interpersonal	128	32.0		
	Other	81	6.2		
			**		
Damage/loss:	Yes	217	5.5	27.28	1
	No	210	23.8		
			**		
Injury:	Yes	89	27.0	12.79	1
	No	338	11.2		
			**		
Victim-complainant characteristics					
Age:	under 16	26	0.0	4.90	2
	16–25	96	14.6		
	25+	293	16.0		
	Do not know	(12)	(8.3)		
Sex:	Male	259	11.6	3.99	1
	Female	168	19.0		
			*		
Race:	White	314	12.1	3.31	1
	Non-white	94	20.2		
	Do not know	(19)	(26.3)		
SES:	Lower	49	30.6	13.65	2
	Working	160	15.6		
	Middle	185	9.7		
	Do not know	(33)	(12.1)		
			**		
Demeanour:	Co-operative	368	13.6	2.26	1
	Unco-operative	48	22.9		
	Do not know	(11)	(9.1)		
Other patrol officer actions					
Advice/assistance:	Yes	72	47.2	71.49	1
	No	355	7.9		
			**		
Official report:	Yes	222	5.9	26.53	1
	No	205	23.9		
			**		

* $p < 0.05$
** $p < 0.01$
χ^2 corrected for continuity in 2 x 2 tables

TABLE 5.8

Incident victim-complainants: stepwise discriminant analysis of mobilization, dispute characteristics, victim-complainant characteristics, and other patrol officer actions against whether or not advice concerning other formal action was given

Step discriminant variables		*F* to enter	Discriminant function coefficients
Advice/assistance:	*Advice/assistance*	104.58	+0.794
	No advice/assistance		
Dispute type:	Other	24.55	−0.323
	Interpersonal		
Personal injury:	*Injury*	3.44	+0.173
	No injury		
Official report:	*No report*	3.15	+0.168
	Report		
Mobilization type:	Proactive	1.35	−0.010
	Reactive		
Sex:	*Male*	1.36	+0.010
	Female		

Centroids: Group I – advice other formal action ($n = 53$) −1.299
Centroids: Group II – no advice other formal action ($n = 300$) +0.229
Percentage correctly classified – 84.4%
Wilk's lambda = 0.701; $\chi^2 = 123.6$; df = 6; $p < 0.001$

As indicated in Table 5.9, decisions by patrol officers to take occurrence reports in conjunction with victim-complainant reports of trouble vary greatly on a number of incident and citizen characteristics.

In contrast to informal advice, formal action via official reports was much less likely in interpersonal disputes than in any other type of dispute. Only 25.8 per cent of victim-complainants in interpersonal incidents had official reports taken by patrol officers, while the figure is 53.0 per cent in automobile disputes, 59.3 per cent in 'other' disputes, and 70.3 per cent in property disputes.

Official reports were much more likely to be taken in relation to victim-complainants involved in incidents where there was property damage or loss. Reports were also somewhat more likely when there was no personal injury to the victim. Reports were particularly likely for victim-complainants in property disputes and particularly unlikely for victim-complainants in interpersonal disputes. We find that men, and persons of higher socio-economic status, were significantly more likely to have official reports taken on their complaints.

Table 5.9 shows also that official reports were much less likely to be taken where informal advice/assistance, or advice to take other formal action, was given.

In Table 5.10 we present a discriminant analysis concerning whether or not an official report was taken. By far the most important predictor is the type of dispute. While eight other factors are also statistically significant, their additional influence is markedly less after the type of dispute has been taken into

TABLE 5.9

Victim-complainants in incident encounters: mobilization, dispute characteristics, victim-complainant characteristics, and other patrol officer actions against proportion subject to official reports

		N	Percentage subject to official reports	χ^2	df
Total sample		427	52.0		
Mobilization:	Proactive	20	50.0	0.00	1
	Reactive	407	52.1		
Dispute type:	Automobile	81	54.3	56.54	3
	Property	137	70.8		
	Interpersonal	128	25.8		
	Other	81	59.3		
			**		
Damage/loss:	Yes	217	67.3	40.09	1
	No	210	36.2		
			**		
Injury:	Yes	89	42.7	3.43	1
	No	338	54.4		
Victim-complainant characteristics					
Age:	Under 16	26	46.2	4.54	2
	16–24	96	61.5		
	25+	293	49.5		
	Do not know	(12)	(50.0)		
Sex:	Male	259	60.6	18.76	1
	Female	168	38.7		
			**		
Race:	White	314	54.1	3.44	1
	Non-white	94	42.6		
	Do not know	(19)	(63.2)		
SES:	Lower	49	28.6	20.56	2
	Working	160	47.5		
	Middle	185	62.7		
	Do not know	(33)	(48.5)		
			**		
Demeanour:	Co-operative	368	53.0	2.54	1
	Unco-operative	48	39.6		
	Do not know	(11)	(72.7)		
Other patrol officer actions					
Advice/assistance:	Yes	72	29.2	16.99	1
	No	355	56.6		
			**		
Advice to take other formal action	Yes	62	21.0	26.53	1
	No	365	57.3		
			**		

** $p < 0.01$

χ^2 corrected for continuity in 2 x 2 tables

TABLE 5.10

Incident victim-complainants: stepwise discriminant analysis of mobilization, dispute characteristics, victim-complainant characteristics, and other patrol officer actions against whether or not an official report was taken

Step discriminant variables		*F* to enter	Discriminant function coefficients
Dispute type:	*Other*	40.31	–0.374
	Interpersonal		
Sex:	*Male*	12.20	–0.339
	Female		
Advice/assistance:	Advice/assistance	8.06	+0.237
	No advice/assistance		
Damage/loss:	*Damage/loss*	6.94	–0.300
	No damage/loss		
Age:	<16 / >24	6.10	+0.322
	16–24		
SES:	*Middle*	5.47	–0.265
	Working/lower		
Race:	*White*	2.09	–0.153
	Non-white		
Advice formal action:	Advice formal action	1.10	+0.121
	No advice formal action		
Demeanour:	Unco-operative	1.06	+0.111
	Co-operative		

Centroids: Group I – no official report ($n = 180$) –0.455
Centroids: Group II – official report ($n = 188$) +0.436
Percentage correctly classified – 68.8%
Wilk's lambda = 0.801; $\chi^2 = 80.18$; df = 9; $p < 0.001$

account. The addition of the victim-complainant's sex adds somewhat, followed in order by whether advice/assistance was given; whether there was property loss/damage; the victim-complainant's age, socio-economic status, and race; whether advice for other formal action was given; and demeanour. Those receiving official reports are involved in disputes other than interpersonal, involved in disputes with some degree of property damage and/or loss, male, aged 16 to 24, middle class, 'white,' co-operative in demeanour, and, not receiving advice/assistance or advice concerning alternative action.

The patterns we found were influenced also by police rules which we were unable to include in the quantitative analysis. Patrol officers handled most interpersonal disputes by means other than official reports. Their work in these situations is to patch up the citizen's disorder by various 'cooling-out' strategies – sometimes informal advice and/or assistance and advice concerning other formal remedies. 'Recipe' rules on interpersonal conflicts, especially among intimates ('domestics'), apparently instruct officers to deal with these situations by means other than the criminal law.[5] Citizens are to be advised about the private-information route and/or non-criminal legal remedies and/or welfare-agency remedies.

On the infrequent occasions when officers invoke a criminal law they are usually corrected by their superior officers. A patrol officer arrested and returned to the divisional station a man whose wife had alleged 'assault occasioning bodily harm' ('AOBH'). Equipped with apparent ample evidence, the patrol officer planned to charge the man with 'AOBH,' but the sergeant ordered him not to do so. The officer was told to write a record-of-arrest report using the non-chargeable 'breach of the peace' section – 31 (1) – of the Criminal Code and to inform the complainant that if she wished criminal charges she would have to proceed via a private information.

The reasons for this practice are well discussed in the literature. Police officers know from experience what researchers have documented (e.g. Vera Institute, 1977): a prior relationship between a victim and suspect substantially decreases the probability that the suspect will be convicted if charged. Of course, compared with property-related offences, there are usually greater problems in sustaining a charge for assault arising out of interpersonal conflicts. Hence, officers routinely try to handle interpersonal troubles by informal means, while property-related troubles are more routinely handled by official reports.[6] As we learn shortly, official reports arising out of interpersonal conflicts are typically produced when the officer wants to 'cover' his decisions in writing.

The variability we have found can be explained in large part by factors we cannot quantify. Features of the encounter, including perceptions of it and police organizational influences, must be taken into account. We now turn to a consideration of these matters.

Citizen Requests and the Production of Organizational Accounts

In handling the complaints of citizens, patrol officers do interpretive work. They interpret who the citizens are and what their complaints are within the context in which they are made. They decide what outcomes they can legitimate to the citizens and to their superiors. While the wishes of the citizens may be taken into account and/or made part of an organizational account, they do not in themselves determine what the officer does.

The officer interprets the situation to make up his mind what he is going to do. He then seeks to justify what he does in terms of the rules of the organization, 'recipe' rules, and/or the law. Often his interpretations and attendant justifications coincide with the wishes of the victim-complainant. When they do not, he must work at getting the victim-complainant to agree with him. His pervasive and persuasive authority gives him the power to do this in a routine manner, although he is always aware that his routines can be upset by the victim-complainant or his superiors.

In this section, we initially establish that contrary to the image portrayed by some researchers (e.g. Black, 1968; Reiss, 1971; Pepinsky, 1975), patrol officers do not routinely accept the definition of the situation put forward by the complainant, and they do not routinely follow whatever action is dictated by the complainant. We present data concerning decisions not to follow citizens' requests and not to undertake any official accounting. Further examples reveal organizational reasons why an officer does take an official report. We examine how reports are written in light of organizational purposes and interpretations of citizen complaints. Finally, we consider the implications of our findings for understanding how matters, including crime, become officially recorded as police business.

Encounters of patrol officers with victim-complainants involve many complex requests, demands, interpretations, and reinterpretations on both sides. It is therefore difficult to quantify victim-complainants' requests and officers' actions. However, we decided to classify requests and actions in incidents if there was a dominant request from the victim-complainant which the patrol officer was asked to respond to in a particular way. We can show on a loose basis that officers frequently deflect these requests or do not respond to them at all. The processes involved can then be depicted through qualitative case materials.

Data for 'special requests' by victim-complainants and officers' actions are documented in Tables 5.11 and 5.12. The 'special requests' include 1) *arrest of suspect*, defined as taking custody of someone present or identified as a suspect; 2) *informal settlement*, defined as any means outside the criminal process for resolving the dispute (e.g. warning or caution of suspect; compensation from suspect to victim); 3) *surveillance*, defined as investigative checks or guarding of persons or property connected with the incident; and 4) *other* requests, including a wide range of favours sought from officers by the citizen. Patrol officers were judged to have followed these requests 1) *entirely*, carrying out what was requested of them; 2) *partially*, carrying out to some degree what was requested, but making some changes (i.e. not complying with all aspects of the request and/or taking some additional action not in accordance with the request); and 3) *not at all*, not carrying out any aspect of what was requested.

Among the 427 victim-complainants encountered in incidents, 38 per cent made a special request. Patrol officers acted *to some degree* on 95 per cent of requests for surveillance, 73 per cent of 'other' requests, and 71 per cent of requests for informal settlements. They followed only *to some degree* requests by victim-complainants for arrest of suspects in 45 per cent of such cases. For all types of requests the officers very often only followed them 'partially'. In sum, patrol officers do not routinely follow victim-complainants' requests. More often than not, they act only after altering the thrust of the request or do not act on the request at all.

Special requests were most likely in interpersonal disputes, followed in order by 'other,' property, and automobile disputes. There was widespread fluctuation in compliance according to dispute type: 90 per cent of requests in

TABLE 5.11

Incident victim-complainant special requests and patrol officer action on requests

	Total		Patrol officer action on requests (percentage)		
Special requests	*N*	%	Entirely	Partially	Not at all
Arrest suspect	38	100.0	26.3	18.4	55.3
Informal settlement	49	100.0	32.7	38.8	28.6
Surveillance	41	100.0	36.6	58.5	4.9
Other	33	100.0	48.5	24.2	27.3
Totals	161	100.0	35.4	36.0	28.6

No special requests: 262; missing information: 4

property disputes were complied with to some degree, 88 per cent in 'other' disputes, 58 per cent in automobile disputes, and 56 per cent in interpersonal disputes. In interpersonal disputes, only 2 of 15 requests for arrest of a suspect were complied with to some degree. Officers complied at least partially with 25 of 37 victim-complainants' requests for an informal settlement in interpersonal disputes. In contrast, in property disputes, they complied at least partially with 12 of 15 requests for arrest of a suspect, and all 5 requests for an informal settlement.

In summary, most (62 per cent) victim-complainants did not make a special request. When requests were made, only slightly more than one-third were followed outright, while a similar proportion were altered and almost one-third were not followed at all. Officers usually acted without taking into account special requests and ignored or altered requests to suit their organizational demands. Clearly victim-complainants were extremely compliant with the ordering brought to the encounter by patrol officers.

One of the accomplishments of patrol officers is to secure routine compliance from victim-complainants in accepting their decisions and the justifications that go with them. Especially when official reports are not taken, this is an important means of keeping their actions discreet and invisible to their superiors. Victim-complainants experience the 'high visibility' of direct dealings with patrol officers and yet routinely accept what officers do, thereby collaborating in keeping officers' activities hidden from the police organization.[7]

Manning (1979: 25) argues that the *context* of disputes is assessed by 'recipe' rules. 'Officers work to do two things: to accomplish work within the premises of the work as they understand them, and to create, if necessary, the proper official paper which will represent events within the official, sanctioned format for such events as they are administratively understood.' 'Paper' may be deemed unnecessary for a number of reasons. It is suspect because it invites scrutiny and can open up the problem of administrative support (Manning, 1979a: 56). The officer may be blamed for reporting a trivial matter, for labelling it one way rather than another, for writing it up as something it is later deemed not to be, and so on. In Rubinstein's view (1973: 40), 'Policemen regard

TABLE 5.12

Incident victim-complainant special requests and patrol officer action on requests, by nature of dispute

			Patrol officer action on requests (percentage)		
Dispute type	Special requests	*N*	Entirely	Partially	Not at all
Automobile	Arrest suspect	5	1	0	4
	Informal settlement	4	1	1	2
	Surveillance	6	3	2	1
	Other	4	3	0	1
	Totals	19	8	3	8
	No request: 62				
	Missing information: 0				
Property	Arrest suspect	15	8	4	3
	Informal settlement	5	4	1	0
	Surveillance	14	5	9	0
	Other	6	4	1	1
	Totals	40	21	15	4
	No request: 95				
	Missing information: 2				
Interpersonal	Arrest suspect	15	0	2	13
	Informal settlement	37	9	16	12
	Surveillance	3	0	3	0
	Other	13	2	6	5
	Totals	68	11	27	30
	No request: 58				
	Missing information: 2				
Other	Arrest suspect	3	1	1	1
	Informal settlement	3	2	1	0
	Surveillance	18	7	10	1
	Other	10	7	1	2
	Totals	34	17	13	4
	No request: 47				
	Missing information: 0				

anything requiring them to commit statements to paper as a threat.' Why write up something if it may create problems for the officer rather than gaining rewards for him and his fellow officers, or personal rewards (e.g. insurance claims) for the victim-complainant? This may be one reason why complaints involving interpersonal disputes are less often recorded than property complaints.

With a strict division of labour in investigative work, not reporting a matter may be a means of keeping something interesting for oneself rather than having it taken over by a superior or detectives.

Another reason for avoiding official reports is the common human desire to avoid work. Patrol officers frequently told research fieldworkers that they did not take an official report because they wished to avoid the work involved.

This practice is termed 'skating' – gliding with ease over the surface of the matter. Sometimes the easiest way to do the work, and avoid repercussions that might upset the routine, is to 'unfound'[8] complaints or otherwise make them unreportable.

Interpersonal disputes are particularly unlikely to result in official reporting and are often handled by offering advice and/or assistance, because they are complex and a wide variety of interpretations are equally believable and easy to legitimate if called into question. If the officer chooses an interpretation that does not call for official recording there is little the victim-complainant can do; he is likely to accept the officer's 'common sense' definition of the matter. The officer's judgment determines the case, and often there is no case at all.

For example, at 2:35 am a patrol officer drove at high speeds along a residential street in response to a dispatch regarding 'someone attempting to enter apartment.' Upon arrival, he was admitted by the 30-year-old female complainant, who explained that she lived there with her young daughter. She reported that someone had knocked on the door and had tried the door handle; when she peered through the door visor, she discovered it was a man dressed only in a bath robe. The complainant said that she feared a sexual attack and that police presence was necessary to investigate the matter. She became visibly upset and began sobbing. The officer immediately suggested that the man may have mistakenly thought it was his own apartment. He then strengthened the force of his interpretation, asserting that the man was 'obviously' a resident of the building, probably on the same floor, and was just a little lost. The officer checked the floor hallway and stairwell and told the complainant to call again if the man reappeared. He did not take an occurrence report; hence there could be no follow-up work by general-investigation detectives. In conversation with the researcher, he said the complainant was unduly alarmed by the circumstances.

In many interpersonal disputes, allegations and counter-allegations make it difficult to label 'victim' and 'suspect' and to generate evidence that would justify a 'criminal' label for the incident. These complexities again create an enabling framework for the officer to impose an interpretation that does not involve official action. The usual method is to recommend the private-information route to the 'victim' who is persistent or simply give up if the 'victim' is not persistent. For example, four people reported that they were assaulted by the bartender of a club 20 minutes prior to their report. The officer drove to the club. One customer told him that one of the complainants was banned from the club; when the bartender asked all four to leave, they refused, and he physically removed them from the premises. The officer accepted this account as a means of justifying to the complainants his decision not to lay a charge. He told them that they could lay a private information by appearing at the divisional police station the following day, but he did not produce an occurrence report on this incident.

Victim-complainants usually accept the officer's decisions, although sometimes their persistence necessitates extra work and the formulation of additional justifications. For example, a patrol officer was dispatched to the parking-lot area of an apartment building regarding 'youths fighting – disorderlies.' He and a back-up officer talked with four male youths and the wife of one of them. Three of the youths said that the fourth youth attempted to take their car for a ride without consent, while the fourth youth (the original complainant) and his wife alleged that one of the others had tried to 'kill' him for no apparent reason. The officers said they accepted the account of the three youths, and they told the fourth youth to 'go home and sober up.'

As far as the patrol officers were concerned, they had ably handled the situation without official paper. However, 25 minutes later they were dispatched to the address of the fourth youth, who had decided to pursue his complaint against the other three. The complainant again argued that the other three should be apprehended, pointing to his cut lip and 'bitten' finger as evidence of the assault. The officers again told him to sober up and added that he could think about laying a private information the next morning if he were still inclined to do so. However, they formulated the options in a way that indicated the only thing to do was to drop the matter. They explicitly advised the complainant not to lay a charge, saying that the other youths would in turn lay a charge against him. Back in the patrol car the officer, in conversation with the researcher, claimed that the encounter had been handled in this manner 'to avoid paper work.' In the unlikely event the complainant did persist, the officer was 'covered' by not being committed in writing to taking sides. If the complainant complained about him, he could discredit the complainant by mobilizing the majority support of the other three youths.

Sometimes patrol officers do not officially report an incident because, in spite of their efforts, they are frustrated by the complexities and the lack of citizen assistance in sorting them out. Even if the allegations are serious, they will not be reported if citizens cannot be mobilized to concur in a particular version of the truth that will legitimate official reporting by the officer.

For example, a patrol officer was dispatched at 1 am to a residential address concerning 'several anonymous complaints – a domestic,' which was relabelled en route as a 'fight.' Upon arrival the officer, backed up by three other patrol officers, discovered a party involving 30 persons of East Indian and Pakistani descent. There was considerable arguing among the citizens present, some of whom were standing on the front lawn.

As the officer was speaking with the owner of the home, another man approached saying, 'Someone hit me – do your duty.' When the officer inquired about the culprit, the complainant informed him that it was a white man who had left the party. The officer then took the owner aside and asked if there had been any white persons at the party. The owner replied that there were no white people present at any time and suggested that the complainant was lying: 'Nobody saw anything. One minute he was OK, the next minute he seemed to have fallen down a few stairs.'

The officer again approached the complainant and told him that if he wanted to lay charges he could do so at the divisional station in the morning. He did not act on 'noise' complaints from surrounding neighbours, justifying this on the grounds that they refused to give their names and addresses as complainants. He departed, making an entry in his notebook with no official report.

Forty minutes later, he was again dispatched to the same address regarding a 'fight,' with the added information that an ambulance had been dispatched. As he approached he saw the ambulance leaving, with another car pulling out behind it. He stopped this car, which contained the owner of the house and another man. A back-up patrol officer stopped the ambulance and said he learned from the attendant that the apparent 'victim' had been punched but was not seriously injured.

The patrol officer questioned the owner of the house, who claimed that he had no knowledge of what happened and added, 'Maybe he fell down the stairs.' The officer returned to the house and sought witnesses, but no one supplied any information. He left the scene and later contacted the 'victim' at the hospital, but the latter refused to provide any information on what had happened or on the identity of the culprit. The officer made no further inquiries. He noted the encounter but did not submit an occurrence report.

Officers also have occasion to write reports and pursue suspects in 'interpersonal' encounters, but tend not to because of 'recipe' rules for handling these disputes, especially 'domestics,' through non-official sources. Unless the officer or his superiors want to record the matter or to 'get' the suspect(s), he is likely to handle the matter without official documentation.

In the 'domestic' area in particular, requests for any type of action are often circumvented or ignored (see Kokis, 1977). For example, husband-and-wife counter-allegations of assault and demands for arrest were rejected by a patrol officer, who offered informal advice and did not take an occurrence report. The husband had called the police. Upon arrival of the officer, he claimed that his wife was very drunk and that when she was drunk she tended to be violent, destroying household property and attacking him and the children. The wife countered by saying that her husband had beat her up while their sons had held her to the floor; she pointed to multiple bruises on her arms and legs, as well as open sores, to support her claim. The patrol officer centred the discussion on the wife's drinking problem. The husband then demanded that the officer take the wife to a hospital 'to dry out,' but the officer said it was not his job to do so. The officer eventually convinced the couple that he could not take any formal action. Afterward another patrol officer, who had provided a back-up, told the officer and researcher that he had given this same couple the same advice on 'three or four' previous occasions. Rather than treating this as an

'AOBH' and possible charge, the officers treated it as a ritualized matter that they could do little about except to remind the citizens involved that they could do little about it.

In these circumstances the criminal law was not a viable option. This was not simply a matter of 'evidence problems,' typically referred to in public debate as a reason for not invoking the criminal law in domestic situations. Rather, the criminal law was an inappropriate means of dealing with the conflict, the origin and depth of which lay elsewhere, and might have exacerbated rather than resolved the problem. While the officers could expect to be called to this address again and have one party or the other attempt to use their authority to order their relationships, they would be likely to continue 'bracketing out' the use of the criminal law in reproducing this order.

While property and other types of disputes are much more often reported than interpersonal disputes, a substantial minority are not reported. The reasons again include the desire to avoid work and to avoid reporting something that will predictably turn out to be trivial or 'unfounded' if investigated further by detectives. Interpretive latitude and the power to make 'common sense' interpretations 'stick' permit officers to act thus.

Patrol officers sometimes submit occurrence reports on property-offence complaints even when nothing is taken or damaged, the loss or damage is minimal, or the complainant is suspected of false reporting. For example, a victim reported a 'break and enter' occurrence at his residence, showing the officer a window screen to his back bedroom that had been pushed in. The officer did not question this account or look for any alternative explanations and subsequently filed a 'break and enter' occurrence report.

In contrast, other officers in similar circumstances give interpretations and justifications that allow them to avoid taking an official report. For example, a patrol officer interviewed a 'break and enter' victim who reported that while she had been away working the previous two nights someone may have entered her house through the front door. The door had a missing panel of glass that would allow someone to slip a hand through and unlock the door. The victim told the officer that she was particularly nervous because she was the victim of a 'break, enter and theft' two weeks earlier. The officer suggested that an offence had not occurred and that she was overreacting. The victim seemed to accept this and appeared grateful when the officer placed a piece of cardboard over the broken pane and suggested that she tie a string across the doorway whenever she went out as a means of discovering if anyone entered during her absence. The officer later told the researcher that there obviously was 'no man around the house,' and he decided that he would not submit an occurrence report.

On another shift, a patrol officer was dispatched to a 'break and enter in progress' after a complaint from a neighbour. The officer sped to the scene with two back-up officers. They searched the residence inside and outside but found no occupants and no signs of an offence. The officer telephoned the complainant, who reported that the owners always left their back door open to allow access for their cat. The officer commented to the researcher, 'Fuck it, if they are going to be that irresponsible to leave their back door open for their cat, I'm not going to take an occurrence on the call.'

When citizens mobilize the police, they usually expect the responding officer to assist them in ways that serve their interests. The officer's organizational agenda sometimes produces actions that leave citizens dissatisfied (see Sparks et al, 1977: chapter 5).

Sometimes an outcome can be arrived at which serves mutual interests but at other times the interests conflict and the citizen is either knowingly, or more often unknowingly, put at a disadvantage. The citizen always invites this latter by calling the police, because he gives up most of his power to direct the course of the encounter and settlement. In Coleman's terms (1973: 3), the citizen who mobilizes the police gives up 'usage rights' (use of his own power resources to resolve the matter in his own interests) in exchange for 'benefit rights' (the right to benefit from the very powerful, organized resources of the police): 'The right to use resources is what is ordinarily meant by power, while the right to benefit is the right to gain from the exercise of power.'[9]

This does not necessarily mean the police are acting improperly when they take over the victim's complaint and use it as police property within their own organizational criteria of priorities, trade-offs, and so on (Christie, 1977; Ericson, 1981). The police and the wider process of criminal law are given a mandate to treat the matter as an offence against the state, to take control of the matter on behalf of the state, and to serve the interests of the state first and foremost over any individual interests.

As we have seen, officers frequently use their power to produce a settlement that is not brought to the attention of the police organization through a written report and does not lead to official investigation of possible suspects. They accomplish this through a 'common sense' redefinition of the situation which complainants come to accept. This redefinition may be accompanied by advice, assistance, and/or the declaration that the new definition of the matter now makes it into something which is not police business.

When patrol officers do decide to make the matter more widely known through official reports, they do so with a consideration for one or more interests: their own or those of the complainant, the police organization, or other bureaucratic organizations. Patrol officers may submit occurrence reports because it enhances their productive appearances. They may construct the proper paper in order to 'cover their ass,' especially where they need to control the definition of events organizationally because they were unable to control them adequately in the encounter.[10] They may produce paper for the direct benefit of a complainant when they perceive some property benefit (e.g. insurance claim) for the victim or to give the victim the *appearance* of something being done. Paper may also be generated to serve the police organization. Particular segments of it may want paper to justify a particular form of action. The division of labour regarding investigation means that paper will be produced to notify and guide supervisors and detectives about specific incidents that might be worthy of further investigation. Patrol officers also produce paper to serve the police organization's mandate to act on behalf of both public and private bureaucracies whose own procedures (for compensation, insurance, and so on) require an official accounting.

The police are sensitive to the need to perpetuate co-operation from citizens through public relations. One of the most obvious methods is by giving the appearance that something can be done even if little or nothing can be done. With very low probabilities for clearing most types of reported crime, especially property crimes, the best the patrol officer can do is record the matter and say that it will be passed on to detectives for investigation. A large part of the 'face work' between officers and victim-complainants involves a careful recording of detail, for appearances' sake (see Skogan, 1975; Greenwood et al, 1975; Sanders, 1977; Ericson, 1981). Patrol officers know that the vast majority of their reports will simply be written off by detectives after a brief follow-up contact with the victim-complainant, or even filed with no further action (see Ericson, 1981: chapters 4 and 5). They justify their efforts as placating the complainant.

On some occasions, patrol officers write reports to appease the citizens involved. For example, a patrol officer eventually took a report on a motor-vehicle collision with damage under $200 that occurred on private property. Organizational procedures and the Highway Traffic Act (see chapter 4, note 10) did not call for an official report. The officer took the report to defuse the hostility between the two drivers.

The officer was informed about the accident by a passing motorist. He drove to the scene and observed two vehicles stopped in the exit of a shopping plaza, one with obvious damage to the rear. As he drove up, one of the drivers approached and asked, 'Would you investigate this accident please?' This citizen (driver 2) was adamant that the other citizen (driver 1) was at fault. Driver 1 claimed that as he was about to leave the plaza, he stopped suddenly and driver 2 hit him in the rear. Driver 2 claimed that driver 1 had stopped suddenly, backed up, and hit him. The officer interjected that since the accident had taken place on private property and the damage was less than $200, he had no jurisdiction in the case. He added that he was not required to take a report, and if he did so it would not make any difference.

The argument worsened to the point where it, rather than the accident, became the problem. The officer separated the two and developed new tactics to enforce their compliance. He asked driver 1 how much he had to drink, implying that if he refused to acquiesce to an informal settlement he might be a candidate for an impaired-driving (or care-and-control) charge. Driver 1 denied having anything to drink. The officer then asked to smell his breath and after doing so again asked him how much he had to drink. Driver 1 replied, 'I just came home from work and I only had one beer.' The officer retorted that by looking at driver 1's face he could tell he had a lot more. Hoping this strategy would defuse driver 1, the officer called driver 2 to join them. Driver 2 suggested that each driver could look after the repair costs on his own car. An argument again ensued, and the officer exclaimed, 'OK, that's it, both of you get in the back of the car and I'll take a report.'

After the details were taken, the officer informed the drivers that he could not assign blame or be used as a witness. The drivers left, with driver 1 throwing his hands up in the air in apparent disgust. The patrol officer said 'You don't look too happy about this.' Driver 1 replied, 'I'm no further ahead than I was before.' The officer reminded him that he had told him taking a report would not change anything. Driver 1 then thanked the officer and departed. The officer, talking to the researcher, characterized driver 1 as a 'stupid asshole' and said, 'I'd bet anything he backed into him. [Driver 2] looked pretty honest.' The officer added that he hated to take accident reports.

Cases of this type illustrate that reports are sometimes taken for situationally specific reasons despite external influences which recommend against doing so. However, most such decisions reflect organizational influences, and the way the reports are written always reflects these influences.

The lack of investigative autonomy available to patrol officers is an impetus to report-writing in some matters. If the victim of an offence describes or even names the alleged culprit, the officer normally records the information for his report but does not pursue the culprit because the division of labour requires him to be back out on patrol. Moreover, the force prefers more experienced police officers (detectives) to investigate reported offences and to decide whether the case is 'founded.' Except in routine cases where the culprits are caught in the act by the complainant (e.g. shoplifting) or by the patrol officer himself (e.g. impaired driving, possession of marijuana), the job of 'making crime' is left up to detectives. Indeed, we saw several minor cases (e.g. shoplifting) turned over to detectives to produce additional information and charges (Ericson, 1981). As we saw in chapter 3, patrol officers generally resent the lack of investigative autonomy because it restricts them from doing interesting work. Yet the role of report-taker rather than investigator is sometimes welcomed because it allows the patrol officer to pass responsibility for key decisions to others.

Many incidents, especially in the property category, reflect the patrol officer's role as report-taker. For example, a woman reported the theft of jewelry worth $650. She suspected one of two workmen who had been doing contract work on her home. She was able to identify this suspect through the second workman, who was a friend of hers. The officer took details and submitted an occurrence report, but he made no effort to contact the suspect or to undertake any other investigative checks.

On another shift, the officer was dispatched to the address of a company that had gone bankrupt and was subject to demonstrations outside the plant by ex-employees who had not been paid. At the scene the complainant, a truck driver with the company, reported an estimated $2,000 damage to a company truck. The company owner was also present, and he demanded that the officer immediately arrest four ex-employees who were demonstrating on the property, and who the owner believed were the culprits for the property damage. The patrol officer – reluctant to aggravate the already tense conflict – took the names, addresses, and dates of birth of the ex-employees, but did not question them as suspects. He recorded their identities in the occurrence report, but only as 'employees' rather than as 'suspects.' The occurrence was eventually turned over to detectives; their reports indicate that they interviewed the ex-employees as suspects for this 'mischief' occurrence.

Specific orders from superior officers shape report-taking activity. The incidents in the last two paragraphs were among many in a division at a time when a senior officer was discouraging patrol officers from taking any form of investigation. To *report* a large volume of occurrences would overload the detective office in another division that also handled the detective work for this division; the added volume might give weight to the argument that a separate detective office was needed for this division.

Reports aimed at 'leaving it up to the detectives' are also taken on specific instructions from sergeants who become involved in the matter. When there is a specific order to take a report for 'covering' purposes, the patrol officer obliges. For example, a patrol officer was dispatched to a home where a woman wanted to lodge a complaint concerning a sexual assault and threats. The woman told the officer that she met the suspect at the hotel where she worked as a stripper. She said she invited the suspect home where she willingly allowed him to embrace and kiss her. He became increasingly aggressive, but was halted by her fiancé, who returned home and confronted the man. At this point the victim called the police and constructed the account to her fiancé that the suspect had grabbed her breasts and threatened to rape her. The fiancé apparently ensured the swift departure of the suspect and encouraged the victim to obtain assistance from the police.

During the interview; both the victim and her fiancé repeatedly asked what type of 'prosecution' would occur, and after a while told the officer to stop wasting his time interviewing them and to go out and catch the 'criminal.' The officer, in the presence of a patrol sergeant and two other patrol officers, took down the details for an 'indecent assault (female)' occurrence report. No attempt was made to apprehend the suspect.

The officer later told the researcher that his interpretation of the victim's characteristics and the nature of the complaint led him to discount the entire matter as something unworthy of an official report. He thought that the victim had constructed the allegations against the suspect when she was 'caught' by her fiancé. Her occupation, her drunken condition, and her statement that she had invited the suspect to her home discredited her account. The officer added that he would not have spent more than five minutes on the incident and would not have taken an official report even for 'covering' purposes if the patrol sergeant had not been present.

Official reports have a 'covering' function for both the patrol officer and the force as a whole. A written account allows the officer to select the facts he deems relevant to construct a version of the incident that is consistent with the decisions he has taken.[11] As long as he does this according to legitimate justifications for decisions, he is usually 'covered' even if later investigations by detectives lead to an alteration in his account. The problem for the patrol officer is to find, and to use appropriately, the correct justifications. As we noted in relation to dispatches (chapter 4), there is a strong tendency to err on the side of caution. Reports are typically constructed to present a negative image *in case* further investigation reveals that image is the correct one, e.g. to present the most serious offence that may have been committed.[12]

For example, patrolling at 3:30 am an officer observed two youths sitting on the parking lot of a closed gas station. As he approached them, he noticed a broken window in the front of the station. He called for a back-up officer and casually began to talk with the youths about their actions. When the second officer arrived the questioning became more accusatory, but the youths denied breaking the window or having any intention of entering the service station. They claimed that they had been drinking a lot and they had chosen this spot to rest. The officers called the gas station proprietor who checked the premises but found nothing missing. In spite of this investigation, the officer decided to submit an occurrence report. Moreover, he chose to label it 'attempt break and enter' rather than 'mischief,' 'damage,' 'suspicious circumstances,' or other less serious labels. He later told the researcher that an occurrence report with this particular label was the best 'cover' in the circumstances.

The favourite 'cover' in vague circumstances is to file a report labelled 'suspicious circumstances.' For example, a patrol officer was dispatched to a jewelry shop regarding a 'theft.' The manager, acting as complainant, stated that no theft had occurred, but he wished to report that three suspicious-looking men had been in the store and appeared to be 'casing' it. The officer accepted the complainant's account and wrote up a 'suspicious circumstances' occurrence report. In addition to the obvious public-relations function, this report covered the officer in the remote event that the complainant's suspicions would turn out to be founded. By reporting the matter according to the complainant's account, the officer provided an informational base to detectives. He had brought the matter to the official attention of the force, thereby displacing the possible allegation that it was his fault the matter had not been investigated more thoroughly.

Patrol officers often do not submit a report after dealing with 'suspicious circumstances.' They can simply make a note in their duty notebook in case they need to recall the matter if later called into account. A cleaner working after hours in a doctor's office called the police to report that when he arrived for work he discovered keys left in the office door and upon checking found that the cash box was unlocked. He did not think anything was missing, but he was very anxious to protect himself against any possibility that he or his cleaning crew might be wrongly accused. The officer did not hold the complainant under suspicion and did not make any other checks concerning the circumstances reported to him. He made a note in his duty book, but did not write an occurrence report.

Official reports can also be taken for reasons unrelated to a complaint. Sometimes they are written to account for time. For example, a man reported that his four-year-old daughter had been missing for slightly more than an hour. The officer initiated a search, which included citizens as well as four patrol officers, a patrol sergeant, a detective inspector, and the canine unit. When a citizen located the girl, the other officers left and the sergeant asked the officer to submit an occurrence report to account for the 'man hours' spent on the case. The officer, who spent one and three-quarter hours on the incident, submitted a report labelled 'assistance.'

Sub-units within the force sometimes encourage the reporting of particular types of incidents, in a particular way. The 'sex offence' detective team were compiling a file of several hundred 'obscene telephone calls' believed to be by the same person. Patrol officers routinely recorded these complaints, repeatedly describing the same mode of operation in their reports to the point where all that was needed to channel them to the detectives' files was writing the first and last name used by the culprit when he made his calls.

Sub-units also encourage reporting of incidents in particular places if they are trying to build a case against the establishment involved. For example, a patrol officer was dispatched to a 'fight in progress' outside a hotel bar. He was met by two badly beaten victims. Both had cuts on their faces and upper bodies, and one was barely conscious when the officer arrived. The victims claimed that they had been attacked by some youths who were refused further drinks after they became 'rowdy' in the hotel bar. The officer talked with the manageress, who said she had cut off the drinks of the culprits and they went outside and engaged in an unprovoked attack on the two victims. The officer, backed up by a duty inspector, patrol sergeant, and three other patrol officers, was very eager to pursue the suspects and lay charges. However, both victims were adamant that they did not want to pursue the matter. They were both reluctant to give the officer even their names, and when they agreed to do so, one victim said, 'I want to sign something that my name can't be used in court.'

Some officers pursued the suspects, who were reported by other youths to be walking along a nearby road. However, they did not arrest or charge them. The patrol officer was apparently not going to submit an occurrence report on the matter, but decided to do so upon instruction from a superior officer who stated, 'Morality [the morality detective squad] is trying to close this place down and they're collecting all the reports out of this place. Turn it over to them.' The officer wrote the occurrence report, using the heading 'Cause Disturbance (Information)':

> At the above noted time, a disturbance broke out downstairs in the [hotel]. Two of the patrons involved then left, and were attacked on the front parking lot by four males. The victims [names, addresses, birth dates] were knocked to the ground and kicked. Both received facial injuries, but refused medical aid.
>
> The four assailants had left upon the writer's arrival. but were walking north on —— Road. Both of the victims stated that they did not wish the matter pursued and wished things left alone.
>
> This report is made by order of Inspector ——.
>
> It is to be sent to the morality squad in order that they have the information on file.
>
> Attention – Morality Squad.

Another reason for taking official reports is because police forces serve large public and private bureaucracies. For example, industrial accidents are routinely recorded to provide the appropriate provincial ministry with an official independent account. Thus, a patrol officer took an occurrence report labelled 'Construction Accident,' after an incident in which a worker allegedly fell off a ladder and suffered head injuries requiring hospitalization. The officer spoke with a witness, who gave details of the accident and the identity of the victim. In his report, the officer offered the judgment that the accident came about because the ladder was not secured properly, and he added that an investigator for the occupational safety branch of the provincial government had been notified and was investigating the matter.

In the private sphere, insurance companies are served through the reporting of property loss, theft, and damage. When complainants mention the need for official reports to bolster their claims for compensation from insurance companies, officers usually oblige. For example, a patrol officer filed a 'property damage' report after an elderly couple complained that someone at some unknown time had apparently knocked paint off the aluminum siding of their house causing an estimated $20 damage. The complainants told the officer that their insurance agent wanted an official police report and that is why they had called the police department.

Patrol officers see report-taking in traffic accidents with damage over $200 as being primarily on behalf of the insurance companies involved. Although there are occasional attempts to avoid paper work by interpreting the damages as being under $200 when other parties claim the damage is over $200, most major accidents are routinely handled by taking accounts from each party and writing up a motor vehicle collision report. While patrol officers sometimes obtain a Highway Traffic Act charge against one of the parties, this is also seen as furthering the work of insurance companies, who thereby have the blame settled for them in working out who must pay the costs.

After a decision to produce an official report, the officer has to decide how he is going to label and describe the incident so as to justify his decisions. He has a great deal of autonomy in doing this. Of course, his definitions and constructions may be checked (and changed) by his supervisors and detectives; indeed, that is a primary function of further investigation by others. However, there is a tendency for other members of the police organization to accept the officer's constructions. The officer writes his reports according to 'recipes' which tell him how to write an acceptable account. Many occurrences are not further investigated by detectives, or are investigated in a cursory manner to 'write them off.' They are filed for statistical purposes without any questioning of the officer's report (Greenwood et al, 1975; Sanders, 1977; Ericson, 1981).

Patrol officers, along with others in the police organization, know the importance of producing and being committed to a particular version of an incident. Despite the many interpretations possible, officers must decide on one interpretation and stand behind it. When they decide to commit their interpretations to paper, the product takes on the status of 'fact' which the organization as a whole becomes committed to. Patrol officers and their colleagues know that 'social order depends upon the co-operative acts of men in sustaining a particular version of the truth' (Silverman, 1970: 134).

Patrol officers are regularly confronted with competing definitions of events from citizens with competing interests who are attempting to influence the patrol officer's judgment. The interests of the police force may demand particular definitions. These competing demands introduce a degree of relativity into decisions. Whose version of reality becomes dominant? How does this come about? This is the practical epistemology of everyday life: what knowledge, transmitted by whom, under what conditions, becomes accepted for the purposes of action?

The patrol officer defines and transmits information from the complainant to the police organization. He decides whether something will be recorded and recognized as official business, and what type of business it is. While he has considerable autonomy, which introduces a degree of arbitrariness, his actions are grounded in reporting rules which come from the law as well as the police organization.

When constructing an official report, the officer keeps in mind its likely route within the bureaucracy. He labels and describes the incident in a way that will influence supervisors and detectives in their decision about further investigation. He omits information that might lead to a type of investigation he deems inappropriate and uses labels and descriptions fitting his assessment of the seriousness of the case.

For example, a patrol officer was initially dispatched to a supermarket in a shopping plaza. The dispatcher labelled the complaint a 'fight,' described the two people involved in it, and instructed the officer to see the manager of the supermarket regarding a knife involved in the incident.

The officer was met in the plaza by a female 'victim' and a male 'complainant' (the victim's common-law husband). The victim reported that while she was shopping alone in the supermarket, she noticed a man 'looking at me funny and flicking his tongue at me.' When she attempted to walk past this man, he grabbed her breast. She jumped away and told the man to 'Fuck off,' to which he replied, 'That's exactly what I'm looking for.' The woman walked away, paid for her purchases, and telephoned her husband to tell him what had occurred.

The woman's husband immediately came to the plaza and had his wife point out the 'suspect.' The husband then confronted the suspect and a fight ensued. During the fight the husband pulled a flick-knife from his pocket, but it was immediately knocked out of his hand by the suspect. The suspect, who was much bigger than the husband, beat him, causing facial cuts and bruises on the face, arms, torso, and legs. As the husband was lying 'dazed' on the floor, the store manager approached and the suspect fled.

After receiving this account from the victim, the officer talked to the husband, who admitted after prompting that he had been aggressive in his approach to the suspect and had drawn a knife on him. In his questioning of the husband, the officer attempted to establish that he was the aggressor and had committed offences (at a minimum common assault/possession of a prohibited weapon). The husband continually asked 'Wouldn't you do the same if it was your wife?' He gave a detailed description of the suspect, adding, 'I hope you catch the guy – I want to charge him to hell.'

The officer retrieved the knife from the store manager, but did not attempt to obtain a detailed account from him or from anyone else in the store. He questioned the husband further about the use of the knife and then decided to consult with a back-up patrol officer who had subsequently arrived. The officers decided not to lay a weapons charge against the husband or to mention the weapon in the occurrence report. They also ignored the original dispatcher definition of a 'fight.' Instead, they decided to focus the report on the woman's original complaint and to label it 'possible sex offender.' While constructing the report, the patrol officer said to the researcher he was writing it in a certain way 'or else the Ds [detectives] will make a big issue of it':

> The victim reported she was shopping in the [store], and while in the area of the ice cream display she noticed the suspect staring at her, flickering his tongue at her. She walked away and while passing the suspect he tried to grab her right breast. She jumped out of his reach and went directly to the check outs. Her common law husband was summoned by the victim a few minutes later, and she pointed out the suspect to him. The complainant spoke with the suspect and warned him to stop his actions. A scuffle ensued, and a few kicks and punches thrown by both men, and the suspect fled on foot.

> The complainant stated he could identify the suspect if he sees him again, however at this point he seemed hesitant in relation to charges.
>
> The area around the mall was checked by uniform cruisers, for suspect, negative results.

Several features effectively controlled any chance for intensive future action. The officer indicated there was a fight, but did not say that the complainant had admitted to being the aggressor and had drawn a knife or that he had suffered bodily injury. Moreover, while the complainant had said, 'I want to charge him to hell,' the officer indicated he was 'hesitant in relation to charges.' The suspect's initial sexual overtures were also not described in detail. The officer reached a settlement he considered just. He confided to the researcher that he agreed with the complainant's way of handling the situation and that the 'score' seemed to be even. He also left this impression with the complainant, to whom he suggested that a charge could have been laid regarding the knife; by implication he should feel fortunate at resolution by means of 'summary justice.'

Officers 'patrol' the facts about the disputes they are called upon to deal with. What initially appears a complex matter with as many shades as a chameleon in a box of crayons ends up black and white in a few sentences in the official report. The many possibilities are reduced to one version which will influence decisions about whether there will be any further investigation, what investigation will be undertaken, the criminal charges likely if a suspect is traced, and the category used in the official version.

Further examples can be provided of different types of disputes. A patrol officer was dispatched to a rural side-road regarding 'vehicle in the ditch – possibly a PI [personal injury].' He discovered a damaged vehicle (estimated $500) but no driver. He suspected that the driver had been impaired and had left to avoid detection. A vehicle registration check uncovered the owner's identity and he proceeded to the owner's residence to interview him.

During the interview, the officer changed his suspicions. The driver, who had apparently not been drinking, said that as his car was rounding a corner he was confronted with an oncoming vehicle driving on the wrong side of the road. This vehicle forced him off the road, but continued on. The driver was now a victim-complainant in an accident with elements of 'careless driving' and 'fail to remain.' He reported that there were no independent witnesses. The officer used this to justify to the complainant his decision not to treat this as a case of 'fail to remain' and/or 'careless driving.' He submitted a motor vehicle collision report, but made no mention of the other driver in the brief description: 'Vehicle was east bound on —; driver attempted to evade oncoming traffic and slid into the ditch. Seat belts prevented injury.'

Even when an officer reports the matter in a particular category (e.g. property offence), he can choose from a number of designations. Thus, he gives varying interpretations of break-and-entry offences. For example, a complainant reported that someone had entered the area of his catering company warehouse where he stored cigarettes. He could not tell if anything had been stolen, but demanded surveillance of the property and investigation of an ex-employee who was known to have a key to the area. The officer listened patiently and wrote an occurrence report for 'suspicious circumstances,' which said there was no clear evidence of an entry, and that the matter was not serious because nothing was reported as stolen.

A victim reported that at some time during the previous two days someone had entered the garage attached to his house and taken the four hub-caps (valued at $85) from his car. The officer, noting in his report that the garage was 'unlocked' (perhaps to indicate why he was not labelling it 'break, enter and theft'), submitted a report for 'theft under $200.'[13]

One victim reported that someone had entered his house and taken a guitar valued at $680, while leaving behind other musical and photographic equipment valued at $3,000. The officer acted surprised upon learning that there were no signs of entry and that the other valuable items had been left behind, but agreed to take a report after the victim claimed that he required a report for insurance purposes. Retrospectively, the officer concluded the victim was probably making a false report for insurance gains, but he nevertheless reported 'theft over $200' (but not 'break, enter and theft').

On another shift, a victim reported that $1,350 worth of coins were missing from his home. He had last seen them 26 days earlier; when he checked the hiding place for them on the day of his complaint, he found they were missing. He reported that there were no signs of entry into the house and that he had thoroughly checked the house but could not find the coins. The officer initially suspected that the victim might be falsely reporting a theft. However, when the victim mentioned that three neighbours bordering on their backyard had had break-and-enters on the same day that he and his wife were absent from their home, the officer shifted his interpretation and accepted the victim's account. Instead of possible 'lost property' or 'theft' reports, the officer submitted a report for 'break, enter and theft.'

In complaints about property loss with no entry victims sometimes insisted that the matter involved a 'theft' rather than 'lost property,' and police interpretations varied. One officer was dispatched to the office of a company district manager regarding a theft. The manager complained that he had been missing his wallet since the previous day and wanted it reported as a theft of $120 to $150 plus credit cards. The officer, questioning the delay in reporting and probing for evidence of theft, received rather vague answers. The victim said he last remembered having the wallet at a shopping plaza on the previous day. The officer convinced the victim that it was more appropriate to regard this as a 'lost property' occurrence and produced a report to that effect. By way of comparison, a gas-station employee reported that he had hidden the station keys while he took a car for a test drive; upon his return 15 minutes later, he found the keys were missing. He reported the matter as a theft, and the officer submitted an occurrence report for theft without any suggestion of 'lost property.'

The many subtleties in report-writing allow patrol officers to justify their actions to supervisors and other officers who might read their reports. There are words or phrases which 'everyone knows' are acceptable designations of how an incident was handled.[14] In our research, a common justification for 'writing off' complaints, particularly interpersonal ones, was to say that this was the wish of the complainant. However, these 'complainant wishes' were sometimes produced by the officer after the complainant had started the transaction with very different intentions.

For example, a patrol officer was checking a park at 6 am when he noticed a parked car with two occupants. His suspicions were aroused when he observed the passenger door open slightly and close again, as if someone wanted to get out but then for some reason decided not to. The officer approached the car and asked the male and female occupants for identification. He noticed that the woman was 'dishevelled' and decided to place the man in the rear of the patrol car while he questioned the woman. She reported that she was picked up by the man in Toronto and driven to this location. She alleged that he had indecently assaulted her and showed the officer that her trousers were torn from the knee to the crotch.

The officer called for a patrol sergeant, who interviewed the victim. The sergeant changed her view of the matter and secured a verbal statement that she did not wish to press charges but only wished a ride back to where she was originally picked up. The sergeant invited the victim to use his car to change into a dress she was carrying in her bag. In private conversation, the sergeant told the officer that 'she seems like a quasi-hooker who has gotten herself in a bit of a spot' and that no charges would be laid because of the victim's wishes. The sergeant and officer also agreed that the victim would fail to appear as a witness if they charged the suspect.

The officer told the man never to bring his 'pick-ups' into the area again and threatened to tell his wife about the incident. The officer drove the woman to the boundary of the police force's area. He later wrote an occurrence report that justified not charging in terms of the victim's 'request':

> [Heading: 'Indecent Assault Female']
> [The victim] got out of the car and stated that suspect had ripped her pants and showed writer that pants were torn in crotch area.
>
> She stated she had been hitch-hiking on Yonge Street Toronto and had been picked up by suspect and driven to above location where he told her to 'put out' or 'she was a dead duck.' She had not been assaulted in any other way than the pants being torn. Suspect denied ripping pants and victim stated she did not wish to press charges. Victim was turned over to —— PD for transport into city and suspect cautioned and released.

'Requests' not to take official action were often sought by officers trying to justify 'writing off' domestic disputes without taking formal action against the alleged culprit. For example, a woman reported to the divisional station to lay a charge against her husband for a domestic incident patrol officers responded to the previous day. On instructions from a staff sergeant, a patrol officer proceeded to interview the victim with the expressed purpose of discouraging her from laying a charge. The main thrust of his statement was that a charge would worsen the conflict with her husband; he recommended she seek the assistance of a lawyer and said he could help her arrange accomodation at the Salvation Army. In a report, the officer said 'She agreed not to lay charges at this time; it was made clear to her that this Department would render all necessary assistance to lay such charges if required.'

In summary, patrol officers exercise considerable power in controlling whether or not a citizen's complaint will be recorded, how it will be recorded, and what its subsequent career is likely to be in the priorities of police business. Our findings have significant implications for the statistics on occurrences and crime the police bureaucracy uses as an indicator of its work and justification of its resources. They also have implications for the way in which criminologists, the media, politicians, and other citizens use police statistics in their assessments of the 'crime problem.' We now turn to an examination of these implications.

Implications for 'Controlology'

In a refinement of the 'labelling' perspective, Ditton (1979) has argued that crime exists only when people decide to seek an official designation of a person's behaviour as criminal. Something is not a crime until it is constituted as such by control agents (the police) and certified as such by the courts. Thus, the study of crime centres on the subject of control, which Ditton refers to as 'controlology.'[15]

There are a number of variable elements in the production of police business, including the discovery of behaviour which might be labelled and treated as police business, the reporting by citizens and patrol officers of that behaviour, and the recording and classification by officers of that behaviour. The great variations in control at each of these stages has been subject to increasing attention.[16] Researchers have concluded that there is a great need for study of the role of police in 'making' or 'unmaking' crime. Sparks et al (1977: 160) state their victimization study findings emphasize that 'there is plenty of scope for such research. They also emphasize the importance of interpreting official criminal statistics as the outcome of a series of social processes and organizational activities; and the extreme dangers of uncritically assuming that the statistics automatically reflect – even approximately – the amounts and types of criminal behaviour which do in fact take place.'

Many complaints are not officially logged. Many calls for service do not result in a dispatch; many dispatches do not result in an official report; many reports do not recommend further action or criminal designations; and, regardless of designation, many reports are filed without any further investigation (see Ericson, 1981: chapters 4 and 5).

The patrol officer clearly has the power to make citizen complaints into non-police business. In reactive minor complaints only 19 per cent resulted in an official report, while in reactive major complaints only 52 per cent did so. The figure for all reactive complaints is 44 per cent. This can be compared with figures of about one-half in a study of 26 American cities (Skogan, 1976), about one-third for London, England (Sparks et al, 1977: chapter 6), and approximately two-thirds in Black's 1970 study.

As both Sparks et al (1977) and McCabe and Sutcliffe (1978) have stressed, policies on reporting can have a substantial influence on the volume of what becomes publicly portrayed as 'crime' and other police business. The police have it within their power to commit 'control waves,' which are then portrayed publicly as 'crime waves' (cf Ditton, 1979: 24).[17] Our own data provide examples of this phenomenon.

The divison of labour increases the probability that patrol officers will submit reports and let their supervisors and detectives decide on further action. This can produce two effects. First, it may increase the number of occurrence reports submitted and thus swell the official statistics on police business. If the patrol officer has more investigative autonomy, he has the opportunity to 'unfound' more complaints; either he will submit fewer reports, or more reports will consist simply of his legitimations for 'unfounding' the complaint. Second, supervisors and detectives may dispose of a greater number of occurrences by marking them 'filed,' 'no crime,' and 'unfounded' (see McCabe and Sutcliffe, 1978: 73; Bottomley and Coleman, 1979: 14–18; Ericson, 1981: chapters 4–5).

Other features of the organization can have a temporary influence on reporting. I mentioned that a senior officer instructed patrol officers to file as many reports as possible, without investigation to 'unfound' them. This strategy was apparently aimed at overloading the detective office in another division which handled the criminal investigation for his division, thereby serving to produce the 'facts' he wanted to support his argument that the force should create a separate detective unit within his division.

One must also consider the 'recipe' rules of the occupational culture concerning the handling of disputes and the production of official paper. A number of features of an encounter, as well as influences external to it, are considered in the context of the 'recipe' rules in order to make a reporting decision. In addition to patrolling the streets, the officer patrols the facts by not reporting them or reporting them to produce an outcome he sees as both just and justifiable.

The quantified data describe patterns in actions by patrol officers in terms of external criteria, including mobilization, the matter in dispute, and status and role of citizens. The qualitative data instruct us how these elements are interpreted by officers and how they, along with aspects of the police organization, are taken into account in the making of decisions and accounting for them.

In the next chapter I document how similar considerations affect dealings of patrol officers with suspects and accused persons. In particular, I stress the importance of looking inside the police organization to see how police business, including the business of crime, is made, literally. Behaviour is just behaviour until it is defined; definitions are just definitions until they are made to 'stick.' 'Making them "stick" requires a different sort of "stick" – power. The more powerful the definer, the "realer" the consequences' (Ditton, 1979: 87). As an organized *force*, the police have the power to make particular definitions of citizens' troubles – and to make them 'stick.'

Notes

1 In this and all subsequent discriminant analyses, cases with missing information on any variable have been excluded. In this section, the age variable has been divided into 1) those under 17 and over 24 years of age and 2) those aged 17 to 24, and the socio-economic status variable has been split into 1) middle-class and 2) lower-or working-class. Here and later the other decisions of the patrol officer are included to determine how much they contribute in the prediction and classification of the decision. We are not simply viewing them as both 'independent' and 'dependent' variables, rather, we simply wish to consider how they contribute to the classification of groups of citizens who did or did not receive given responses.

2 Sparks et al (1977: 120) report that personal injury increases the chances a victim will make a complaint to the police; also, the greater the degree of property loss, the greater the chance the victim will complain.

3 While we did consider separately victim-complainant 'special requests' of patrol officers (see Tables 5.11 and 5.12), we did not include this as an independent variable for the cross-tabulation and discriminant analyses. These requests vary greatly and cannot be reduced to two or three categories. We might have taken the requests to 'arrest a suspect' and related this variable to actions against suspects, but these requests were few (38), and we would have had to analyse separately situations in which 1) suspects were present, 2) suspects were apprehendable, 3) suspects were not apprehendable and would have been pursued, if at all, by detectives. Also, as we argue in our qualitative analysis, preferences of victims could be interpreted and transformed by officers.

4 Here and later, the dispute-type variable has been divided into 1) 'interpersonal' disputes and 2) all 'other' types of disputes (combined automobile, property, other). The age variable is split into those 1) under 16 and over 24 and 2) 16 to 24. The SES variable is divided into 1) the 'middle' and 2) the 'working/lower' group.

5 McCabe and Sutcliffe (1978: 58n) cite a Greater London (England) police force order: 'In minor cases, where the identity of the offender is known, particularly when the Police have no knowledge of the matter and it arises from a dispute between relations, neighbors etc., the Police should leave the complainant to apply for a summons and should only arrest the offender if he refuses to desist, or a breach of the peace may otherwise occur.'

6 This differs radically from much of the 'policy talk' in Canada about 'diversion' and 'violence' (e.g. Law Reform Commission of Canada, 1974, 1975). The official approach is to divert minor property complaints from the criminal process and to concentrate law enforcement and correctional attention on violence. Our data indicate that the police are much more likely to make property disputes official and 'criminal,' while dealing informally with most complaints of violence and leaving them unofficial.

7 Wiley and Hudik (1974) suggest that a citizen's co-operation depends upon the value he places on police actions and the formulations of the police officer. If the citizen is co-operative, the officer is likely to respond in kind. Sheley and Harris (1976) suggest that citizens co-operate not because of the reward for co-operation, but because they know the probable costs of not co-operating with the police.

8 Rubinstein (1973: 145) observes, 'Unfounding calls is one of the ways policemen have of reducing the amount of paper work they are obliged to do and also curbing the rate of reported crime. When a patrolman tells his dispatcher that a job is unfounded, he is claiming that his investigation has not substantiated the initial claim of the person who called for a police officer. Frequently this is the case, but often enough it is not.'

9 Several copies of official reports are made for various purposes within the police force, but a copy is not made for the complainant. The complainant may not know even whether or not a report is filed and is unlikely to know how a report is labelled or what account is constructed by the officer to justify his designations and decisions.

10 ' "Necessary paper" is defined by external pressures as much as by features of the incident. In other words, paper that is written is written at such time that one needs to show paper work. Sometimes, this action of generating the proper paper is called "covering your ass". Thus, the remarkable discretion of the officer is constantly in working tandem with the complex web of internal rules and guidelines' (Manning, 1979a: 54–5).

11 This production of accounts can be viewed as part of the micro-politics of defining deviance. Similar processes also occur on the macro- level of conflict among different interest groups (Schur, 1980: especially chapter 3).

12 According to a statement dated February 1981 and sent to the researchers by the chief of police of the force studied: 'In order to give direction to the uniform patrol officer as to the manner in which an occurrence report is labelled, he is given instruction during his recruit orientation classes as to the categories of incidents and the necessity for labelling the occurrence with the most serious offence.'

13 In other cases we observed, entries into open garages were recorded as 'break and enter' offences according to Criminal Code sec 306.

14 For example, McCabe and Sutcliffe (1978: 20n) observe: 'In Oxford and Salford ... most [written note] entries concerning domestic complaints ended with the expression "advice given". What the advice was and how it was given was not specified. The question, "What is the advice?" addressed to a number of policemen from many parts of the country who were attending a conference on police matters, seemed to require no answer since it was well understood to be a placebo if not for the complainant at least for supervisory officers.'

15 'The reaction is *constitutive* of the criminal (or deviant) act. In fact, the reaction *is* the "commission" of the act. Accordingly, the *idea* of a "dark figure" of offences committed without a reaction is an unnecessary absurdity ... So what, in *all* cases, makes an act a crime? *Control.* In sum, it is not the offend*er* who "commits" the crime: it is the offend*ed* ... "Crime" is ... *not* an activity engaged in by an offender, it is one formulated ... by others. Similarly, "criminal activity" is the activity of calling activities crimes' Ditton (1979: 20–3).

16 For detailed discussion of original and published data on the process of discovery, reporting, and recording, see Bottomley and Coleman (1979, 1980).

17 Sparks et al (1977: 155) point out in relation to their findings: 'In the case of burglary and thefts in dwelling houses ... only about one offence in five is recorded. Thus, a 5 per cent increase in the *proportion* recorded would by itself result in over a 20 per cent increase in the *numbers* recorded, which is more than enough to give the impression of a "crime wave". In the case of assaults and other thefts, the effect would be even more drastic: on our findings, a 5 per cent increase in the proportion of such offences recorded would at least treble their numbers in the police statistics, even if the total volume of offences actually committed remained unchanged.'

Bibliography

Biderman, A. et al. 1967 *Report on a Pilot Study in the District of Columbia on Victimization and Attitudes Toward Law Enforcement and Administration of Justice: Field Surveys I.* Washington, DC: United States Government Printing Office

Bittner, E. 1970 *The Functions of the Police in Modern Society.* Rockville, Md.: NIMH

Black, D. 1968 'Police Encounters and Social Organization: An Observation Study,' PhD dissertation, University of Michigan

– 1971 'The Social Organization of Arrest,' *Stanford Law Review* 23: 1087–1111

– 1972 'The Boundaries of Legal Sociology,' *Yale Law Journal* 81(6): 1086–1110

– 1976 *The Behavior of Law.* New York: Academic Press

Bottomley, A. 1973 *Decisions in the Penal Process.* London: Martin Robertson

Bottomley, A. and Coleman, C. 1979 'Police Effectiveness and the Public: The Limitations of Official Crime Rates.' Paper presented to the Cambridge Conference on Police Effectiveness, Cambridge, England, 11–13 July

219a

Chappell, D. et al. 1977 'A Comparative Study of Forcible Rape Offenses Known to the Police in Boston and Los Angeles,' in D. Chappell et al *Forcibie Rape*. New York: Columbia University Press, pp 227–44

Christie, N. 1977 'Conflicts as Property,' *British Journal of Criminology* 17: 1–15

Coleman, J. 1973 'Loss of Power,' *American Sociological Review* 38: 1–17

Cumming, E. et al. 1970 'Policeman as Philosopher, Guide and Friend,' in A. Niederhoffer and A. Blumberg ed *The Ambivalent Force*. Waltham, Mass.: Ginn, pp 184–92

Ditton, J. 1979 *Controlology: Beyond the New Criminology*. London: Macmillan

Downes, D. 1979 'Praxis Makes Perfect: A Critique of Critical Criminology,' in D. Downes and P. Rock ed *Deviant Interpretations*. Oxford: Martin Robertson, pp 1–16

Ennis, P. 1967 *Criminal Victimization in the United States: A Report of a National Survey*. Washington DC: United States Government Printing Office

Ericson, R. 1981 *Making Crime: A Study of Detective Work*. Toronto: Butterworths

Greenwood, P. et al. 1975 *The Criminal Investigation Process. Volume III: Observations and Analysis*. Santa Monica: Rand Corp.

Hudson, J. 1970 'Police–Citizen Encounters that Lead to Citizen Complaints,' *Social Problems* 18: 179–93

Jorgensen, B. 1979 *Transferring Trouble: The Initiation of Reactive Policing*. Unpublished research report, Centre of Criminology, University of Toronto

Kokis, R. 1977 'Domestic Violence: A Study of Police Non-Enforcement.' MA dissertation, Centre of Criminology, University of Toronto

McCabe, S. and Sutcliffe, F. 1978 *Defining Crime: A Study of Police Decisions*. Oxford: Basil Blackwell

Manning, P. 1979 'Organization and Environment: Influences on Police Work.' Paper presented to the Cambridge Conference on Police Effectiveness, Cambridge, England, 11–13 July

– 1979a 'The Social Control of Police Work,' in S. Holdaway ed *The British Police*. London: Edward Arnold

Meyer, J. 1974 'Patterns of Reporting Non-Criminal Incidents to the Police,' *Criminology* 12: 70–83

Pepinsky, H. 1975 'Police Decision-Making,' in D. Gottfredson ed *Decision Making in the Criminal Justice System: Reviews and Essays*. Rockville, Md.: NIMH, pp 21–52

Punch, M. 1979 *Policing the Inner City*. London: Macmillan

219b

Reiss, A. 1971 *The Police and the Public*. New Haven: Yale University Press

Rubinstein, J. 1973 *City Police*. New York: Farrer, Strauss and Giroux

Sanders, W. 1977 *Detective Work*. New York: Free Press

Schur, E. 1980 *The Politics of Deviance: Stigma Contests and the Uses of Power*. Englewood Cliffs, NJ: Prentice-Hall

Shearing, C. and Leon, J. 1978 'Reconsidering the Police Role: A Challenge to a Challenge of a Popular Conception,' *Canadian Journal of Criminology and Corrections* 19: 331–45

Sheley, J. and Harris, A. 1976 'Communication: On Police-Citizen Encounters,' *Social Problems* 23: 630–31

Silverman, D. 1970 *The Theory of Organizations*. London: Heinemann

Skogan, W. 1975 'Public Policy and Public Evaluations of Criminal Justice System Performance,' in J. Gardiner and M. Mulkey ed *Crime and Criminal Justice: Issues in Public Policy Analysis*. Lexington, Mass.: Lexington Books

– 1976 'Crime and Crime Rates,' in W. Skogan ed *Sample Surveys of Victims of Crimes*. Cambridge, Mass.: Ballinger Press

Sparks, R. et al. 1977 *Surveying Victims: A Study of the Measurement of Criminal Victimization, Perceptions of Crime, and Attitudes to Criminal Justice*. London: Wiley

Vera Institute. 1977 *Felony Arrests: Their Prosecution and Disposition in New York City's Courts*. New York: Vera Institute

Wiley, M. and Hudik, T. 1974 'Police-Citizen encounters: A Field Test of Exchange Theory,' *Social Problems* 22: 119–27

[5] Order out of Court II: The Position of the Accused and the Plea Decision

---

> The weak are always forced to decide between alternatives they have not chosen themselves.
>
> Dietrich Bonhoeffer, 'Miscellaneous Thoughts,' *Letters and Papers from Prison* (1953)

> It is always thus, impelled by a state of mind which is destined not to last, that we make our irrevocable decisions.
>
> Marcel Proust, *Remembrance of Things Past: Within a Budding Grove* (1918)

The Views of the Accused on Plea Transactions

The accused is excluded from the process of plea transaction. Therefore, his perceptions of this process are at a distance from the phenomenon and must be based upon what his lawyer relates to him and the outcome produced in court.

While accused persons who engaged lawyers did so because they thought it would bring some advantage, they rarely mentioned having the lawyer participate in out-of-court plea transactions as a reason for engaging the lawyer. Among the 75 interviewed accused who engaged a lawyer, only 9 said that they retained the lawyer for purposes of out-of-court plea transaction, and 5 of these 9 also stated other reasons for having a lawyer. Furthermore, when talking about the functions of having a lawyer, only 15 made any mention of plea transactions. Four accused said that one function of the lawyer is to conduct plea discussions with the prosecution for concessions, 6 said that the lawyer should conduct plea discussions only if it is in the accused's best interests, and 5 explicitly stated that plea discussions should *not* be one of the lawyer's functions.

In sum, the accused did not typically think of their lawyer's work in terms of out-of-court plea transactions. This may be due to the fact that these transactions were not open to the accused for direct participation, or even observation. Moreover, if the lawyer provided the accused with an account of the transaction, he gave little knowledge and no insight. Thus, when an accused was asked how his lawyer was able to arrange for the withdrawal of two charges, he replied, 'That's what puzzles me. I asked him and he said, "Don't worry about it. It has been taken care of." '

Interestingly, while the accused rarely discussed lawyer participation in plea transactions as a reason for engaging a lawyer, or as a significant component of the lawyer's role, they were often aware of what their lawyers had transacted out of court in their own cases. Among the 61 accused for whom we have both lawyer interviews and accused interviews, there was a high degree of agreement (approximately 80 per cent) concerning whether or not a plea transaction took place. In 15 instances the lawyer and accused both stated no plea transaction took place. In 3 instances the accused believed a plea transaction took place but the lawyer said there was none. In the 43 instances in which the lawyer said that a plea transaction took place, all but 9 accused said they were aware of it. Furthermore, in the 34 instances in which the lawyer and accused concurred that there was a plea transaction, there was no disagreement about the nature of the transaction in 21 instances, partial disagreement in 11 instances, and total disagreement in only 2 instances. These data, when compared with the accounts of their lawyers, indicate that the accused were usually informed that transactions took place, and frequently informed about the general topics discussed.

A scrutiny of the cases involved in this comparison provides further insight. In 1 case where the accused did not mention a plea transaction while the lawyer said there was one leading to charge and sentencing concessions, the accused was a lawyer who refused comment on the matter but was probably aware of what took place. In all 3 cases in which the lawyer did not mention a discussion but the accused thought one had taken place, the accused believed, in light of the sentences received, that their lawyers had bargained for sentencing concessions. As we document in chapter 6, many accused saw their lawyer's work, and most other aspects of the criminal process, in terms of the observable order in court and the outcomes that were announced (rather than decided) in that context. In the 2 instances where there was total disagreement on the nature of the discussion, the confusion was over whether the plea agreement had been for a charge reduction or a charge withdrawal. Among the 11 cases where there were only partial agreements as to the nature of the discussion, 6 involved the lawyer saying there had been a sentence concession as well as charge reductions or withdrawals, while the accused were unaware of the sentence concession.

In all but two cases the accused believed that their lawyers had initiated the plea discussions with the police and/or crown attorney. Since lawyers and not law enforcement agents were seen as the initiators of plea discussions, the accused were thereby encouraged to believe that plea discussions held out the promise of advantage they would otherwise have been unlikely to receive. It also fostered the view that lawyers were working in the best interests of their clients.

The question of who initiated the discussion was usually of little importance; all parties agreed a discussion was necessary, and the limits to the arrangement were not a function of who initiated it. The point we are making is that the accused believed his lawyer had taken the initiative to enter into these discussions and that he would do so only in the search for some advantage to the accused. This contrasts with the experiences of the accused in 'dealing' with the police which, in 38 of 39 instances reported by the accused, were initiated by the police and most often seen as initiated for the purpose of bringing relative advantage to the police (see chapter 2).

As Polstein (1962: 41) states in his 'practical guide' for lawyers entitled, 'How to "Settle" a Criminal Case,' after the 'deal' has been struck 'the client still has to be sold the idea he is getting a bargain.' Since there were usually no substantial bargains to be gained from plea discussion, this selling job required some skilful impression management on the part of the lawyers. The lawyer's task was to formulate the matter so that the accused saw concessions and therefore went along with the agreement for a guilty plea.

The accused are interested in ends, not means.[1] As an accused said when he was asked about his lawyer's involvement in plea discussions, 'I wasn't really interested in that, how *he got* charges dropped or anything. I was just interested what he was going to do but I didn't care how he did it.' Similarly, another accused was content with the plea discussions his lawyer engaged in, whatever they were:

A: Everything was taken care of beforehand, which is all right.
Q: Okay. Now, do you have any idea what he talked about with the crown attorney?
A: No idea, that's, you know, that's his job.

...

A: [My lawyer] made the decision and then he came up and said, 'Okay, plead guilty to careless and he'll drop the other ones.' 'Fine' – that's what I said, 'Fine with me.'
Q: You mostly took advice from him?
A: Oh yeah, I let him do everything, yeah I didn't say anything, whatever he says is fine with me.
Q: Now why did you do that, why did you let him do the thinking?
A: That's what he's paid for.

In most cases this reasoning was reasonable. The accused knew that they were excluded from plea discussions, and that even if they were included they would have had difficulty understanding all the ramifications. They knew also that tinkering with the details was of no benefit in itself, and that it could only be measured by the end product. From the lawyer's viewpoint the task was to convince the accused that the end product was more than just a by-product, that it was only possible because of the lawyer's efforts. This task was greatly facilitated by the dependent position of the accused in having to rely upon what his lawyer said about the transactions.

Apart from the hope that the sentence outcome would match or better the expectations of the accused and thereby cast a favourable light on the lawyer's efforts, the lawyer could use certain elements of the plea agreement to impress upon his client that some leniency was being exercised. For example, even though charge withdrawals represented no real concessions from the crown, the lawyer could present them to his client as if they did. A good illustration of this is the case of an accused who was originally charged with 12 property offences and who eventually pleaded guilty to 5 of them after a plea agreement between his lawyer and the crown. By all accounts of the lawyer for this accused and the lawyers for three co-accused, the police had overcharged in this case. In relation to this accused, charges of mischief and possession of stolen property over $200 had been laid which were admitted to by the co-accused and for which he was not responsible. These charges were among those withdrawn, but according to the lawyer this was no bargain. Moreover, 10 theft under $200 charges all arose out of the same incident and could have been covered by 1 charge. The evidence was deemed poor on several of these theft counts, especially since the detective returned most of the stolen property to the victims after anticipating that there would be a guilty plea agreement. The lawyer viewed the entire plea discussion as 'meaningless' because it corrected only the overcharging: 'In retrospect, the negotiation was only as to the extent of the number of counts that he was to plead guilty to. I think that I made it clear [to the crown attorney and detective] that it was really only 1 count. So it was meaningless. It was just a play of numbers or words.'

The lawyer also stated, 'I knew it wouldn't make any difference in the sentence anyways, but the accused might think it's great.' However, the accused apparently did not think it was great and told his lawyer he wanted to plead guilty on two counts only. According to the accused, the lawyer told him that if he did not plead guilty to the five counts, the crown attorney would proceed to trial on all the original charges; moreover, the lawyer gave him a prediction that the crown attorney would be able to secure convictions on all twelve. When this prediction was contrasted with the prediction that guilty pleas to the five counts would likely result in a non-custodial sentence, the accused complied: 'I figured well, that's the way *they* want it, go ahead with it. I'll get it over with and I won't have anything to worry about after that.'

These examples indicate that one of the influences on the accused in pleading guilty was a plea agreement worked out by the lawyer and urged upon the accused. Plea settlements arranged by lawyers were potentially a significant factor influencing the plea decision of the accused, but there were many other influences that had also to be taken into account by the accused. We now turn to a consideration of plea decisions by the accused and examine the role of plea agreements among other elements.

The Plea Decision

The plea decision encapsulates the criminal process. In deciding on plea, the accused potentially takes into account what has taken place before – e.g. transactions with the police, including whether a statement was given, and transactions with a lawyer, including whether the lawyer came up with a plea agreement – and what will happen afterwards, including predictions about what would happen if there is a trial and what the sentence outcome is likely to be. In what follows we present the plea and finding outcomes for each interviewed accused person; consider whether particular pleas were entered because the accused were commited to them, or for some other reason; enumerate the reasons of the accused for entering the pleas they did; and ascertain whether in retrospect the accused saw problems with the pleas they entered which might have led them to a different course of action if they had it to do over again.

As enumerated in Table 5.1, 70 of 101 accused entered guilty pleas and received that finding for at least some of the charges they were facing.[2] Another 13 accused entered not guilty pleas on the charge(s) they were facing, but were convicted on at least some of them. An additional 6 accused entered not guilty pleas for the charge(s) they were facing, and 4 had their charge(s) dismissed while 2 had the charge(s) acquitted. One accused pleaded guilty to some charges and not guilty to others and received convictions after a withdrawal of some charges. Finally, 11 of 101 accused had their charge(s) withdrawn by the crown prior to a finding being reached in their case.

If from the law enforcers' perspective we take as the criterion of 'success' conviction on something from the original charges, then there is a very high 'success' rate.[3] Among the 101 accused, 84 were convicted on something. Among those who were not convicted, only 6 of 17 successfully defended their position in court after entering not guilty pleas, while the remainder avoided the court's disposition because the crown attorney withdrew the charge(s). Thus, 93 per cent (84 of 90) of accused who had their case go to the point of disposition in court were convicted.

TABLE 5.1

Plea and finding for each interviewed accused person

Plea and finding	Number
Guilty of 1+ charge(s) after withdrawal of 1+ charge(s)	32
Guilty of 1 charge as originally charged	24
Guilty of 2+ charges as originally charged	7
Guilty of 1 charge after a charge reduction	3
Guilty of 2+ charges after a charge reduction	2
Guilty after a reduction and withdrawal of some charges	2
Guilty of some, not guilty of others – conviction for some, withdrawal of some	1
Not guilty – convicted	7
Not guilty – dismissed	4
Not guilty – acquitted for some/convicted of others	3
Not guilty – acquitted	2
Not guilty – acquitted for some/convicted of some/some withdrawn	1
Not guilty – convicted of some/some withdrawn	1
Not guilty – convicted on reduced category	1
Charge(s) withdrawn	11
Total	101

This finding suggests that the agents of law enforcement put together a criminal case in a way that usually ensured a conviction outcome. Moreover, since a large majority of accused entered guilty pleas, it suggests that the matter of conviction was usually determined out of court. What we wish to understand is why the large majority of accused conceded to 'the other side' when they had a legal right not to, and how their reasons reflected their position within the order of things. We agree with Cousineau and Verdun-Jones (1979: especially 296) that the rate of guilty pleas is a crude and imprecise measure of out-of-court settlements, although it has been used by many researchers and commentators on the topic of plea transactions. What we are arguing is that the case is constructed ('framed') in such a way that by the time he comes to the plea decision the accused more often than not has no real decision to take. This construction is of course largely an accomplishment of the police and the resources at their disposal, although it is often solidified through the plea transactions among the police, crown attorney, and defence lawyer.

Pleading Guilty while Maintaining Innocence

In Table 5.2 we consider the plea decisions taken by the accused according to whether or not they admitted guilt to the research interviewer. Of course, an admission of guilt in a research interview does not take into account conceptions of legal guilt that might stand up in the courtroom, but it does give an

TABLE 5.2

Admission of guilt by the accused in research interview, plea, and finding of court

	Number
Admission of guilt in research interview	
Guilty plea(s) and finding(s)	54
Not guilty plea(s) – found not guilty on some or all	4
Not guilty plea(s) – found guilty on all	2
All charges withdrawn	5
Total	65
No admission of guilt in research interview	
Guilty plea(s) and finding(s)	16
Not guilty plea(s) – found guilty	8
Not guilty plea(s) – found not guilty on some or all	6
All charges withdrawn	6
Total	36

indication of whether or not the accused felt they were innocent. The vast majority (54 of 65) of accused who admitted to their offence(s) in interview pleaded guilty. Among the six who admitted to their offence(s) in interview and pleaded not guilty in court, four obtained dismissals or acquittals on at least some charges and two were found guilty as charged.

Among the 36 persons who did not admit to their offences in research interviews, 16 nevertheless pleaded guilty as charged. By way of comparison, Baldwin and McConville (1977: 62) found, in an interview sample of 121 persons who changed their pleas to guilty after initially deciding to plead not guilty, that 33 (27.3 per cent) claimed innocence on all charges, 12 (9.9 per cent) claimed innocence on some charges, 13 (10.7 per cent) made a 'token claim' of innocence, and 12 (9.9 per cent) were uncertain about their innocence. In an interview study of 118 young incarcerated offenders, Arcuri (1976: 184) reports that less than 10 per cent claimed innocence. Bottoms and McClean (1976: 120) said that 18 per cent of their interviewed accused retrospectively claimed innocence after pleading guilty.

One reason for pleading guilty while still feeling innocent was the perceived risk of facing worse consequences if a not guilty plea was entered and the person was found guilty.[4] This was usually considered in the context of a lawyer-arranged plea settlement with the crown that was formulated to the accused in an 'offer you can't refuse' manner. For example, an accused charged with 'wounding' maintained both to the police and in interview that he had been arbitrarily selected out as the culprit, and that the 'victim' was more the aggressor as evidenced by the more serious cuts and bruises on the accused: 'I didn't assault, I was being assaulted that night, and I just can't figure things out.' The accused related in interview that he had argued with his lawyer about the decision. He said he wanted to plead not guilty, 'But my lawyer [said] ... you should plead guilty because if you plead not guilty and they find you guilty then they might look at you a little more stiffly when they sentence you.' In interview, the lawyer confirmed that his client wanted to plead not guilty and added that he 'was unrealistic about his position.' In order to introduce a sense of 'realism' into his client, the lawyer said, 'I told him that if he got convicted of wounding he might get a penitentiary term.' The lawyer arranged an agreement with the detective and crown attorney to have his client plead guilty to the lesser included offence of 'assault occasioning bodily harm' (not requiring the specific element of intention necessary in the wounding charge), even though he admitted in interview that 'there's some little question here whether the actual bodily harm took place ... the crown didn't prove that very well.' Suggesting that a guilty plea to the reduced charge would bring a lower range of sentence, the lawyer convinced his client of the wisdom of a guilty plea. The accused was sentenced to six months' imprisonment.

A woman charged with obstructing police when she allegedly interfered with officers arresting her husband during a domestic dispute felt pressured into a guilty plea by her lawyer's arguments that to do otherwise would bring more serious consequences. The police later added a charge of assaulting police, which was then used by the crown attorney as a lever in plea discussions with the lawyer. The crown attorney offered the withdrawal of the charge of assaulting police and no specific sentence recommendation in exchange for a guilty plea to the charge of obstructing police. The accused said that the lawyer tried to convince her to plead guilty by telling her the facts were against her; for example, '[He said] you don't have to really be physical with them for them to consider it assault.' The lawyer added in interview that part of the persuasion was in terms of the consequences of not guilty pleas: 'Well I believe she was a bit taken aback [by the suggestion of a guilty plea] ... but I persuaded her that it might be in her interest to do so because here, you see, you're taking a chance, you plead not guilty then the evidence is laid, she might be convicted of both counts.' The lawyer related that he felt quite proper in urging the accused to plead guilty because, '[I must] consider what is in the best interest of the client ... It's not what the client says, you know, it's what comes out in court.'

The lawyer very clearly asserted that he was pleading his client guilty even though she perceived herself to be innocent. He also believed he had convinced her of the strategic wisdom of this decision, even if she was not personally convinced. The accused said that she believed there might have been more serious consequences if she pleaded not guilty, and that at this stage – nine months after the original charge – she was mainly concerned with getting the matter over with:

It's one of the reasons why I pleaded guilty because ... it was going on for nearly a year, you know, and it really bothered me mentally to have this sort of thing hanging over my head. You know, you just wanted to get it over and done with, whatever happened ... it was going to be that day ...

I know I didn't do anything ... but ... the law is set up in a way that, I mean, if I didn't plead guilty, what if they found me guilty, you know? ... I'm not that versed with the law, what is what, what they could come up with, you know. I figure well if this is the way to get over with it I'll just get over with it ... In a way I felt, you know, cheated, I've cheated on myself, I shouldn't have said it [guilty plea], but I said it because I wanted to get rid of it, I wanted to get it over and done with, something dragging on for a year.

The situation of this accused reflects two features present in the case of other accused who pleaded guilty while maintaining innocence. First, it was a matter of deferring to the lawyer's judgment because the accused had no other source of knowledge and opinion to rely upon. Indeed, accused who felt not guilty sometimes conceded to the lawyer's suggestion of a guilty plea even though there were no arrangements with the crown which the lawyer could use to urge the accused into a guilty plea. Second, it reflects the pressure which some accused felt to plead guilty simply to get over the delays awaiting trial.

In the case of one accused, avoiding delay was more important than convictions for three offences he claimed he did not commit. He was charged with being unlawfully at large (which he admitted to), two counts of attempt robbery, and one count of break, enter and theft (all of which he did not admit to). As recorded in chapter 2, this accused said he was told by the detective that if he did not confess to these offences he would be charged with attempt robbery rather than attempt theft. The accused decided not to confess to something he persistently claimed he did not do. However, after a period of awaiting trial in custody he became willing to say he was guilty to expedite the conclusion of the case.

In interview, the accused said he had been falsely accused in the statement of his co-accused. He believed that in the face of this evidence he might have difficulty proving his innocence. However, his main concern was to have the matter settled in order to avoid months of 'dead time' in custody awaiting trial, and he said he pleaded guilty for this reason. His lawyer obtained a reduction of the two attempt robbery charges to attempt theft, apparently because a co-accused was being charged only with attempt theft, but this did not seem to be a factor in the accused's decision to plead guilty:

Q: Were you satisfied with that kind of 'deal'?

A: Well, I guess I had to be, you know.

Q: Well, what kind of deal would you have liked?

A: Drop them all ... except for the one I'm guilty of ... unlawfully at large.

...

Q: When did you first decide you were going to plead guilty to them?
A: Well, I had no choice ... I read the statements [of co-accused] against me – three statements against me. So I was –
Q: And you decided then you were going to plead [guilty]?
A: Yeah, well, I had no choice right?
Q: Did you ever consider pleading not guilty?
A: Oh, yeah. But then I figured maybe they'd find me guilty, you know.
Q: Because of the statements?
A: Yeah, and then I'd be doing a longer time ... all that dead time ... six months, seven months dead time.

The lawyer for the accused stated in interview that he felt that some charges were highly suspect, but he decided to accept his client's wish to plead guilty to get it over with. In particular, the lawyer questioned the break, enter and theft charge:

> Well, the way I dealt with [my client] was that I was in court that day on other matters. I got a message from the cells, or the gentleman from the Salvation Army, that [my client] wanted to see me. I went and talked to him, he informed me of the charges, he informed me as to what he'd like to do. I told him that it was in his interest that the matter go over for consideration so I could evaluate the charges and the evidence. he said, 'No,' he wished to have the matters dealt with today regardless. He then advised me that, as to certain charges that he was not guilty of but – at least the break and enter he said – he gave me a defence, a possible defence to the break and enter to which he said he wasn't guilty or didn't do, he gave me a possible defence. I told him from what he told me he had a valid defence and he still insisted he wanted to plead guilty because he knew he was going to go down on something and he sort of has a sense of knowledge that whatever he goes down on is going to have the same effect. I got him to sign a written instruction saying that, notwithstanding I told him he has a good defence, he intends to plead guilty to certain charges.

The lawyer was less certain about the possible innocence of his client on the attempt robbery charges. The lawyer's solution to the situation came from a lunchtime meeting with the crown attorney, the lawyer for a co-accused, and the police. The lawyer, noticing a discrepancy in accounts between his client and the police, decided that the police account was justifiable, and therefore went for a guilty plea 'package.' In doing this, the lawyer seemed to accept what he had previously stated was his client's view, that he was 'going to go down for something [and] ... whatever he goes down on is going to have the same effect':

> [At the meeting] there was sort of a feeling that the matter should be all wrapped up together ... I spoke with the officer ... [and] I found out that what my client had told me and what the officer had told me was somewhat in

> conflict. However, if my client was to be believed he still had a valid defence. The accused's record was substantial and the crown offered at that time to take a plea to two counts of attempt theft rather than the two counts of attempt robbery which were the purse snatchings. I felt that quite legally – the accused never gave me a defence to the purse snatchings although he indicated that the people who the purses came from might have had problems identifying him (they never gave any statements to the police) – I felt that they were actually robberies subject to the issue of identification and in view of that I suppose because of what the officer had told me, I felt a little bit more at ease taking the plea in the sense that I felt that the crown had a valid case to put before the jury and my client's chances were somewhat reduced as to success on a not guilty plea ... On the break and enter charge, there was no statement but the officer informed me that he was informed that there was fingerprint evidence. Now the officer very fairly said he understands there were fingerprints and it implicates my client but he also said he's not swearing to that because he'd have to talk to the identification officer, OK. Knowing the particular officer and knowing what my accused, my client had told me, I felt I suppose more at ease of accepting my client's instructions and consequently, because of the reduction of the charges from a robbery to an attempt theft, the attempt theft under, you know, I don't think he could, he couldn't have done better than that, you know, even on trial.

The accused's strategy of pleading guilty to avoid 'dead time' awaiting trial was very successful, as he only spent three weeks in jail from the time of arrest to the time of conviction, and another two weeks before he was sentenced to 18 months definite and 18 months indefinite, concurrent on all charges.

One of three co-suspects who implicated this accused in 'purse snatching' offences said that although he himself was not guilty of two 'purse snatchings' he nevertheless was willing to plead guilty to them to protect his friends who were the culprits. He believed that guilty pleas on these two offences would likely make little difference on his overall sentence since he was facing five other charges. He said that his lawyer advised him to plead not guilty on these two offences, but he ignored his lawyer's advice. The lawyer related in interview that he believed his client was innocent of the two 'purse snatching' charges. The lawyer also expressed suspicion about why one of the four co-suspects was never charged and suggested that this person may have been granted leniency as an informant against the others.[5] Nevertheless, the lawyer apparently made no inquiries with the police along these lines. He accepted the wish of the accused to plead guilty to these two offences along with five others, although he eventually arranged a plea settlement whereby three counts (including one of the two 'purse snatchings') were withdrawn in exchange for guilty pleas to four counts.

Among the idiosyncratic reasons for pleading guilty while maintaining innocence was an accused's explanation that she became very nervous in court and pleaded guilty to a charge she was planning to plead not guilty on. She was arrested and charged for theft under $200 (shoplifting), and when a search revealed that she was in possession of allegedly stolen identification she was also charged with possession of stolen property. She maintained in interview that the identification was not stolen, but when she appeared in court without a lawyer she found it difficult to understand the proceedings and entered guilty pleas to both charges.

Another unrepresented accused had problems of understanding as well as a strategic reason for entering a guilty plea even though he maintained innocence. He was charged with possession of stolen property over $200 after he was caught driving a vehicle the police believed to have been stolen. He maintained he borrowed the vehicle from someone to whom he thought it belonged, and he maintained innocence from the time he dealt with the police through to the retrospective interview with our researcher. At three different points during the interview he said one reason for pleading guilty was his belief that once a person is found with stolen property it is a strict liability situation.[6] For example, at one point he stated, 'I was innocent, I didn't know the car was stolen' but then went on to say, 'There is no way around it as long as you've got it in your hand, or if you are sitting in a [allegedly stolen] car, that's it.' When the accused was asked why he did not explain to the judge that he did not know the borrowed vehicle was stolen, he replied, 'Doesn't make any difference. You've got to plead guilty to it so even if you're innocent beyond a shadow of doubt, you're guilty.'

The accused related another reason for entering a guilty plea. He said he was charged with two other offences in another jurisdiction, and that he was pleading guilty to them. As a parolee, he predicted he was going back to the penitentiary on these convictions; therefore, he wanted to expedite the process rather than face the 'dead time' awaiting trial on the possession charge, which in any case he felt would not have much influence on his sentence. By pleading guilty to the possession charge he could have it transferred to the other jurisdiction for sentencing on all three and thereby speed up his re-entry to the pentitentiary to begin serving his time there.

In the main, people who pleaded guilty while maintaining innocence decided to plead guilty because they saw no other option, because they thought it would not have a significant impact on their overall sentence in connection with other convictions they were facing at the same time, and/or because they perceived some personal advantage in pleading guilty (e.g. expediting the disposition or protecting a friend). Some of these elements entered also into the decisions of people who admitted in interview to their offences and who decided to plead guilty rather than contest the matter.

Reasons for Pleading Guilty

Among the 71 people who entered a plea of guilty to one or more charges, the most frequently mentioned reason was 'I was guilty.' Among the 31 (44 per cent) people who gave this response, 11 gave no other reason while 20 combined it with another reason. By way of comparison, Bottoms and McClean (1976: 112) report that 41 per cent of their interviewed defendants said they pleaded guilty because 'I was guilty' and 58 per cent said they pleaded guilty because of the police case against them.

Most of those who said 'I was guilty' were charged with offences which were apparently supported with substantial evidence that the accused believed he could not reasonably challenge. For example, an accused charged with impaired/over 80 mg pleaded guilty to impaired care and control, without legal representation. He stated, 'I had to plead guilty pretty well ... It was open and shut, I mean uh, you blow in the breathalyser, what can you do about that?' He said that he planned to plead guilty from the night of his arrest: 'What the hell ... what could I plead? Stupidity? Insanity?' This accused was among the many who saw the matter as foreclosed from the point of first contact with the police. They could not think of any reasonable alternative but to submit to police actions at the time of arrest. Similarly, they could not see any reasonable way to challenge the police action of charging once they reached the court stage. These accused immediately concluded that a conviction was in order, basing their conclusion on the realization that they did not have a choice in any case.

The second most frequently mentioned reason for pleading guilty was to get the court process over with as soon as possible in order to avoid the uncertainties and anxieties associated with delays. The 22 accused who gave this reason all offered it in conjunction with some other reason; in particular, along with a feeling of being guilty anyway (5), a belief that the matter was already foreclosed because of a written statement of confession (5), or the promise of leniency from the crown attorney (8).

Among those who said that they were guilty and wanted to get the matter over with quickly was an accused charged with possessing a small amount of marijuana. Without legal representation, he pleaded guilty on his first court appearance even though the crown attorney could not produce the drug analysis certificate: 'I wanted to get it over with, I didn't want to come to court in another three months, I knew it was hash ... The only thing I could see in pleading not guilty was just a lot of hassles, you know, go into court another day and get a lawyer and all that and there's just no point, I figured well I'll take what's coming to me.'

Eight accused said they decided to plead guilty to get the matter over with after an expedient and apparently lenient plea settlement worked out between their lawyer and the crown. For them, the choice was between a not guilty plea after remand for several months – with a significant chance of still being found guilty and possibly facing a harsher sentence than if a guilty plea had been entered – versus a guilty plea to get the matter over within the predictable scope of what the lawyer said about the agreement. Not surprisingly, these persons opted for expediency, especially since their lawyers formulated the settlement in comparatively attractive terms.

For example, an accused was charged with break, enter and theft and mischief, in connection with an incident he was allegedly involved in along with two accomplices. After three remands over two months, the accused said he was told by his lawyer that 'If I wanted to plead not guilty then okay, there still was a 50-50 chance on either side, but it would have been remanded again until after Christmas.' The accused believed the excessive delays were caused by the crown attorney, who required a police officer witness who had been unavailable because of an accident. He was offered a withdrawal of the mischief charge and a reduction of the break, enter and theft charge to attempt break and enter in exchange for a guilty plea. The accused accepted the offer even though he said he had been planning to plead not guilty up to that date. According to the accused's lawyer, his client would have been willing to plead guilty to the higher category (break, enter and theft) at this stage because he was so fed up with the dealings.

The pressures to get it over with were of course particularly marked in the case of those who were in custody awaiting trial. An accused in custody on charges of assault occasioning bodily harm, weapons dangerous, choking, and forceible seizure had 10 court appearances over 3 months. On his tenth appearance his lawyer arranged a plea settlement whereby the crown would withdraw the charges of weapons dangerous and forcible seizure in exchange for a guilty plea to two counts of assault occasioning bodily harm. The accused said his lawyer advised him to accept this arrangement. According to the accused, this 'advice' included telling the accused that if he pleaded guilty he could expect a sentence of 18 months in jail, and that if he did not go along with it he was facing another six months in custody awaiting trial plus the chance of being found guilty and receiving a more severe sentence. In interview, the lawyer described how he formulated the matter to the accused:

> I told him that 'You [are] looking at life ... Don't kid yourself, you're playing around with a penitentiary term' ... Enter a plea [and] there's a good chance you'll stay within a reformatory setting ... You understand that we could go to trial and you could get convicted of common assault. You're looking at about three or four months of doing dead time before your trial and you could still get up to a year, and you're gambling that [at a minimum] versus life. Do you really want to waive the trial?' he said, 'Yes.'

Not surprisingly, the accused did 'waive the trial' and entered guilty pleas on two counts of assault occasioning bodily harm (one of which was substituted for the 'choking' charge). He was sentenced to a total of 18 months' prison definite and 6 months' prison indefinite.

Fifteen accused mentioned as a reason for pleading guilty the fact that they had signed a written statement of confession to the police.[7] This reason was invariably combined with another reason – most often a desire to get it over with (five), a declaration of being guilty (three), or a plea agreement arranged between his lawyer and the crown (three).

Most of these accused equated their written statement of confession to the police with a guilty plea; that is, they felt they had 'pleaded guilty' to the police and that this foreclosed the matter of conviction because they were unable to contradict their statement to the police once they reached court. This was expressed in different ways in different circumstances, but the essential feeling of foreclosure was the same. For example, an accused stated '[Detective's first and last name] is the one I pleaded guilty to.' Another accused indicated at various points in the interview that his plea decision was foreclosed at the point of signing the confession statement:

> [Initially discussing why he did not call a third party]
> I signed a statement, a plea of guilty, so I figured there's no sense in getting a lawyer.
> [Discussing why he would not elect up and plead not guilty]
> I was guilty of it, you know. There's no sense in lying about it. I signed a statement and that. Probably if I did plead not guilty they would have been harder on me.
> [Discussing what he would do differently in retrospect]
> I'd get my lawyer before I'd do anything next time ... because I was talking to [my lawyer] and he says, 'You never plead guilty or anything. You're always innocent 'til proven guilty.' So, next time if anything comes in [I] don't sign nothing or anything 'til I talk to my lawyer ... If I had to do it all over again I wouldn't have been signing any statements or anything else, and I would plead not guilty.

Seven of the nine persons who gave as their first-mentioned reason for pleading guilty the fact that they had given the police a written statement of confession said that if they had it to do over again, they would plead not guilty by challenging the statement, or not give one in the first place. In light of this, it is important to enquire into why the 15 accused who said they pleaded guilty because of statements of confession to the police originally provided those statements. Four accused said they provided the statements as part of a 'leniency deal' with the police, 3 because they feared physical abuse at the hands of the police, and 2 because they feared further police investigations of their activities. These 9 accused can be viewed as having been pressured into their confessions and as having extended this into a guilty plea decision. Among the other 6 accused there were not similar signs of pressure:

3 said they gave written statements of confession because they were 'guilty,' and 3 said that other evidence was obviously against them and it was therefore expedient to provide a statement.

As indicated by the response of the accused cited above, the lawyer sometimes encouraged the view that statements of confession foreclosed the matter of conviction. In another case the accused, charged with one count of robbery, said he decided to plead guilty because his lawyer 'said I was already convicted on my statement.' In some cases this undoubtedly appeared as realistic advice, based on the prediction that the evidence was clearly in favour of the crown and that a guilty plea might be taken as a sign of co-operation that would pay off in a more lenient disposition than might otherwise be expected. However, as we discussed in chapters 2 and 3, in most cases the lawyer readily accepted the statement of confession as 'fact' with little or no effort at enquiring into how that fact was constructed. In some cases this undoubtedly led the lawyer to perpetuate the view that the statement had foreclosed the matter, when he might have used it as a basis for opening up quite different matters.

Several lawyers indicated in interview that they routinely accepted statements of confession as 'fact,' making guilty pleas inevitable, even though they were told of some irregularity by their client or otherwise believed there was some basis for suspicion about how the statements were produced. These lawyers displayed an unwillingness to upset their relationships with criminal control agents for the sake of defending persons whom they believed were guilty of something in any case. For example, a lawyer for two co-accused believed that the statements were improperly obtained and that one of his clients was not guilty to two of the charges he had given statements on. However, when he was asked at the conclusion of the case to comment on the police methods in obtaining the statements, the lawyer indicated that he made no effort to challenge them.

L: I don't know what the police did. Both accused said that they were beaten.
Q: Yes, you mentioned that at lunch.
L: Yes, that's all I know, if they were beaten that's obviously inappropriate.
Q: Did both of them give statements?
L: They both gave statements and they both said that's why they gave statements, because they were frightened.
Q: Do you believe it?
L: To some extent, yes.

Again, the feeling of this lawyer seemed to be that his clients should be convicted on something and that the important matter was to arrange what that something would be through plea transactions with the crown. It was of little use, and of possible harm, to challenge openly police procedures when everyone agreed that there should be a conviction on something.

In some cases the lawyers said that they did make enquiries into the production of the statements but satisfied themselves that everything was in order. In the case of co-accused who were both charged with and entered guilty pleas on one count of break, enter and theft, the nature of the enquiry and the basis for satisfaction were again indicative of the typical approach of lawyers. The lawyer for both co-accused said that he viewed the charges as legitimate because both of his clients had given the police written statements of confession on them. The lawyer initially described the police procedures as 'entirely proper and entirely in order,' although his later discussion of the statement-taking process revealed that they should only have been described as 'entirely *on* order': '[My clients] indicated to me that they felt obliged to make the statement. Uh, they indicated that they felt under some pressure to make the statement, but in going over it with them, I, we satisfied ourselves, all of us – that the statement was not coerced from them ... They did not feel that there were any threats of violence or anything like that against them. They just felt that if they wanted to get out of custody they had to make a statement.'[8]

It was not a practice of lawyers to challenge the admissibility of statements through *voir dire* hearings in court. Only one lawyer initiated this form of challenge, and his actions proved unsuccessful. Indeed, the only person to have his statement to the police ruled inadmissible in court was an accused who defended himself without legal representation. He argued that he had been threatened with other charges and continued detention until he confessed, and the judge accepted his argument as a ground for ruling that the statement was inadmissible. In comparison, a co-accused who alleged the same police practices in obtaining a statement from him did not challenge the statement because his lawyer advised against it. In interview, his lawyer stated that his client alleged improper police tactics in securing the confession, but the lawyer did not take these allegations seriously and made no effort to challenge the police either in or out of court: 'The information that I had received from [my client] and through one of the co-accused that I spoke with was that there were techniques that I might call "harrassing," "bullying," and yet I feel quite certain that no court would upset them. I think the technique that was used, was, "Look, we know you're guilty and you're not getting out of here until you sign the statement." There was also an allegation by one of the accused that they'd asked permission to call a lawyer first and that it was refused ... [My client] was concerned that there might be some abuse. But, it was his first contact with the police in this fashion and I would suspect that, you know, anybody in for the first time is going to feel intimidated.'

In sum, one accused felt intimidated and did something about it on his own: his statement was ruled inadmissible, and he was acquitted on one charge against him while the other charge was dismissed. His co-accused felt intimidated and consulted his lawyer: his lawyer passed off the complaints to inexperience in the ways of the system and had his client plead guilty to one charge (possession of stolen property under $200) as part of an agreement with the crown which involved the withdrawal of two other charges (possession under $200, theft under $200).

As we have previously argued, lawyers are unlikely to throw off balance a process which they help to engineer and from which they benefit. Lawyers routinely *accept* the 'facts' as they are constructed by the police, and consequently the 'truths' built upon these facts, even if they may not entirely *agree* with them. Lawyers inure themselves to the consistency of police accounts, because consistency means expediency; this is the case even if expediency might be at the expense of the accused. As ongoing members, lawyers do not wish to upset the ordering of justice; their primary commitment is to keep their client in order throughout the process in order to receive the 'going rate.'

Fifteen accused said that their lawyers' advice to them to plead guilty was at least part of their reason for pleading guilty. In two cases this was the only reason given. In the 13 cases where this was combined with other reasons, the most frequent additional reasons were 'I was guilty' (4), a plea arrangement for withdrawal of charges by the crown (3), getting the matter disposed of quickly (2), and the belief that a guilty plea would have a beneficial effect on sentence by not wasting the court's resources (2).

Only one accused said he pleaded guilty based on his lawyer's advice that nothing else could be done because of his statement of confession. This masks the complexity of the issues surrounding lawyers' advice and points to the advantage of having interviews with lawyers and tape-recorded data on plea transactions in addition to interviews with the accused. Research based solely on interviews with the accused may well underestimate the role of the lawyer in the guilty plea decision.

Twenty-two accused said that their decision to plead guilty was at least partly due to a plea agreement worked out with the crown. Nine spoke of charge withdrawal agreements, seven spoke of charge reduction agreements, one spoke of a charge withdrawal and reduction agreement, and five spoke of sentence recommendation agreements. These reasons for pleading guilty were invariably stated in combination with other reasons, in particular a desire to get the matter over with (eight), lawyer's advice (three), and the belief that a guilty plea would have a beneficial effect by not wasting the court's resources (three).

In comparison, Baldwin and McConville (1977: 28) report that in a sample of 121 accused persons who changed their plea to guilty at the last instance, 22 (18.2 per cent) said they did so because of an explicit 'plea bargain' entailing some form of sentence leniency. Empirical evidence suggests that judges do offer more lenient sentences in exchange for guilty pleas. Baldwin and McConville (1978) matched persons who had changed their pleas from guilty to not guilty late in the proceedings to persons who had pleaded guilty from the beginning and to those who had pleaded not guilty but were convicted, with respect to sex, age, offence, number of counts, record, and previous incarcerations. They found that 64.6 per cent of the late changes received custodial sentences compared with 50 per cent of those who planned guilty pleas from the beginning and 69.3 per cent of those convicted after pleading not guilty. Nardulli (1978) reports similar results in comparing guilty pleas to trials before a judge alone and trials before a jury, for the offences of murder, armed robbery, and trafficking in heroin. Custodial sentences were from two and one-half to four and one-half times greater after a conviction from a jury trial compared with a guilty plea. Sentences after a conviction in a bench trial were between the other two forms of hearing.

While 'lawyer's advice' was only infrequently mentioned along with a plea arrangement as a reason for pleading guilty, lawyers were instrumental in making the arrangements and then convincing the accused that the arrangements should be accepted. As documented in chapter 4, the typical practice was for lawyers to arrange a plea agreement for their clients and then to convince their clients that it was indeed a 'deal.' Since the accused was rarely in a position to judge the advantages or disadvantages of the arrangement, he typically went along with whatever his lawyer said was in order. As Baldwin and McConville (1977: especially 45ff) document, lawyers frequently formulate the matter in a way that effectively leaves the accused with no choice but to plead guilty. While the offer is one that could be refused, it is not likely to be refused because the accused acts solely on the basis of trusting his lawyer's judgments in out-of-court transactions with the crown.

In most cases it was routine for the lawyer to make the plea arrangement and then to get the accused's nodding agreement. Indeed, several lawyers took the view that once they were satisfied with the arrangement, they could order the accused to accept it. As we recorded in chapter 3, some lawyers said explicitly they would not allow their relationship with their clients to be otherwise. Other lawyers indicated their views in other ways. For example, an accused was charged with impaired/over 80 mg and break, enter and theft. The break, enter and theft arose when the accused allegedly broke into a garage compound to retrieve his motorcycle after it had been impounded by the police following the impaired/over 80 mg arrest. In talking with the police officer and crown attorney involved in the case, the lawyer made the plea arrangement and then confidently assured them that his client would go along with it. The lawyer simply proclaimed that he would order his client to agree and went on to concur with the detective's view that the accused was of a lower order:

L: What do you want, impaired or over 80?

CA: I'm easy.

L: How about over 80?

CA: I'll take the over 80.
L: Okay. What about the other charges, he's go ah –
Detective: How about just ah –
L: Mischief.
D: Yeah.
L: That's what he did, ah, broke a lock ...
D: It was his own bike.
L: Yeah, his own bike.
CA: So really a mischief.
D: Actually.
CA: You got him on a theft, charged him with a theft.
D: Yeah.
CA: We just got one where the fellow stole his own car.
D: Pardon?
CA: We just convicted a guy where he stole his own car.
D: Yeah. Like it's technically under s.4. Oh yeah, you've got the other file there.
CA: He's going to plead on the mischief, eh?
L: Yeah, he'll plead on that. As soon as he gets here and I tell him he's pleading to mischief.
D: It's just being dumb.
L: It's known as the unproclaimed stupid asses' section of the Criminal Code.

In interview, the lawyer described his client as 'passive' and agreeable to whatever the lawyer said was an offer. The lawyer also said that if he told his client to plead guilty to break, enter and theft, his client would have done so. Of course, given his exclusion from the plea transaction and his dependent position in relation to his lawyer, the accused could hardly be anything but passive and compliant. To reiterate, contrary to the view of the accused person as imperceptive, ignorant, frightened, and therefore passive (e.g. Dell, 1971), we see the accused's passivity as a reflection of his powerlessness within the ordering of justice.

Twelve accused who pleaded guilty gave as one reason for doing so the desire to create a favourable impression by not wasting the court's time in a trial. This reason was invariably combined with another reason, most frequently saying 'I was guilty' (three), as part of a plea arrangement with the crown (three), and on the advice of a lawyer (two). Most of these accused were aware of the legal fact that a guilty plea could bring sentence leniency because it shows a measure of contrition, a deference to the order of things. They learned of this through their lawyers. An example was provided by an accused who said his lawyer advised him to plead guilty because, 'He said that if I pleaded not guilty and they found me guilty, then I would have got more time for holding up the court, you know, remands and stuff like that.'[9]

Among the remaining reasons given for pleading guilty, five could be generally categorized as involving a belief that there was compelling evidence against the accused. Three persons said they wished to protect other persons who were culprits and therefore 'took the rap.'

Reasons for Pleading Not Guilty

Among the 20 persons who entered not guilty pleas, 15 said they did so because they were innocent. Among the other 5, 4 did not protest innocence but indicated that they had a plausible defence and/or were defending their legal right to a trial, while 1 provided no reason for pleading not guilty. In sum, most persons who pleaded not guilty said they did so because of a feeling of innocence rather than as a strategy to get off more lightly on something they admitted to doing. If they were seeking leniency, accused persons were more likely to plead guilty in the hope that they could parlay their co-operation into a lighter sentence.

Persons who said they pleaded not guilty because they felt they were innocent sometimes saw other benefits in going to trial. An accused charged with a fellow-worker for allegedly causing a disturbance at a strike picket line related that there were wider issues of labour unionism at stake and viewed his case as a union cause being fought by his union-hired lawyer. A first offender charged with mischief said that in spite of being innocent he did consider pleading guilty at one stage in order to get the matter over with; however, he continued with his decision to plead not guilty because he wanted to avoid having a criminal record.

Only one person took the view that he was out to manipulate the system and hired an expensive lawyer to 'get him off' completely on impaired/over 80 mg charges. The others who perceived that they might be factually guilty were committed to the idea that they still had to be proven guilty legally. For example, a person charged with driving while her licence was suspended, and then with failure to appear in court on this initial charge, took the attitude that she had 'nothing to lose' by pleading not guilty. She argued that there was a bureaucratic mix-up over non-payment of a fine which led to the licence suspension and that her failure to appear in court was an 'honest mistake' she had made in mixing up the court date.

Lawyers were not always successful at resisting wishes to plead not guilty, sometimes accepted these wishes, and occasionally encouraged them. However, only one accused said he explicitly overruled his lawyer's advice to plead guilty. He was charged with two counts of assault occasioning bodily harm and one count of weapons dangerous arising out of the same incident involving two victims. He believed that he was no more the 'offender' than the 'victims' and decided to plead not guilty because 'I guess I had to give them a fight ... Why not? Instead of just going up there and pleading guilty.'

The lawyer believed his client was factually guilty and said that he had a preconception of his client's guilt because of his reputation as a 'punk.' The lawyer felt his client was just 'playing games' by pleading not guilty: 'He has an almost oriental fatalism about the police and courts, you know. He got caught and he's going to screw the system around so long as he can and eventually, you know, take his lumps.' In most cases fatalism led the accused to give up at an early point; in this case, the accused was still fatalistic but decided to prolong the inevitable by forcing the game to the end.

The lawyer said he advised his client to accept a guilty plea arrangement. The lawyer predicted that the accused would have received 60 days via the guilty plea route, arguing 'There is a rule of thumb, I guess, that in cases which have an emotional overtone that you are much better off to plead guilty because of the sort of dull recitation of facts in a monotone by the crown attorney doesn't sound anywhere as near as severe as when the judge has an emotional interplay with the witness.' The lawyer said he told his client that a not guilty plea entailed the risk of antagonizing the judge and getting a heavier sentence, but the accused refused to accept the idea of a guilty plea arrangement with the crown. In the end, the accused was convicted on one count of assault occasioning bodily harm after the other two charges were dismissed, and he received a four-month reformatory term.

In another case the accused said he turned down a tentative plea agreement offer, but he had some backing from his lawyer rather than being faced with 'an offer you can't refuse.' He was charged along with a co-accused with possession of a weapon for the purpose of committing an indictable offence. Both accused adamantly maintained their innocence. The co-accused was in a particularly precarious position because he was a parolee who faced a three-year penitentiary term if his parole was revoked upon conviction for an indictable offence. At one point the crown attorney offered a plea settlement whereby the accused would plead guilty to the offence and the charge against the co-accused would be dismissed. The lawyer for the accused said he consulted with his client about his offer and they agreed to refuse it, and the lawyer said he countered with an offer that was not taken up. The counter offer was that 'they both could plead guilty to a summary conviction offence of being in possession of a weapon or something like that which would have avoided all these problems [parole revocation for the co-accused; excessive delay], but I kind of felt in the circumstances that they were kind of pushing a charge that there really wasn't a lot of substance to.' The accused said he would have no part of any 'deal' whether or not it might benefit the co-accused, and he had no difficulty in convincing his lawyer of this:

A: They had been talking to the crown, [the co-accused's] lawyer had been, because the fact was that [the co-accused] has just gotten off parole, forty months parole, so if he got convicted he would have to do his forty months parole plus

> whatever for this. So they wanted us to see if I could plead guilty and the crown said I would just get a fine – so [if] I pleaded guilty [co-accused] would be found not guilty. And I said, 'No because I won't change my story. Why should I? I'm telling the truth.' And at my preliminary hearing the judge took five minutes to decide if he should drop the charges on me or not, so I almost walked once, why should I decide to plead guilty now. And our lawyers, my lawyer told me, he says, 'Don't make a deal because you are going to beat it, there is no way they can convict you on what they have.'
>
> Q: Both lawyers said this?
>
> A: Yeah, so ... the crown just wanted our conviction, some kind of conviction.
>
> Q: Why did he want that?
>
> A: Well that's his job, to get a conviction.
>
> Q: At any point did any of you – your lawyers or you or [co-accused] at all consider the deal?
>
> A: No, they just asked me to think about it. How good a friend I would be saving [co-accused's] neck, if we were found guilty; but my lawyer told me that, and I knew myself, as far as I was concerned that they just didn't have what they needed to convict us.

Both accused were acquitted.

In a few cases accused persons who seriously contemplated guilty pleas to get the matter over with were actively talked into not guilty pleas by their lawyers. For example, an accused charged with theft under $200 after a 'shoplifting' incident said he wanted to plead guilty so that he could relieve his anxiety about the case and not lose more time from work caused by additional court appearances. He said that he decided to plead not guilty after talking with a duty counsel:

> Like the two witnesses was there, you know. I said I had no chance to win the case. And he [duty counsel] said 'Try to plead not guilty' you know. So that is what I did, I pled not guilty because he told me. If it was my decison I would have pled guilty already, even the second time. Because when I got out through the door, you know I said, 'I am going to plead guilty.' And he stopped me again and he said, 'Why do you want to plead guilty?' So you know, well I said, 'They are going to fine me.' And he said to me, 'It's the judge's decision what he is going to do to you, fine you or not.' So I said, 'If they are going to fine me the same, I am going to plead guilty so to get it over with.'

This accused was found guilty and fined $75. In contrast, another accused charged with theft under $200 in similar circumstances pleaded not guilty on the advice of his legal aid lawyer and eventually had the charge dismissed after a trial.

Another accused who said he benefitted greatly from the advice of a duty counsel to plead not guilty was charged with common nuisance after an incident in which he and a co-accused had allegedly thrown beer bottles from a high-rise apartment balcony on to police cars. The accused, who went to court unrepresented, said he had direct discussions with the police and crown attorney about an out-of-court plea agreement:

A: [The crown attorney said] if I plead guilty, that [he'll] go for a mischief charge.
Q: If you plead guilty to common nuisance?
A: Yeah, he'll drop it down to mischief. And then he said, 'If you plead not guilty, [I'll] put it up to criminal negligence.' So I didn't know. I had to think about that for a while. If I would've pleaded guilty, I would have been [convicted] you know. If I pleaded not guilty – they never had no evidence on me at all for this. They were just going nuts.
Q: Yeah.
A: So, I was going to plead guilty, 'cause I didn't know –
Q: To common nuisance?
A: Right. I was going to plead guilty, and thinking maybe I can get off easier ... I thought if I had pleaded not guilty, I would have got [convicted], and you know, I would have got screwed or something.
Q: Yeah. So when did you decide you weren't going to plead guilty to common nuisance?
A: Well, I talked to the – what is he called?
Q: Duty counsel.
A: Duty counsel.
Q: So this is right after [the crown attorney] was trying to make this deal with you, you went in to talk to duty counsel? What did duty counsel say?
A: He goes, 'They're just trying to make deals with you. If you've never done it, go ahead with it [trial].' he says, 'They're scared.' I says, 'I know they're scared.' He says, 'Just go in there.' And I say, 'I want to get it over with right now. And I'm going to plead not guilty.' And so that's what I did.

The crown attorney substituted a mischief charge for the common nuisance charge and the case went to trial. The accused succeeded in having the charge dismissed.

These examples clearly point out that defence lawyers were not invariably oriented to the expediency of having accused persons plead guilty regardless of the crown's case. In a few instances it was the lawyer who forced the matter to trial as the most reasonable way of dealing with the case, even against the client's inclinations. Furthermore, as documented earlier, some lawyers involved in out-of-court plea negotiations with the crown *threatened* a trial as part of their strategy to have a plea settlement that was of possible advantage to their clients.

The Plea Decision in Retrospect

All the accused who entered not guilty pleas said that if they had to do it over again they would still plead not guilty. Even the seven accused who were convicted as originally charged after pleading not guilty said they would still plead not guilty if they were faced with the same decision again.

In contrast, 22 of 70 people who pleaded guilty said that if they had the decision to make again, they would enter not guilty pleas. Among this group, 11 pleaded guilty as originally charged, 9 pleaded guilty after the crown withdrew at least one charge, and 2 pleaded guilty after the crown reduced the charges. This indicates that dissatisfaction with the guilty plea decision was as prevalent among those who entered into a plea agreement with the crown as among those who did not.

In order to consider the reasons why these 22 accused would in retrospect change their plea to not guilty, it is instructive to examine the reasons they originally gave for pleading guilty. In Table 5.3 we cross-tabulate the first-mentioned reason for pleading guilty and whether or not in retrospect the accused would plead the same. This table includes the responses of 69 persons who originally pleaded guilty, excluding a person for whom there is no information.

The vast majority (20 of 33) of people who gave as a first-mentioned reason for pleading guilty the declaration 'I was guilty' would still plead the same if they had to do it over again. In contrast only 2 of 9 who said they pleaded guilty because of signing a statement of confession said they would still plead guilty. These persons had become educated during the course of their case to the fact that silence can be rewarding. They realized too late that it is extremely difficult to challenge a statement once given because it entails contradicting yourself and attacking the institutionalized credibility of the police. These accused came to appreciate that saying something to the police usually means there is little that can be said later; silence with the police at least keeps open the possibility of saying something in your defence at a later stage.

Among the six who gave as a first reason for pleading guilty the desire to get the matter over with, four said that in retrospect they would still have pleaded guilty. The two who would change their plea to not guilty were dissatisfied with the sentencing outcome and felt that they could secure a more lenient outcome via a not guilty plea. Both persons who gave as a first reason for pleading guilty a desire not to waste the court's time, in the hopes that it would yield leniency, said, in retrospect, that they would plead not guilty; again, the leniency they originally predicted was not perceived as forthcoming.

Among the 12 accused who gave as a first reason for pleading guilty a plea agreement worked out with the crown, 9 said that in retrospect they would still plead guilty. All 5 involved in agreements for charge withdrawal would still plead guilty, 3 of 5 involved in agreements for charge reduction would still plead guilty, and 1 of 2 involved in a promise of sentence recommendation would still plead guilty. In sum the majority of these accused were

TABLE 5.3

First-mentioned reason for pleading guilty and whether or not accused said in retrospect he would plead the same

First-mentioned reason for pleading guilty	Total		Whether accused said in retrospect he would plead the same: Yes		No	
	N	%	*N*	%	*N*	%
I was guilty	23	33.3	20	42.6	3	13.6
Already signed police statement	9	13.1	2	4.3	7	31.5
Advised by lawyer	9	13.1	5	10.6	4	18.2
Get it over	6	8.7	4	8.5	2	9.1
Crown withdrew charge(s)	5	7.2	5	10.6	0	0.0
Crown reduced charge(s)	5	7.2	3	6.4	2	9.1
Crown recommended lenient sentence	2	2.9	1	2.1	1	4.7
Did not wish to waste court's time	2	2.9	0	0.0	2	9.1
Deal protecting accomplice	2	2.9	2	4.3	0	0.0
Defence strategy fell through	1	1.5	1	2.1	0	0.0
Other	5	7.2	4	8.5	1	4.7
Total	69	100.0	47	100.0	22	100.0

satisfied with their guilty plea arrangement with the crown attorney. However, it must be emphasized that this satisfaction was grounded in their powerless position at a distance from the process by which the plea decision was made for them by their lawyers. They were left to make their judgments of satisfaction in their lawyer's terms, paying special attention to the sentencing outcome in comparison with what they were led to expect.

Among the 47 who said they would still plead guilty if they had it to do over again, all but 7 gave the same reason as they originally gave for pleading guilty. The 7 who gave different reasons all commented on the outcome 'working out well' from their perspective.

In conclusion we can say that in a minority of cases the accused's decision to plead guilty was finally made *because of* an agreement made via the plea discussion among the lawyer, the crown attorney, and the police. Other studies have also shown that plea decisions by the accused are sometimes arrived at out of apparent 'bargains' struck between lawyers and law enforcers, although the extent of the practice varies enormously by jurisdiction. Regardless of the figures produced, reports on the quantity of plea discussions leading to plea agreements (whether deemed bargains or not) are lacking if they consider only samples of persons who plead guilty and ignore the complex processes that have taken place up to the plea decision. For example, if we consider our sample of 101 interviewed accused, we find that

20 per cent found it worthwhile to plead not guilty, mainly because they felt they were innocent but also in a few cases because they thought it was worth the effort to contest it or because it was not possible for their lawyers to reach a guilty plea agreement with the crown after an attempt to do so. Another 10 per cent had their charges withdrawn by the crown attorney prior to the point at which a plea decision had to be finalized. Among the 70 per cent who did enter guilty pleas, the clear majority (70 per cent) said they did so for reasons other than the nature of the agreement worked out with the crown. Paramount among these reasons was a realization of being guilty and/or a desire to get the matter over with as quickly as possible, two reasons which also undoubtedly framed the decisions of the other actors in the process. Many of these persons had extinguished their chances for future dealing when they signed a statement of confession to the police.

As we have demonstrated in our analysis of the process of plea discussion, most of the discussions involved routine administrative sorting out of evidence and relevant charges with little or no advantage accruing. The agreements involved mainly the altering of charges that were either questionable or insignificant in light of the main charges against the accused, and thus no 'big deal.' The agreements did allow the lawyers to *display* to clients that something was done and to sharpen their ability to predict the range of sentence. A substantial minority of accused said they were persuaded to plead guilty in light of these plea agreements, but nearly always in conjunction with other factors.

It is surprising that the accused do not mention more often the plea agreement arranged by their lawyers as a primary reason for pleading guilty. One explanation is that the ordering of justice vis-à-vis the accused is much more subtle than what other researchers have depicted. From the point of police contact the accused is managed in a way that makes him feel powerless, especially in the plea decision. Therefore, by the time his lawyer approaches him with a plea agreement it is not a 'deciding factor' in pleading guilty because he already been prepared for the realization that there is no choice. When he is thus prepared, even the hint of a concession in the plea agreement is likely to encourage him to think he has received a bargain. He has been made into a satisfied customer, not appreciating that in the process it is he who has been 'customized.'

178a Notes to pp 117–56

Notes: Order out of Court II: The Position of the Accused and the Plea Decision

1 For further documentation, see chapters 3 and 6. In Arcuri's (1976: 182) study, almost two-thirds of the respondents judged the plea bargaining in their own case as 'fair' on the grounds that it apparently brought them a lighter sentence and/or a lesser number of convictions than they thought they would have had otherwise.

2 Other studies in Canada have documented a lower rate of guilty pleas. Friedland (1965: 89) presents a figure of 69 per cent for magistrates' courts in the city of Toronto in 1964; Hann (1973: 313) states that only 43.5 per cent of defendants in magistrates' courts in Toronto studied in 1970–71 pleaded guilty; and MacKaay (1976: 31) reports that in 1975, 62.3 per cent of defendants at the Montreal court house pleaded guilty, while at the Montreal Municipal Hall court the figure was 51 per cent. The Sheffield, England, study by Bottoms and McClean (1976: 105, 108) reports a rate of 93 per cent guilty pleas in the lower (magistrates') courts and 65 per cent in the higher (county) courts. Most American jurisdictions report guilty plea rates near or over 90 per cent. See Heumann (1978) re Connecticut; Vera Institute (1977) re New York City; Law Enforcement Assistance Administration (1978) for US survey data.

3 Of course, as mentioned in chapter 2 and as analysed elsewhere (Ericson 1981, 1982), the police sometimes have other ends in mind apart from conviction when they decide to lay a charge. A charge can be used to obtain bail conditions and attendant controls over a suspect, to harass, to hold a suspect for investigation on other matters, to 'lever' the suspect to return stolen property, to cool out participants in a hostile interpersonal conflict, etc. From the police viewpoint, in cases with one of these elements the conviction outcome is of secondary or no importance.

4 In Canada there is authority that a plea of guilty should be considered as a mitigating factor with respect to sentencing: *R.* v *de Haan* (1967), 52 Cr App R 25; *R.* v *Johnston and Tremayne* (1970) 4 CCC 64 (Ont CA). Salhany (1978) states that the basis of this ruling is that pleading guilty is not only in the public interest but is also a sign of remorse on the part of the accused. However, the court has also ruled that a plea of not guilty should not be held against the accused: 'It is quite improper to use language which may convey that a man is being sentenced because he had pleaded not guilty, or because he has run his defence in a particular way. It is, however, of course proper to give a man a lesser sentence if he has shown genuine remorse amongst other things by pleading guilty'; *R.* v *Harper* (1967) 3 ALL ER 619 (CCA).

5 Our observational data on the police confirm that one of the four co-suspects in this case was not charged at all in exchange for information and a written statement implicating the other three (see Ericson 1981: chapter 6).

6 Criminal Code sec 312, which deals with possession of stolen property, includes a requirement of guilty knowledge as part of the definition of the offence.

7 Cf Baldwin and McConville's recent research study (Royal Commission on Criminal Procedure, 1980b) in which they report that over 90 per cent of defendants who made written statements to the police in Birmingham, and 76 per cent in London, pleaded guilty at trial.

8 The law of confession in Canada makes any threat or promise regarding release as a means of inducing a confession grounds for ruling that statement of confession inadmissible in court (Kaufman, 1974).

9 See chapter 5, note 4. Several accused believed a not guilty plea resulting in a finding of guilt would lead to a more severe penalty than a guilty plea because the judge would see it as 'lying' and take it as another indication of the 'dishonest' character of the accused. In a separate question on the effect of plea on judges' sentencing decisions, several accused expressed this belief, even to the point of describing a not guilty plea as 'perjury.'

Bibliography

Arcuri, A. 1976 'Lawyers, Judges and Plea Bargaining: Some New Data on Inmates' Views,' *International Journal of Criminology and Penology*, 4:177–9

Baldwin, J. and M. McConville 1977 *Negotiated Justice: Pressures on Defendents to Plead Guilty*. London: Martin Robertson

– 1978 'The Influence of the Sentencing Discount in Inducing Guilty Pleas,' in J. Baldwin and A. Bottomley (ed) *Criminal Justice: Selected Readings*. London: Martin Robertson

Bottoms. A.E. and J.D. McClean 1976 *Defendants in the Criminal Process*. London: Routledge and Kegan Paul

Cousineau, D. and S. Verdun-Jones 1979 'Evaluating Research into Plea Bargaining in Canada and the United States: Pitfalls Facing the Policy Makers,' *Canadian Journal of Criminology*, 21: 293–309

Dell, S. 1971 *Silence in Court*. London: Bell

Ericson, R.V. 1981 *Making Crime: A Study of Police Detective Work*. Toronto: Butterworths

Friedland, M. 1965 *Detention before Trial*. Toronto: University of Toronto Press

Hann, R. 1973 *Decision Making in the Canadian Criminal Court System: A Systems Analysis*. Centre of Criminology, University of Toronto

Heumann, M. 1978 *Plea Bargaining: The Experience of Prosecutors, Judges and Defence Attorneys*. Chicago: Chicago University Press

Kaufman, F. 1974 *Admissibility of Confessions*. Toronto: Carswell

MacKaay, E. 1976 The Path of Justice. Groupe de Recherche en Jurimetrue, Faculté de Droit, Université de Montréal

Nardulli, P. 1978 'Plea Bargaining: An Organizational Perspective,' *Journal of Criminal Justice*, 6: 217–31

Polstein, R. 1962 'How to "Settle" a Criminal Case', *The Practical Lawyer* 8(1): 35–44

Salhany, R.E. 1978 *Canadian Criminal Procedure*, 3rd ed. Agincourt, Ontario: Canada Law Book

Vera Institute 1977 *Felony Arrests: Their Prosecution and Disposition in New York City's Courts*. New York: Vera Institute

[6]
Patrolling the Facts: Secrecy and Publicity in Police Work*

ABSTRACT

This paper examines the role of the police as news sources in Canada. Analysis focuses on the ways in which the police patrol the regions of their organization to which journalists can have access, and on the forms of enclosure they effect over knowledge about their activities. The analysis builds upon theoretical foundations laid by Goffman and Giddens regarding privacy and revelation, illustrating that their social psychological formulations can be extended to the organizational and sociological levels. A typology is developed to distinguish police practices in back region enclosure (secrecy), back region disclosure (confidence), front region enclosure (censorship), and front region disclosure (publicity). Journalists' efforts to overcome the spatial, social and cultural barriers erected by the police are delineated. Consideration is given to the ways in which journalists police the police: how news texts 'play back' into the police organization and affect relations and practices there, including renewed efforts to patrol the facts. The process is shown to be equivocal and problematic, respecting the fact that information is the most difficult thing to guard because it can be taken without leaving its place.

THE POLICE AS GUARDIANS OF SYMBOLIC ORDER

The police are usually conceived in material and physical terms. They are seen to be at the forefront of the coercive arm of the state, the embodiment of the state's monopoly on the legitimate use of force. As law enforcers, the police are equipped with the technological and legal means to coerce citizens who victimize other citizens. As preventers of crime, the police are equipped with the technological and legal means of deployment and surveillance. As social service agents, the police are equipped with the 'velvet glove' of service provision and welfare referral aimed at managing trouble and preventing harms. In each of these conventional conceptions the order that is the goal of policing is also conceived in physical or material terms. It is something that we are supposed to see or experience, for example, orderly streets, and peace and tranquillity in domestic settings. It is therefore also something that we are supposed to be able to measure, for example crime prevented, and arrests made.

With this focus we tend to forget that the police are also out to patrol the facts, to reproduce various symbolic orders. They guard the facts about their coercive operations. They shield aspects of their deployment strategies, including their priorities, and whom they are targeting as threats. They are protective of facts about their investigations, including how they respond to calls, the decisions they take on whether to write reports and how to formulate them, and the choices they take on whether to prosecute and how to make the case. They gloss the facts of their effectiveness, including their success in deterring crime, and in clearing crime by arrest.

This shielding, protecting and glossing takes place not only on the street-level of police work, but also on the administrative-level of producing organizational and occupational ideologies. At this higher level policing becomes a matter of the heart as well as the head, playing on dominant themes in the culture to ensure that the police have a dominant place culturally, and thereby also socially and politically. Whether through funerals of slain police officers, lectures to school children, displays in shopping malls, or the normal crime discourse of the popular news media, the police traffic in images that they are indeed the thin blue line between order and chaos. In this role the police are reproducers of the symbolic order of their organization and occupation.

The concern of this paper is with the police as reproducers of symbolic order, how they patrol the facts of their operations and in doing so produce an ideology of policing. A key site for addressing this topic is the organization of transactions between police and journalists. Why do the police have such significance in public political culture and in popular culture, leading to substantial media attention? How do journalists organize to obtain and publish knowledge about the police? What do the police themselves regard as fit for public consumption and what do they think should be kept secret? How do the police organize to defend their organization against incursions from journalists and to obtain only publicity they think is helpful? How does publicity affect police organizations? What are the implications for public understanding of the police and crime?

The ideas and research reported here are part of a wider comparative study of secrecy and publicity in various state and private sector organizations (Ericson *et al.* 1989). The broader theoretical dimensions of this research relate to power/knowledge relations within and between organizations and institutions. This research is concerned with the micropolitics of meaning and accounting practices, including the organization of conflicts over meaning, and how meaning-contests are strategically managed in terms of tactics for achieving secrecy, confidences, censorship and publicity. The research remains sensitive to the fact that knowledge control is at best equivocal and elusive, respecting the wisdom of Goffman that, 'Amongst all the things of this world, information is the hardest to guard, since it can be stolen without removing it' (quoted in Meyrowitz, 1985). A related focus is the relevance of knowledge control for legal control on several levels — personal, professional, institutional, and cultural — including the constitution of authority and the consolidation of interests on each of these levels.

THE POLICE IN PUBLIC CULTURE

The police beat is a major focus of news coverage for several reasons. The police are able to supply a steady stream of stories that are entertaining, dramatic, amusing and titillating. In particular, low-budget news operations look to the police for a predictable supply of material to fill out their news space and time (Chibnall 1977; Fishman 1980, 1981). In addition to their contributions to popular culture, the police are also newsworthy because of their place in political culture. They are a barometer by which the citizen assesses the state as a moral agent, including how it is likely to act in lesser exercises of authority. In many countries, such as Canada, the police have become a national political symbol, embodying the traditional constitutional concern with 'peace, order and good government.' However, the police are not simply passive, objectified by other political forces. They have become involved themselves as an active political force. In the context of substantial growth, bureaucratization, specialization and centralization (Ericson 1982; McMahon and Ericson 1987), there has occurred what Reiner (1983, 1985) terms the politicization of the police

> Their overt intervention into the public political arena in order to change the *content* of rules both within the police organization and in the wider society.

The police see themselves, and are seen by other major political groups and organizations, as key players in democratization processes in society, the object and forum of political conflicts, stability, and change (Van Outrive and Fijnaut 1983).

In this context there arises a cultural and political affinity between the police and the news media. Both claim to be operating in the public interest (Chibnall 1977). They both wish to acknowledge order (Ericson *et al.* forthcoming), to appear as representatives and defenders of established institutions and consensus. Since responsible news reporting is to promote the public interest, it follows that it will also promote police interests.

The police and the media also have an affinity as agencies of social control. In their own 'investigative' policing function,

> journalists do not merely reflect others' efforts to designate deviance and effect control, but are actively involved themselves as social-control agents. As such, journalists play a key role in constituting visions of order, stability, and change, and in influencing the control practices that accord with these visions. In sum, journalists are central agents in the reproduction of order. (Ericson *et al.* 1987: 1)

The police themselves view the media as social control agents. Therefore, the police try to incorporate the news media as *part of* the policing apparatus. They do so by giving journalists physical space within police buildings, by taking them into account in organization charts, directives and planning, and by making them a part of the everyday social and cultural practices in the police organization.

These close affinities and involvements between journalists and police inevitably entail conflicts and efforts to control each other. There are efforts by the news media to police the police. Always within range of the media searchlight, the police are vulnerable to having their procedural strays focused upon and controlled through the pressure of publicity. In face of this the police work to control the news media. They do so defensively, fending off media incursions into their social, cultural and physical space. They do so offensively, trying to disseminate helpful news in order to harness media power to their advantage.

By all accounts the police have become more active, indeed pro-active, in this regard. They have enhanced their ideological arm by increasing the size and jurisdiction of their public relations units. They have hired civilian staff for their public relations units, including experienced ex-journalists with the requisite knowledge to control other journalists. They have opened up the number of ranks within the force authorized to speak to reporters. In the particular jurisdiction analysed in this paper, police officers pointed to a major shift toward pro actively selling the police. This was articulated by two senior officers

> I think it's a common concept today by most progressive organizations that it's necessary to tell your story and sell yourself to whoever you see you are trying to provide a product or a service . . . [We] are quite progressive I think . . . [We] identified

> a need for the police force to sell themselves and to sell or put on an attractive image before the public about what the police force was trying to do, and how they were trying to do it, and I think this is pretty well an accepted way of operating for business in North America.
>
> We [now] initiate more press releases. We try to think out in advance something that's going to happen in the future and how we'll handle the media, so I guess we've increased where we stimulate the media . . . I mean they know that I'm looking for ink to sell the police. I'm trying to get some free marketing.

THE ORGANIZATION OF REPORTERS

There were two cultures of reporters on the police beat we studied (compare Chibnall 1977; see also Fishman 1980). There was an 'inner circle' and an 'outer circle', distinguished by both police and journalists according to the type of organization they represented and the type of knowledge they were after. A comparison of these two cultures furthers our understanding of how knowledge sources and the uses of knowledge are related to physical space and social and cultural relations.

The inner circle was exclusive to journalists from popular news outlets. These reporters were after 'spot news' about crime incidents, the 'eternal recurrence' (Rock 1973) of describing serious crimes, naming the people involved, and reporting the outcome of investigations, the 'normal crime discourse' (Wheeler 1986; Fishman 1981) available in the major news occurrence releases supplied by the police public relations unit, or investigative units. They also developed stories sympathetic to the lot of police officers, describing what it is like to be on the streets 'fighting' crime.

In order to obtain these types of knowledge inner circle reporters developed close relations with police officers. The police station was their place of work. They had office space at police headquarters, and most of them made no use of the office facilities of their newsrooms but simply filed stories directly from police headquarters or a field location. They functioned as their own assignment editors, using police radio feeds, scanner radios, and date files to decide what they would cover on a given day. There were many sources of social and cultural affinity between inner circle reporters and police officers. Many reporters on the beat had been there for years, including one person who had spent three decades reporting on police. Reporters had 'wanted posters' regarding notorious criminal suspects on their desks. They addressed officers on a first-name basis. They wrote articles for police newspapers and magazines, sat on a committee to select the police officer of the month for a special civic award, and arranged parties at major hotels for journalists and police. They served as consultants to police officers regarding the preparation of information for news release or for other formats. They collaborated in various forms of information control that would help their police sources, for example editing out harmful information, writing stories favourable to the police when there were serious allegations of police misconduct, crediting officers with 'good pinches,' and participating in law enforcement crackdown campaigns.

Given the types of knowledge inner circle reporters were after, reciprocity seemed inevitable, and it worked. Inner circle reporters were given preferential treatment and 'scoops' as long as their knowledge was confined to factual updates and empathetic understanding of the police officer's lot. As the head of an investigative unit informed us in interview, referring to inner circle reporters

> I'll call them if I want to sell my men. If I want to give a good pinch, because my men have done a good job, then I'll contact them all. And I don't have any preference on how I contact them. As a matter of fact they answer each others' phones. So it's to put the police image up good.

While inner circle reporters succeeded in obtaining the types of knowledge they were after, it was at the expense of respect among other journalists. They were seen as being too close to their sources, captured by such perjorative terms as 'spit collectors'. For members of the inner circle, when the values of journalism and the values of the police culture collided, the police culture prevailed.

The outer circle was exclusive to journalists who represented quality news outlets. These outlets gave relatively little attention to crime incidents, but focused instead on policing the police in terms of procedural propriety, inefficiency and mismanagement. As a result their reporters were distanced from the police spatially, socially and culturally. They did not use the office space for reporters at police headquarters, and they were ostracized by inner circle reporters. They were in frequent conflict with various officers and units in the police force, and this sometimes led to hostile exchanges at the management level. They were frequently cut off from access to knowledge within the police force, and therefore they relied on informants outside the force, including citizens who had been aggrieved by the police, and citizens' interest groups opposed to some aspect of police operations. They were generally unconcerned about lack of access to legitimate police channels of knowledge because they were not after the types of knowledge provided by those channels.

POLICE ORGANIZATION

FIGURE I: *Regions and closures*

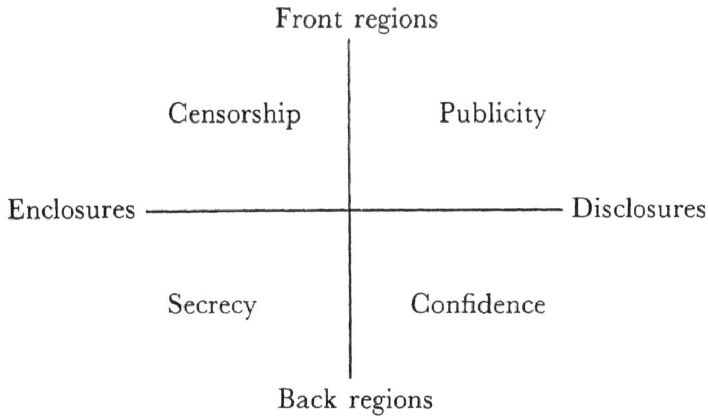

Figure I presents a model of organizational regions and closures which is useful for classifying the ways in which the police organize to deal with journalists. This model follows the pioneering work of Goffman (1959), and its elaboration by Giddens (1984: 122–6), but with refinements related to the present analysis. Goffman and Giddens were concerned with the social psychological level of presentation of self. They examined how an individual's presentation of self is dependent upon having spatial regions for the preservation of privacy, alternating with public places for the staging of appearances. In addition to these social psychological aspects, the present analysis examines the sociological level of how organizations protect and present their activities by policing spatial regions and knowledge.

Secrecy entails enclosure on knowledge in the back regions of the organization. All organizations require some workable level of privacy in order to be able to organize at all (Bok 1982; Reiss 1987; Rock 1988). There is a need for places, spaces, and matters upon or into which others may not intrude without consent. This is a fundamental aspect of the capacity to act, to create a degree of predictability that will reduce equivocality and lessen vulnerability. It is also necessary for the maintenance of a competitive advantage over one's enemies, or organizations in the same business, who might gain unfairly if they are able to intrude on discussions and plans.

The police have a particular bent toward reticence and secrecy. This is the case even *within* a police force, as various individuals, sub-units, and ranks work hard to keep information from each other in order to preserve their autonomy and to gain credit (Punch 1983,

1985; Ericson 1981, 1982). Secrecy is an engrained part of police culture, necessary for the capacity to act (e.g. to provide reasonable accounts to superiors and the courts that are credible and 'cover-ass'), and necessary for maintaining a competitive advantage (e.g. to gain personal and sub-unit credit for investigative successes).

Secrecy is also demanded legally. For example in Ontario the *Police Act* explicitly prohibits any sworn police officer from saying anything about police work to persons outside the force without prior authorization. Laws concerning contempt of court circumscribe what police officers are willing to say about their investigations or about the people involved prior to revelations in the courtroom. Laws concerning libel are also a good reason for police officers to stay mum about people who are merely suspects or only under legal accusation rather than certified offenders.

The police force also channels officers' accounts into particular grooves. In a force we studied there were several pages of written directives stating who in the force was authorized to speak and what topics and details they could and could not address (Ericson *et al.* 1989: 98–102). Persons of the rank of Inspector or above could speak to reporters; persons of lower rank were required to obtain permission before speaking to reporters. The public relations unit of the police force acted as a clearing house for releases to the news media, and for arranging interviews, news conferences, lectures, and so on. The public relations unit also prepared the major occurrence news releases that were designed to limit reporters to what the police thought they should know (Wheeler 1986). Reporters were otherwise very limited in the methodologies they could employ. There was no direct observation of police activities, except in the form of one-day ridealongs that allowed the reporter to write an empathetic story about the police officer's lot. There was no systematic analysis of police files; we witnessed a request by a news organization to have a reporter do a systematic analysis of police files on rape cases, but the request was denied and the reporter was told he could only have access to past major occurrence news releases on rape cases.

In the context of these various restrictions, the police patrolled the facts regarding anything that they thought might give an advantage to the 'criminal element,' anything that might jeopardize an investigation, and anything that might be unfair to a suspect, accused, witness or victim. Of course these reasons for secrecy were also justifications that were routinely invoked to put off an inquiring reporter (cf. Brandt 1969; Scott and Lyman 1970). There was also considerable effort to patrol the facts regarding policy, such as deployment strategies and budget allocations.

Accounts were also tailored to fit into prevailing cultural sensitivities and sensibilities. For example, officers were advised to limit talking about the criminal activities of particular groups if such talk might be construed as having racist overtones. Women officers, and officers whose ethnic background was in the minority, were specially selected as spokespersons for particular events or issues to make the force appear sensitive to the demographic mosaic of the city. During a moral panic about attacks on women in the city (see Voumvakis and Ericson 1984), which extended for several months and which brought enormous pressure on the police to solve the murders involved, it was deemed difficult to communicate police statistics indicating there was no increase in female murder victims based on trends over the previous decade. The police feared that reporting such data might appear as a slight, in the context of the dominant media frame of the fear being experienced by women in the city, and in the context of the wider political culture with its emphasis on the status of women. As an officer in the public relations unit said in interview

> Our murders of women that year in this city were half of what they were the previous year. But first of all, how do you play a statistical game with a young girl's life? It is just a dangerous thing to do.

For the police, secrecy is not easy to manage. There was an ongoing struggle with outer circle reporters, and especially with reporters from one newspaper which had longstanding hostilities with the police as a result of exposure of police brutality in the mid-1970s.

The police constantly fear the sting of negative publicity, which can overcome any particular desire they might have to keep information from a news organization. A reporter informed us that when he was working for a newspaper in another town, the local police chief became upset at stories that were unfavourable to the police and said he was going to prohibit his officers from releasing any information to reporters from the newspaper. Following a serious car accident, a reporter called the police but was denied any information. The newspaper editor then ran a front page story with the headline, 'SEVERAL INJURED IN SERIOUS ACCIDENT, WE THINK,' relating that reporters had heard about the accident but the police had refused information about it. The police chief called the newspaper and expressed even greater anger than he had before. The editor informed him that for each day the police refused to give the newspaper information, he would run a front-page box with the headline, 'POLICE REPORT NO CRIME IN THE PAST 24 HOURS'. This had the intended effect of reopening access to police information, at least via official channels.

This story illustrates that anything approaching total control of information is not easy to accomplish. Moreover, in the large police bureaucracy a lot of autonomy resides with the lower-ranking officers who perform the work. Police organizations resemble symbolic or mock bureaucracies, where only the appearance of control, not the reality, is actually possible (Van Maanen 1980, 1983). In an organization with hundreds of units and thousands of members, porosity is the norm and leaks are frequent. Reporters routinely circumvent the public affairs unit and other official channels to further their stories. This is illustrated in the following story about a 'hitman' turned police informant.

A reporter persisted in giving coverage to an underworld 'hitman' who had become a police informer in exchange for not being prosecuted for an alleged murder. The reporter kept trying to raise the visibility of this exchange and the identity of the informer in face of the police desire to keep the whole affair from publicity. As he became excluded from police cooperation the reporter used alternative sources, including the informer's wife. Seeking to keep the matter 'alive' in every way possible, the reporter reported an instance in which the police arranged for the couple to meet in a hotel room, and failed to intervene when they heard their informer assaulting his wife in a 'domestic'. To the reporter, this failure to control the informer's violence was another instance of the general immunity the police were granting to him. To the police, this was 'the final straw' in a continuing series of incursions into their exclusive back regions. A police respondent gave an overview of this matter, indicating that trust was defined ultimately in terms of interests

> [Names reporter], we had an incident with him over the guarding of the hit man . . . He didn't seem to be satisfied with cooperation all forces were giving him . . . So he was doing a little bit of his own, through [the informer's] common-law wife. He got an 'in' with her, and he wasn't taking into account who she was and what she was. And as a result of that he started doing outside articles that were really hindering our investigation, and he was told that. Said, 'Look, it's your story, we'll help you.' But a lot of the people we were trying to charge did not know what [the informer] looked like, and we were sending him with an undercover policeman back into this area in order to get the evidence that we required, through body packs and everything else. But no, he wouldn't let up, you see, and as a result of that we had to curtail it. We could [have] pick[ed] up maybe a lot more evidence that we wanted. But it became so obvious that he was making it very difficult for the safety of our undercover men, never mind the [informer]. . . . [A] headline that really came out way out of context, was where [the informer] met his common-law wife. He wanted to meet her, and she agreed to it, in a hotel room, and our officers were in the next room. And as a result of it, they

> had a domestic, and he dinged her, and of course the headline came out, 'POLICE STAND BY WHILE KEY WITNESS ASSAULTS GIRL,' words to that effect. So I talked to him and I said, 'You know you just put two officers' careers in jeopardy. They're under investigation . . . that they permitted this man to assault his common-law wife.' And I said, 'You should be on the Ann Landers column because I can give you domestics every night.' And that's what it boiled down to, is a domestic. 'And yet you've blown this out of context . . . He's not under arrest. We're only guarding him. If he didn't want to stay with us tomorrow, you know, he could go and take his chances of getting shot by someone. Versus she agreed to meet him and she wanted to meet him.' . . . It was a misleading headline. It subjected my men to a lot of report-writing [internally], anxiety for their families, and the whole bit. And as a result of that . . . we had a meeting with the Attorney General and the RCMP, the OPP, all up in the Attorney General's office. And all because of [names reporter]. And we told him right there and then, right in that room, I said to him, 'You know you have jeopardized the lives of the undercover operation, and not only that you have jeopardized the career of my two officers.' I said, 'Do you know how many seconds it takes to ding somebody? Split seconds.' And I said, 'And they're in another room. They have a right to be in the room if they want to meet and make love or what they want to do together.' And yet, the headline shows that police stood by while this woman gets assaulted. I really, I lost my trust in the man.

According to a senior executive in the reporter's newspaper, this reporter experienced considerable difficulties obtaining knowledge from police during and after his work on this story. The executive said it took him a year to re-establish relations with one police force. From the police viewpoint, the reporter was interfering with their opportunity to clear crimes and convict offenders of greater value than the immunity they had granted to the informer. From the news organization's perspective, it was important to question the value of granting immunity to someone who had allegedly killed and assaulted, in order to get at others. In identifying a procedural stray, the news organization was questioning police values and whether they could be trusted. With the interest of efficient suppression of crime at heart, the police did not appreciate the reporter's values and decided that he could not be trusted.

News sources are constantly faced with the dilemma of whether to try to keep something secret, or to disclose to defend against counter-knowledge from internal leaks or outside sources. One option is to provide reporters with knowledge in *confidence*. Confidence is the revelation of a private matter with mutual trust that it will not be disclosed to others at all, or until an appropriate time and place.

Police officers were generally of the opinion that because of the porosity of their organization, the best means to control knowledge in the back regions is to establish relations of trust and reciprocity with reporters. This was the basis of their relations with inner circle reporters. They were often quite free with information to inner circle reporters, knowing that they would keep it 'off the record' entirely or until it was appropriate to publish it. Sometimes the deal was explicit: keeping the information from public knowledge for a period, in exchange for an exclusive or 'scoop' when the police decided it could be made public. Most often it was implicit: experienced inner circle reporters knew what the police would want to be kept off the record and they obliged without comment. There were occasions when inner circle reporters were not, in their terms, 'kicking-back all the news' to their newsrooms, and they tried to coerce other reporters outside the circle into following suit.

The confidences between inner circle reporters and the police had a particular irony. By working hard to establish the trust of the police, inner circle reporters put themselves in a position of being very knowledgeable about many aspects of policing. However, the very basis for achieving trust was their willingness not to divulge what they learned. The very methodology they adopted to be trusted and to enhance their knowledge also limited the knowledge they could make public. As Rubinstein (1973: 7) has observed, 'The reporter is always an outsider whose access to the police is assured by his pledge not to reveal what he knows of police work.'

Another means by which the police can control the potential damage of publicity is through *censorship*. Censorship is a restriction on publishing more broadly that which is made public in one narrower context. In some respects everything that is made public is censored in some way, through selection, omission, framing, and interpretation.

The law is one major source of censorship. As mentioned previously, laws of criminal procedure, contempt of court, and libel, circumscribe the knowledge the police officer will communicate publicly, except that which has been officially imprinted legally. In this respect the law itself provides a procedure not to know, and is effective in controlling public discussion within its genre. As Brodeur (1983: 509–10) has observed in a different context

> As any police officer can bear witness to, knowledge and legal proof are two different things; the first notion concerns the substance of the facts, whereas the second is a question of formal procedure . . . To confuse a lack of compelling evidence . . . with a lack of reliable information . . . only strengthens the tendency to repress knowledge.

The law is also used on another level to enclose on what the police officer will communicate publicly. Police officers routinely invoke the frame that they are 'law officers' and are unable to offer knowledge or express opinions that are outside of that frame. This was articulated by a female police officer regarding the law relating to abortion

> If you're going to be truly professional and represent the police department, you're not there because of your moral standpoint. I may disagree wholeheartedly with abortion but the law states *this*, OK! I may vote for a particular M.P. because his wishes are what mine are on the abortion issue, but if I get on television and I'm representing the police department, I state what the law is. That's what my function is. I'm a police officer, I enforce the law as it stands, good or bad. The more I enforce the bad laws, the more the public outcry and the faster it gets changed. But I'm not there to discuss anything about how I feel about it . . . It's against the law. It's very plain and simple.

The realism in this officer's view was indicated in the recent case of an officer from the same force who refused duty to stand outside a free-standing abortion clinic where there had been frequent clashes between pro-choice and pro-life groups. This officer said he was morally opposed to abortion and could not undertake a duty that entailed protecting an abortion clinic. He was subsequently subject to a disciplinary hearing, and dismissed from the force (Toronto *Star*, 28 January 1988, p. A22).

Police officers' accounts are also censored through the official formats for presenting information to reporters. There were strict encoding procedures for major occurrence news reports and for news releases, in accordance with particular forms and their classifications and categories. These forms included particular things and excluded other things, so that the accounts they contained were both performative and promotional in character (Fishman 1980, 1981; Wheeler 1986). As performative documents, they constituted crime and control not as they happen, but as the force wanted crime and control understood publicly. As promotional documents, they constituted the world as rife with crime and the police as *the* vehicle for keeping the lid on it, making the role of the police seem self-evident, and their efforts at crime control appear objective, compassionate and effective. Indeed these documents were probably more effective than the 'good news' activities of the public affairs unit because they appeared to be objective and not self-laudatory. Here the medium was the message, literally.

The ability of the police to enclose on knowledge and yet appear open to publicity explains a major policy change in the force studied. The change was toward more contact with the media, and allowing more lower-ranking officers to talk to the media. Patrolling the facts through particular formats of publicity was seen as more effective than secrecy in many instances. A senior officer said that with the shift to more 'openness,' 'We've tried to give them what they want, but in a more controlled environment.' Another senior officer was more pithy: 'I think the more we disclose, the more we control.'

INFLUENCES OF NEWS

Most research on the effects of the news media examines the effects on the general public, or some vulnerable segment of it such as children. Psychologists generally operate with the view that bad news (e.g. about crime and violence) causes bad behaviour (e.g. more violence). Sociologists generally operate with the view that bad news provides good lessons about the moral boundaries of society. Another approach is to examine the specific negative and positive influences of publicity on the organizations and people who are the subjects of news reports. This is based on a view that news is primarily a communication between journalists and their regular sources, and other citizens are mere spectators (Tuchman 1978).

Police officers in the force studied experienced a range of negative influences from the news media. Reporters sometimes interfered with investigations literally by meddling in some material aspect of the scene of the crime. News reports tipped off suspects about police strategies, creating difficulty in capturing them and bringing evidence against them. News reports that gave specific details of evidence carried the risk of affecting a suspect's confession and its reliability for court. Pressures to solve highly publicized crimes were said to have real effects on the investigative units concerned, including transfer of officers out of the units. Crimes that were subject to continuing stories, and especially media-created crime waves, were blamed for bringing a heavier workload as a result of additional calls from members of the public who were fearful and suspicious. Officers repeatedly expressed a concern that the image of the force and their occupation was tarnished in particular reports, but they were constrained from responding because of legal and administrative impediments.

Police officers also had worries in terms of individual careers. Cases were pointed to where the pressure of negative publicity had forced changes in assignment, and early retirement or resignations. The policing the police orientation of outer circle journalists was especially upsetting, as indicated in the previously related 'hitman' case. An officer gave a personal example of being involved in a court case in which publicity was given to the fact that the lawyer for the accused alleged that the officer had committed acts of theft, sexual misconduct, and conspiracy to obstruct justice. This led to an investigation by the police internal affairs unit. Although the investigation concluded the allegations were unfounded, the officer said the news media did not publish any follow-up stories to record this fact, and he felt a lingering stigma among fellow officers, friends, and peers in the legal community.

Police officers also enumerated positive benefits of publicity in terms of the same dimensions. The news media were seen as being very helpful regarding some aspects of dealing with investigations and emergency situations. The news media are a valued means of mobilizing general public awareness about emergency situations to be avoided and precautions to be taken. They function as the contemporary equivalent of the 'wanted poster' by publishing photographs and descriptions of suspects. They provide a similar service regarding missing persons, sometimes extending the dissemination of photographs to newspaper delivery vans and street-corner boxes. Television stations supply video records of street demonstrations, picket-lines, funerals, and so on, from which police can identify troublesome people. At times the media will go further, actively participating with the police in investigating or controlling a problem (Ericson *et al.* 1987). In this regard a television network's policy handbook is revealing. At one point the handbook says that journalists are not to use deceptive practices, but at another point it states that practices such as the use of hidden cameras and microphones are acceptable if the target is anti-social behaviour and 'the public interest' is at stake. The examples of anti-social behaviour given are selling drugs to children and certain types of street demonstrations. Here the police and the media are conceived as having a common policing task, in the public interest.

The media were also seen by the police to be a helpful agency of social control regarding the prevention of crime. Police officers praised the media for their participation in law enforcement crackdowns, such as an annual Christmas-time blitz on impaired driving, and major drug 'busts.' They also pointed to instances in which journalists had selected or omitted facts as these had an assumed bearing on general deterrence.

The media also proved helpful in boosting force morale. Inner circle reporters obliged requests to single out particular officers and units for credit. They did so on an everyday basis by citing arrests by officers and units involved in particular crimes, and in the institutionalized format of sitting on the committee to give an award to the police officer of the month.

Line police officers said that they had learned to use the news media to pressure the senior administration and the police commission into particular actions (see also Punch 1985). This was usually done through the police association, whose officers had learned how to convert particular events in the public political culture into advantages for the working conditions of police officers. For example, an officer described in interview how the administration and police commission had been reluctant to supply officers with protective body armour. The occasion of the shooting of a police officer was deemed opportune for generating publicity that would pressure the administration into supplying the equipment.

> [T]here are quite a few occasions where, and in quotes, I 'use' the press to the best advantage . . . [for example] protective body armour. And of course with management we had been attempting through negotiation and meeting after meeting to get some movement from them and all they were doing was paying us lip service. I think almost not genuinely concerned enough, or they felt that the expenditure didn't warrant the product that would provide the safety for our police officers. And so that was just at the time that one of our officers was shot, in fact two of them were shot . . . And shortly after that . . . an Ontario Provincial Police officer . . . was killed . . . and it was at that point that, well here it goes, we'll give it full volley. And so we got into the area of protective body armour and that every likelihood this officer would not have received a serious gun shot wound if he had been wearing armour, and blahblahblahblahblah, and that we had asked the government to become involved in testing different materials, different products . . . One thing led to another, and the amount of pressure that was coming on our politicians and our police force! The public, hell, they were, in fact maybe it went a little too far at times but there were different groups donating money and wanting to take up different charitable campaigns and events and all the rest of it to get dollars and to provide protective armour for the police officers. And of course about a year down the road it was targeted for another provincial election, and of course the government at that time was in a minority position, provincially. So everything tied in well and we got some very good coverage and as a result . . . out of 5,300 [police officers] over 5,000 have protective body armour . . . I'm almost waiting for an issue or something to come up that can be somewhat controversial . . . Management is just acquiescing on almost every one of our proposals. Anything that might get a bit of light publicity, they would rather pay the bucks than have some controversy in the media . . . [in relation to the protective body armour publicity campaign] it put them in a position where they couldn't do anything but come out favorably, in front, you know, 'for the boys in blue, because we love you.' It makes nice rhetoric but I don't think they really believe it . . . [I]f it wasn't for the media, we wouldn't have the protective body armour. They were an integral

> part of the chess game, and at least what I've found is that our Board of Commissioners, our senior officers, municipal government, provincial government, don't want bad publicity or bad light, or be viewed like that. And they'll respond affirmatively if the issue is right, and of course we wouldn't go to the press with an issue that we want, oh maybe some frivolous item, where the public can't identify with it . . . Holsters was one issue. What we had was legitimately a 'widow maker.' We had attempted in numerous different ways . . . to get a holster that was adequate and that would ensure that for the most part that an assailant couldn't draw a police officer's revolver from the holster. And geez we've had it in negotiations for years and with little or no success. So finally we said, 'Hey, you know, it's the same strategy again.' And I know the [Police] Commission is well aware of it now. And so when a situation arises, refer to it, like, 'widow maker,' that's a nice catchy little phrase and people like to to go, you know, 'widow maker.' I mean they'll read it and think, 'Why the hell, why have they got an $11 holster when a $50 holster is going to save their lives?'

This example illustrates how one part of an organization can use publicity to pressure another part of the organization into taking a particular action. It also shows how the police use the media to enhance their material resources. The formula is as follows. Bad news (the shooting of police officers) provides the occasion (e.g. the wounded officer's struggle to survive; the funeral of the slain officer) to dramatically display the police as a core symbol in political culture (cf. Manning 1977; Taylor 1986). In turn the political cultural context is provided for the police to 'press' for more resources, which in the context are difficult for the administration to deny.

This example also illustrates how the police can enhance their ideological resources through the media. However, such dramatic occasions are not required for ideological purposes. Ideological enhancement is achievable much more routinely through the normal crime discourse of crime incident reporting; good news items on advances in police technology, new programmes, and heroic acts; crime prevention displays in shopping plazas and schools; and school essay contests which glorify the image of the police. A public relations officer described his elation at having the winning entries in a school essay contest published in a mass circulation newspaper

> We had hoped to have released this feature information on a Monday . . . about two kids who won an essay contest Metro-wide about police. But the *Star* got word of it early, got copies of the essays, and I thought they'd treat it as a feature . . . And they thought, u-huh, no, front-page stuff on the Saturday *Star*. A

> matter of fact they guaranteed me, they got a middle-management guy on the phone, he says, 'You get this for me and set it all up. And get the people out by the police car and everything else, and make copies of the essay. Front page of the Saturday *Star*.' And 'cash registers', numbers started to go up in my mind. Front page of the Saturday *Star*, I think, what is it, 575,000 issues, provincial [-wide distribution]. And I'm adding this up in my mind, 'cause it was for a benefit and I wanted publicity. So I said, 'Sure!' and I think I set the thing up for them and they read it back to me. It was front page. I mean you couldn't ask for better coverage. Did you see the front page of the *Sun* this morning? It's a coloured picture of a mounted policeman, with our horse and with the police museum which is opening up. And I thought to myself, I mean, who can get that kind of coverage on the front page of a major paper like that?

PUBLIC KNOWLEDGE OF POLICE AND CRIME

The police viewed their publicity mandate in terms of myth and ceremony. They were not concerned as much with public understanding of their work as with whether the news helped them with their work, and with the image of the force and the occupation. Indeed they were not overly concerned about distorting aspects of crime and their approaches to controlling it, recognizing that organizations can thrive on useful myths.

The primary factor in the accomplishment of helpful myths was the self-enclosure of inner-circle journalists, in the context of police-erected regions and closures for secrecy, confidences, censorship and publicity. In relation to inner circle reporters the police were primary definers. Reporters accepted what was given to them without reflecting upon how those facts had been constructed by the police for the purposes of publicity. This is perhaps why, for inner circle reporters, the sharing of facts among each other was routine and taken for granted. The approach of journalists to facts was articulated in interview by a news executive.

> The great thing that we believe in, much as the courts believe . . . that the police are always right, except in extraordinary circumstances. That is an unalterable fact, that the police are not a bunch of shysters and not a bunch of crooks, but essentially the epitome of the fine, upstanding citizen who has observed and recorded accurately. If we can't take information from them without having to verify, we're in deep trouble. Aren't we?

Accepting certain facts at face value, reporters fail to ask potentially significant questions regarding organizational structures and processes. For example, a reporter helped a citizen obtain a police report on an incident involving him so that he could use it in a court case pertaining to a separate but related matter. The reporter rested content with her 'press moves mountains' story regarding how she had managed to obtain something from the police that had previously been denied to the citizen. She did not follow-up with an analysis, for example, of why the complainant is routinely excluded from receiving a copy of the report that labels and describes the complaint and what the police did about it. Is it because complaints are police property? Is it because the police can do little or nothing about most complaints and do not want to make this fact evident to complainants? Is it because routine disclosure would lead to conflicts over interpretation and meaning and create a lot of organizational trouble for the police?

Through their procedures not to know reporters routinely reproduce police ideology. A reporter was observing demonstrators outside a courtroom. The demonstrators were protesting that the police had created and escalated a situation at an anti-nuclear arms demonstration that led to the laying of 62 criminal charges, for which the accused presently stood trial inside the court building. The reporter began arguing with the demonstrators, and at one point exclaimed, 'The police don't judge the law, they merely enforce it!' If the reporter had reflected on his own judgments that day, including his decision not to include the demonstration outside the court building as part of his report on the court case, he would have appreciated that his statement was as vacuous as saying, 'Reporters don't judge the news, they merely report it.'

A television reporter returned from the scene of an anti-nuclear arms demonstration and proceeded to the video-editing room to prepare the visuals for his story. He came across a shot of police officers dragging demonstrators through manure that had been deposited by police horses. The reporter decided not to include this shot in his story, justifying his decision to the studio technician by saying that it was unfair to represent the way the police handled the entire demonstration with this particular shot. The reporter said nothing about the demonstrators' sense of fairness regarding how they were handled by the police.

As introduced previously, the most fundamental way in which police ideology is reproduced by journalists is through daily reporting of crime incidents and their investigation. In crime reporting journalists routinely translate policing into the popular mythology of 'good guys' and 'bad guys,' 'white hats' and 'black hats.' As Hartley (1982: 106) observes in a different context, this translation means that the news

> produces a way of understanding which proposes that not only is it possible for the events to be made sense of in this accessible, commonsense way, but that this is *necessarily* what they mean, of

themselves . . . However, the strategies it has evolved [to maintain autonomy from sources] . . . and the language it takes from out of 'our' mouths to make sense of the world *for* us, do not secure it from other social forces. The impartiality and autonomy of news production are real and are actively struggled for by news people. The function of that hard-won space is to guarantee that the meanings constructed there are not mere propaganda, either for the government, the 'establishment' or anyone else. In the process the sense that is made of the world turns out to be much more ideologically active and productive for the maintenance of one particular (dominant) 'reality' than 'mere' propaganda would be. For propaganda is contestable, whereas, as common sense tells us, 'nature' is not.

CONCLUSIONS

The police expend considerable resources in patrolling the facts of their operations. As well as being crime preventers, law enforcers, and social service agents, the police are information workers with a keen sense of the importance of how their information is made into knowledge (Ericson and Shearing 1986). They strategically organize physical facilities, cultural sensibilities and social relations to construct silence about most of their activities. These same spatial, cultural, and social resources also enable the police to narrow publicity into acceptable channels, making it both of practical use and productive ideologically.

The perfection of the art of public relations is to routinize the process to the point where journalists engage in self-enclosure, censoring themselves. In our observations the police come close to perfection with inner circle reporters from popular news outlets. These reporters routinely reproduced the performative and promotional character of police news releases. However, the process was much more equivocal and problematic with outer circle reporters from quality news outlets, who were interested in focusing the media searchlight on procedural strays to police the police. In relation to outer circle journalists the police were involved in a perpetual dance of secrecy and revelation, constantly forced to refine their accountability to achieve accountability in the public culture. Even for powerful institutions such as the police, patrolling the facts is inevitably difficult and partial because information can be moved and interpreted so freely even while it remains in its place.

Richard V. Ericson
Centre of Criminology
University of Toronto

NOTE

* Earlier versions of this paper were presented as a public lecture at the University of Manitoba, March 1988, and to the World Congress on Criminology, Hamburg, September 1988. I am grateful to Pat Baranek and Janet Chan for their work on the research programme which provided some of the empirical materials used in this paper. The research programme was funded by grants from the Social Sciences and Humanities Research Council of Canada and the Solicitor General of Canada.

BIBLIOGRAPHY

Bok, S. 1982. *Secrets: On the Ethics of Concealment and Revelation.* New York: Pantheon.

Brandt, R. 1969. 'A Ultilitarian Theory of Excuses'. *Philosophical Review* 78: 337–61.

Brodeur, J.-P. 1983. 'High Policing: Remarks about the Policing of Political Activities'. *Social Problems* 30: 507–20.

Chibnall, S. 1977. *Law-and-Order News.* London: Tavistock.

Ericson, R. 1981. *Making Crime: A Study of Detective Work.* Toronto: Butterworth.

Ericson, R. 1982. *Reproducing Order: A Study of Police Patrol Work.* Toronto: University of Toronto Press.

Ericson, R. and **C. Shearing**. 'The Scientification of Police Work', in G. Bohme and N. Stehr, (eds), *The Knowledge Society: The Growing Impact of Scientific Knowledge on Social Relations.* Sociology of the Sciences Yearbook, 10: 129–59. Dordrecht: Reidel.

Ericson, R., P. Baranek, and **J. Chan.** 1987. *Visualizing Deviance: A Study of News Organization.* Milton Keynes: Open University Press.

Ericson, R., P. Baranek, and **J. Chan.** 1989. *Negotiating Control: A Study of News Sources.* Milton Keynes: Open University Press.

Ericson, R., P. Baranek, and **J. Chan.** [forthcoming] *Acknowledging Order: A Study of News Content.*

Fishman, M. 1980. *Manufacturing the News.* Austin: University of Texas Press.

Fishman, M. 1981. 'Police News: Constructing an Image of Crime'. *Urban Life*, 9: 371–94.

Giddens, A. 1984. *The Constitution of Society.* Cambridge: Polity.

Goffman, E. 1959. *The Presentation of Self in Everyday Life.* New York: Doubleday.

Hartley, J. 1982. *Understanding News.* London: Methuen.

McMahon, M. and **R. Ericson.** 1987. 'Reforming the Police and Policing Reform', in R. Ratner and J. McMullan, (eds), *State Control: Criminal Justice Politics in Canada*, pp. 38–68. Vancouver: University of British Columbia Press.

Manning, P. 1977. *Police Work.* Cambridge, Mass.: MIT Press.

Meyrowitz, J. 1985. *No Sense of Place.* New York: Oxford University Press.

Punch, M., (ed.) 1983. *Control in the Police Organization.* Cambridge, Mass.: MIT Press.

Punch, M. 1985. *Conduct Unbecoming: The Social Construction of Police Deviance and Control.* London: Tavistock.

Reiner, R. 1983. 'The Politicization of the Police in Britain', in M. Punch, (ed.), *Control in the Police Organization*, pp. 126–48. Cambridge, Mass.: MIT Press.

Reiner, R. 1985. *The Politics of the Police.* Brighton: Wheatsheaf Books.

Reiss, A. 1987. 'The Legitimacy of Intrusion into Private Space', in C. Shearing and P. Stenning, (eds), *Private Policing*; pp. 19–44. Beverly Hills: Sage.

Rock, P. 1973. 'News as Eternal Recurrence', in S. Cohen and J. Young, (eds), *The Manufacture of News*, pp. 73–80. London: Constable.

Rock, P. 1988. 'On the Birth of Organizations', *Canadian Journal of Sociology* 13: 359–84.

Rubinstein, J. 1973. *City Police.* New York: Farrar, Strauss and Giroux.

Scott, M., and **S. Lyman.** 1970.

'Accounts, Deviance and Social Disorder', in J. Douglas, (ed.), *Deviance and Respectability: The Social Construction of Moral Meanings*, pp. 89–119. New York: Basic Books.

Taylor, I. 1986. 'Martyrdom and Surveillance: Ideological and Social Problems of Police in Canada in the 1980s'. *Crime and Social Justice*, 26: 60–74.

Tuchman, G. 1978. *Making News*. New York: Free Press.

Van Maanen, J. 1980. 'Beyond Account: The Personal Impact of Police Shootings'. *The Annals of the American Academy of Political and Social Sciences* 425: 145–56.

Van Maanen, J. 1983. 'The Boss: First-Line Supervision in an American Police Agency', in M. Punch, (ed.), *Control in the Police Organization*, pp. 275–317. Cambridge, Mass.: MIT Press.

Van Outrive, L., and **C. Fijnaut**. 1983. 'Police and the Organization of Prevention', in M. Punch, (ed.), *Control in the Police Organization*, pp. 47–59. Cambridge, Mass.: MIT Press.

Voumvakis, S., and **R. Ericson**. 1984. *News Accounts of Attacks on Women*. Toronto: Centre of Criminology, University of Toronto.

Wheeler, G. 1986. 'Reporting Crime: The News Release as Textual Mediator of Police/Media Relations'. MA dissertation, Centre of Criminology, University of Toronto.

[7]
Media and Markets

Medium Differences

In the news process, reality is not a solid but a fluid. All knowledge is mediated by a medium, whether print, television, or radio. The medium does not stand apart from the work as a technological apparatus through which news operatives simply transmit their messages. Rather, the medium is 'any process, technique or technology that produces something visible from something invisible ... Media provide a means to visualize, identify, and locate meaning. Although media rely on symbols for communications, they also do something more: media arrange, define, and communicate meaning' (Altheide 1985: 39). As such, the particular medium the news operative uses is integral to his or her work, and he or she helps to constitute its meanings and uses. While the medium constrains the formats in which knowledge can be presented, it is also a means of discovery, creativity, and innovation. While the medium frames discourse, it also accomplishes it.

In this section we contemplate how the newspaper, television, and radio news media each have a distinctive influence on news discourse. We consider how each medium influences the use of particular news formats, sources, knowledge, and topics. This consideration provides the necessary analytical framework for our empirical inquiry into how news of crime, law, and justice varies by medium.

FORMATS

How something is communicated precedes what is communicated. Newspapers, television, and radio have distinct formats. Each medium has different procedures for the selection, transmission, and reception of knowledge. Each medium differs in how it transcends the limits of time and space to make news available, and thereby creates a different social environment and context for thinking. Format differences yield variation in content, and ultimately, different consequences for the knowledge structure of society (Altheide 1985; Meyrowitz 1985; Crisell 1986). Thus how communications are mediated by formats has an importance beyond particular expressions of economic and political power in news accounts. This is the importance of 'media power' (Altheide 1985).

The news reality of each medium is a matter of *how* it presents knowledge in its established formats, rather than of *what* it presents. Aspects of format fundamentally delimit and shape the news product: for example, the time available for a broadcast-news bulletin and the space available in a newspaper; the sequencing of broadcast-news items and the layout of a newspaper; the technologies associated with the medium; and the beats available as routine rounds for acquiring preselected material from sources that is itself formatted for the purposes of the reporter's medium. The format requirements are paramount. Content must always fit the format, and it is therefore always secondary to the format.

> Any medium's first commitment is to itself as a legitimate format for the definition, recognition, and communication of meaning ... Whatever defines a particular medium, e.g. sound for radio and visuals for TV, will essentially define and shape how the event's temporal and spatial features will be translated into those of the listener or viewer. Furthermore, whatever content is produced, e.g. people, places, things, will be subservient to and largely a result of these format considerations. And, whatever elements of format are deemed the most important will weigh disproportionately on the resulting messages. (Altheide 1985: 40, 56)

A fuller appreciation of media and formats can be derived from a detailed comparison of the capacities and limitations of newspaper, television, and radio formats as summarized in table 2.1.

A basic point of comparison, from which several other points follow, is that the newspaper is a visual medium, television both visual and audio, and radio audio. The fact that radio has no visual capacity and is therefore 'a *blind* medium' (Crisell 1986: 3) is fundamental. Television can transmit printed material: some cable-television stations present nothing but news in print, and newscasts use printed vistas to identify sources and to highlight key points in a story. Newspapers can use still photographs, graphics, and visually 'catchy' headlines, captions, and layouts. While television and

TABLE 2.1
A comparison of newspapers, television, and radio news formats

Newspaper	Television	Radio
Visual	Visual and audio	Audio
Weak validation of context	Strong validation of context	Some validation of context
Least redundancy/ simplification	Considerable redundancy/ simplification	Most redundancy/ simplification
Considerable imaginative work	Least imaginative work	Most imaginative work
Narrative/symbolic/ abstraction	Most dramatization/ entertaining/concrete	Considerable abstraction dramatization/ entertaining/concrete
Least personalization	Most personalization	Considerable personalization
Structure with space	Structure with time	Structure with time
Least immediacy/past tense	Considerable immediacy/ present tense	Most immediacy/present tense
Largest number of items	Intermediate number of items	Least number of items
Longest items	Intermediate length of items	Shortest items
Linear/sequential	Mosaic/episodic	Mosaic/episodic
Static	Dynamic/continuous	Dynamic/continuous
Consistent/permanent/ a record	Ephemeral/evanescent	Ephemeral/evanescent
Self-pacing	Imposes own pace	Imposes own pace
Individual/primary activity	More social/secondary activity	Most social/secondary activity

newspaper words and visuals can gloss a lot, radio words gloss everything because there is no opportunity for visual interpretation of individual character and interactional contexts.

As their medium lacks a visual capacity, radio journalists are more limited in their ability to convey connotative meanings. There is, of course, a great deal of connotative potential in the use of words alone. As Monaco (1981: 131) observes, 'If denotation were the only measure of the power of a language, for example, then English – which has a vocabulary of a million or so words and is the largest language in history – would be over three times more powerful than French – which has only 300,000 or so words. But French makes up for its "limited" vocabulary with a noticeably greater use of connotation.' A particular skill required of the radio announcer is to keep the audience engaged by dropping in witty and entertaining connotations as he or she talks (Goffman 1981: chap. 5; Crisell 1986). Nevertheless, radio talk, and especially radio-news talk, must be presented within a very limited, simple, 'perfected' form, not only to be engaged and understood, but also so as not to connote meanings that might give offence to some segment of the audience (Goffman 1981: chap. 5). While music and other background sounds can be used in radio news (Crisell 1986), they are not used often.

Language use in newspapers is similarly restricted, but the restrictions are not as great. The newspaper has considerable latitude in arriving at connotative meanings by contrasting and juxtaposing pictures, headlines, and stories in its page layouts. 'In both television and the newspapers – especially the popular tabloids – there is as much attention given to, and signification in, the spatial composition as the sequence of verbal/written signs. The composition within the TV screen puts different iconic signs together so that they modify or reinforce each other's signification. The same is true of the combination of headline and picture and story in newspapers. We read them simultaneously, and this is where a picture can indeed be worth a thousand ideological words' (Hartley 1982: 31).

The film and video technologies of television greatly enhance its connotative capacity. The television journalist can use camera angles, lighting, and background staging 'props,' and editing to connote meaning. The television journalist can also combine visuals with sound – words, music, background noise – to connote ideologically (Fiske and Hartley 1978, chap. 3; Ericson, Baranek, and Chan 1987: chaps. 7 and 8).

The visual capacity of television allows it to bind its messages to the context in which they were produced. Through the use of sounds from the context of production, radio also has some capacity in this regard. 'Quotes in a newspaper may have nothing to do with the place in which the words were spoken, but a recording of a speech also captures aspects of the physical environment in which the speech was made' (Meyrowitz 1985: 122). Newspapers are limited to the use of still photographs, and these provide a relatively weak means of tying messages to context.

The greater the capacity to bind messages to context, the greater the validation powers of the medium. Television appears most valid because statements made by its sources can be contextualized in the real places in which they were made. As politicians who preen themselves for television interviews know best (Ericson, Baranek, and Chan 1989: chap. 4), television can capture not only the offices and assembly rooms where important decisions are made, but also the source's dress, demeanour, and direct reaction to questions, from which readings of character are made. Television's capacity to bind messages to context and thereby validate its messages accounts for the fact that survey research in Canada, Britain, and the United States consistently shows that readers find television news more believable, fair, and influential than radio news or newspapers (Glasgow University Media Group [GUMG] 1976: 1ff; Royal Commission on Newspapers [RCN] 1981b: 35; Robinson and Levy 1986; Fiske 1987).

Radio, too, has some power of validation, although extra effort is required to accomplish it. The radio journalist must establish context by describing the environment in which events are occurring, and by using surrounding messages, source clips, and news items. Background sounds associated with the context in which statements are made also provide validity, although these are used indexically rather than iconically. Radio sounds require 'textual pointing – support from the dialogue or narrative' (Crisell 1986: 51). The context of all radio sounds is provided by the script, just as the context of all television sounds and visuals is 'anchored' by the script (Barthes 1977: 39). While radio and television are validated through the ability to use 'actualities,' it is the written text that directs one to the meaning of those actualities and anchors them in a framework.

Newspaper journalists have a limited ability to do the same thing, for example, by writing pointed captions for still photographs. A still photograph of a demolished car wrapped around a tree, with the caption 'Drunk driving tragedy,' can serve as a poignant reminder about the 'terror' of impaired driving. Without the caption, the picture would be polysemous and serve as a reminder of the 'terror' of uncertain signs. Outside the use of still photographs, which is limited (see chapter 7), newspapers must rely upon the visual aspects of their layout (juxtaposing stories, using bold-type headlines, etc.) to magnify the contexts of their stories and to give them force and validity. Popular newspapers in particular use layouts in this way, while quality newspapers rely more upon the authority of their sources to validate what it is they have to say and to lend authority to the newspaper itself.

Compared to most other cultural products, news is quite redundant and simplified. Newspapers are the least redundant and simplified because they have the capacity to present long and complex items in a literate mode. They present detailed features either singly or in a series. They also present stories on a continuing basis, using a wide range of sources (characters) in detailed and subtle narratives. Whether in features or in complex continuing stories, newspapers are more capable of introducing experts and their specialist knowledge than is television or radio news.

Television news is much more simplified and redundant than that in newspapers. It tends towards the concrete and dramatic and has great difficulty in being subtle. Its representations are sometimes 'cartoon stick-figure like' (Gitlin 1980). While television can use its visual capacity to establish context and to present written materials on the screen, this is of little help when it comes to detail and expert knowledge. It is difficult to watch and listen to detailed, specialized knowledge being conveyed because the television-audience member, unlike the newspaper reader, has no chance for retrieval, for introducing his or her own redundancy, unless he or she goes to the trouble and expense of recording the material and playing it over. While specialist knowledge is conveyed on television, it is revealing that 'ideas' programs – such as 'Realities' on TVOntario and 'Ideas' on CBC Radio – provide follow-up printed transcripts of what was said so that the reader can introduce his or her own redundancy at leisure. It is also revealing that in televised distance-education programs, such as those offered by the Open University and the BBC in Britain, the written textual materials are paramount and the broadcast materials are secondary. 'Paulu has pointed out that students of the Open University are expected to spend 65 per cent of their time reading and only 10 per cent of their time listening or viewing (1981: 270); more recently Bates has conceded that broadcasting is a relatively minor component of its teaching system (1984: 139)' (Crisell 1986: 114).

Lacking television's visual capacity, radio is forced to be even more simplified and redundant. 'Radio is the art of communicating meaning at first hearing' (Crisell 1986, quoting Lawrence Gillian of BBC Radio). Communicating meaning at first hearing is difficult because our ears are not terribly 'intelligent.' We tend to miss a lot and forget even more when what we hear is not augmented by something seen. Hence radio talk is reduced to being, as far as possible, simple, redundant, and without the errors typical in natural conversation. Radio is a kind of 'perfect speech machine' (Goffman 1981: chap. 5).

> It is a general truth that much language is written down precisely because its meaning is too complex to be assimilated by ear ... And it is certainly the case that radio language will not be easily followed unless it is syntactically fairly simple or else fairly concrete in subject-matter ... [when] ideas and arguments become more abstract and their expression is premeditated, or when they require sustained explanation or specialist knowledge, the radio medium is less effective (McWhinnie 1959: 49–50). The BBC's Audience Research Department once tested a group of people on how much they could understand of a talk intended for the 'average' Light Programme listener: the average listener in the group could correctly answer only 28 per cent of the questions which were asked about the talk after it was broadcast (Silvey 1974: 141). Indeed it has been observed that the importance of the radio interviewer is not only as the poser of questions but as the interpreter of answers, the 'plain man' who in brief paraphrases renders the complex or

> specialist responses of the expert into language intelligible to the lay public (Cardiff 1980: 38). (Crisell 1986: 62; see also Goffman 1981: esp. 241)

The radio listener must make up for being blind by using his or her imagination. The visualization function of imagination is to an extent provided for by the visual capacities of television and newspapers. In relation to radio, however, the listener must supply the visualization, that is, making something visible to the mind because it is not visible to the eye. This includes imagining the setting, the characters, and even the facts of the matter. The listener must interpret the words as symbols of what they represent, and the voice (accent, stress) as an index of the character who is speaking. In radio, 'speech must be regarded as both typographic and photographic, as equivalent not only of the newspaper text but in many cases of its photographs' (Crisell 1986: 88). As Crisell (ibid: 116) also observes, radio 'is the only medium in which reality is in some sense directly presented yet must *at the same time* be imagined.'

While the visual capacity of television means that the television viewer has to do less imaginative work, there is still a considerable amount of visualization required (Fiske 1987: chap. 5). While television news *seems* to present reality more or less directly, it is nevertheless a highly mediated product that is produced out of considerable imaginative work by journalists and sources, and requires considerable imaginative work by its audience members. The following observation of Monaco (1981: 136–7) regarding the imaginative work required of the cinema viewer is equally applicable to the role of the television-audience member.

> Just as, in general, our sense of cinema's connotation depends on understood comparisons of the image with images that were not chosen (paradigmatic) and images that came before and after (syntagmatic), so our sense of the cultural connotations depend on understood comparisons of the part with the whole (synecdoche) and associated details with ideas (metonymy). Cinema is an art and a medium of extensions and indexes. Much of its meaning comes not from what we see (or hear) but from what we don't see or, more accurately, from an ongoing process of comparison of what we see with what we don't see. This is ironic, considering that cinema at first glance seems to be an art that is all too evident, one that is often criticized for 'leaving nothing to the imagination.' Quite the contrary is true.

Newspapers invite some conceptualization and abstraction, whereas radio and especially television must deal with the concrete and do so in a dramatic and entertaining way. Newspapers can be somewhat discursive, while radio and television tend to be more expressive and 'presentational' (Meyrowitz 1985: 93ff), providing 'experience' and tertiary understanding.

Television in particular is rich in its expressive dimensions, allowing a reading of people and how they answer that is unavailable to the other media, especially newspapers. As Meyrowitz (ibid: 103, 108) observes, it is therefore acceptable for a politician to appear on television reading a speech everyone knows was prepared by someone else, but it would not be acceptable for that someone else to appear on television reading a speech everyone knows was prepared by the politician. Moreover, television allows certain charismatic characters – such as the Polish Solidarity leader Lech Walesa – to become *powerful* communicators expressively, even though they are rather inarticulate discursively.

Newspapers try to convey reality by being 'realistic' in discursive terms, while radio and especially television try to convey reality by 'realism' in dramatic terms. Radio (Pietropaolo 1982) and television (Fiske and Hartley 1978; Fiske 1987) therefore are much more attuned to entertaining presentations. Television producers are directed to treat news as theatre and to keep the entertaining features uppermost (Epstein 1974; Cayley 1982). While snippets of information are dropped in along the way, and form the basis for doing the story in the first place, an entertaining angle and visuals provide the frame (Ericson, Baranek, and Chan 1987). Even serious matters must be treated in this way, 'lightened' more than 'enlightening,' 'livened' more than 'enlivening.' This is why, in Postman's (1985) view, television is contributing to the Huxleian nightmare that we are 'amusing ourselves to death.'

Personalization is part of the entertainment formula, especially in broadcast media. People tune in to radio and television to spend time with their favourite personalities, whether they be soap-opera stars, news anchorpersons, sports heroes, or regular news sources. In the broadcast-news media, there is also the tendency to simplify stories by personalizing them through the eyes of people involved. While newspapers also personalize to a considerable degree – for example, people like to read a regular column by their favourite opinionated columnist, and they like to read about their favourite television personalities in the newspaper – they arguably do so less often because the medium does not have the same expressive and dramatic dimensions of tertiary understanding available to radio and especially to television.

Television and radio use time as the major structuring agent, whereas newspapers use space. The auditory codes of television and radio exist in time, and give the sense that they are dealing in the 'here and now.' They are 'present-tense,' seeming 'to be an account of what *is* happening rather than a record of what *has* happened' (Crisell 1986).

Some of the differences among media in this regard relate to the practicalities of production. Newspaper production – even with the aid of electronic media such as word processors and computer-assisted editing and printing techniques – is still relatively cumbersome and slow. As a result, newspapers cannot compete in terms of immediacy. The very latest news has the least chance of making it into the newspaper ahead of broadcast media. While it has been argued that television is much more immediate than is the newspaper (e.g., RCN 1981b: 105), television journalists are encumbered by the need to obtain visuals and to edit them as scripted. To achieve a predictable supply, most of what television journalists cover is prescheduled and pre-scripted, and a lot of what they broadcast is prepackaged and days old (Epstein 1974; Schlesinger 1978; Ericson, Baranek, and Chan 1987).

Radio is most instantaneous and spontaneous. Radio can link an event and listeners very quickly. For example, radio can report a traffic jam quickly so that the knowledge is very helpful to listeners; by the time television and newspaper journalists are able to report it, the problem is likely to be over and therefore the knowledge is unhelpful. Moreover, radio listeners are often in a better position to receive the knowledge, since radio can be attended to in a greater variety of settings (e.g., while driving an automobile, while working) than can newspapers or television. Radio also has a 'rotating feature' (Altheide 1985: 54) whereby key items are repeated in frequent newscasts or special bulletins so that they are unlikely to be missed by anyone who is tuned into the station even for a relatively short time. Nevertheless, radio news is often less immediate than it seems. In face of limited budgets, radio journalists also do a lot of prescheduling and pre-scripting in a narrow range of preselected beats. While radio provides the illusion of 'fresh talk' (Goffman 1981: 172), the reality is usually scripted talk that narrows the speaker into the redundant grooves and recurrent paths of story themes and language.

The need to structure in time, and to hold audience attention through successive items, means that television and radio journalists are limited to a few items per newscast, and to brief items. In comparison, newspaper journalists have scope for a much larger number of items and for longer items, knowing that their readers will pick and choose among them. In a given day's news output, newspapers have a substantial number of items, television considerably less, and radio less still. Television and radio make up for this through other 'information programming' formats, including documentaries, talk shows, and investigative features. However, within the news genre itself broadcast media tend to limit themselves to a few items. For example, a ten-minute radio newscast, at 160–180 words per minute, is equivalent in words to only one and one-half columns of a newspaper (Crisell 1986: 71). The main evening television-news show typically contains fewer words than a single page of a broadsheet quality newspaper. While it is contentious as to whether more words provide more knowledge, it is clear that the brevity of broadcast-news shows and items indicates how limited they are in discursive potential.

The newspaper page layout allows for a mosaic-like, creative juxtaposition on a given page, although the overall presentation in print is linear and sequential, especially within the story. In contrast, television and radio are much more mosaic-like in their presentation as well as between items. They make a collage of very brief (ten- to fifteen-second) clips from sources and journalists to capture a sense of what has gone on and who the key players seem to be. While several items are sometimes combined into a 'wrap' with a theme, the presentation is still episodic and sometimes even strobe-like in effect. Reduced to the condition of advertising, and even overlapping with it (Fiske and Hartley 1978; Postman 1985), broadcast news paints an abstract mosaic of the world even while appearing to be closest to reality and to involve little imaginative work.

Television and radio have the related feature of presenting their picture of the world in motion. Their clips and items are presented continuously and therefore have a dynamic quality, in contrast to the newspaper, which is relatively static. This feature relates also to the element of immediacy raised earlier. In motion, television and radio seem to be very much in the present tense. Static, newspapers seem to be very much in the past tense. As Williams (1989) observed, while you can 'read all about it' in newspapers, the newspaper statement that 'a man was shot' has a less immediate and realistic quality than television-news pictures of a man *being* shot.

Researchers of broadcast news have shown that a lot can be read into it if only one takes the time to record it, stop its motion, and keep it still. When broadcast news is not captured in this way, it imposes its own pace, and people experience it as ephemeral and evanescent. All television-news sources have had the experience of having a friend say, 'I saw you on television last night but I can't remember what you said. What was it about?' The image lingers, but most of the details have evaporated. In contrast, newspapers are characterized by self-pacing. Readers can repeatedly review a permanent *record* that is consistent in presentation and tone. As a record, the newspaper functions not only as a reference work of the activities of contemporary élites (RCN 1981g; Ericson, Baranek, and Chan 1989), but also a rich source for social historians. Crisell (1986: 72–4) ably summarizes comparative dimensions of these elements.

> The language of newspapers is permanent: the reader sets her own pace and can reread what she has missed or cannot understand. This means that the press is capable of considerable linguistic variety. It can therefore divide the heterogeneous audience with which every mass medium is confronted into different intellectual levels by providing different kinds of newspapers for different kinds of reader ... The language of radio is evanescent. The radio newsreader sets an arbitrary pace and his words dissolve into thin air ... This means that however complex the material – and complexity is especially

> likely in news, documentary and educational programmes – it must be expressed in language which is fairly simple and straightforward in style and diction. Since radio lacks the linguistic range of newspapers we would expect it to be less capable of providing different levels of output for different kinds of listeners and to remain confronted with a largely heterogeneous audience. This certainly seems to be the case with television, whose language code is also evanescent ... In both television and radio the heterogeneous nature of the viewers imposes constraints and restraints on the referential power of the message, but the nature of the contact makes a prior, even more basic imposition for it requires that the message should be relatively simple: and it must be even simpler in the case of radio since it is unassisted by visual codes and must therefore be apprehensible through ear alone.

The newspaper is read more as a primary activity and individually. While it may be read while doing other things – talking on the telephone, chatting to one's husband, listening to the radio, hectoring one's children, watching television – it is often read in isolation from all other social activities. In contrast, television and especially radio are typically used as secondary activities while doing something else, and this frequently includes being in the presence of other people. Most radios, and some television sets, are portable and can be used while driving, working, lying on the beach, etc. They accompany the flow of the day, providing a 'presence' and an 'aural environment' (Monaco 1981: 375) or 'sound' whose function goes beyond particular content. Meyrowitz's (1985: 90) observations on television in this regard are also applicable to radio.

> A great part of the social significance of television ... may be less in what is *on* television than in the very existence of television as a shared arena. Television provides the largest simultaneous perception of a message that humanity has ever experienced ... Recognition of television's role as a new public arena solves a number of mysteries surrounding television viewing, including: why people complain so bitterly about television content but continue to watch so much of it, why many Americans say they turn to television for 'most' of their news even though – by any objective standard – there is remarkably little news on television, and why people who purchase video tape machines often discover they have little interest in creating 'libraries' of their favourite television programs.

SOURCES

We have already considered how media format requirements influence journalists in their selection and use of sources (pp. 16–17; Altheide 1985;

Ericson, Baranek, and Chan 1987). Media format requirements also influence sources in their selection and use of journalists (Ericson, Baranek, and Chan 1989; Schlesinger 1988, 1989). Through their procedures for controlling knowledge, different sources create different media environments, more suitable to one medium than others. For example, we found that, because of the nature of legal discourse, the fact that electronic media were excluded from the courtroom, and the ways in which reporters were effectively excluded from back regions where case settlements were negotiated, the court beat was primarily print-oriented (Ericson, Baranek, and Chan 1989). In contrast, on the police beat, the major-occurrence news releases, with updates on crimes and investigations, were especially attuned to the hourly update requirements of radio stations and therefore radio reporters were at the core of the reporters' subculture on the police beat (ibid). A further contrast was provided on the legislature beat, where politicians and their officials favoured television because of the assumed size and breadth of television's audience and the impact of its images (ibid). While radio reporters had a leading place on the police beat, they were referred to as mere 'spit collectors' at the legislature, indicating the fact that they picked up only residual material from interviews and questions framed by reporters working in other media. Different news requirements of different sources *vis-à-vis* medium format capabilities lead them to favour a particular medium, and variation in content across media is the result.

Each medium offers sources different formats for expressing their authority. Meyrowitz (1985) argues that a print-oriented society is supportive of hierarchy based on specialized and compartmentalized knowledge, whereas electronic media, especially television, tend to undermine claims to authority based on specialized knowledge and thereby foster a levelling and democratic effect.

> In a print society, the graded complexity of print data and the highly compartmentalized nature of print audiences leads to high esteem for 'experts' (the 'top' in the field) and 'specialists' (people whose knowledge is focused in one tiny cluster of information about a particular subject) ... [In the electronic society] messages from all bodies of knowledge are more equally accessible to all people. While such messages, especially as presented on radio and television, often offer more 'awareness' than 'understanding,' the new communication pattern works to undermine the stature of authorities whose knowledge and skills are based on isolated communication networks. (ibid: 326–7)

Meyrowitz's observations help explain the fact that while politicians and other members of the élite gravitate towards television to express their authority, they turn to the newspaper as a source of authority. When it comes to actually using knowledge available in the news in the course of their activities, members of élites who are regular news sources favour the quality newspaper. For example, in a survey of 602 élite decision-makers, 55 per cent said they relied on daily newspapers, especially the *Globe and Mail*, while only 22 per cent expressed a preference for television, 13 per cent for radio (mainly the CBC), and 10 per cent for periodicals (RCN 1981b).

KNOWLEDGE

The format requirements of a medium create an affinity with particular types of knowledge. Newspapers, television, and radio vary in the degree to which they each rely on knowledge that is primary (factual, asking 'What happened?'), secondary (explanatory, asking 'Why did it happen?'), tertiary (emotional, empathetic, asking 'What was it like to be involved in what happened?'), and evaluative (moral, asking 'Was what happened good or bad?'), and involves recommendations (asking 'What should be done about what happened?').

The distinction among these types of knowledge in any given news item is a matter of context, not syntax (Runciman 1983: 38). The journalist, like the novelist, uses various source clips, including his or her own, as part of a spoken dialogue to sustain a narrative. 'Whatever an individual character may say, its meaning will be determined not by his or her intentions or situation, but by placing of the interview in the overall context of the story. The terms he or she uses may be taken approvingly, or be contradicted and appear to be cynical, short-sighted, or bloody-minded ... All the individual voices, like individual notes in a musical score, are then orchestrated together with the overall news story. The effect of this on the narrative is to provide it with authenticity, the *reality effect*' (Hartley 1982: 109–10).

While the intended effect of the news story is to make consumers believe that they are witnesses to reality, reality is always inferential. What appears as iconic is actually the result of a process in which journalists and sources have necessarily gone beyond the knowledge apprehended by them, reconstructing it in ways that displace the observed world. The reality is that the news is embedded in the criteria of rational acceptability of news practice, and as such it is not mind- or discourse-independent. News discourse is not about objects; it constitutes objects. News reality depends on how the comments of journalists and sources have been contextualized in the narrative, and ultimately on how this contextualization is visualized by the consumer.

This context-dependency means that it is not a straightforward matter to specify what is a fact, explanation, empathetic understanding, evaluation, or recommendation. For example, depending on the context, the word 'inconsiderate' can be used as part of a statement of fact, explanation, evaluation, or prediction (Putnam 1981: 138–9; see also Dworkin 1986). The same can be said for many words that appear regularly in news discourse, including words taken from the discourses of professions that deal with social problems. For example, the psychiatrist's use of 'psychotic' and the sociologist's use of 'exploitation' vary in their knowledge-use, depending on their context within the text. Thus the term 'psychotic' can involve a mere report, an explanation, a prediction, and/or an evaluation (Runciman 1983: 38). As Putnam (1981: 139) observes, 'When we think of facts and values as independent we typically think of "facts" as stated in some physicalistic or bureaucratic jargon, and the "values" as being stated in the most abstract value terms, e.g., "good," "bad." The independence of value from fact is harder to maintain when the facts themselves are of the order of "inconsiderate," "thinks only about himself," "would do anything for money."'

These considerations indicate that even primary (factual) understanding can be polysemous. Reformulation of the factual depends on the methods people use to attribute meaning to the world, including especially the medium formats and language they use for what they observe. A fact cannot be photographed. In examining a photograph, we select certain features and express them in the forms and linguistic terms available to us. All factual empirical statements are entwined with interpretation (in the case of science, see Ryle 1949; Mulkay 1979; Brannigan 1981). In accomplishing primary understanding, the journalist does not simply reproduce the interpretations of his or her sources, he or she gives them a 'constructive interpretation' (Dworkin 1986: esp. chap. 4). That is, his or her interpretations contest and pass judgment on the interpretations of his or her sources. Similarly news consumers engage in 'constructive interpretation,' reading in an interpretation that contests and passes judgment on the interpretations of journalists. We know things only in terms of their significance to us. We always have to propound the world in which our description makes sense (Geertz 1983). Even the simplest facts are differentially interpreted in different contexts (Monaco 1981: 122; Fiske 1987: chap. 5). The reading or interpretation of facts gives them a fictive character, yet such fictions are essential to making sense of a communication and its context. As Crisell (1986: 124) observes with respect to radio, 'however factual the events which the commentator describes, they must be "created" in the listener's mind, very probably in a form which is in many respects different from the reality itself, and are in that sense a "fiction."'

Consider that statements that are descriptive on one level may also be read as evaluative. This is so because the very language we use to describe the world depends on our values (Putnam 1981). Thus descriptive terms may also bear evaluations and yet be assessed as 'fair comment' by journalists. As Hartley (1982: 27) observes, 'the sign *moderate* may be used to denote a politician or union leader, but it also connotes approval of their status and therefore of that individual. Much of the media's attention is devoted to giving people labels that denote their job or status, but these also connote the attitude or value they attach to it. The trick is to make multi-accentual connotation look like uni-accentual denotation.'

Another reason why factual or descriptive statements are read evaluatively is because the facts that people construct are related to the moral conclusions they draw (Midgley 1982). The use of facts in making moral judgments best explains why sources take the news so seriously even though they are very sceptical about its factual accuracy (Ericson, Baranek, and Chan 1989). Sources are sensitive to 'the cultural significance of mass communication for assessment of one's moral qualities by others. In this sense all media reports are sanctionable as public documents and thereby call for an accounting (Scott and Lyman 1968)' (Altheide 1985: 192). The news is taken seriously because of its moral power, not because it is the best available source of primary facts.

The news media frequently value the facts through tertiary (emotional, empathetic) understanding, addressing the question, 'What is it like to be involved in what happened?' Sources provide 'emotional exhibitions' (Wagner-Pacifici 1986: 95) as part of the performance of their authority and how they wish others to value the facts of what happened. Television and radio have greater scope in this regard, including the use of emotive music on radio and emotive music and visuals on television (Epstein 1974: 242; Crisell 1986; Carriere and Ericson 1989: chap. 3). In the extreme, tertiary knowledge is a synthetic creation of sources and journalists that can intrude on or even extinguish other knowledge potentially available in the news item. When this occurs the news consumer is left with the feeling that 'we had the experience but missed the meaning' (T.S. Eliot, quoted by Gitlin 1980: 233).

The valuing of facts is also a matter of medium. News accounts involve technologically mediated metaphorical reconstructions that emphasize particular emotions and social and political realities. For example, on television 'an apparently direct or iconic representation of reality is more accurately a metaphorical reconstitution of that reality in the terms of the television medium. The similarity we perceive between signifier and signified should be thought of as a *constructed equivalence*; the metaphoric real world shown on television does not *display* the real world but *displaces* it' (Fiske and Hartley 1978: 48).

In contributing to the valuing of facts, each medium thus bears ideological functions (Elliott 1979; Altheide 1985; Meyrowitz 1985). 'For example, TV news information has a certain look and rhythm to it. As long as this is associated with news and the contexts of these special effects are not exploited, then it looks fine, complete, good enough, even true ... [It] can be regarded as a feature of rational ideology in its own right, and, therefore, is far more persuasive and consequential than run-of-the-mill political preferences' (Altheide 1985: 234). The medium itself takes on a familiar, credible, authoritative character that makes the knowledge it presents seem acceptable, as if what it offers is all that one needs to know. This ideological power of a medium can transcend political and economic power in framing how people see events and in influencing actions taken in relation to those events (ibid: 71ff; Meyrowitz 1985; Ericson, Baranek, and Chan 1987, 1989).

Market Differences

News formats, sources, and knowledge also vary in accordance with the market orientation of media organizations. Newspapers in particular pursue distinct markets. 'Popular' newspapers seek acceptance through seeming to be close to reality. Their formats thus incorporate iconic elements, including pictures, brief items on simple themes, strongly opinionated columns on simple themes, colloquial expressions, and parochial interests. These elements are combined in an entertaining and lively manner. The presentation of material in an entertaining manner does not contradict the sense of being close to reality, but rather underpins it. Playing on the heart, and on lower regions of the anatomy, popular newspapers are able to effect a sense of what it is 'really' like to be involved in a situation. Material that is lively also seems 'alive,' and thus real.

'Quality' newspapers, by contrast, seek acceptance through more 'literary' and symbolic means. Their formats include longer items, features, and continuing stories on complex matters affecting business and political élites on a national and international scale. There is a concern with being a source of record both at the moment and historically, resulting in close attention to language and to mechanisms for correcting errors that exhume accuracy and authority.

There are also newspapers that try to encompass both ends of the spectrum, to be all things to all people. For example, in Toronto, while the *Sun* is explicitly a popular newspaper and the *Globe and Mail* is explicitly a quality newspaper, the *Star* is a mass newspaper that includes elements of both and is read *in addition to* the others (RCN 1981c: 70–1). Instead of finding a particular limited niche in the market, the mass newspaper tries to be the market itself.

An appeal to the mass market is more characteristic of broadcast media, especially television, because of their medium formats. There is particular pressure on broadcast outlets to appear popular when advertising revenue is a consideration. For reasons we shall outline shortly, and document in substantive chapters that follow, television news is least able to offer distinct popular and quality products. However, as Crisell (1986: 48–9) has shown, there is scope within radio to make news distinctly popular or quality in character.

FORMATS

The need to sell markets leads to particular news formats. News that is relatively discursive, and unadorned with sensational and dramatic constructions, fails to hold readers and therefore fails to sell goods (Seaton 1980: 96–7). Hence news, like the advertising system that supports it, moves in the direction of non-discursive, entertaining formats of presentation. Fifty years ago the Gallup organization discovered that 'more people read comic strips than the news,' and this 'led advertisers to exploit emotional symbols and techniques' (Draper 1986: 15). The success of this exploitation in advertising has had a recursive influence on news producers who use the techniques of advertising to hold their readers for advertising. For example, the news focus on sensational crimes is in part explained by their entertainment value. A survey of newspapers in Ontario found that the greater the advertising space in the newspaper the greater the emphasis on crime news (Dussuyer 1979: 100). A television news producer informed us that 'news must be packaged in a glittering way so that viewers who have just finished watching Carol Burnett will stay tuned for the news. In noting that the 'Newshour' rating had gone up to 24 per cent of the audience in the previous eighteen months, this producer observed that Kellogg's does not spend most of its money on cornflakes, but rather on the cornflakes box' (Ericson, Baranek, and Chan 1987: 86).

Advertising offers no opportunity for assessing products on the basis of truth claims. Its claims are neither true nor false, just more interesting or less interesting, more imaginative or less imaginative, more beautiful or less beautiful. Television news in particular takes on these characteristics of advertising. It offers brief clips that show people making claims to authority, knowledge, and doing good, but this is largely presentational and non-discursive and as such does not allow for judgments of truth (Meyrowitz 1985; Postman 1985). Viewed this way, news is indeed a 'social hallucinogen' for a commercial culture in which the 'boundaries between news, entertainment, public relations and advertising, always fluid historically, are now becoming almost invisible' (D. Schiller 1986: 36, 21).

Advertising affects news organizations in other ways. In at least one newspaper chain in Canada, favourable news treatment for advertisers has been reinforced by promoting advertising managers to the publisher's chair and to other senior and influential positions that affect editorial content (RCN 1981b: 69; RCN 1981c: 100). People in the news business, of course, appreciate that news and advertising are entwined. For example, in commenting on a newspaper's decision to refuse two advertisements, the Ontario Press Council declared, 'Advertising is a form of news and the paper has a responsibility to publish advertising news whether it agrees with it or not' (RCN 1981b: 77). Ask an academic colleague why he bought a copy of the local popular newspaper and he will tell you that it has the best selection of advertisements for stereo equipment.

Distinctive quality and popular news products, and the organizational differences associated with them, may be more applicable to radio news, and especially to newspapers, than to television news. Research has shown repeatedly that television news production and products are similar. Epstein (1974) reported no substantial differences in the approach and coverage of the three national television networks in the United States, and the Glasgow University Group (1976) reported similarities in industrial news coverage among the BBC1, BBC2, and ITN channels in Britain. A study of television news comparing Ireland, Sweden, and Nigeria (Golding and Elliott 1979) concluded that there was a 'broad similarity of news production practices and of the news values embodied in the output of these three quite diverse societies, despite the distinctive relationships of broadcasting to the state in each case. The study presented broadcast news as an "international genre" with significant national variations, and argued for an understanding of news as ideology, in its emphasis upon consensus, in its alignment with the assumptions and preoccupations of the powerful, and on its inherent inability to provide "a portrayal of social change" or to reveal "the operation of power within and between societies"' (Golding, Murdock, and Schlesinger 1986: 4–5). These findings suggest that the format requirements of the television medium may predominate in limiting the range of what it is possible to present (Altheide 1985).

The format limitations of the television medium are a major reason why television news is directed at a mass audience. A newspaper can build its readership by appealing to an aggregate of minorities, each of whom will select and read only particular sections and items from the total volume available in the newspaper. Television must do the selecting of items for its audience and hold its attention through the newscast. Therefore television includes material that is attractive to the widest possible range of people, which means an appeal to the lowest-common-denominator mass audience. Whereas individual newspapers are assumed to be the competing parts of the market, individual broadcasters are assumed to be the market-place itself' (Epstein 1974: 64). Competition is for a share of the total audience – people with their television sets on during a time segment – rather than for a share of a more specialized or narrow market. Television has the greatest capacity for this popular appeal because of its pictorial strength, sense of realism, and simple language. Television news is accessible to virtually everyone, including young children (Meyrowitz 1985: chap. 13). The popular formula of dramatic, entertaining, simple, and short items is adopted by television journalists to fulfil the competitive requirements for audience share, and form takes precedence over content (Elliott 1978, 1979). Hence television journalists converge on similar topics, sources and story angles, and the popular/quality distinction is blurred.

Some of the format requirements of radio create a popular tendency in its newscasts. Like their counterparts in television, radio journalists must select items for their listeners, and hold their attention through the newscast with limited language and dramatic structuring. This means that radio news shows are relatively short and each item is brief; that coverage focuses on dramatic events and conflict; and that such techniques as alternating voices and sound actualities are used to strengthen the auditory appeal. These components combine to enhance the listener's ability to visualize what is being said, to make the radio news story as 'photographic' as it can be without the actual capacity to present a visual.

In spite of these tendencies, the radio medium does not preclude a quality orientation. Radio cannot be like the quality press. Its language is not that of the quality London *Times* or Toronto *Globe and Mail.* Because it is auditory, radio news must use a more limited vocabulary and a less complicated syntax than the *Times* or *Globe and Mail.* But neither is radio language that of the popular English *Sun* or Toronto *Sun.* Radio news has a greater need for a more objective, and a less individualistic, emotive, and opinionated tone than popular newspapers exhibit.

Crisell's (1986: chap. 4) detailed comparison of a popular newscast and a quality newscast, both emanating from the BBC radio network, shows clearly that the popular/quality distinction holds for radio. In language, presentation, content, and some aspects of format, popular and quality radio newscasts are very different. 'For all the linguistic compression which the medium imposes, its inability to editorialize and its need to use its voices not only for reportage but also as actuality, radio news does succeed to a remarkable extent in paralleling and evoking the differences between the popular and quality newspapers' (ibid: 99). For example, Crisell's analysis shows that in the popular radio outlet he studied, the newscast is presented as an enclave within an existing entertainment (pop music) show. It therefore tends to assimilate news to the wider broadcasting context of its entertainment programming. This assimilation is indicated, for example, by the title for the show – 'Newsbeat' – and by the fact that the show frequently ends with an item on pop music, such as an interview with a pop star. This packaging is based on the assumption that people listen to the station for the music, not the news, and so the news is in essence made part of a 'newsic' formula. In contrast the quality radio outlet studied by Crisell has a more discrete, self-contained, and much longer news show. The news show is therefore a program in its own right, rather than, in effect, an extended news summary. It is presented with greater detail and complexity on the assumption that people tune in because they want news, that they are seeking knowledge and detail rather than merely the station's 'sound.'

The format of newspapers allows their journalists to focus on various special interests, and thereby to increase circulation through the aggregate of interest groups who buy it for their particular purposes. Alternatively, newspapers can tailor their coverage to the interests of a single narrow or specialized group, who can be sold to advertisers whose products and services are of special interest to the group. These possibilities exist in particular because the newspaper is capable of linguistic variety, has a permanency to its language, and provides the self-pacing such permanency allows. The basic distinction is between the popular newspaper which is simple in structure and colloquial in its use of vocabulary, and gives more emphasis to emotive or tertiary understanding, and the quality newspaper, which tends towards great complexity in structure, 'literary' use of vocabulary, and primary and secondary (explanatory) understanding presented in an 'objective' tone.

While newspapers retain these flexible features of their format, there have been encroachments on the autonomy of their formats from the broadcast media, especially from television. All newspaper journalists have been affected by how television formats dominate particular beats, such as the legislature (RCN 1981b: 135; Meyrowitz 1985; Ericson, Baranek, and Chan 1989). They have also been affected by the peculiar conception of objectivity fostered in broadcast news, where an allegation is quoted from one source, a counterpoint is made by a spokesperson for the organization subject to the allegation, and truth is held to reside somewhere in between (Epstein 1974; Tuchman 1978; Ericson, Baranek, and Chan 1987). This approach has increased the expectation of impartiality in all media and has made the bias of newspapers appear increasingly improper (A. Smith 1980: 179).

Popular newspapers in particular have changed in tune with television formats. They are explicitly formatted in terms of television, and serve as a complement to television. The Toronto *Sun* has been described as the closest thing to television in print. Various executives in popular newspaper organizations have acknowledged the impact of television. 'John Hamilton, publisher of the Calgary *Albertan* at the time it was converted into a tabloid in 1977, said "Our format of tight editing rules related to young people brought up on television. They're used to brief presentation of news." Pierre Péladeau, whose two daily tabs have half Canada's tabloid circulation and enjoyed the fast growth of any Canadian newspaper in the 1970s, sees them as a complement to television' (RCN 1981b: 82). Entwined with this influence of television on newspaper formats is television's impact on newspaper marketing. The growth of life-style, entertainment, and sports sections of newspapers is associated with the spread of television, as is the 'zoning' of special supplements within a newspaper to different market areas. More fundamentally, television has become predominant in framing and demarcating the market that newspapers must feed into. 'The modern newspaper is essentially reaching out towards the *television* audience, a demographically defined audience, paid for by advertisers, which requires the kind of detail that turns into spectacle or reveals the panorama of events lying behind the reports that have already reached the audience in aural and/or visual terms' (A. Smith 1980: 241).

SOURCES

Market considerations, blended with media format requirements, have a substantial influence on the selection and use of sources.

Given their tendency towards non-discursive, entertaining, and simple accounts of events, outlets oriented to the popular market are likely to use fewer sources. They are also likely to rely more heavily on particular types of sources offering particular types of knowledge: officials who provide them with primary facts already formatted for their medium/market, and individual citizens who offer tertiary understanding that fits their 'vox pop' format.

The subtleties and nuances of source selection and use vary with the local market environment. In large urban markets with dozens of news outlets, there is sometimes a condition of 'overproduction.' This condition leads news outlets to pursue more unique stories with unofficial or minority-status sources in an effort to capture at least some of the market seeming to be different.

Advertising is a major factor in source selection. Those who advertise regularly are often given favourable treatment in news items and features about the wonders of their company and its products. This is especially the case with smaller, local newspapers and radio stations, and with feature sections of large newspapers such as those dealing with entertainment, travel, and real estate (RCN 1981b: 69; RCN 1981c: 100). Private-sector sources themselves treat the news accordingly, seeing access primarily in terms of their own marketing needs (Ericson, Baranek, and Chan 1989).

Sources in government are also oriented to their own marketing needs, blending news with advertising in the hope that the public will remain faithful to the belief that they are good public servants. However, with sources in government there is not a crude exchange of advertising revenue for news space that serves marketing functions, but rather a tit-for-tat subtle favouritism with particular outlets because their formats best fit the source's needs (Ericson, Baranek, and Chan 1989). For example, the police favour popular news outlets because these outlets offer a format suitable for communication of the primary facts of major occurrences at the core of police-defined newsworthiness (Ericson 1989; Wheeler 1986; Fishman 1981; Chibnall 1977). The police shy away from quality outlets because these outlets largely eschew the reporting of crime incidents in favour of a focus on police mismanagement and procedural propriety. Moreover, quality outlets, especially quality newspapers, search out a greater number of sources and a more diverse range of source types, and present them more discursively to make innuendo about police deviance. The police therefore perceive quality news outlets as a threat rather than as an ally, and erect different physical, social, and cultural barriers to the access of journalists from quality outlets than is accorded to journalists from popular outlets (Ericson 1989). The different needs of news sources and news organizations in terms of media/market format considerations are clearly reflected in content.

KNOWLEDGE

The news media have always been criticized for pandering to their readership to create and sustain a market share. John Stuart Mill described journalism as 'the vilest and most degrading of all trades because more of affection and hypocrisy and more subservience to the basic feelings of others are necessary for carrying it on, than for any other trade, from that of a brothel-keeper up.' In recent times there are complaints that journalism is done by market survey (RCN 1981b): deciphering what news readers want to fit with their 'life-styles,' which can in turn be linked to 'life-style' advertising. While reporters have little detailed knowledge of their readership (Schlesinger 1978; D. Clarke 1981; Ericson, Baranek, and Chan 1987), editors' expectations are framed by market considerations and they assign and edit accordingly (Seaton 1980). Hence news outlets with the same market orientation are likely to cover the same events, to talk to the same most influential sources involved in those events, and to formulate stories in similar terms. The result is pack journalism and convergence in news content.

These forces of convergence can also foster divergence. For example, the ascendancy of broadcast media has been accompanied by an advertising-driven need to appeal to a mass audience. In face of this need some newspapers try to appeal to a more limited readership that is attractive to particular advertisers. For example, quality newspapers take up an investigative and adversarial style that articulates with the institutional concerns of upscale readers who in turn are a market for upscale advertisers. The *Globe and Mail* has evolved to such a place within the Toronto news-media market. While finding a market niche in these terms leads to divergence in topics and sources on one level, on another level the product may not be different from more popular renditions of news. The popular news outlet continues its traditional formula identified by Mill, using salacious gossip, titillation, and sensationalism to allow its readers to be vicarious voyeurs, and then denouncing the very people and activities it preys upon (Roshier 1973). The quality news outlet does the same thing, only its targets are those prostituting themselves for the high life in established institutions (political corruption) more than those engaged in the low life of illicit prostitutions (vice and 'normal crime').

Ultimately the market orientation a news outlet tries to find for itself combines with its medium-format consideration to yield a distinct process of knowledge flow, system of knowledge, and type of knowledge. The popular format is characteristic of all television outlets because of medium considerations, and is chosen by particular radio and newspaper outlets for marketing purposes. It features particular knowledge: factual updating (largely bureaucratic constructs), evaluation and tertiary understanding (largely from the people as 'vox pop'), both of which are personalized and dramatized. Enclosed in these terms, the popular format is preferred by particular sources, especially the police, politicians, and others whose primary interest is helpful news and positive images (Ericson, Baranek, and Chan 1989). The quality format suits particular newspapers and radio outlets, but is available to television in a more limited way because of medium constraints. The quality news outlet features a more discursive presentation of knowledge: multiple institutional sources who offer greater depth in the form of explanation of events as well as evaluations and recommendations pertaining to legal change and political reform. Relatively more open in these terms, the quality format is preferred by particular sources, especially those who can benefit from particular instances of adversarial-style journalism to bring about the legal changes and political reforms they desire.

The market orientation a news outlet finds for itself also combines with its medium-format considerations to lead it in particular ideological directions. Popular news outlets tend towards strong ideological positions that are stated explicitly. For example, in their everyday crime reporting, they are strongly pro-police and pro–law and order; in their everyday international reporting they are strongly nationalistic and anti-communist. Quality news outlets offer their ideologies more gently. They appear more liberal, offering a greater number and wider range of sources and opinions, arriving at a particular ideological position only after a managed dialogue and debate.

Sources of Convergence

Our emphasis in this chapter has been on differences in media and market orientation of news outlets as these differences have a bearing on news formats, sources, knowledge, and topics. The emphasis on differences has provided an analytical starting-point for our empirical inquiry into how news of crime, law, and justice varies by medium and markets. However, we would be remiss if we failed to give weight to the many influences on news production that may yield similar news content across media and markets. We have already indicated some sources of convergence, including the important point that some factors that precipitate differences can also serve in contradictory ways to produce convergence. At this point it is worthwhile to make the sources of convergence more evident as they inform the empirical investigation that follows.

> We have the greatest, most sophisticated system for mass communication of any society that we know about, yet somehow mass communication becomes more and more synonymous with less communication ... We have the mistaken, conduit-metaphor influenced view that the more signals we can create, and the more signals we can preserve, the more ideas we 'transfer' and 'store.' We neglect the crucial human ability to reconstruct thought patterns on the basis of signals and this ability founders ... The conduit metaphor is leading us down a technological and social blind alley. That blind alley is mass communications systems coupled with mass neglect of the internal, human systems responsible for nine-tenths of the work in communicating. We think we are 'capturing ideas in words,' and funnelling them out to the greatest public in the history of the world. But if there are no ideas 'within' this endless flood of words then all we are doing is replaying the myth of Babel – centering it, this time, around a broadcasting tower. (Reddy 1979: 310)

Reddy articulates a pervasive sentiment that more media outlets have not brought better knowledge, and may be narrowing and trivializing public discourse (see also Postman 1985). In spite of the capabilities of each medium, and the competitive quest of news outlets for a different product that will secure a niche in the market-place, if anything the proliferation of news outlets may offer less diversity, not more. Why does the large urban news market-place – like the beer market-place or the automobile market-place – offer such a rich variety of brand names and yet end up being so bland?

One answer lies in monopoly capitalism and its relation to markets. In the case of newspapers, chains have become increasingly dominant, at least in the North American context (A. Smith 1980: 45–6; RCN 1981b: 9). The effect of the advertising-based chain monopolies has been to encourage journalism's peculiar version of objectivity, neutrality, and fairness, where overt and diverse opinion is reduced and blandness is produced. 'The professional code of the editor, and journalists as a whole, has been profoundly influenced by the evolution of the distribution methods of newspapers and their successive delineations of appropriate markets' (A. Smith 1979: 193). While 'narrowcasting' has expanded in recent years, the attitude in broadcasting is still " 'Least Objectionable Programming" (LOP). That is, the key is to design a program that is least likely to be turned *off*, rather than a program viewers will activity seek out' (Meyrowitz 1985: 73). Even the Public Broadcasting System in the United States is dependent on corporate donors and therefore tends towards programming that will not offend and that is lacking in political relevance. It is difficult to show a direct link between advertising and particular features of news content. However, it is revealing that readers perceive the news as having been influenced by news organizations catering to advertisers. In survey research conducted for the Royal Commission on Newspapers (1981b: 36–7), 72 per cent of respondents said they believed newspapers play down facts in news items that might offend advertisers.

News outlets operating with different market orientations but within the same medium may converge in their coverage because of medium-format requirements. As addressed earlier (pp. 37–8), the format requirements of television make television-news production and products very similar, not only between outlets within a local market, but also between national networks and even in international comparisons. Television outlets compete head-on for a share of the total audience rather than dividing up into more narrow or specialized markets, and this inevitably leads all outlets into the popular formula of dramatic, entertaining, short, and simple items which are, in any event, most suited to the medium.

The impact of one medium upon another medium is also a source of convergence. As considered previously (pp. 39–40), television has had a major impact on newspapers. Some popular newspapers are explicitly formatted as the closest thing to television in print. They emphasize the visual, with display headlines, still photographs, and captions in bold type taking up more space in a story than the written narrative. More broadly, television has had a fundamental impact on newspaper marketing, essentially framing and demarcating the market that newspapers feed into.

Practices in news production also foster convergence. The knowledgeability of journalists – the norms, values, and precedents of the craft – leads them to focus on similar topics, sources, and angles regardless of the medium or market orientation of their news organization (Schlesinger 1978; Tuchman 1978; Ericson, Baranek, and Chan 1987). The journalist's 'nose' for news seems to be the same, even if the details of what is required for each medium and market vary. It is the shared knowledgeability of journalists that leads to 'pack journalism': reporters covering news conferences, public hearings such as court cases or legislative proceedings, and continuing stories such as election campaigns, tend to focus on similar angles, use the same sources, and even reproduce the same 'quotable quotes.' It is as if journalists sometimes do no more than reflect a reality that is self-evident, at least to them. It is as if all that is required is to send one reporter to scoop up the facts, while the rest can simply polish them off and turn them into the symbolic gems required by their particular medium and market.

Pack journalism is compounded by the fact that journalists view existing news stories as their primary source of knowledge about newsworthiness (ibid). Broadcast journalists in particular rely on newspaper stories for their own ideas and assignments, with the result that 'newspapers are more of a source than a competitor' (Schlesinger 1978: 85). At some *n*th-level removed from what they are reporting on, broadcast journalists use newspaper reports verbatim, as background detail that they cite without attribution, for matching stories suitable to their medium, and as second-day leads that seek to further the story through a different angle, or at least a different twist. 'Newsmen come to see the print media as purveyors of *original* material while radio and TV extend or recirculate information, in the form of current affairs discussion or follow-up interviews. So newsmen turn to print media for information, and strengthen the pattern of dependence' (RCN 1981a: 2). As far as journalists are concerned, it is as if all one really needs to know is contained in the news, and one's only job is to repackage it in the different containers available in one's medium and market to make it appear new.

These journalistic practices are related to resources. The fewer the resources of a news outlet, the more it is dependent on a predictable supply of material from source bureaucracies and from other news outlets, and the greater the number of steps it is removed from the events reported on. Among the news media, radio stations tend to have the least journalistic resources and therefore are most dependent in this regard. Television stations are in an intermediate position, while newspapers have the most journalistic resources. Thus radio, with least resources, produces fewer items, shorter items, and more simple items that reproduce the bare essentials of stories as framed by sources and/or by previous newspaper stories. However, the limited aspects of radio news are not only a matter of resources. The radio medium is restrictive to the point where it may not be worthwhile for a radio organization to multiply the resources of its news division. Increased resources might not enhance its product greatly, and may even have a negative impact; for example, long items with multiple sources on complex matters might lead people to switch off mentally or literally.

A limited budget and therefore circumscribed content are characteristic of popular news outlets more than of quality news outlets. However, this is not a straightforward matter. For example, in our observation of the court beat in Toronto, we discovered that a popular newspaper and a quality newspaper each devoted limited resources to the beat, especially in comparison to a mass-market newspaper. As a result, the reporter for the quality newspaper and the reporters for the popular newspaper helped each other routinely, exchanging cases to cover, story angles and ideas, quotations from sources, and basic factual details. There was no similar exchange with reporters from the mass-market newspaper. The exchanges resulted in a convergence in coverage between the popular and quality newspapers (Ericson, Baranek, and Chan 1989: chap. 2).

Sources are another point of convergence (ibid). By restricting reporters to particular times and places, and by enclosing on knowledge, sources can effectively circumscribe news stories to a narrow range so that 'pack journalism' is the only possible outcome. While particular sources may favour particular media and markets on particular occasions, on other occasions they may offer a news release to all outlets, so that the only choice for those outlets is to report what everyone else has or not report at all.

In summary, there is a large number of medium and market considerations that yield both convergence and divergence in news coverage. We keep these considerations in mind as we embark upon our empirical investigation into how news formats, sources, topics, and knowledge vary across different media and markets. In this chapter, we have raised many of the relevant issues through an overview of the current state of knowledge. In the next chapter, we crystallize this overview into questions for research, and then describe the research project we designed to address them.

46a

References

Altheide, D. 1985. *Media Power.* Beverly Hills: Sage
Barthes, R. 1977. *Image – Music – Text,* trans. S. Heath. Glasgow: Fontana
Bates, A. 1984. *Broadcasting in Education.* London: Constable
Brannigan, A. 1981. *The Social Basis of Scientific Discoveries.* Cambridge: Cambridge University Press
Cardiff, D. 1980. 'The Serious and the Popular: Aspects of the Evolution of Style in Radio Talk:, 1928–1939,' *Media, Culture and Society* 2.
Carriere, K., and R. Ericson. 1989. *Crime Stoppers: A Study in the Organization of Community Policing.* Toronto: Centre of Criminology, University of Toronto
Cayley, D. 1982. 'Making Sense of the News,' *Sources,* Spring: 126–8, 130–3, 136–7
Chibnall, S. 1977. *Law-and-Order News.* London: Tavistock
Clarke, D. 1981. 'Second-Hand News: Production and Reproduction at a Major Ontario Television Station,' in L. Salter, ed., *Communication Studies in Canada,* pp. 20–51. Toronto: Butterworths
Crisell, A. 1986. *Understanding Radio.* London: Methuen
Draper, R. 1986. 'The Faithless Shepherd,' *New York Review of Books,* 26 June, pp. 14–18
Dussuyer, I. 1979. *Crime News: A Study of 40 Ontario Newspapers.* Toronto: Centre of Criminology, University of Toronto
Dworkin, R. 1986. *Law's Empire.* Cambridge, Mass.: Harvard University Press
Elliott, P. 1978'. 'Professional Ideology and Organizational Change: The Journalist since 1800,' in G. Boyce et al., *Newspaper History.* London: Constable
– 1979. 'Media Organizations and Occupations: An Overview,' in 1. Curran, ed., *Mass Communication and Society,* pp. 142–73. Beverly Hills: Sage
Epstein, E. 1974. *News from Nowhere.* New York: Vintage
Ericson, R. 1989. 'Patrolling the Facts: Secrecy and Publicity in Police Work,' *British Journal of Sociology* 40: 205–26
Ericson, R., P. Baranek, and J. Chan. 1987. *Visualizing Deviance: A Study of News Organization.* Toronto: University of Toronto Press; Milton Keynes: Open University Press
– 1989. *Negotiating Control: A Study of News Sources.* Toronto: University of Toronto Press; Milton Keynes: Open University Press
Fishman, M. 1981. 'Police News: Constructing an Image of Crime,' *Urban Life* 9: 371–94

46b

Fiske. J, 1987. *Television Culture.* London: Methuen
Fiske, J., and J. Hartley. 1978. *Reading Television.* London: Methuen
Geertz, C. 1983. *Local Knowledge.* New York: Basic Books
Gitlin, T. 1980. *The Whole World Is Watching.* Berkeley: University of California Press
Glasgow University Media Group. 1976. *Bad News.* London: Routledge
Goffman, E. 1981. *Forms of Talk.* Philadelphia: University of Pennsylvania
Golding, P., and P. Elliott 1979. *Making the News.* London: Longman
Golding, P., G. Murdock, and P. Schlesinger. 1986. *Communicating Politics: Mass Communications and the Political Process.* Leicester: University of Leicester Press
Hartley, J. 1982. *Understanding News.* London: Methuen
McWhinnie, D. 1959. *The Art of Radio.* London: Faber and Faber
Meyrowitz, J. 1985. *No Sense of Place: The Impact of Electronic Media on Social Behavior.* New York: Oxford University Press
Midgley, M. 1982. 'Moral Melodrama,' *Times Higher Education Supplement,* 16 April, p. 10
Monaco, J. 1981. *How to Read a Film: The Art, Technology, Language. History and Theory of Film and Media.* Oxford: Oxford University Press
Mulkay, M. 1979. *Science and the Sociology of Knowledge.* London: Allen and Unwin
Paulu, B. 1981. *Television and Radio in the United Kingdom.* London: Macmillan
Pietropaolo, D. 1982. 'Structuring "Truth": The Uses of Drama in "Information" Radio,' *Canadian Theatre Review* 36: 52–6
Postman, N. 1985. *Amusing Ourselves to Death: Public Discourse in the Age of Show Business.* New York: Viking
Putnam, H. 1981. *Reason, Truth, and History.* Cambridge: Cambridge University Press
Reddy, M. 1979. 'The Conduit Metaphor – A Case of Frame Conflict in Our Language about Language,' in A. Ortony, ed., *Metaphor and Thought,* pp. 284–310. Cambridge: Cambridge University Press
Robinson, J., and M. Levy. 1986. *The Main Source: Learning from Television News.* Beverly Hills: Sage
Roshier, B. 1973. 'The Selection of Crime News by the Press,' in S. Cohen and J. Young, eds., *The Manufacture of News,* pp. 28–39. London: Constable
Royal Commission on Newspapers. 1981a. *Canadian News Sources.* Ottawa: Research Studies on the Newspaper Industry, Supply and Services Canada
– 1981b. *Final Report.* Ottawa: Supply and Services Canada
– 1981c. *The Journalists.* Ottawa: Research Studies on the Newspaper Industry, Supply and Services Canada

46c

– 1981g. *Newspapers and Their Readers.* Ottawa: Research Studies on the Newspaper Industry, Supply and Services Canada

Runciman, W.G. 1983. *A Treatise on Social Theory.* Vol. 1: *The Methodology of Social Theory.* Cambridge: Cambridge University Press

Ryle, G. 1949. *The Concept of Mind.* London: Hutchinson

Schiller, D. 1986. 'Transformations of News in the u.s. Information Market,' in P. Golding, G. Murdock, and P. Schlesinger, eds., *Communicating Politics,* pp. 19–36. Leicester: Leicester University Press

Schlesinger, P. 1978. *Putting Reality Together: BBC News.* London: Constable

– 1988. 'Rethinking the Sociology of Journalism: Source Strategies and the Limits of Media Centrism.' Paper to the Economic and Social Research Council Workshop on Classic Issues of Mass Communication Research, Madingley Hall, Cambridge

– 1989. 'Crime and Mass Media: Theoretical Issues.' Paper to the British Criminology Conference, Bristol

Scott, M., and S. Lyman. 1968. 'Accounts,' *American Sociological Review* 33: 46–62

Seaton, J. 1980. 'Politics and Television,''Economy *and Society* 9: 90–107

Silvey, R. 1974. *Who's Listening?* London: Allen and Unwin

Smith, A. 1979. 'Technology and Control: The Interactive Dimensions of Journalism,' in J. Curran et al., eds., *Mass Communication and Society,* pp. 174–94. Beverly Hills: Sage

– 1980. *Goodbye Gutenberg: The Newspaper Revolution of the 1980s.* New York: Oxford University Press

Tuchman, G. 1978. *Making News.* New York: Free Press

Wagner-Pacifici, R. 1986. *The Moro Morality Play: Terrorism as Social Drama.* Chicago: University of Chicago Press

Wheeler, G. 1986. 'Reporting Crime: The News Release as Textual Mediator of Police/Media Relations,' MA thesis, Centre of Criminology, University of Toronto

Williams, R. 1989. *Raymond Williams on Television: Selected Writings.* Toronto: Between the Lines

[8]
How Journalists Visualize Fact

ABSTRACT: Fact is a product of the communication practices of journalists. Journalists rarely have the resources or access to penetrate their sources' informational worlds to establish facts independently. Moreover, the norms of objectivity in journalism often preclude efforts to establish facts independent of sources' accounts. Therefore, journalists visualize the fact value of a story on the basis of a source's face value as an authoritative, normative witness to events. While television visuals offer a greater capacity for believability, the need for an orderly visual narrative leads to staged news events, retakes, reenactments, use of stock footage, and other fakes. These communication practices blur distinctions between fact, value, information, and knowledge and have literary properties. Like literary fiction, news requires the willing suspension of disbelief in order to have its knowledge accepted. This important literary character of news may be fading as the news institution breaks down into segmented markets and specialized information services.

COMMUNICATION does not stand apart from reality. There is not, first, reality and then, second, communication about it. Communication participates in the formation and change of reality.

VISUALIZING FACT

Fact—defined simply as that which is accepted as reality—is an artifact of communication practices. People use communication media (Thompson 1995; Altheide 1995), language (Meyrowitz 1994), trust (Luhmann 1979; Mistzal 1996), and institutions (Ericson 1991, 1994) to make facts, understand, organize experience, and take action. They produce facts, information, and knowledge as a capacity for action (Stehr and Ericson 1992).

There is no real distinction between facts, information, and knowledge. They are all a result of interpretation through communication practices that give them meaning in the contexts of their use. This view differs sharply from statements such as the following one by Bell (1985):

> Information is news, facts, statistics, reports, legislation, tax-codes, judicial decisions, resolutions, and the like, and it is quite obvious that we have had an "explosion" of these. . . . But that is not necessarily (or even usually) knowledge. Knowledge is interpretation in context, exegesis, relatedness, and conceptualization, the form of argument. (17)

News and other "information" designated by Bell are indeed knowledge, in his own sense that they have been interpreted in context and given particular meanings. They may be given different meanings as they are transformed and used in additional contexts, but that does not make them knowledge in the additional contexts as distinct from information or fact in the original context. They are knowledge in all contexts, in the sense of being given an objectivated, real meaning that is used in action and has social consequences.

Visualizing is a concept that captures the communication practices of journalists as they make facts. Through the accounts of journalists and their sources, facts are made visible in the minds of audience members even if they are not visible to their eyes. News accounts visualize what happened, why it happened, what it was like to be involved, what should be done about it, and whether any or all of this is good or bad.

The focus on what is good or bad means that a great deal of what journalists visualize is deviance: the behavior of a thing or person straying from the norm. Deviance is a defining characteristic of what journalists regard as newsworthy and, as such, becomes inextricably linked with their communication practices. Deviance and control are not only woven into the seamless web of news reporting but are actually part of its fiber: they define not only the object and central character of news stories as morality plays but also the methodological approaches of journalists as they work on their stories (Ericson, Baranek, and Chan 1987).

In visualizing deviance, journalists inevitably blend fact and value. The norm is a factual standard established with the help of science, such as a risk threshold regarding environmental pollution or a dangerous offender. But the norm is also a powerful ethical constraint, so that any declaration of a factual standard also bears the imprint of moral evaluation. Journalists are perpetually making up normal people and normal events as a touchstone for evaluating the human condition, using "a power as old as Aristotle to bridge the fact/value distinction, whispering in your ear that what is normal is also all right" (Hacking 1990, 170).

The journalist proceeds like a fiction writer, imaginatively construing the facts as they fit the communication practices of news. His or her main task is to quote sources' accounts of events, behaviors, and documents that are not made visible otherwise. This is the case even in television, as journalists and their sources mainly give talking-head accounts of the facts rather than being everywhere as an eyewitness to reality as it happens (Glasgow University Media Group 1976; Ericson, Baranek, and Chan 1991). The journalist-as-novelist imagines typical demands on organizations and their key actors on a particular occasion, and then proceeds through questioning or listening to choose interview quotations and to construct factuality. The story is told in terms of his or her sense of what the sources represent in the roles in which they have been socially cast, carrying on the ancient tradition of Thucydides as enunciated in the *Peloponnesian War*:

> It was in all cases difficult to carry [speeches] word-for-word in one's memory, so my habit has been to make the speakers say what was in my opinion demanded of them by the various occasions: of course adhering as closely as possible to the general sense of what was said.

In summary, journalism has a set of communication practices that blur the distinction between fact, information, and knowledge, collapse fact and value, and have literary properties. Examination of specific communication practices in journalism reveals the fact of fiction in news but also how fiction nevertheless provides knowledge as a capacity for action.

CREDIBLE SOURCES

Journalists establish factuality by using credible sources who make statements that can be quoted as fact without further investigation. The journalist rarely has the time, material resources, or access to penetrate the source's back region informational world to establish the facts independently (Fishman 1980; Schlesinger 1987; Ericson, Baranek, and Chan 1989). Moreover, as will be addressed, the peculiar norms of objectivity in journalism often preclude efforts to establish facts independent of sources' accounts. The journalist must establish the fact value of a story on the basis of a source's face value as a normative witness to events.

The credibility of sources is established through institutionalized forms of authority and knowledge. Sources are typically predetermined as authorized knowers by the source organization itself, within its own hierarchy of credibility. The source organization selects the best person to represent its interests in the news event, regardless of whether that person is in the best position to know the facts of the matter. Journalists also turn to those with expert knowledge and experiential knowledge in the field in question, and to official bodies without a direct stake in a conflict. As a result, news represents political power as residing in formal institutions, such as electoral politics, legislatures, and law enforcement agencies. This emphasis tends to erase other powerful groups, such as private sector corporations that wish to stay out of the news (Golding, Murdock, and Schlesinger 1986), and marginalizes oppositional groups as at best theatrical and at worst irrational and illegitimate (Gitlin 1980; Hackett and Zhao 1996).

QUOTATION AND VERIFICATION

Journalists also produce factuality through their peculiar means of making the accounts of sources seem objective. Facts are clearly attributed to official sources, often in point-counterpoint format. These attributions make the journalists seem to be operating in a detached, impartial, independent, fair, and balanced manner. News production is a perpetual process of authorizing facts through official sources. Official authorization provides the orderly world of news accounts in contrast to the chaos of rumor, innuendo, mudslinging, and lawsuits.

Journalists follow the institutional grooves of authorized accusation. For example, a source's allegation against another person or organization is not treated as fact unless the allegation is officially deemed fact by law enforcers or other constituted authorities. This practice is, of course, guided in part by the law of defamation and libel, which is in effect the law of authorized accusation. However, it is guided more routinely by the official organization of the process being reported on.

For example, court reporting is organized to display the formal legal rationality of the courtroom process rather than the fish market rationality of the plea bargaining process (Chibnall 1977; Drechsel 1983; Ericson, Baranek, and Chan 1989). There is a preference for obtaining quotations from the accused, witnesses, and victims who are testifying under oath rather than through separate interviews outside of the courtroom. On the other hand, many facts are accepted from the prosecutor without attribution or independent checks, in part to save time and in part because it is important to the journalist's own authority as a narrator to appear to be in command of some basic facts. Thus it would be peculiar for the journalist to report, "According to the prosecutor, the accused is 27 years old and charged with robbery," because to name the prosecutor as authority in this context is to raise doubt about the prosecutor's authority and thus the validity of the facts. On the other hand, the journalist would most likely name the prosecutor if he or she referred to the accused as "a known con artist" because the journalist would not want to be seen as making that attribution without further knowledge of the accused's actual record.

Ethnographic research reveals that verification practices vary by the power of the sources the facts are about (Ericson, Baranek, and Chan 1987). A story involving a powerful source facing a serious allegation requires two or three independent checks from other reliable sources. If a less powerful source is involved, one such check will do. When the source is a marginal member of society, no such checks are required, although the journalist should know where to obtain a credible verification if called upon to do so.

News that is already published or broadcast has credibility as a source of verification. This was institutionalized in the former two-agency rule of the British Broadcasting Corporation: "No report should be treated as adequately confirmed if it had not appeared independently on the tape of two news agencies" (Schlesinger 1987, 90). There is also a hierarchy of credibility among news outlets regarding reliable sources. Newspapers of record, such as the *New York Times*, or news agencies of repute, such as Reuters, are assumed to be factually accurate. In routine news production, materials from other news outlets are lifted and reproduced verbatim without attribution. For example, many local broadcast outlets are known as rip-and-read operations that take stories from newspapers and broadcast them as simply the facts without reference to the source (Ericson, Baranek, and Chan 1987).

Verification through access to documents of the source organization being reported on is relatively rare. In spite of regular protests from journalists that they do not have enough freedom of access to information, they have much more access to sources' documents than they take advantage of (Ericson, Baranek, and Chan 1989). Journalists shy away from documents for two main reasons. First, documents require interpretive work that is troublesome because the journalist lacks expert knowledge that would help to interpret them and because there is always room for error in interpretation. Second, factuality for journalists is in any case grounded in having a source person in the know say it is so. Indeed, probing documents for the discovery of competing facts can soften the hard facts of source quotations and may even lead to the conclusion that there is no story to report because the documentary evidence settles the conflict.

Journalists frequently operate within a binary-opposition format of allegations from one source and the counterpoint response of the other source. Within this format, there are many situations in which journalists choose not to forgo their story by obtaining an accessible document that will disconfirm one side and result in no story (Ericson, Baranek, and Chan 1987, 258-64).

> Since a correspondent is required to present contrasting points of view, even if he finds the views of one side to be valid and those of the other side to be false and misleading . . . any attempt to resolve a controversial issue and find "the truth" can become self-defeating. (Epstein 1974, 68)

Thus what journalists regard as objective can undercut both what is truthful and what is ethical (Hackett and Zhao 1996). As indicated by the following remarks of a television news producer, journalists end up reporting what should be the facts of the matter.

> The *final* test is to go and ask the opinion of the institution or the individual that's had the statement made about him, . . . to get their side of it. Because there are some statements that are in dispute. A statement that's in dispute is a fact, but you don't know what side of it is a fact. (Ericson, Baranek, and Chan 1987, 291)

FRAMING

Journalists must tell their story within a narrative framework that has salience in popular reality (Goffman 1974; Hartley 1996). While a journalist may work hard to establish a frame and to relate it to an ongoing theme or issue, once the frame is established, there is a strong disinclination to consider information or alternative frames that do not seem to fit into the picture. Potentially relevant facts are routinely ignored because they would make the story too complicated; the journalist already has his or her story; and/or the journalist is disinterested in the possible story that might be derived from the additional facts.

Research on news accounts of crime waves has demonstrated how journalists frame facts (Cohen 1971; Fishman 1980; Pearson 1983; Voumvakis and Ericson 1984; Orcutt and Turner 1993). An illustration is provided in an ethnographic account of how a crime wave story was handled by a local television outlet (Ericson, Baranek, and Chan 1987, 173-78).

An assignment editor handed a reporter a newspaper story about a significant increase in thefts from pleasure boats in the city's harbor, and asked her to produce a second-day lead for the story. However, in spite of her best efforts, and with concern about expending valuable camera crew resources without producing a story, she was unable to verify that thefts from boats had increased. Police officials denied the problem, and a visit to seven marinas and yacht clubs along the waterfront failed to yield one source who believed there was a problem. The assignment editor did not heed the reporter's early indication that there was no problem and asked her to persist because, in the words of the reporter, "Around here, as I'm sure you've learned, newspapers are everything—they think if it is in print it must be accurate." In this case, the only frame possible was an increase in thefts from boats, indicating a serious problem that required more intensive control remedies. Normal crime is not news; only abnormal crime is. If there is no deviance, there is no story.

There was one possible source of deviance in this story that was not pursued. There was no perceived possibility of reporting on the newspaper journalist's deviance in reporting doubtful facts. Police documents on thefts from boats and a systematic survey of boat owners were not imagined as possible sources to correct the facts of the matter. To have pursued a frame critical of the newspaper account would have exposed the everyday fact of fiction in news reports in too blatant a manner. As the television station producer remarked about the questionable newspaper facts, "I mean, that happens so frequently that it's something we're not going to get into, unless it becomes a major concern" (Ericson, Baranek, and Chan 1987, 176).

As opposed to direct criticism, correction, or contradiction, accounts found wanting are ignored or a story with improved information is published without specific reference to the faulty account in the other news outlet. Of course, this is also usual practice in other fields, such as science, where "publication in a journal in no way establishes that a claim has been accepted by the scientific community. . . . claims which are found wanting are seldom publicly refuted. They are usually ignored instead" (Mulkay 1979, 57).

TELEVISION VISUALS

The visual capacity of television news gives it greater believability than newspapers and radio news (Robinson and Levy 1986; Meyrowitz 1991). Television visuals offer strong validation of the context of the story, and a more direct reading of the moral character and authority of sources. They also offer a sense of immediacy and seem to be in real time or present tense. Combined with the redundant and simplified scripts of television news items, they require little imaginative work by the viewer. Nevertheless, the believability of television news is a strategic accomplishment of the journalists involved. Their news stories are staged productions, complete with props and a cast of journalists and sources as actors. A news producer's manual for the national broadcasting corporation in Canada directs simply to "treat news as theatre" (Cayley 1982, 136).

The theatrical production of television news includes the staging of sources' authority in highly controlled contexts. The news conference is the most controlled context, with authorities who are preselected and preened stating in a matter-of-fact manner what appears to be the case. When a source is interviewed individually, care is taken to visualize the authority of his or her office. Various props are used to sustain the dominant cultural impression that good people work hard and use all available technologies to be knowledgeable and efficient: computers are at hand, books appear in the background, and documents are piled on the desk. If television crews are allowed inside private space to convey what goes on there, it is still in the terms of public cultural expectations of how authority should appear.

Television journalists also help to stage authority in the midst of conflict and chaos. Demonstrations by social movement activists are typically staged rituals in which they, for example, burn figures in effigy, spray paint in bright colors, carry colorful placards, and block transportation routes in order to be pictured under arrest by police. Even riot coverage is contained by the police arranging for television cameras to be positioned behind their lines in order to show that they are invincible, that they are indeed the thin blue line between order and chaos (Holloran, Elliott, and Murdock 1970; Tumber 1982).

Television news staging is inevitable for a number of reasons. There are problems with crew timing and availability. Technical difficulties arise with respect to lighting, sound, and focus. There is the need to appear normal and natural, which is far easier to accomplish through staged events, retakes, reenactments, and the use of stock footage than through simply letting the camera roll as cinema verité.

What journalists term fakes—retakes, reenactments, and the use of stock visuals—help enormously with the flow of the visual narrative in face of the pragmatic problems in producing daily television news. Fakes come in handy when the reporter faces a distant event, an event that has already occurred, an event occurring in a private space that cannot be penetrated, or an encroaching deadline. For example, in reporting on the release of a local government report concerning domestic violence, a journalist did not have time to obtain shots of local police and therefore used five-month-old stock footage of a domestic response team in a distant foreign city (Ericson, Baranek, and Chan 1987, 278). Even ethnographers studying television news production get used as actors in the staging of those productions (91). The only concern of journalists in using such material is to avoid any indication that things are staged, for example, obvious inconsistencies regarding seasons, dress, and signage, or repeated use of the same stock clips.

While visuals are important, they are usually secondary to the script in the visualizations of television journalists. The visual material can become paramount when it is exceptionally dramatic, immediate, and/or exclusive. A shot of a person leaping from a building that is engulfed by flames may speak for itself. However, most visual material comprises talking heads of people speaking for themselves, more like the newspaper photograph that pictures sources who are part of the printed text (Ericson, Baranek, and Chan 1991, 221-23).

Most often, visuals contribute to factuality by picturing events that support the scripted narrative (Ericson, Baranek, and Chan 1987). Thus, in covering a fire in a high-rise apartment building, a reporter included a shot of a woman looking up fearfully at the fire, with a voice-over that relatives were waiting anxiously to learn the fate of their loved ones. The fact was that this woman was worried about her cat still being in her apartment. Another journalist was doing a story on fear among women, in the context of a reported series of attacks on women. She decided to take shots of a secluded area in a park where a woman had been raped while sunbathing in her swimsuit. On location, there were approximately one hundred men, women, and children in the area. The journalist had the cameraman isolate two women in swimsuits sitting on a bench, with no other people in the background. This clip was later used in the story, suggesting that even after the rape there were women foolhardy enough to be in this presumably secluded area of the park wearing only scanty clothing.

THE FACT OF FICTION

The same television network that directed its journalists to "treat news as theatre" also provided a policy book that said journalists must ensure that

> what in fact results from selection and editing is a compression of reality, a slice of reality—which must nonetheless reflect the essential truth without distortion. . . . Production techniques may not be used to distort reality nor to have the effect of producing editorial comment. (Canadian Broadcasting Corporation n.d.)

A mandate to dramatically reflect the facts may seem contradictory, but it is not if we appreciate the fact of fiction in journalism. Every use of language, every classification has an element of fiction because it is not the thing itself. As Nietzsche observed, "What can be thought of must certainly be a fiction." Fiction is bound up with our ways of imaginatively construing the world, of visualizing what something is in order to know it and act upon it. Organized life depends upon acting as if things are as they have been imaginatively construed. The law requires legal fictions to take and justify action. Rhode Island was once declared a peninsula to settle a legal case (Fuller 1967; Scheppele 1988). Historians require regulative fictions, "the imposition of plot on time" (Kermode 1966, 43). Quantitative social scientists use dummy variables to fill in the facts, while ethnographers tell stories that are fashioned within their own narrative frames (Geertz 1973; Clifford and Marcus 1986). The same holds for the practices of physical and natural scientists (Knorr-Cetina 1981).

In the case of literary fiction, to which news is most akin, the essence is what Coleridge once termed the "willing suspension of disbelief" so that the material can be engaged as if it is reality. Literary fictions are "consciously false" (Varhinger 1968) and hence not intended to deceive. In this light, perhaps the best analogy for news is that it is like the Victorian novel: fiction that functions to report facts about the world. Indeed, explicitly fictional entertainment programs can sometimes do more to report the facts than the news itself. Schlesinger, Murdock, and Elliot (1983) found that in the face of U.K. government legal restrictions on journalists interviewing Irish Republican Army terrorists, the reality of the terrorism was more accurately portrayed in fictional entertainment programs.

There is no distinct genre of literary journalism, in spite of efforts to make it distinctive (Kerrane and Yagoda 1997; Sims and Kramer 1995). All journalism is literary in that it employs fictions to discover and apprehend the world. Fictions give order to the world and are essential to the creation of an orderly world of fact. We experience events with a sense of randomness, except when we attend to them closely and analyze them as patterns. News provides analysis in this sense, using fictions to order its products and how those products depict the world. "The randomness of events occurring daily around the world is presented by the daily newscasts as a structured, artistically contrived unity" (Pietropaolo 1982, 53).

Like the novel, news is also a fantasy. As with fiction, fantasy does not mean that it is all made up with whim and fancy or that it is intended to deceive. Rather, it is grounded in fact, reality, a way in which people both make sense of their experiences and make their social worlds. Fantasy is also a method for

> the imaginative and creative interpretation of events that fulfills a psychological or rhetorical need. The Greek root is *phantaskikos* and means to be able to present or show to the mind, to make visible. A fantasy theme is a way for people to present a show to the group mind, to make visible (understandable) a common experience and invest it with an emotional tone. (Bormann 1983, 99-122)

Metaphors, tropes, and other figurative language are important means of accomplishing this imaginative and creative work. Fires *rage*, communities are *battlefronts* over planning and zoning decisions, and elections are reported using boxing metaphors. It is not only that one news picture is used to say a thousand words but also that one news word can visualize a thousand others.

> In metaphor one has, of course, a stratification of meaning, in which incongruity of sense on one level produces an influx of significance on another. As Percy has pointed out, the feature of metaphor that has most troubled philosophers is that it is "wrong." The power of a metaphor derives precisely from the interplay between the discordant meanings it symbolically coerces into a unitary conceptual framework and from the degree to which that coercion is successful in overcoming the psychic resistance such semantic tension inevitably generates in anyone in a position to perceive it. When it works, a metaphor transforms a false identification . . . into an apt analogy. (Geertz 1973, 210-11)

Neither the visual fakes of television journalists nor the figurative language of all journalists should be seen as deception or forgery. They are simulation devices that add unity, coherence, plausibility, and order to the news. Figurative language is a creative means of making news items recognizable in terms of the presumed common sense (Shearing and Ericson 1991). It gives meaning and flow to events in the recognizable terms of news discourse.

THE FUTURE OF FACT

Fact has a strong future. However, its power or capacity for action perpetually shifts between different institutions as they struggle to maintain the power of their respective discourses.

Hard facts continue to have a prominent role in governing modern society. The hard facts of the sciences of probability determine risk thresholds, provide the basis of legal regulation, and help people to tame chance and take risks (Hacking 1990). The hard facts of consumer marketing, credit cards, and police surveillance systems allow institutions to govern at a distance and to include or exclude people as they see fit (Gandy 1993; Turow 1997; Slater 1997; Ericson and Haggerty 1997).

Perhaps the news and other literary discourses are not faring so well in this orderly world of hard fact. News inevitably falls down when it is held up to the hard facts of normal science. Consider the prevailing research methodology for studying news content. The facts of news are compared with other measures of reality, for example, asking whether crime in the media reflects the reality of police statistics and crime victimization surveys (Sherizen 1978; Ditton and Duffy 1983; Sacco 1995). Of course, discrepancies are found, with the mass media overrepresenting murder and other forms of serious violent crime and underreporting burglary and other forms of property crime. But why would anyone expect the cultural products of the news media to reflect other facts about crime? Police statistics themselves do not mirror the reality of crime but are cultural, legal, and social constructs produced by the police for organizational purposes (Kitsuse 1964; Ericson 1993). Each institution has a peculiar discourse for rendering and valuing facts.

The news institution itself is breaking down into specialized information services that feed the reflexive frenzy of other institutions and individuals who demand facts about risk for their own instrumental purposes. Market segmentation of print media and narrowcasting of broadcast media create knowledge-based inequality that is "breaking up America" (Turow 1997; Schiller 1989; Webster 1995).

There is a need to appreciate news for what it is, a form of literary fiction that provides valuable facts about the human condition. There is a parallel need to ascertain the relative position of the news institution in comparison to other institutions as a producer of valuable facts. Such knowledge may well lead us to worry that the literary powers of journalism are losing ground in a society that is increasingly governed through the utilitarian morality of probability statistics and actuarial justice. The morality plays that result from how journalists visualize fact remain vital to the mentalities and sensibilities of modern society.

References

Altheide, David. 1995. *An Ecology of Communication: Cultural Formats of Control*. New York: Aldine de Gruyter.

Bell, Daniel. 1985. Gutenberg and the Computer. *Encounter* (May):15-20.

Bormann, Ernest. 1983. Symbolic Convergence: Organizational Communication and Culture. In *Communication and Organizations*, ed. Linda Putnam and Michael Pacanowsky. Beverly Hills, CA: Sage.

Canadian Broadcasting Corporation. n.d. Internal policy manual.

Cayley, David. 1982. Making Sense of the News. *Sources* (Spring):126-28, 130-33, 136-37.

Chibnall, Steven. 1977. *Law-and-Order News*. London: Tavistock.

Clifford, James and George Marcus, eds. 1986. *Writing Culture: The Poetics and Politics of Ethnography*. Berkeley: University of California Press.

Cohen, Stanley. 1971. *Folk Devils and Moral Panics*. London: Paladin.

Ditton, Jason and James Duffy. 1983. Bias in the Newspaper Reporting of Crime News. *British Journal of Criminology* 23:159-65.

Drechsel, Robert. 1983. *News Making in the Trial Courts*. New York: Longman.

Epstein, Edward. 1974. *News from Nowhere*. New York: Vintage.

Ericson, Richard. 1991. Mass Media, Crime, Law and Justice: An Institutional Approach. *British Journal of Criminology* 31:219-49.

———. 1993. *Making Crime: A Study of Detective Work*. Toronto: University of Toronto Press.

———. 1994. An Institutional Perspective on News Media Access and Control. In *Controlling Broadcasting*, ed. Meryl Aldridge and Nicholas Hewitt. Manchester: University of Manchester Press.

Ericson, Richard, Patricia Baranek, and Janet Chan. 1987. *Visualizing Deviance: A Study of News Organization*. Toronto: University of Toronto Press; Milton Keynes: Open University Press.

———. 1989. *Negotiating Control: A Study of News Sources*. Toronto: University of Toronto Press; Milton Keynes: Open University Press.

———. 1991. *Representing Order: Crime, Law and Justice in the News Media*. Toronto: University of Toronto Press; Milton Keynes: Open University Press.

Ericson, Richard and Kevin Haggerty. 1997. *Policing the Risk Society*. Toronto: University of Toronto Press; Oxford: Oxford University Press.

Fishman, Mark. 1980. *Manufacturing the News*. Austin: University of Texas Press.

Fuller, Lon. 1967. *Legal Fictions*. Stanford, CA: Stanford University Press.

Gandy, Oscar. 1993. *The Panoptic Sort: A Political Economy of Personal Information*. Boulder, CO: Westview Press.

Geertz, Clifford. 1973. *The Interpretation of Cultures*. New York: Basic Books.

Gitlin, Todd. 1980. *The Whole World Is Watching*. Berkeley: University of California Press.

Glasgow University Media Group. 1976. *Bad News*. London: Routledge.

Goffman, Erving. 1974. *Frame Analysis: An Essay on the Organization of Experience*. Cambridge, MA: Harvard University Press.

Golding, Peter, Graham Murdock, and Philip Schlesinger. 1986. *Communicating Politics*. Leicester: University of Leicester Press.

Hackett, Robert and Yuezhi Zhao. 1996. Are Ethics Enough? "Objective" Journalism and Sustainable Democracy. In *Journalism Ethics in a Changing World*, ed. Valeria Alia, Brian Brennan, and Barry Hoffmaster. Halifax: Fernwood.

Hacking, Ian. 1990. *The Taming of Chance*. New York: Cambridge University Press.

Hartley, John. 1996. *Popular Reality*. London: Arnold.

Holloran, James, Philip Elliott, and Graham Murdock. 1970. *Demonstrations and Communication*. New York: Penguin.

Kermode, Frank. 1966. *The Sense of an Ending: Studies in the Theory of Fiction*. New York: Oxford University Press.

Kerrane, Kevin and Ben Yagoda, eds. 1997. *The Art of Fact: An Historical Anthology of Literary Journalism*. New York: Scribner.

Kitsuse, John. 1964. Social Reactions to Deviant Behavior: Problems of Theory and Method. *Social Problems* 9: 247-56.

Knorr-Cetina, Karen. 1981. *The Manufacture of Knowledge: An Essay on the Constructivist and Contextual Nature of Science*. Oxford: Pergamon.

Luhmann, Niklas. 1979. *Trust and Power*. New York: John Wiley.

Meyrowitz, Joshua. 1991. The Questionable Reality of Media. In *Ways of Knowing: The Reality Club*, ed. John Brockman. New York: Prentice Hall.

———. 1994. Medium Theory. In *Communication Theory Today*, ed. David Crowley and David Mitchell. Stanford, CA: Stanford University Press.

Mistzal, Barbara. 1996. *Trust in Modern Societies*. Cambridge: Polity.

Mulkay, Michael. 1979. *Science and the Sociology of Knowledge*. London: Allen & Unwin.

Orcutt, James and Blake Turner. 1993. Shocking Numbers and Graphic Accounts: Quantified Images of Drug Problems in the Print Media. *Social Problems* 40:190-206.

Pearson, Geoffrey. 1983. *Hooligan: A History of Respectable Fears*. London: Macmillan.

Pietropaolo, Dimitri. 1982. Structuring "Truth": The Uses of Drama in "Information" Radio. *Canadian Theatre Review* 36:52-56.

Robinson, John and Mark Levy. 1986. *The Main Source: Learning from Television News*. Newbury Park, CA: Sage.

Sacco, Vincent F. 1995. Media Constructions of Crime. *The Annals* of the American Academy of Political and Social Science 539(May):141-54.

Scheppele, Kim. 1988. *Legal Secrets*. Chicago: University of Chicago Press.

Schiller, Herbert. 1989. *Culture, Inc.: The Corporate Takeover of Public Expression*. New York: Oxford University Press.

Schlesinger, Philip. 1987. *Putting "Reality" Together: B.B.C. News*. London: Methuen.

Schlesinger, Philip, Graham Murdock, and Philip Elliott. 1983. *Televising Terrorism*. London: Comedia.

Shearing, Clifford and Richard Ericson. 1991. Culture as Figurative Action. *British Journal of Sociology* 42: 481-506.

Sherizen, Sanford. 1978. Social Creation of Crime News: All the News Fitted to Print. In *Deviance and Mass Media*, ed. Charles Winick. Beverly Hills, CA: Sage.

Sims, Norman and Mark Kramer, eds. 1995. *Literary Journalism: A New Collection of the Best American Nonfiction*. New York: Ballantine.

Slater, Donald. 1997. *Consumer Culture and Modernity*. Cambridge: Polity.

Stehr, Nico and Richard Ericson, eds. 1992. *The Culture and Power of Knowledge*. New York: Walter de Gruyter.

Thompson, John. 1995. *The Media and Modernity*. Stanford, CA: Stanford University Press.

Tumber, Howard. 1982. *Television and the Riots*. London: British Film Institute.

Turow, Joseph. 1997. *Breaking up America: Advertisers and the New Media World*. Chicago: University of Chicago Press.

Varhinger, Hans. 1968. *The Philosophy of the As If: A System of the Theoretical, Practical, and Religious Fictions of Mankind*. New York: Routledge.

Voumvakis, Sophia and Richard Ericson. 1984. *News Accounts of Attacks on Women*. Toronto: University of Toronto, Centre of Criminology.

Webster, Frank. 1995. *Theories of the Information Society*. New York: Routledge.

[9]
The Moral Hazards of Neo-Liberalism: Lessons from the Private Insurance Industry

Abstract

The key tenets of neo-liberalism regarding risk, governance, and responsibility are critically evaluated through an empirical study of the private insurance industry. Recent tendencies in this industry towards increasing segmentation of consumers regarding risk, and towards an expansion of private policing of insurance fraud, are analysed. The definition of moral hazard is broadened to include all parties in the insurance relationship, not just the insured. Moral hazards embedded in the social organization of private insurance lead to various kinds of immoral risky behaviour by insureds, insurance companies, and their employees, and to intensified efforts to regulate this behaviour. The analysis concludes with some critical observations about the neo-liberal emphasis on minimal state, market fundamentalism, risk-taking, individual responsibility, and acceptance of inequality.

Keywords: insurance; risk; neo-liberalism; governance; moral hazard; insurance fraud.

The discourse of neo-liberalism calls for new configurations of risk. While it occurs in different inflections as the political platform of recent Western governments, neo-liberalism has also penetrated to a more fundamental level. It is a prescription for ordering social relations that increasingly pervades contemporary public and private institutions and the lives of individuals. In this article we use an empirical study of the private insurance industry in order to evaluate the key tenets of neo-liberalism regarding risk, governance, and responsibility.

Neo-liberalism is a model for governance beyond the state. This model has five basic points. First, there is to be a minimal state. People are presumed to have enough self-restraint, willingness to share, and capacity for self-governance at levels of organization beyond the state that civil society can be a self-generating basis of social solidarity. Second, market fundamentalism is stressed. A 'free market' is supposed to provide security and prosperity by encouraging fragmented individuals and collectivities to participate in market relations that stimulate economic growth and, in the case of insurance, manage risk. Third, emphasis is placed not only on risk management but also on risk taking. As participants in fast-moving and fluctuating markets, people must become educated, knowledgeable, reflexive risk takers who are adaptable to transitions in their lives. Fourth, individual responsibility is underscored. Each individual is to be her own political economy, an informed, self-sufficient consumer of labour markets, personal security markets, and other consuming interests. Fifth, within a regime of responsible risk taking, all differences, and the inequalities that result from them, are seen as a matter of choice. Conceived as a choice, inequality is also seen as inevitable.

The private insurance industry is an ideal institution within which to examine these basic points about neo-liberalism. While neo-liberalism preaches self-reliance in managing risk, some risks are too large for individuals to self-insure. In these cases, neo-liberalism spotlights private insurance as the responsible market-based alternative, as opposed to depending on the state for managing risk. Indeed, private insurance has become a central institution of governance beyond the state, a key institution for aspects of governance such as risk management, security provision and population management. Private insurance configures risk in all other important institutions, not only by defining and managing risks, but ironically, as we will discuss, by creating them.

Remarkably, insurance remains an under-researched institution in social science, especially among sociologists and criminologists (Strange 1996: 122). Our article draws on empirical material from an extensive ongoing study of the insurance institution which addresses this gap. For this study, we have conducted extensive observational research, completed 224 open-focused interviews and gathered several hundred documents.[1] In this article, we illustrate our arguments with examples drawn from the private insurance industry in Canada, the United States, and Britain.

The following points concerning the private insurance industry are discussed. Our research shows, first, how, in the neo-liberal era, the contemporary private insurance industry is characterized by increasing risk segmentation or the unpooling of risks. We also explore, how, as a central institution of governance beyond the state, private insurance is an industry that is increasingly deeply involved in policing and the management of crime risks. As such, it exemplifies many of the theoretical arguments about crime in risk society (Ericson and Haggerty 1997; O'Malley 1998). First, crime is an artefact of how an institution organizes to deal with it: crime is literally 'made' (Ericson 1993) through the risk management practices of the institution concerned. Second, this crime is dealt with very largely by expanding private policing systems beyond the state's criminal justice system. Third, these policing systems not only govern crime but govern through crime (Simon 1997). That is, in developing risk information systems in the name of crime management, they also serve other governmental purposes in population management.

Our empirical research leads us to offer an expanded definition of the moral hazard resulting from insurance relationships. Neo-liberal critics reject the welfare state as resulting in intractable problems with moral hazard. However, our empirical material reveals that, ironically, the private insurance institution is shot through with immoral risky behaviour. Our analysis allows us to conclude with some critical observations about the neo-liberal emphasis on minimal state, market fundamentalism, risk-taking, individual responsibility, and acceptance of inequality.

The unpooling of risks

Private insurance can operate to socialize risk. However, our data show that a tendency in insurance which has become increasingly pronounced in the era of neo-liberalism is that of more and more risk segmentation or the unpooling of risks. One of the ironies of insurance is that, while it is supposed to pool risks, in practice it tends to unpool them, breaking down the larger pool of potential insured in search of smaller, less risky pools, which are more advantageous for some, while excluding others (Gowri 1997). Premiums within these smaller pools can be kept lower and claims service can be higher, but only for those fortunate enough to be included.

The insurance industry uses sophisticated surveillance systems – surveillance defined simply as technologies for the production of knowledge about populations useful in their administration (Dandeker 1990; Ericson and Haggerty 1997) – in order to 'panoptically sort' (Gandy 1993) individuals into pools of standard, sub-standard, and uninsurable risks. These systems are there to magnify differences among individuals in order to achieve greater precision in the commodification of insurance products and exclusion of those who do not fit (Simon 1987). An insurance company's mandate is to discriminate on merit, for example favouring policyholders who foster loss reduction; and on prudent decisions that keep the company solvent and hopefully prosperous. Its task is not a redistribution of resources among insured persons nor equal treatment, but only equitable treatment within the community of interest it has pooled (Gowri 1997: 151–3).

The recent trend towards more risk segmentation or unpooling within private insurance stems in part from the increasingly detailed risk information (e.g. financial, medical) which is available to actuaries and underwriters, both concerning individual insureds and concerning trends in populations. However, it is also one of several industry responses to the same global competitive pressures that have led to the advent of neo-liberal discourse. One source of these pressures has been the entrance of banks into the insurance market-place. As a vice-president of one large insurance company said:

> We've got regulatory barriers breaking down in what was a very protected marketplace, we've got new competitors . . . trying to find ways they can target a market share . . . [the banks have] invested extensively in customer information and customer segmentation. And if you think of the wealth of information that a bank would have with all the transactions that are going through, they would have a good sense of income levels, of debt patterns, of payment patterns. They've used this very much to segment customers. . . . As insurers, we're going to have to take niche positions in terms of which markets we're going to be experts in, and focus all our energies and resources in those markets.

Experts we spoke to outlined a history (or 'revolution', as one put it) in increasing differentiation and risk segmentation of consumers in various insurance markets, as insurers have increasingly sought to create and target-market to 'preferred' and 'super-preferred' risks or otherwise to profit from an increasing calibration of risk. Segmentation is simultaneously a process of marketing and one of risk assessment or underwriting, because preferred risks are doubly desirable as insurance clients: they are seen to be both affluent consumers, on the one hand, and less risky in terms of claims, on the other. However, insurers also profit by pooling substandard risks, as insureds in the resulting pool, with little market choice, are compelled to purchase insurance under the most substandard of arrangements.

This tendency and some of its social consequences were epitomized in a private-sector vehicle insurance market we studied, by a local company which found a niche market in substandard driving risks. The niche market is people for whom vehicle insurance is mandatory, but who have difficulty obtaining it because of their poor driving records. The large multinational companies that dominate the general insurance market do not want these poor risks, leaving room for the local company to create a very profitable business.

The company is highly profitable for four reasons. First, as just mentioned, there is no competition. Second, the insurer covers liability claims against these drivers only to a modest level. Third, the insurer provides financing of premium payments at high interest to consumers who frequently cannot afford to pay up front and therefore have no choice but to pay this interest. Fourth, the company charges very high premiums. Unwanted risks are simply priced too high, although this is rare because, in the words of a company official, 'My attitude is a good risk is one that pays high enough premium'. Moreover, the insurance regulators in the jurisdiction allow the company to circumvent the fairness criteria that apply to companies filing rates for standard risks by allowing separate rates to be filed for the non-standard risks. The regulators thereby effectively constitute the company as an unfairness company. An official of the company explained in interview:

> If you file rates for a standard type of risk, you can't file a rate for a non-standard risk because you have to set the rate levels that are going to be fair for all types of drivers. So where a company is, say, identifying the better risk

> and they set a rate for liability insurance at say $800, they don't want to insure the bad risk because they can't get enough money for it [because of the fairness criteria]. So our base rate might be $1500 and we only insure the bad ones who come to us.

There is a ruthless de-selection of the poor once they are insured with the company. As mentioned above, many policyholders cannot afford to pay the full cost of the policy up front, and so must finance their premiums through the insurance company, at profitable interest rates considerably above market level. Moreover, they are required to pay two months' premium in advance on a twelve-month contract, and to have their subsequent monthly payments made automatically through an electronic pre-authorization system from their bank account. In fact, approximately 40 per cent of the policyholders cannot keep up this payment schedule; thus 40 per cent of the company's auto insurance policies are cancelled at some time during the twelve-month contract period for non-payment of the premium. Many of these cancelled policyholders thus join the ranks of the estimated 10 to 15 per cent of drivers in the jurisdiction who drive illegally without insurance. This situation poses a problem for the police because the insurance card is issued for twelve months: the driver can still show the police officer what looks like a valid card even after it has been cancelled. In sum, these arrangements enable and encourage motorists with poor driving records to drive without valid insurance, putting themselves and other drivers at risk, although not the insurance company, which is no longer liable once the drivers' policies are cancelled. While some police officers have learned that all insurance cards from this company are 'red flags' indicating high risk drivers and are therefore likely to do further investigative checks, this approach is by no means uniform.

Given its approach and substandard risk clientele, this company does not even bother employing regular insurance adjusters on staff or on contract, adjusters who would be skilled in dealing with claims relatively gently and diplomatically. Instead, this company contracts with a firm of private investigators located in the same office building as the insurance company's headquarters, in order to ensure a much tougher approach with this particular clientele. As ex-police officers, these private investigators are especially adept at detecting fraudulent claims and at having clients see the wisdom of withdrawing such claims. They are also skilled at the preparation of evidence, and work closely with their former police department colleagues in prosecuting the company's clients. This represents a very strong contrast with the more diplomatic approach to claims which we found is adopted by insurance firms targeting more upscale risk segments.

While this company is heralded as an exemplary business success in a jurisdiction that is strongly neo-liberal, its ethos and practices ramify throughout the insurance industry. A leading actuarial scientist in the jurisdiction had the following observations on the changes he had witnessed with the ascendancy of neo-liberalism:

> The whole idea of insurance works on the pooling of risk. . . . Those categories of the collective were very broad even fifteen years ago. . . . You'd have to have a couple of claims in a short period of time to see your premium change very much. Now it is going with the philosophy of the rest of society that you are responsible. . . . The whole concept of a pure accident is almost disappearing. There is no pure accident any more. If you have a claim, you are partially at fault. And you need to change risk categories. . . . [This is a] move to more and more slicing and individualization, and more and more passing the responsibility back to the claimant. If it goes too far people will say that this isn't insurance any more. . . . As soon as I have a claim my premium goes up. So over the next six years I pay the claim. Well heck, I can run my bank account to do that.

Moral hazard

These ever-refined processes of risk selection are also related to intensified efforts to regulate moral hazard. Our empirical research on the industry has led us to offer a new, expanded definition of this term. We define moral hazard as the ways in which an insurance relationship fosters behaviour by *any* party in the relationship that immorally increases risk to others. This definition of moral hazard is broader than the one typically used by insurers themselves, as well as by some researchers (see generally Heimer 1985; Reichman 1986; Baker 1996). It is typically only the insured who is seen as influenced by moral hazard. In this definition, being insured is seen to reduce the insured's incentive to avoid risky behaviour or to minimize loss through preventive security, with negative consequences for insurers. Our broader definition stems from our empirical finding that how private insurance is socially organized also offers incentives to other parties in the insurance relationship to engage in risky behaviour with immoral consequences. Indeed, insurers themselves are often influenced in ways which encourage them to put others at risk, including their policyholders, employees, competitors, and governments.

Moral hazard influences on the insured party will increase if the cultural relationship is strained, for example if the insurer is seen as distant and anonymous or there are discrepancies between sales stories and claims stories that create a sense of bad faith; if there is a lot at stake in the economic relationship regarding premiums paid and benefits sought; if there is an opportunity created because of inadequate selection of the insured population and/or inadequate policing of the claims process; and if the insured is able to morally neutralize her behaviour as just in the circumstances. We have observed that many parallel factors are also at work concerning the influence of moral hazard on insurance companies and their employees: for example, a cushion from the consequences of risk, very high economic stakes, low visibility and inadequate policing, and readily available justifications to morally neutralize their risky behaviour.

The welfare state as a source of moral hazard

Neo-liberal criticism of the welfare state is based on the view that welfarism generates intractable problems of moral hazard. In making this argument neo-liberals are quite comfortable with sociological explanations that emphasize structural conditions, institutional arrangements, and social relationships. State welfare systems are said to create a cultural relationship of dependency on social security. Instead of the desirable emphasis on risk-taking and enterprise, there is risk minimization, avoidance, and aversion that create human and institutional inertia. There is an economic relationship in which people pay substantial 'premiums' (taxes, social security payments, etc.) and expect returns over time. The state not only offers substantial and generous benefits, it is the ultimate deep pocket. There is situational opportunity to take advantage of this economic relationship because of bureaucratic inefficiency. For example, the risks insured do not fit the need, the wrong groups are insured, and claims are not adequately policed. This bureaucratic inefficiency is compounded by aspects of professional interest: professionals in the social security system receive very substantial salaries and benefits, and often have iatrogenic effects. Most pervasive of all is the welfare state's strong emphasis on social justice, with its values of welfarism, trust, and the promise of security, which make it easy for someone to morally neutralize a questionable claim to a social insurance benefit.

Taken to the extreme, neo-liberal arguments about the welfare state as a source of moral hazard suggest that we would be better off with no state insurance provision at all. Welfare provision is said to contain several ironies that defeat its purpose and compound rather than correct the risks it is supposed to offset. First, as argued so vehemently by the law and economics ideological arm of neo-liberalism, state insurance systems will make people less self-sufficient and less responsible for self and others (Arnott and Stiglitz 1991). Second, taken too far, state insurance schemes might ironically reduce safety and security. This logic suggests that the less the welfare provision, the more there will be a responsible workforce above the poverty line; the less workers' compensation for disabilities incurred at work, the greater the workplace safety; the less the availability of disability insurance in general, the greater the availability of an able, responsible workforce (see Baker 1996: 238, in criticism). Third, and embodying these other ironies, the welfare state is said to work against its own purposes of collective responsibility and welfare. Neo-liberal advocates argue that greater welfare can be provided through the minimal state and market economy of responsible risk takers than through the welfare state (e.g. Marsland 1996).

The third way argues in the same way. For example, Giddens (1998: 114–15) describes the moral hazards of welfare, and initially says the problem is not so much dependency as situational opportunism for financial gain. However, he then contends that dependency cultures are created by welfare state insurance systems. He cites Lindbeck (1995) to assert that the higher the benefits, the greater the risk of moral hazard, including fraud, to the point where benefit dependency becomes taken-for-granted behaviour.

Moral hazard and the private insurance industry

Giddens, in keeping with most social scientists, is silent about the private insurance industry and its moral hazard problems and responses. Our empirical study provides much evidence that moral hazard is embedded in the institutional arrangements, social relationships, and moral economies of private insurance. We begin by discussing claims fraud and insurance company practices in that area.

It is very difficult to establish the epidemiology of claims fraud. In Canada, industry associations and spokespersons regularly proclaim things such as 'insurance fraud is the second leading source of criminal profits next to drugs', and that 10 to 20 per cent of all claims are fraudulent. However, these figures are made up. A lot of claims fraud is simply undetected and remains part of the dark figure of crime.

In addition, a great deal of claims fraud is suspected by loss adjusters but ignored. For example, in a vehicle hit-and-run insurance claims centre we studied, out of an average of sixty-five claims each day, about six were judged to be fraudulent claims based on material damage assessment. These claims were denied on the spot. However, an additional thirteen claims on average were believed to be fraudulent but not investigated further because the company decided it was more expedient to pay the claim.

Cases involving personal injuries and disabilities are even more ambiguous and difficult to assess. Studies of bodily injury claims arising from vehicle crashes in Massachusetts (Weisberg and Derrig 1991, 1992) judged 32 per cent (n = 597) of one sample and 47 per cent (n = 1,154) of another sample to have involved dishonesty in the claim. Several disability insurers we interviewed pointed to the fact that disability claims increase with recession, lay-offs and rightsizing of companies. For example, a disability insurance broker said that two pending hospital closings in her city had led to a significant increase in insurance claims from employees desperate for sources of income in face of losing their jobs. There are also concentrated contexts of using disability insurance for special benefit. A video produced by a television station in collaboration with the US National Insurance Crime Bureau reports that disability insurance claims have been a preferred route for Long Island police officers wishing to ease into other activities. Evidently more than 1,000 officers have been receiving disability benefits of approximately $32 million annually. Surveillance video footage has captured some of these officers engaged in activities that seem to belie their disabilities. These activities included hang gliding, lifeguarding, rodeo riding, and professional wrestling.

There are many reasons why a claims adjuster must tread lightly even when a fraudulent claim is suspected. First, there is often a great deal of ambiguity regarding the evidence for what is claimed. Exaggeration or soft fraud is easy to visualize but difficult to investigate and take action against. Second, in an industry where the operating philosophy is moral utilitarianism and therefore the supreme value is efficiency, it is often judged more expedient to make 'nuisance payments' rather than investigate. The hit-and-run claims centre example above is a case in point. Furthermore, the loss can be absorbed in future higher premiums to the claimant and across the pool of insured persons. Third, and pervading the above considerations, is public relations. The claims process is also part of the sales process, since the primary thing an insurance company is selling is its promise to pay (Baker 1994: 1401). Indeed, an insurance company may want to keep its dishonest customers because they continue to pay premiums that the company needs to invest and make profits. It is sometimes easier not to bite the hand that feeds, even if one's own hand is nibbled at from time-to-time.

The expansion of insurance fraud policing

Insurance claims fraud is a classic case of 'making crime' (Ericson 1993). It is an artefact of how the insurance industry organizes to deal with it. As related to us by a senior official in an insurance crime control organization:

> The scary part is, as we continue to increase the fight, we continually uncover more and more fraud. So people say, 'You are putting all these dollars in there, but the problem is increasing.' You can't say something is fraudulent until you find it. There's been such a growth in 'insurance fraud'. It has probably always been there, it is just that more has been uncovered than ever before.

This official is pointing to the fact that there has been a substantial expansion of private policing personnel and technologies in the private insurance industry in the past few years. For example, Special Investigation Units (SIUs) of private police within insurance companies in the United States multiplied between 1992 and 1997. In 1992, approximately 240 companies had SIUs. However, by 1997 approximately 1,200 companies had such units. This expansion in SIUs has been accompanied by the hiring of more investigators within each company's SIU. During the same five-year period one major company's SIU grew from approximately 300 to 1,200 investigators. This expansion was fostered by the establishment of the National Insurance Crime Bureau in 1992. The first director was a former US Army general who had worked in the Pentagon in the Bush administration's war on drugs, and talked in similar terms about insurance fraud as a threat to the nation (Dornstein 1996: 332).

While the companies indicate that this explosion in private insurance claims policing is simply a response to an exploding fraud problem, one US industry executive offered an alternative reason for it. He indicated to us that this contemporary boom in fraud policing has been driven by increased pressure on the companies to keep premiums down. In the past, increased claims costs could simply be passed on to the consumer in higher premiums. The executive indicated, however, that new laws in California and other states which restrict premium increases forced the companies to take stronger anti-fraud measures instead to reduce claims costs, and to bolster their competitive position and profits.

The scope of claims policing can be appreciated by considering a Canadian provincial automobile insurance company we studied. This company receives around $1.2 billion in personal injury claims arising from vehicle crashes each year. This amounts to slightly more than 1 per cent of the entire provincial economy, which is approximately $100 billion annually. Moreover, almost half of the dollar value of these claims is with respect to soft tissue injuries, such as 'whiplash associated disorder', which are extremely perplexing for the health professions to diagnose and treat.

This company has also recently been operating under a government-mandated freeze in premium increases, which has prompted a heavy crackdown on fraud as one method to contain costs, very similar to the American situation described above. The response of the insurance company, in keeping with other disability insurers facing similar problems, has been to develop its own SIU along with new and tightened procedures for adjusters and case management staff. Moreover, it is a major contractor with the private investigation firms in the province, who are primarily used to conduct photo surveillance on claimants to ascertain whether they are engaged in physical tasks that would belie their claimed disabilities. In 1995 there were approximately 4,400 such assignments. There is also an effort to mobilize neighbours, fellow employees and others as informants, for example through an informant-tip line.

A parallel effort is made to police health service providers. There is increasing centralization and control of which health professionals can supply specified health services. Health profession billing is filed electronically and subject to ongoing dataveillance. New manuals for health professionals are being developed to regulate the service and ensure that the service providers function as allies of the insurer in the claims management process. For example, a manual for doctors dealing with whiplash-associated disorders is 212 pages in length. It features not only details on diagnoses and treatments, but repeated instructions on how to detect fraudulent claims and malingerers who would rather collect disability payments than return to work. It lists 'factitious disorder' as one of several 'illness behaviour' syndromes:

> Malingering or Factitious Disorder. A conscious or willful invention or distortion of symptoms to achieve secondary gain, usually a financial gain. (It should be pointed out that it is not easy to detect malingering, as it can sometimes appear the same as previously discussed syndromes). The difference between malingering, and the other psychological issues is that in malingering the person knows they are faking an illness or injury, and why – usually for money or to avoid traumatization or abuse.

Some disability insurers have tried to enhance detection of 'factitious disorder' by having claimants undergo a series of physical movement tests that measure their ability to squeeze, grip, lift, and so on. For example, there is now on the market a sophisticated computer-based measurement technology that does reliability checks on each physical movement tested. Each physical movement is tested three times, and crosschecked against other physical movements tested and self-reported levels of pain. This technology has been developed not only as a kind of lie detector of the body, but also to regulate health professionals who vary widely in assessments using more primitive means.

In summary, the advent of neo-liberalism has been accompanied by a 'control wave' (Ditton 1979) of private insurance claims policing that may well prove as intensive and intrusive as that directed at state welfare and social insurance systems. The problems of moral hazard and the need for intensive policing do not go away in a society more oriented towards private markets in insurance and security. Moreover, there are additional moral hazard problems and attendant policing needs at the level of insurance company operations.

Company fraud

It is not only state welfare bureaucracies that generate fraud and other undue losses because of internal dimensions of their culture, economic relationships, opportunity structures, and provisions for social justice. Private insurance companies also experience inefficient systems unable to respond to the nature of risk, professionals who benefit exceptionally from their status and income, and criminogenic structures. Indeed, moral hazard leading to fraud is endemic to some of the ways in which the insurance industry organizes and conducts business. A focus on various dimensions of insurance mis-selling – selling the wrong product, too much of the product, or a product on unfavourable terms – will illustrate some dimensions of moral hazard at the level of organizational structures and practices.

Mis-selling in the form of sales fraud is institutionalized in the marketing of life insurance and associated investment products. There are many ways in which mis-selling materializes, depending on the features of the product and the organization of the distribution system. Michael Clarke (1999) provides a chronicle of the large-scale and systematic mis-selling scandals in the United Kingdom life insurance industry. In the present context we consider only the basic organizational features of life insurance sales distribution that are conducive to mis-selling.

The traditional system for life insurance sales involves recruitment of neophytes who are required to produce a substantial list of 'prospects' from among their family, friends, and acquaintances. There may be some salary in the start-up period, but otherwise the sales staff including sales managers are commission-dependent. As a result, they have a strong incentive to sell products that yield higher premiums for the company and higher commissions for themselves. For example, as is widely acknowledged in the industry, it is often the case that consumers, particularly those who are on limited budgets, are best off with a simple term life policy that carries only death benefits. However, an effort is made to sell instead investment-based policies, such as whole life or universal life products, because they are more lucrative to the company and sales staff. These products do potentially allow the policy to accumulate value. Nevertheless, they are based on investment assumptions that often fail to materialize – as occurred in the North American 'vanishing premiums' mis-selling cases – or that have a modest yield in comparison with other ways the consumer could invest her money. They do have guaranteed high yield for the company and for the sales agents, who are pressured to neutralize the moral bonds they have to their family, friends, and acquaintances in order to coax them into inappropriate purchases. Ostensibly for training, more senior sales personnel often accompany the new agents when they sell to family and friends, and play a major role in closing the deal.

The commission structure is thus a major source of moral hazard influencing life insurance sales people, providing incentives for selling practices that put the consumer at risk of making a dubious insurance purchase. One telling admission of this point came from a company we studied that sold group insurance. This company also sold individual life policies to selected clients who were contacts for group sales. The company had adopted a slogan indicating that they were 'people you can trust'. Asked to explain this slogan, a company executive gave the example that the salesperson who sold these individual policies to key clients was paid a straight salary, rather than any commissions. Scrapping the commissions in this case removed the moral hazard of encouraging the salesperson to mis-sell to these favoured clients, whose goodwill was needed for the group business. As the company executive told us, 'This guy's not motivated to sell the wrong product. . . . I couldn't afford to have my individual guy selling the president of the hospital a whole life policy which turns out to be the wrong product and it's too expensive . . . because our guy makes 50 per cent commission in the first year'.

Not surprisingly, the life insurance industry is characterized by very high turnover in sales staff. Approximately one-half leave within a year (Clarke 1999: 95–6, 153), typically because they have either exhausted their list of prospects or developed a distaste for using unethical sales practices.

In fact, the high turnover of agents is advantageous for the industry as it leads to a constant stream of new prospective customers who are personal contacts of newly hired agents. One former life insurance agent told us a fairly typical story:

> I was young, just out of [university] and a pretty slick manager got me going [as an agent] and, you know, wanted me to go out and hit my friends up for, you know, to buy policies...At first they really pushed that, you know, if you believe in the product you should sell it to your family members, your friends, because they need it, everybody needs this product because it's very important and they were very slick at doing that. I didn't like it for the reason that at times they tried to push the products that really wouldn't fit with the person. . . . Because the commission on term insurance was not the best, they really didn't push that part of the business. . . . And somebody who's got a young family they need the protection and you should be pushing term insurance for them always and they just didn't like that.
>
> I think probably there's a one in twenty success rate in that industry. . . . I think it was just a volume type business where they get, snap people up, they'll

> promise them a whole bunch and then a lot of people realized that that just wasn't their bag. . . . People who started with me they were dropping out, plus people who had been in the business for, like you know, a couple of years too, you could see they were dropping out too.

At an insurance company's sales meeting we observed, the district manager instructed his sales managers and agents on how to sell a life insurance policy designed to have investment value and to avoid some estate taxes that would otherwise be due to government. He emphasized that clients are often impressed by a policy that returns enough in effect to pay for itself. Such clients overlook the fact that, if they invested the same amount themselves in higher yielding and equally safe financial products, they would be much better off. He used the example of a farmer's son, who, the district manager said, is likely to be ignorant of the 'time value' (long-term investment value) of the money he will spend on insurance premiums:

> About 30 per cent of the policies being sold now are starting to have return of premium on them. People just love that concept, I'm not sure why. The farming son, he's probably going to put out $300,000 to $400,000 over the life of the policy. If they can get that money back, the way a farmer thinks, they don't worry about the time value of the money or anything like that. If they can get their principal back they're more than happy.

Imprudent investments

The 'time value' of money is precisely what the insurance industry thrives on. While they manage their 'loss ratio' (claims paid against premiums received) as best they can through policing of the claims process and through reinsurance, their profits are primarily derived from investment of premium dollars. While their clients are encouraged to be prudent risk minimizers – by purchasing policies that promise to take care of dependents in the event of untimely disabilities and death, and to provide some conservative investment yield – insurance companies themselves are risk takers in speculative investment markets. Their risk taking is both facilitated and cushioned by various mechanisms that effectively insure them. These mechanisms include, for example, industry-funded regulatory regimes and policyholder compensation schemes, as well as corporate liability rules that protect some (e.g. directors and officers, policyholders) more than others (e.g. creditors). As the following example suggests, such mechanisms are a source of moral hazard, reducing incentives for company directors and officials to avoid risky investments.

An example of how much risk a major insurance company is willing to take in investment markets is provided by the case of Confederation Life (McQueen 1996).[2] As of the mid-1990s, Confederation Life was the largest-ever North American insurance company failure, and the fourth largest financial institution failure worldwide. At the point of collapse, it faced unmet liability to life and health insurance policyholders of $450 million in Canada ($275 million of which was covered by the industry policyholder compensation scheme, CompCorp), and $800 million in the United States. Trade creditors, bond and commercial bond holders faced unmet liabilities of $1.3 billion.

Confederation Life had diversified enormously in the 1980s, exemplifying Milton Friedman's (1970) view that 'The social responsibility of business is to make profits'. For example, it developed a wide range of new insurance products, operated a trust company, operated a lease financing company, invested in derivatives, and invested in real estate. The major problem was its participation in speculative real estate markets and the way in which it used its trust company operation in this regard. By 1989, 74 per cent of its assets were tied up in real estate-related investments (compared to 30 to 40 per cent for other major Canadian life and health insurance companies), and these investments were debt-financed to exceptional levels (141 per cent of surplus, compared to, for example, 4 per cent in the case of Sun Life of Canada). Moreover, in the very high interest rate environment of the time, they were paying around 12 per cent interest on this debt and therefore required ongoing investment returns of at least 15 per cent to be profitable. When the capital value of their real estate holdings dropped 40 per cent by 1994, they were left holding properties and debt that proved too much to bear. As a senior federal regulator indicated to us in an interview, Confederation Life had a 'mismatch problem': too much investment in commercial property mortgages without proper expertise, financed with short-term commercial bonds:

> And that is something you don't do! A management problem. Way too aggressive. They thought they would just keep receiving these commercial notes and people would just come in. It doesn't happen. They are downgraded and no one wants to touch this any more.

During the period of imprudent investment, Confederation Life made significant changes to its insurance sales structure and practices. It eliminated its 'captive' (career) sales agent system and moved into distribution through various broker and agent commission sales networks. These new sales agents, inexperienced with the company, were asked to sell new products they were also unfamiliar with. Indeed, 75 per cent of the products were new, and sensitive to the interest rate environment. Forced to be aggressive in fields they knew little about, agents inevitably participated in various forms of mis-selling. Their mis-selling was underpinned by sales documents in the United States that misrepresented the sources of consumer protection available to policyholders. Not surprisingly, class action suits followed in a number of states, including Georgia, New York, and New Jersey. Company employees also suffered. While they may previously have trusted the company and felt secure in its employ, they eventually lost jobs, insurance benefit packages, and a sense of worth. Retired employees on company pensions also lost some benefits.

The Government of Canada, not wanting to add a moral hazard to its relationship with the insurance industry, refused to help finance a restructuring of the company. Moreover, its regulators did very little at any point along the way. The Superintendent of the federal regulatory agency responsible said:

> Failure is a fact of life in the United States. . . . In Canada, we have difficulty coming to terms with it. In Canada, when people lose money there is a need to search for a villain who is always by definition not the person who loses the money. We have to mature as a country and part of that maturity is to allow failure of financial services companies.
>
> (quoted by McQueen 1996: 258)

Other companies did little to protect Confederation Life, or indeed their own image as vultures. Instead, the major industry players jostled, negotiated, and then circled as vultures to acquire the profitable areas of business that remained in the Confederation Life portfolios. As McQueen (1996: 231) observes, the $275 million industry payout to policyholders under the CompCorp scheme was in effect a business expense for the companies participating in the ensuing acquisition process. None of the Confederation Life directors and officers faced sanctions beyond the shame of what was seen in retrospect as too much risk taking. The President of Confederation Life could offer nothing more than a farewell dinner speech at which he bore testimony to our neo-liberal future: 'As I look into the new century, I sense a return to those older values that drove people to be self-reliant, to take the responsibility for their own future and that of their families' (ibid.: 158).

Insuring the insurers

The Confederation Life story raises the question of relationships among insurance companies. They are effectively left to govern each other – either directly, or through industry-funded regulatory agencies and industry associations – but to do so in a neo-liberal environment of fierce competition, mergers, and acquisitions. A key feature of the relationship among insurance companies is that they take out insurance with each other. A given company may decide to reinsure because it does not have enough capacity to take on a given risk itself, or because it wants to distribute the risks in its overall portfolio. Industry-funded compensation schemes for policyholders, such as the CompCorp scheme, also constitute a form of reinsurance in that they provide for the indemnification of the policyholders of a company that proves unable to meet its contractual obligations. The world of reinsurance and compensation schemes is also ripe with moral hazards. Insurance companies involved in reinsurance contracts want to ensure that they are taking risks and laying off risks with companies that are prudent, have good contractual practices, are well managed, work with other reinsurers of high standing, and so on. To this end, they inspect and audit each other, and work through reinsurance brokers who provide ongoing intelligence about other companies. With large premiums and claims stakes involved, there is often distrust and concern about other insurance companies as policyholders, just as there is regarding individuals as policyholders.

To illustrate moral hazards at this level we can consider efforts to insure natural hazards. The (mis)selling of earthquake insurance in British Columbia is a case in point. While the science of earthquake risk is very shaky (Brun *et al.* 1997), and in spite of the fact that there has not been an earthquake that has caused serious damage to the built environment of the province, there is public perception of considerable risk. Hence, about 60 per cent of the property-insured population in the province purchase earthquake coverage. In contrast, in the Province of Quebec, which has about the same risk as British Columbia according to scientific evidence (ibid.), only about 3 per cent of the property-insured population purchases earthquake coverage.

Earthquake insurance coverage is sold in British Columbia even though there is explicit acknowledgement by the industry that a number of the companies involved would become insolvent if there was a medium-sized or greater earthquake in Vancouver. The failure of these companies would occur even after taking into account their reinsurance arrangements. The moral hazard problem posed by this situation is that companies that are more prudent in financing earthquake coverage will be obligated to compensate policyholders of the imprudent companies through the industry-funded Property and Casualty Insurance Compensation scheme. Such compensation is likely to be at very high levels, causing some of the more prudent companies to collapse as well in a house-of-cards effect. Reinsurers would also be affected to some degree. Meanwhile the provincial and federal governments, who would ultimately provide some financial relief following a major earthquake disaster, support this (mis)selling by the private insurance industry because it provides at least some reserve capital in case such a disaster occurs. Moreover, government does not wish to say explicitly that it will cover everything through disaster relief because such a statement would pose the ultimate moral hazard, for example reducing incentives to ensure that buildings, bridges, roads, and other infrastructures are earthquake-resistant.

The conduct of market conduct

The insurance industry is the first to recognize the myriad moral hazard problems embedded in the ways in which sells its products, invests, and insures itself. As a result, just as the industry devises sophisticated surveillance technologies to address moral hazard problems in its relationships with the populations it insures, so too it invokes a variety of surveillance technologies to police its own operatives.

Market conduct audits are administered through several mechanisms. First, government regulators set standards and monitor sales staff recruitment, training, and sales practices. For example, in the troublesome field of life insurance sales, regulators now typically require a waiting period (e.g. two weeks) during which the consumer can change her mind before the contract is finally bound;

and they also typically require the life insurance company to send a follow-up questionnaire to the consumer to ascertain her comprehension of her purchase. Second, industry associations set rules of underwriting and marketing. Since these associations are typically dominated by the largest companies in the given market, the rules they set in this regard tend to prevail regardless of what other, lesser companies may wish. Third, reinsurers are an important source of market conduct auditing. Since they themselves are taking on a significant share of a given risk, and often the biggest share relative to the primary insurer, they do regular monitoring of their own insurance partners as well as site inspections of their consumer files and practices. Fourth, companies do their own internal audits of market conduct. These audits are not simply actuarial and accounting exercises, but sometimes also involve use of their own Special Investigation Unit operatives to ferret out internal fraud and systematic corruption.

Insurance companies have been able to address some of their market conduct moral hazards as part of the fundamental restructuring of the industry that has been transpiring. This restructuring is being driven by economic globalization; technological changes, including information systems that have proven too costly for some companies to bear; the integration of the traditional four pillars of financial services (banks, trust companies, insurance companies, and securities dealing), and in particular the entry of banks into the insurance business; and attendant competition resulting in an acceleration in mergers and acquisitions. This re-structuring is allowing a neo-liberal rightsizing of career insurance employment, and a reorganization of relationships to independent brokers, that gives the insurance companies more direct auditing capacity over sales agents and their practices.

These changes are illustrated, for example, by a new agency distribution system that some insurance companies are developing whereby former captive agents, as well as other recruits, become in effect franchise holders of a local insurance agency operation. The franchise holder, with some minor exceptions, can sell only the one insurance company's designated products. Through this franchise system the agent-turned-franchise holder assumes a great deal more of the financial risk for the company's local operations. While constituted as an independent entrepreneur in assuming such risk, the franchise holder is nevertheless heavily regulated through very detailed rules for agency operation, backed up by 'mystery shopping' surveillance by company operatives who pose as customers. There are also stringent controls over selection of preferred insurable populations, for example making the commission paid partly dependent on the overall claims record of the agency.

Insurance company auditing of the sales process is even tighter in the case of the direct sales call centre operations that are proliferating. These operations, in keeping with call centres more generally, provide continuous surveillance of every sales act and ongoing performance calculations of the agent's sales record. All sales calls are recorded for playback if problems arise, for spot-check inspections, and for ongoing training in effective sales practices. In an insurance sales call centre we examined, there was a weekly training session involving the sales team coach and each of her sales agents individually. Each agent went through selected tape-recorded sales calls with the coach to assess the call against a 50-point checklist. This call centre also posted weekly performance statistics around the office, listing the percentage of sales 'hits' by each agent within the team in baseball batting average fashion, as well as a league table comparing the weekly performance of each team. It is difficult to imagine a more directly surveilled and audited environment.

Insurance operatives are also subject to inspections, surveillance, and training requirements through various forms of insurance that they purchase as part of their business operations. Directors and officers insurance, employment practices insurance, and errors and omissions insurance are all common in insurance companies, just as they are in other spheres of corporate activity. These types of insurance identify significant moral hazards in insurance company operations, and alter premiums, deductibles, exclusions, and riders accordingly. One barometer of the market conduct and solvency of an insurance company is the conditions under which it is able to insure itself via reinsurance, as well as directors and officers, employment practices, and errors and omissions insurances.

In spite of these complex and sophisticated means of surveillance regarding company fraud and moral hazard, significant problems persist. These surveillance mechanisms structure, shape, and manage moral hazards rather than eliminate them.

To summarize then, the trend is towards more and more segmentation and de-selection of insured populations, creating greater inequality in contract conditions and classes of the insurance poor and uninsured. This trend is consistent with neo-liberal marketing trends more generally, which are fragmenting populations into increasingly specialized communities of interest to the point of 'breaking up America' (Turow 1997; see also Slater 1997). Company-organized mis-selling is also rife. Furthermore, while insurers-as-bookmakers heavily regulate their gambling at the level of what risks they will insure and for whom, as investors they are subject to enabling conditions and sometimes gamble wildly on what turns out in retrospect to be folly. Not surprisingly, all the above practices lead insurance companies to see each other as morally hazardous, especially when it comes to partnerships in reinsurance and in compensation schemes for policyholders.

The moral hazards of neo-liberalism

We are now in a position to examine the basic features of neo-liberalism – minimal state, market fundamentalism, risk taking, individual responsibility, and acceptance of inequality – in light of our understanding of moral hazards in insurance as well as some additional considerations about the role of the insurance institution in society.

Neo-liberalism conjures a view of civil society as a self-generating mechanism of social solidarity. In fact, civil society requires massive intervention by the insurance institution in the absence of such solidarity. While state intervention itself has been reduced somewhat, at least in some areas of social insurance provision, governance is not diminished but rather changed and elaborated upon through the insurance institution. Insurance becomes *the* institution of governance, providing administrative and policing capacities for risk management, population management, social security and social cohesion. This is governance-at-a-distance, embedding surveillance and power in centres of calculation and networks of risk communication between insurance and other institutions (Latour 1987; Castels 1996, 1997, 1998; Ericson and Haggerty 1997).

Private insurance, as we have seen, bears many of the institutional tendencies and problems critics attribute to the welfare state. It poses difficult and sometimes intractable problems of moral hazard among both its insured populations and its own agents. Instead of social solidarity and community as 'a moral field binding persons into durable relations' (Rose 1997: 6), private insurance increasingly fragments populations into selective risk-rated communities with a price tag. This tendency marks the confluence, on the one hand, of niche marketing by insurers to survive in the neo-liberal marketplace and, on the other, intensified efforts to cope with private insurance's moral hazard problems by ever more finely tuning risk assessments of populations. As we saw in the case of the insurer of substandard driver risks, and in the comments of the actuarial expert in the same jurisdiction, the irony of unpooling risks has reached extreme forms in contemporary insurance markets.

The neo-liberal 'free market' promises security and prosperity by having fragmented individuals and collectivities participate in market relations that stimulate economic growth. On the one hand, the existence of the enormous surveillance apparatus of the insurance industry indicates that the market is not very fundamental. The insurance institution must intervene in the market in much the same way as the state. Substantial private policing operations and surveillance technologies are used to regulate moral hazards. On the other hand, the insurance industry and its associated private security suppliers turn the surveillance technologies into market commodities. The result is a commodification of some forms of security that were previously seen as the responsibility of the state. State security provision is increasingly subject to the cost of supplements, for example through private policing, private health insurance, and private pensions. It is also subject to new partnerships, often expressed through visions of 'community' as in community policing, community health, and community facilities for pensioners. There are also exclusive private markets for security products, especially preventive security devices that are a condition of property and casualty insurance contracts. These market supplements, partnerships, and exclusive products are supposed to blend into 'mutually reinforcing interests of personal security, private profit and public good' (Rose 1996: 342).

Those with a stake in a private property insurance relationship are contractually induced into buying loss reduction technologies, ranging from better locks to electronic alarms, surveillance cameras, and private police (O'Malley 1991). Those with a stake in a life and health insurance relationship are contractually induced into fitness and wellness practices (Staples 1997: 114–15). In this respect, every potential victim is also a suspect, suspected of not doing enough to reduce loss. And, every actual victim is also an offender, found not to have done enough to reduce loss and therefore subject to insurance sanctioning of higher premiums, higher deductibles, exclusion clauses, and, if there is too much recidivism, no insurance at all.

On the other hand, as we have seen, a great deal of fraud and other loss through moral hazard is tolerated and even fostered in insurance relationships. As Garland (1997: 187) observes, part of the responsibility of the neo-liberal *homo prudens* is to recognize which losses are not only inevitable but necessary for the smooth flow of social and economic life. Surveillance for preventive security has limits, as does law enforcement. Seen in this light, one can appreciate the following statement by Mr Large, then chair of the UK Securities and Investment Review Board, addressing the mis-selling of life insurance and pension schemes: 'We want to avoid over-regulation and too great an emphasis on prescription in all areas of financial services. Some hazards and dangers will always be there. Human nature will not change. People will still commit fraud' (*Money Marketing* 10 October 1995).

The policing mechanisms of insurance-as-governance are not designed simply to act on economic subjects of interest, but also to act through them. That is, these mechanisms mobilize both insurance operatives and insured persons as knowledgeable and reflexive risk assessors, risk minimizers, and risk takers. This enterprise goes well beyond the regulation of fraud *per se*. It generates all manner of surveillance that serves in turn much wider governmental purposes of population management (Simon 1997).

Neo-liberalism fosters a move away from the social security society of risk minimization, avoidance, and aversion, a move away from the human and institutional inertia that society is said to create. Instead, we are to become a risk-taking society of knowledgeable, responsible, reflexive risk takers. Insurance is a central institution in this regard. The markets in insurance and related security products are at the core of 'reflexive modernization' (Beck *et al.* 1994), forcing people constantly to look at themselves in the hall of mirrors of their risk attributes. Insurance also provides a 'safety net' when things go wrong in risk-taking enterprises, and participates in life course decisions about work, mortgages, child-rearing, investment, retirement, and so on.

There has been a significant shift in moral language from 'welfare' to 'safety net'. In turn, there are many new concepts within the discourse of 'safety net' to encourage people to see state support as only very temporary relief from their efforts to get ahead by taking risks. For example, in Canada the state unemployment insurance scheme has been relabelled 'employment insurance' to indicate that one must always be working, even when the work is seeking work. State political discourse as well as private marketing of (in)security perpetually reinforces the need to insure, save, and invest for the possible disabilities of life. Abilities are fostered to a limited extent by the 'social investment state', whose only promise is to commodify people as 'human resources' within the utilitarian morality of neo-liberalism. New Labour in the UK even suggests that the trope of 'trampoline' is better than 'safety net' because people become entangled in nets whereas what they should be doing is bouncing back immediately (Giddens 1998). Of course this view ignores how exhausting trampolines are even for the most fit, as well as the possibility that the less fit will miss the mark and become seriously disabled when they fall through one of the holes on the edge. The state also promises to provide the better off with some safety against the marginal populations who might threaten their hard-won freedoms, although again most of the protection in this regard must be bought on the private market in the form of gated communities, surveillance technologies, private police, and private insurances.

Under neo-liberalism, private insurance products are also part of risk taking. For example, life insurance is no longer only an exercise in thrift, aimed at avoidance of the possibility that one's dependants will be left in poverty or unable to afford a decent funeral (Zelizer 1997). It is also an investment, blending with mutual funds, tax planning, and other speculative products that promote individual responsibility for financial futures. This role of life insurance in planning one's personal political economy is emphasized in the financial self-help books that have flooded the market (Foot 1996). It also forms part of the new travelling circuses called 'financial forums' whose marquees promise enough reflexive knowledge of risk taking to allow one to leave the big top with a 'diploma in financial security' from 'The University of Money' (Rayher 1998). Facilitated by state governments desperate for tax revenues, lottery and casino gambling become 'a saint rather than a sinner' (O'Malley 1997: 41–2). While such gambling helps to educate the poor in neo-liberal risk-taking sensibilities, the poor have the most to lose because they risk becoming further entangled in the safety net or, worse still, falling through the holes at the edge of the trampoline.

The risk-taking aspects of insurance point to another irony. There are many ways in which insurance inevitably results in moral hazard. For example, as we saw in the case of speculative investment gambling by Confederation Life, corporate limited liability laws and practices may be viewed as a source of moral hazard because they facilitate risk taking that transfers risks to creditors. A product such as health insurance is highly socially desirable despite extensive problems with moral hazard. While it entails substantial fraud and other financial losses on one level, it results, on other levels, in enormous social gains, such as greater productivity, well-being, and social responsibility. In most circumstances it is a matter of where the moral hazard problem will be located among the parties to the risk-taking relationship. Reducing the moral hazard problem for one party may increase it for another. For example, a strict products liability regime is likely to create a moral hazard problem at the level of consumers, but every reduction in strictness will amplify the moral hazard problem at the level of manufacturers (Baker 1996: 272–3; see also Gowri 1997).

If moral hazard is institutionalized and inevitable, then the central political question becomes: who should be made responsible for conditions that people suffer – states, private insurers, employers, families, or the individuals themselves (ibid.)? The neo-liberal answer to this question is uncomplicated. The individual is responsible. She is to be her own political economy, an informed, self-sufficient consumer of insurance and other security products. Neo-liberalism fits comfortably with the economic individualism of private insurance, and they constitute each other in discourse and practice. Insurance is required to the extent the individual is defined as an autonomous economic unit. Insurance is required for risks that are classified as the problem of the individual, classifications that the insurance institution itself contributes to because it perpetuates conventions that individuals are to be responsible for risks. 'Thus, ironically, purchasing an insurance can be understood as a way to protect oneself against the effects of the existence of the insurance system' (Gowri 1997: 196).

As documented in our analysis of moral hazard and its regulation, individual responsibility for risk does not occur spontaneously but must be actively governed. Indeed, the active management of responsible choice in risk taking is at the core of neo-liberal governance. Insurance links individual self-governance to institutional discourses and practices of governance for risk taking and security provision. This is 'institutionalized individualism' through which 'people are invited to constitute themselves as individuals: to plan, understand, design themselves as individuals' (Beck 1998). The governance of institutionalized individualism does offer people choice and agency (Garland 1997), but not freedom or liberty (Rose 1999, 2000). Freedom and liberty are based on the capacity to choose actions without external constraints, but there are real constraints in insurance regimes and other institutions of governance they connect with.

As introduced in the above discussion of a moral language shift from 'welfare' to 'safety net', the insurance institution plays a significant role in the political language of neo-liberal responsibility. Increasingly, 'risk', 'security', 'market', 'responsibility' and so on are not only technical terms used by insurance operatives, but also part of the everyday lexicon of self-governing subjects (O'Malley 1997: 30–1). Insurance operatives themselves are subject to politically correct language in this regard. This language control is aimed at altering the public discourse of responsibility and, in turn, institutional and individual practices in attributing responsibility. For example, in a large vehicle insurance company we studied, operatives were explicitly required to refer to vehicle 'crashes' rather than 'accidents' because 'accidents' connotes a lack of responsibility whereas 'crashes' leaves open the attribution of responsibility (cf. Green 1997).

Moral hazard is itself used as a 'responsibilizing' concept of individual rational choice by the law and economics intellectual arm of neo-liberalism (Baker 1996). As Baker (1996: 276–7) observes, it is based on a number of problematic assumptions, such as that money compensates for loss; people are rational (money) loss minimizers; insured people have effective control over themselves and their property; and, preventive security is effective. As such, it ignores other levels of analysis and possibilities, for example the ways in which other institutions contribute to safety and security; the cognition of contracting parties; the cultural meanings of money beyond narrow instrumentalism (Zelizer 1997); cultural interpretations of what else apart from money is valued;

the subjective meaning of losses such as pain; and, the inevitability of certain moral hazards in insurance relationships.

The political language of individual responsibility fostered by the insurance industry – including the way in which it conceptualizes moral hazard as a problem only at the level of individual insureds – shifts thought and action away from the loftier levels of moral order and collective responsibilities. Just as one hardly ever thinks of welfare any more, only safety nets or trampolines, so one hardly ever thinks of higher moral codes any more, only situational ethics. As Rose (1997: 16) observes, neo-liberalism fosters the applied ethics of being responsible 'as the practical shaping by the individual of the daily practices of his or her life'. In this light the politically correct language of neo-liberal responsibility may well change 'moral hazard' to 'ethical hazard'.

The emphasis on individual responsibility under neo-liberalism accompanies changing conceptions of rights. Individual rights are circumscribed, except as they pertain to the expression of personal voice, competence, and self-sufficiency; that is, as exemplars of neo-liberalism. 'No rights without responsibilities' (Giddens 1998: 65) means rights will be granted only to those who meet their ethical obligations of self-sufficiency. Individual legal rights diminish in favour of system rights to knowledge useful in the administration of populations. This trend is evident not only in the surveillance systems of the insurance industry, but also in associated institutions. For example, in the criminal justice institution the law of criminal procedure lessens rights for suspects and accused persons, and enhances system rights to surveillance that facilitate population management more generally (Ericson 1994a, 1994b; Ericson and Haggerty 1997). Perhaps the most extreme example of this point is the recent decision by the state of Iceland to contract with a pharmaceutical company to develop DNA sampling, research, and databases on the entire Icelandic population.

The neo-liberal focus on individual responsibility leads to the view that there should be less protection for those who suffer a loss that they themselves cannot pay for, rather than placing the onus on institutions to compensate for loss and provide safe and healthy environments. The intensified policing of disability claims addressed earlier is a case in point. This policing is focused on blaming the victim, rather than on fostering economic prosperity for the less well-off that is a proven strong correlate of healthy populations (Sullivan *et al.* 1997).

Neo-liberalism chooses inequality. Within a neo-liberal regime of responsible risk taking all difference, and the inequalities that result from it, is seen as a matter of choice. If one ends up poor, unemployed, and unfulfilled, it is because of poorly thought-out risk decisions. Again, self-help books convey the neo-liberal sensibility. In *Facing the Future*, Worzel (1994) counsels that 'In the 1990s jobs are like all-terrain vehicles. You are the driver and there are no roads. You determine the direction, the speed, the state of repair, and you're responsible for everything good or bad that happens along the way.'

Seen as a choice, inequality is also seen as inevitable. Where neo-liberalism has been the strongest – in the United States, the United Kingdom, and New Zealand – wealth inequality has increased and been the greatest (Giddens 1998:

106; see also Atkinson 2000). Wealth inequality is accompanied by employment and income inequality, with ongoing 'rightsizing' as well as knowledge/service industry divisions. Entitlement (rights) inequality also prospers because there are to be no rights without individual responsibilities, and because rights are now determined by each private institution in terms of its own risk management criteria of inclusion and exclusion.

Private insurance exemplifies these dimensions of inequality as it constitutes fragmented and unequal communities of policyholders. It constitutes communities of difference, constantly unpooling risks in the very process of trying to create its saleable commodity of good selection pools. It is not in the business of redistributing resources among the insured, but rather of discriminating in favour of those who contribute to the goodness of the pool and the prosperity of the company. It would be acting immorally if it did otherwise. Thus it constitutes communities of interest, user-pay communities into which entrance is purchased with cash, not collective sentiments. As always, there is choice: the rich can afford to self-insure, the poor can gamble in desperation.

In a risk society organized through probability statistics and the taming of chance (Hacking 1990), insurers appear to be simply responding to the facts in ways that are ethically and commercially necessary (Gowri 1997). In fact, they are also a difference machine, constituting a world of fragmented interests in increasingly refined calibrations of deselection. The deselected insurance poor, who cannot afford the insurance premiums necessary to buy their way into social and economic networks of risk-taking, are left for the state to handle, along with the uninsurable catastrophes (Beck 1992a, 1992b). Faced with the most intractable problems of risk, the state is bound to experience recurrent legitimation crises, which only heighten demands for neo-liberal solutions beyond the state.

Acknowledgements

Earlier versions of this paper were presented by Richard Ericson to a conference on 'Crime, Risk and Neo-Liberalism', City University of New York; to the Visiting Fellows Colloquium, All Souls College, Oxford; to the Department of Sociology, London School of Economics and Political Science; and to the Centre for Law and Society, University of Edinburgh. He thanks Kevin Stenson, Bob Sullivan, Paul Rock, Martin West, and James Sheptycki for organizing those occasions, and all those present who provided critical comments. The authors also thank Pat O'Malley, Tom Baker, Paul Rock, and Ian Loader for their detailed comments on an earlier draft of this paper.

Notes

1 We have conducted 224 open-focused interviews in Canada and the United States. Interviewees included people with a wide range of responsibilities in the insurance

industry, professionals in expert systems that serve the industry, representatives of consumer associations, members of the general public who were consumers, industry regulators, senior civil servants, and members of parliament. Observational research included attending industry conferences, and observing sales operations, loss prevention operations, and claims-related examination practices. The research was funded by the Social Sciences and Humanities Research Council of Canada, the Canada Council Killam Research Fellowship Program, and the Visiting Fellows Program of All Souls College.

2 The account of the Confederation Life failure relies heavily on the excellent analysis by McQueen (1996).

References

Arnott, R. and **Stiglitz, J.** (1991) 'Moral hazard and nonmarket institutions: dysfunctional crowding out or peer monitoring?', *American Economic Review* 81(1): 179.

Atkinson, A. (2000) 'Can welfare states compete in a global economy?', in R. Ericson and N. Stehr (eds) *Governing Modern Societies*, Toronto: University of Toronto Press.

Baker, T. (1994) 'Constructing the insurance relationship: sales stories, claims stories, and insurance contract damages', *Texas Law Review* 75: 1395–434.

——(1996) 'On the genealogy of moral hazard', *Texas Law Review* 72: 237–92.

Beck, U. (1992a) *Risk Society: Toward a New Modernity*, London: Sage.

——(1992b) 'Modern society as a risk society', in N. Stehr and R. Ericson (eds) *The Culture and Power of Knowledge*, Berlin and New York: de Gruyter, pp. 199–214.

——(1998) 'The cosmopolitan manifesto', *New Statesman*, 20 March.

——, **Giddens, A.** and **Lash, S.** (1994) *Reflexive Modernization: Politics, Tradition and Aesthetics in the Modern Social Order*, Cambridge: Polity Press.

Brun, S., Etkin, D., Law, D., Wallace, L. and **White, R.** (1997) *Coping with Natural Hazards in Canada: Scientific, Government and Insurance Industry Perspectives*, Toronto: Institute of Environmental Studies, University of Toronto.

Castels, M. (1996) *The Information Age: Economy, Society and Culture.* Volume I: *The Rise of the Network Society*, Oxford: Blackwell.

——(1997) *The Information Age: Economy, Society and Culture.* Volume II: *The Power of Identity*, Oxford: Blackwell.

——(1998) *The Information Age: Economy, Society and Culture.* Volume III: *End of Millennium*, Oxford: Blackwell.

Clarke, M. (1999) *Citizens' Financial Futures: The Regulation of Retail Financial Services in Britain*, Aldershot: Gower.

Dandeker, C. (1990) *Surveillance, Power and Modernity: Bureaucracy and Discipline from 1700 to the Present Day*, New York: St. Martin's Press.

Ditton, J. (1979) *Controlology: Beyond the New Criminology*, London: Macmillan.

Dornstein, K. (1996) *Accidentally on Purpose: The Making of a Personal Injury Underworld in America*, New York: St. Martin's Press.

Ericson, R. (1993) *Making Crime: A Study of Detective Work*, 2nd edn, Toronto: University of Toronto Press.

——(1994a) 'The Royal Commission on Criminal Justice System Surveillance', in M. McConville and L. Bridges (eds) *Criminal Justice in Crisis*, Aldershot: Edward Elgar, pp. 113–40.

——(1994b) 'The decline of innocence', *University of British Columbia Law Review* 28: 367–83.

——and **Haggerty, K.** (1997) *Policing the Risk Society*, Toronto: University of Toronto Press; Oxford: Oxford University Press.

Friedman, M. (1988) 'The social responsibility of business is to increase its profits', in T. Donaldson and P. Werhane (eds) *Ethical Issues in Business: A Philosophical Approach*, Englewood Cliffs, NJ: Prentice-Hall.

Foot, D. (1996) *Boom, Bust and Echo: How to Profit from the Coming Demographic Shift*, Toronto: Macfarlane Walter & Ross.

Gandy, O. (1993) *The Panoptic Sort: A Political Economy of Personal Information*, Boulder, CO: Westview.

Garland, D. (1997) '"Governmentality" and the problem of crime: Foucault, criminology, sociology', *Theoretical Criminology* 1: 173–214.

Giddens, A. (1998) *The Third Way: The Renewal of Social Democracy*, Cambridge: Polity Press.

Gowri, A. (1997) 'The irony of insurance: community and commodity', PhD dissertation, University of Southern California.

Green, J. (1997) *Risk and Misfortune: The Social Construction of Accidents*, London: UCL Press.

Hacking, I. (1990) *The Taming of Chance*, Cambridge: Cambridge University Press.

Heimer, C. (1985) *Reactive Risk and Rational Action: Managing Moral Hazard in Insurance Contracts*, Berkeley, CA: University of California Press.

Latour, B. (1987) *Science in Action*, Cambridge, MA: Harvard University Press.

Lindbeck, A. (1995) 'Hazardous welfare state dynamics', *American Economic Review* 85(2): 9.

McQueen, R. (1996) *Who Killed Confederation Life?*, Toronto: McClelland & Stewart.

Marsland, D. (1996) *Welfare or Welfare State?*, Basingstoke: Macmillan.

O'Malley, P. (1991) 'Legal networks and domestic security', *Studies in Law, Politics and Society* 11: 171–90.

——(1997) 'Governing thrift: insurance, technology, political rationalities and working class security', unpublished paper, School of Law and Legal Studies, LaTrobe University.

——(ed.) (1998) *Crime and the Risk Society*, Aldershot: Dartmouth.

Rayher, J. (1998) 'Governing the future: marketing financial security', MA thesis, Department of Anthropology and Sociology, University of British Columbia.

Reichman, N. (1986) 'Managing crime risks: towards an insurance based model of social control', in S. Spitzer and A. Scull (eds) *Research in Law, Deviance and Social Control*, Greenwich, CT: JAI Press, pp. 151–72.

Rose, N. (1996) 'The death of the social? Re-figuring the territory of government', *Economy and Society* 25: 327–56.

——(1997) 'Between authority and liberty: governing virtue in a free society', paper presented to a conference on Civil Society, Communitarianism, Third Sector, Helsinki, October.

——(1999) *Powers of Freedom: Reframing Political Thought*, Cambridge: Cambridge University Press.

——(2000) 'Governing liberty', in R. Ericson and N. Stehr (eds) *Governing Modern Societies*, Toronto: University of Toronto Press, pp. 141–76.

Simon, J. (1987) 'The emergence of risk society: insurance, law and the state', *Socialist Review* 95: 61–89

——(1997) 'Governing through crime', in George Fisher and Lawrence Friedman (eds) *The Crime Conundrum: Essays on Criminal Justice*, Boulder, CO: Westview, pp. 171–90.

Slater, D. (1997) *Consumer Culture and Modernity*, Cambridge: Polity Press.

Staples, W. (1997) *The Culture of Surveillance: Discipline and Social Control in the United States*, New York: St. Martin's Press.

Strange, S. (1996) *The Retreat of the State: The Diffusion of Power in the World Economy*, Cambridge: Cambridge University Press.

Sullivan, T., Shainblum E. and **Frank J.** (1997) 'Multicausality and the future of workers' compensation', paper to The Third International Congress on Medical-Legal Aspects of Work Injury.

Turow, J. (1997) *Breaking Up America: Advertisers and the New Media World*, Chicago: University of Chicago Press.

Weisberg, H. and **Derrig, R.** (1991) 'Fraud and automobile insurance: a report

on bodily injury claims in Massachusetts', *Journal of Insurance Regulation* 9: 497–541.
—— and —— (1992) 'Massachusetts bodily injury tort reform', *Journal of Insurance Regulation* 10: 384–440.

Worzel, R. (1994) *Facing the Future: The Seven Forces Revolutionizing our Lives*, Toronto: Stoddart.

Zelizer, V. (1997) *The Social Meaning of Money*, Princeton, NJ: Princeton University Press.

[10]
The Policing of Risk

Risk Communication

Risk refers to such external dangers as a natural disaster, technological catastrophe, and threatening behavior by human beings. The system for communicating risk—its people, rules, formats, and technologies—is a part of the social meaning of risk. That is, threats and dangers are recognized, responded to, and made real through the human invention and use of risk classifications and technologies.

Risk-communication systems are not simply conduits through which knowledge of risk is transferred. Rather, they have their own logics and autonomous processes. They are themselves the producers of new risks, because it is through them that risks are recognized, subject to calculation, and acted upon. They govern institutional relations, and they affect what individuals and organizations are able to accomplish.

Risk society is comprised of institutions that organize on the basis of knowledge of risk. These institutions expend a significant proportion of their resources on the production and distribution of knowledge of risk. This knowledge is used to manage populations, provide security, and take risks.

The Forms of Policing

The police are at the fulcrum of risk communication among institutions. They are first and foremost knowledge workers who think and act within the risk-communication systems of other institutions. An appreciation of the changing role of police within risk-communication systems can be gleaned from an examination of changes to their official forms for reporting occurrences. Changes to the occurrence report forms of a large urban police organization we studied illustrate the shift from an open narrative format to fixed-choice risk classifications.

Before 1939 the occurrence report was simply written on a blank sheet of paper. The reporting officer was required to compose a narrative of his investigation without the aid of any classification format. The first step in formalization of the occurrence report took place in 1939 (figure 1). The neophyte form was headed "Occurrence Report" and had spaces for the date, subject, occurrence number, file number, and inspector's signature indicating approval of the narrative. But the investigating police officer was still required to compose a narrative of the "once upon a time there was a theft" variety, as is illustrated by the narrative from 1939 reproduced in figure 1. This form remained in place until the 1960s.

Figure 2 reproduces the offence report as it appeared in 1964. Here we see the beginning of enclosed formatting. There are twenty-eight items in addition to the narrative. These relate to investigative details such as the victim's profile and how the crime was carried out. Apparently safecracking was a problem at the time, as it is given its own section. Vehicular information is also singled out as relevant to investigations. In addition, there are classifications related to the nascent effort to risk-manage police officers' activities and efficiency. For example, knowledge must be provided about how the matter came to police attention ("How Received: Radio, Station, Citizen, On View"), and about its disposition ("Case Declared: Unfounded, Cleared by Arrest, Cleared Otherwise, Inactive Not Cleared, Investigation Continuing"). The narrative space is now reduced to half the page.

Figure 3 reproduces the occurrence report in use in 1981. While officers could add a "continuation report" that included a space for a narrative, figure 3 is entirely formatted in fixed-closure terms. It calls for precise detail on the offence and when it occurred, and on the modus operandi ("M.O"). It requires a detailed population profiling of victims, and an even more detailed population profiling of accused persons, suspects, and missing-person "subjects." The population of vehicles is also subject to extensive classification and validation. The population of investigating police officers is profiled by recording how they were notified about the occurrence, how they processed the case—for instance, by applying for a warrant, issuing an appearance notice to the accused, serving a subpoena, issuing a victim services card, or entering information on the CPIC (Canadian Police Information Centre) national computerized police data system—and what the outcome of the case was. This profiling is also furthered by providing space

OCCURRENCE REPORT

City Police Headquarters
Province, May 31st. 1939

Chief Constable

Subject: Re Theft of dresses

Occ.
No.______
File No.______

I beg to report that on March 23rd, 1939, Mrs [Victim] reported the theft of three dresses to the value of $5.94, from the soft drink counter at Woolworth's Store, these dresses were taken on Saturday the 11th of March.

About a week after they were taken one of the dresses was exchanged at the dress shop where they had been purchased by [the Victim].

On interviewing the Clerk that had sold the dresses I learned that a girl from Woolworth's had exchanged this dress, I took the Clerk to Woolworth's store and she pointed out [Miss X] who was in charge of the soft drink counter as the girl that had exchanged it.

[Miss X] stated that on the date the dresses were stolen a foreign woman who was described as about 35 to 40 yrs. old, dark comp. slim build and wearing winter clothing had spoken to her, she asked her for her address and she said that she would send her something from the farm, a few days later this woman sent the dress to her asking her to return it to the dress shop, get a refund of the money and return it to her, she sent a letter with the parcel which [Miss X] produced when she returned the dress, this letter was destroyed when it served it's purpose and [Miss X] stated that she was not sure of the name but it started with P and ended with uik, this woman lived on a farm in the district.

[Miss X] promised to get in touch with the police when she saw this woman again in the City, she was discharged from Woolworth's on account of this matter and stated that she did not get a chance to see her again.

As [the victim] called at this Office a few days ago, Miss X was again interviewed and gave the same story as previously mentioned, she is living above a store, 4th Ave. and 1st St. E., she is working in the Restaurant on the corner of 6th Ave. and 4th St. E.

Miss X appears very anxious to get this matter cleared and if she ever sees this woman she will notify this Dept., Mr. Y was looking after her interests in regard to this matter.

Examined and forwarded

Respectfully submitted,

.... Inspector

Detective.

Figure 1. Police Occurrence Report Form, 1939

CASE NO.

OFFENCE REPORT

1. OFFENCE				2. DIVISION	3. DATE AND TIME OF THIS REPORT	
4. PLACE OF OCCURRENCE					PATROL AREA	REPORT ZONE
5. TIME OF OCCURRENCE	DAY	DATE	MONTH	YEAR	HOUR	RELIEF
6. VICTIM (IF FIRM, NAME AND TYPE OF BUSINESS)				7. HOME ADDRESS		8. HOME PHONE
				9. BUSINESS ADDRESS		10. BUS. PHONE
11. DESCRIPTION OF VICTIM	SEX	AGE	RACE OR NATIONALITY	OCCUPATION		MARITAL STATUS
12. REPORTED BY (NAME AND RELATIONSHIP TO VICTIM)				ADDRESS		PHONE

13. TYPE OF PREMISES (PREMISES USED FOR)	14. HOW ATTACKED (HOW COMMITED—ENTRANCE GAINED)
15. MEANS OF ATTACK (WEAPONS—TOOLS USED)	16. OBJECT OF ATTACK (MOTIVE—TYPE OF PROPERTY STOLEN)

17. SAFE ATTACKED YES ☐ NO ☐	EXPLOSIVES	TORCH	PUNCH	PEEL	WORKED COMB	CARRIED AWAY	OTHER (DESCRIBE)
18. TRADE MARKS							

19. DESC. OF VEHICLE USED	YEAR	MAKE	MODEL	COLOR	LICENSE UNUSUAL FEATURES
20. DETAILS AND WITNESSES:					

21. REPORT BY				22. ACCOMPANIED BY		23. C.I.B. PERSONNEL IN ATTENDANCE	
24. HOW RECEIVED	RADIO	STATION	CITIZEN	ON VIEW	DATE AND TIME REPORTED	APPROVED BY	
CASE DECLARED	UNFOUNDED	CLRD BY ARREST	CLRD OTHERWISE	IN-ACTIVE NOT CLRD	INVSTGN. CONT.		SIGNATURE
BULLENTIN NO.	CANCELLED	CIRCULAR NO.	CANCELLED	TABULATED			TYPED BY

Figure 2. Police Occurrence Report Form, 1964

for supervisory checks, including the warning "No approval unless all facts embodied. Approving officer will be held responsible."

By the early 1990s this process of the formalization of police reports had advanced to a "paperless" computerized occurrence report system. Officers are no longer required to fill out occurrence reports by hand, but rather do

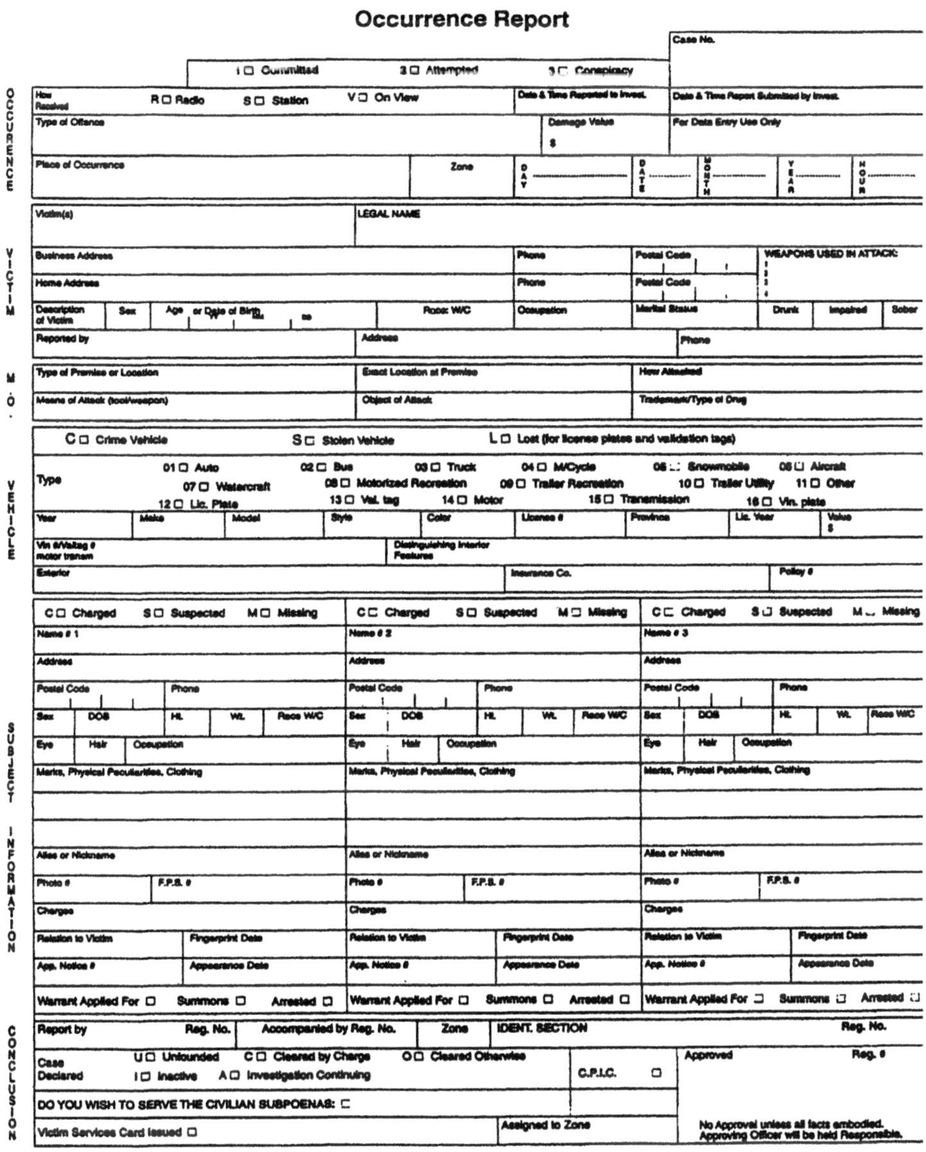

Occurrence Report

Case No.

1 ☐ Committed 2 ☐ Attempted 3 ☐ Conspiracy

OCCURRENCE

How Received R ☐ Radio S ☐ Station V ☐ On View | Date & Time Reported to Invest. | Date & Time Report Submitted by Invest.

Type of Offence | Damage Value $ | For Data Entry Use Only

Place of Occurrence | Zone | DAY | DATE | MONTH | YEAR | HOUR

VICTIM

Victim(s) | LEGAL NAME

Business Address | Phone | Postal Code | WEAPONS USED IN ATTACK:

Home Address | Phone | Postal Code

Description of Victim | Sex | Age or Date of Birth | Race: W/C | Occupation | Marital Status | Drunk | Impaired | Sober

Reported by | Address | Phone

M.O.

Type of Premise or Location | Exact Location at Premise | How Attacked

Means of Attack (tool/weapon) | Object of Attack | Trademark/Type of Drug

VEHICLE

C ☐ Crime Vehicle S ☐ Stolen Vehicle L ☐ Lost (for license plates and validation tags)

Type: 01 ☐ Auto 02 ☐ Bus 03 ☐ Truck 04 ☐ M/Cycle 05 ☐ Snowmobile 06 ☐ Aircraft 07 ☐ Watercraft 08 ☐ Motorized Recreation 09 ☐ Trailer Recreation 10 ☐ Trailer Utility 11 ☐ Other 12 ☐ Lic. Plate 13 ☐ Val. tag 14 ☐ Motor 15 ☐ Transmission 16 ☐ Vin. plate

Year | Make | Model | Style | Color | License # | Province | Lic. Year | Value $

Vin #/Valtag # motor transm | Distinguishing Interior Features

Exterior | Insurance Co. | Policy #

SUBJECT INFORMATION

C ☐ Charged S ☐ Suspected M ☐ Missing (×3)

Name # 1 | Name # 2 | Name # 3

Address

Postal Code | Phone

Sex | DOB | Ht. | Wt. | Race W/C

Eye | Hair | Occupation

Marks, Physical Peculiarities, Clothing

Alias or Nickname

Photo # | F.P.S. #

Charges

Relation to Victim | Fingerprint Date

App. Notice # | Appearance Date

Warrant Applied For ☐ Summons ☐ Arrested ☐

CONCLUSION

Report by | Reg. No. | Accompanied by Reg. No. | Zone | IDENT. SECTION | Reg. No.

Case Declared U ☐ Unfounded C ☐ Cleared by Charge O ☐ Cleared Otherwise 1 ☐ Inactive A ☐ Investigation Continuing | C.P.I.C. ☐ | Approved | Reg. #

DO YOU WISH TO SERVE THE CIVILIAN SUBPOENAS: ☐

Victim Services Card Issued ☐ | Assigned to Zone | No Approval unless all facts embodied. Approving Officer will be held Responsible.

Figure 3. Police Occurrence Report Form, 1981

so electronically using highly specific categories and codes. Fully printed out, the present occurrence report runs to twelve pages of fixed-choice classifications.

We interviewed a veteran member of this police organization and discussed the changes that had taken place over time in report formatting. He attributed the changes to the combined effects of computerization and the demand for knowledge from external institutions:

> When I joined, the [general occurrence] report was one 8.5 by 11 [page] that was folded into three, and the boxed information would then be on that much . . . and now we're up to twelve pages. . . . Computers are driving it. The fact that we *can* now collect vast amounts of data. . . . The more information you have, the more information people want, so you gather more, so they want more, and you just keep going and going and going.

The lengthening of a given police form and the proliferation of classifications within it has been accompanied by an enormous expansion in the number and nature of forms. For example, by 1992 the Royal Canadian Mounted Police (RCMP) had, because of the many federal, provincial, and municipal government jurisdictions and private sector institutions it served, approximately twenty-one hundred operational forms and a staff of six hundred full-time knowledge workers in a special "Informatics" division.

A single new reporting requirement can have a dramatic impact on police personnel allocation and resources. For example, in England and Wales there is a requirement that all police audiotape of interviews with suspects must be summarized on a standard form. The time devoted to this one knowledge-work requirement is estimated to be equal to the full-time efforts of fourteen hundred police officers, the equivalent of about 1 percent of the entire constabulary of England and Wales (Royal Commission on Criminal Justice 1993)!

Further appreciation of how the police have embraced risk can be gleaned from considering their reporting of vehicle collisions. In figure 4 we reproduce the 1991 Alberta Collision Report Form. This form requires the police to provide fine-grained detail on the background to the collision, the parties involved, the vehicles, the vehicle owners, and road and environmental conditions at the time. It comes with a forty-eight-page *Alberta Manual on Classification and Reporting of Vehicle Collisions,* which provides highly specific coding instructions for each category and classification on the form. The form and the manual together turn the investigating officer into, in effect, a social scientist field worker guided by fixed-choice criteria designed to facilitate systematic observation. Thus formatted, the officer is bound to report the collision within the constraints imposed by the risk-relevant criteria of external institutions. Every detail of context, people, vehicles, roads, and environments is registered and subsequently

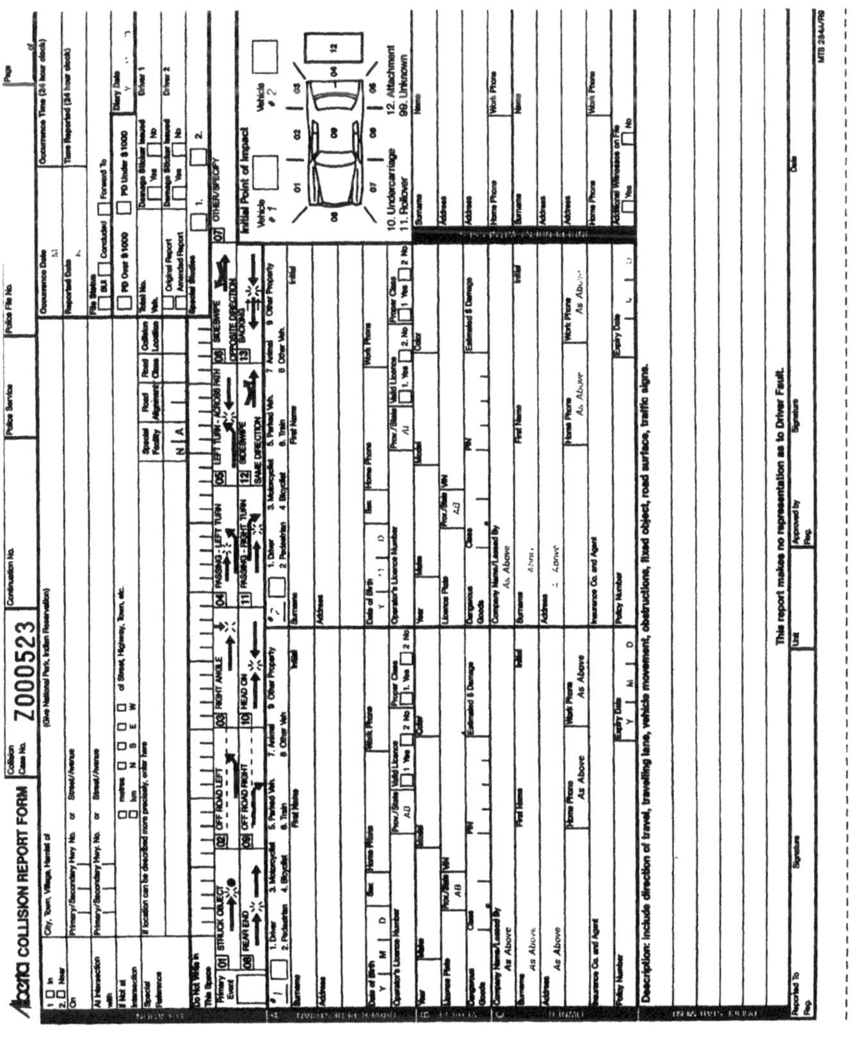

Fig. 4. Traffic Collision Report Form, 1991

Please Select One Item From Each Of The Sections Listed Below. (X)

Alberta COLLISION REPORT FORM | Collision Case No. Z000523 | Police Service | Police File No.

Object Identification

1 2		1 2	
	01. Passenger Car		13. Fixed Object
	02. Pick-Up/Van <4500kg		14. Train
	03. Mini-Van/MPV		15. Animal
	04. Truck >4500kg		16. Motorhome
	05. Truck Tractor		17. Construction Equipment
	06. Motorcycle/Scooter		18. Emergency Vehicle
	07. Pedestrian		19. Farm Equipment
	08. Bicycle		20. Off-Highway Vehicle
	09. School Bus		21. Motorized Snow Vehicle
	10. Transit Bus		22. Moped
	11. Intercity Bus		98. Other/Specify
	12. Other Bus		99. Unknown

Light Conditions (Choose one in A and one in B)

1 2	A	1 2	B
	01. Daylight		01. No Artificial Light
	02. Sunglare		02. Artificial Light
	03. Darkness		99. Unknown
	99. Unknown		

Traffic Control Device

1 2		1 2	
	01. None Present		07. School Bus
	02. Traffic Signal/Lights		08. Lane Control Signal
	03. Stop Sign		09. RR Crossing
	04. Yield Sign		98. Other/Specify
	05. Merge Sign		
	06. Pedestrian Cross-Walk		99. Unknown

Contributing Road Condition

1 2		1 2	
	01. No Unusual Condition		05. Oily Pavement
	02. Under Const./Maint.		06. Soft/Sharp Shoulder
	03. Hole/Ruts/Bumps		98. Other/Specify
	04. Slippery When Wet		99. Unknown

Environmental Condition

	01. Clear		05. Fog/Smog/Smoke/Dust
	02. Raining		06. High Wind
	03. Hail/Sleet		98. Other/Specify
	04. Snow		99. Unknown

Surface Condition

	01. Dry		05. Muddy
	02. Wet		98. Other/Specify
	03. Slush/Snow/Ice		
	04. Loose Surface Mat.		99. Unknown

INSTRUCTIONS

This form is **NOT** to be used if there has been **A FATALITY OR INJURY, A HIT AND RUN CRASH, OR A CRASH INVOLVING A NATIONAL SAFETY CODE VEHICLE** (school bus, truck >4500 kg, truck tractor).

PLEASE HAVE YOUR DRIVER'S LICENCE, VEHICLE REGISTRATION, INSURANCE (PINK) CARD, AND THE VEHICLE WHICH WAS INVOLVED IN THE COLLISION WHEN REPORTING TO THE POLICE.

EACH DRIVER SHALL COMPLETE EITHER THE BLUE OR YELLOW SECTIONS OF THIS FORM ONLY.

A. DRIVER INFORMATION
OPERATOR LICENCE NUMBER - This number should appear on the top portion of your Alberta Driver's Licence (Example: 123456-999)

B. VEHICLE INFORMATION
Please take the following information from your vehicle registration documents:

YEAR: Enter the year of vehicle using the last two digits only. ("86" for a 1986 vehicle)
MAKE MODEL: EXAMPLE: Ford Bronco or Chev Camaro.
COLOR: Enter the color(s) of the vehicle as per registration.
LICENCE PLATE: This is the plate number on your vehicle.
VIN: This is your vehicle identification number found on your vehicle registration.
This number is a long one, please make sure you have copied it correctly.

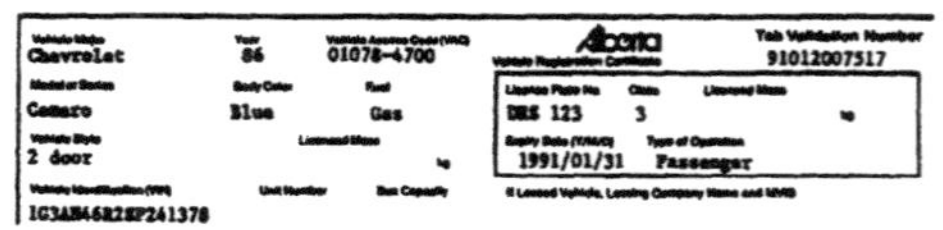

C. WHO OWNS THIS VEHICLE?
Please use your insurance pink card to assist you in completing the following:
Owner Name and Address.
Insurance Co./Agent:
Write the name of the insurance company and the agent in this area.
For example: XXX Insurance Inc., Protect Agencies Inc.
Policy Number: Write the policy number from the area on the pink card.

D. Please select only **ONE** item from <u>each</u> of the sections listed: Check only the <u>one</u> which best describes.

Printed on Recycled Paper

POLICE COPY

Fig. 4. *Continued*

risk profiled to ascertain the norm and the anomaly. That is, the job of the police, and of all other institutions connected with the collision event, is to ensure that the event is interpreted in terms of whether it is or is not a "normal accident," for a "normal accident" is no accident at all but, indeed, a collision.

Myriad institutions require knowledge of collisions as part of their risk-management systems, and they each influence the risk-communication format of this collision report. For example, the government motor vehicles registry requires risk knowledge regarding driver records, traffic engineering problems, collision prevention, and automobile industry compliance with safety standards. The automobile industry requires risk knowledge regarding the safety of its vehicles for compliance and product improvement. Insurance companies require risk knowledge to allocate liability in the particular case, develop risk ratings for drivers and vehicles in general, establish premium and deductible levels, establish levels of compensation, and undertake collision prevention initiatives. The criminal courts require risk knowledge if the collision results from a driving-related offense. Last and least, the police administration requires risk knowledge to measure the productivity records of its officers and to allocate resources.

The Police and Crime Risks

Risk communication is central to all aspects of police work. The police are not only involved in law enforcement, order maintenance, and social service, but in all of these roles they are also knowledge workers engaged in the production and distribution of knowledge of risk.

Risk-communication work certainly takes up a lot more police time and has greater salience than criminal law enforcement. For example, in an analysis of British Crime Survey data, Skogan (1990:9) found that the activity that required the most police time with citizens was the exchange of information, either citizens giving police noncrime related information (16 percent of contacts) or asking police for information (23 percent of contacts). Reporting crime accounted for only 18 percent of contacts.

It is extremely rare for a patrol officer to encounter a serious crime in progress (Clarke and Hough 1984). While patrol officers are proactive, it is mainly to obtain knowledge about possible suspects who appear out of place and time, or for regulatory matters such as traffic and liquor violations (Ericson 1982). Reactive calls for police services are also mainly about noncriminal matters. Up to 75 percent of calls for service are screened out without being forwarded to patrol officers for further action (Jorgensen 1981; Manning 1988). Even when there is a crime call, what operators define as serious crime is changed by officers to a minor incident or no crime in one-third to one-half of all instances (Comrie and Kings 1975; Ericson 1982; Manning 1988). What officers often find at the scene is not serious crime but a kaleidoscope of trouble that requires them to provide some combination of counsel, assistance, expertise, coercion, referral, and persuasion, and to make a report (Cumming, Cumming, and Edell 1965; Ericson 1982). For patrol officers, at least, direct involvement in crime work takes up as little as 3 percent of their working time (Comrie and Kings 1975; Ericson 1982).

There are, of course, criminal investigation specialists in police organizations—detectives—who devote all their time to crime work. However, detectives also spend relatively little time on direct criminal investigation. Draper (1978:31) estimated that only about 10 percent of the investigator's time was spent this way. Ericson (1993:45) found that detectives spent almost half their time in the office and that much more time was devoted to recording investigative activities than to actual investigation work.

On average, a patrol officer in Canada records one indictable crime occurrence a week, makes one indictable crime arrest every three weeks, and secures one indictable crime conviction every nine months (McMahon 1992). Even in New York City, which has an extraordinary high rate of serious crime, officers spend a relatively small amount of time dealing with crime and capturing criminals. Walsh (1986) found that among 156 patrol officers assigned to a high-crime area in New York City, 40 percent did not make a single felony arrest in a year and 69 percent made no more than three felony arrests in a year.

The police simply have an incapacity to do much about crime directly. This incapacity is related to the institution of privacy, which limits them in developing evidence to detect and solve cases (Stinchcombe 1963; Reiss 1987). They are also limited by their own resources and by a criminal justice system that is designed more to divert cases than to prosecute fully or heavily.

Attrition within the criminal justice is captured in figures 5 and 6. These data derive from the criminal statistics for England and Wales and 1994 British Crime Survey (Barclay, Tavaras, and Prout 1995). Figure 5 shows that for a range of crimes against individuals and their property—including criminal damage, theft of a motor vehicle, theft from a motor vehicle (including attempts), bicycle theft, domestic burglary, wounding, robbery, and theft from the person—less than half (47 percent) are reported to the police and only 27 percent are actually recorded by the police. Only 4.9 percent are cleared up by police after investigation. A mere 2.7 percent are

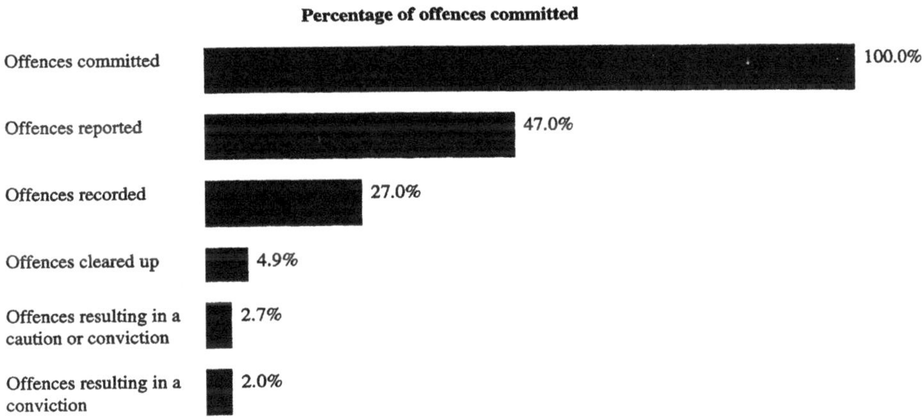

Fig. 5. Attrition within the Criminal Justice System: Crimes against Individuals and Their Property (criminal damage; theft of a motor vehicle; theft from a motor vehicle, including attempts; bicycle theft; domestic burglary; wounding; robbery; theft from the person)

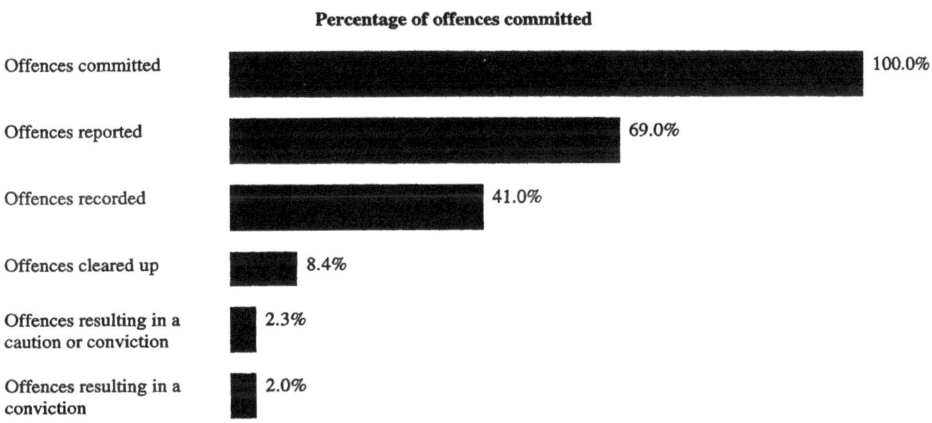

Fig. 6. Attrition within the Criminal Justice System: Domestic Burglary

cleared by either a police caution of the suspect or conviction of an offender, and 2.0 percent result in the conviction of an offender. Figure 6 shows that for domestic burglary, 69 percent are reported to the police but only 41 percent are actually recorded by them. Moreover, only 8.4 percent are cleared up by police after investigation, with 2.3 percent resulting in either a police caution of the suspect or conviction of an offender, and 2.0 percent resulting in the conviction of an offender.

Given such a low clearance rate for property crimes, the main task of the police is to provide good risk-management data for insurance purposes. The occurrence reports themselves are designed to suit the risk-knowledge requirements of insurance companies, and in many jurisdictions the insurance companies pay for the police reports they obtain. A police official engaged in negotiation with insurers over the change of occurrence reports said to us in interview, "Insurance companies now pay to get their form and so the form should look more like something they are buying rather than just a photocopy of something we are providing them—how to put it so that it could be more logical for insurance companies because they're actually the external customer."

In the management of property crime, the criminal law and its enforcement apparatus gives way to insurance law and its risk-management regime. Insurance law, embodied in property insurance contracts, provides a series of inducements for the householder or commercial property owner to become self-policing agents of preventive security. Premium levels, deductibles, exclusion, and policy limits all turn property holders into watchers as well as the watched, and the bearers of their own control. Insurance law steps in where criminal law is unable to meet the needs of the parties concerned, and the police become risk-knowledge brokers to the insurance system. As O'Malley (1991:172) remarks in analyzing this situation in the Australian context, "To protect its profits, especially against forms of moral hazard that are not prohibited under criminal law (and thus potentially subject to state policing), the insurance company must establish its own legal order within the framework of the insurance contract. The insurance contract (and more recently, the law of insurance contracts) establishes the coercive conditions for the operation of an enforcement network aimed at disciplining householders, in order to minimize the assumed moral hazard." A leading actuarial scientist in Canada described in an interview how, over the past fifteen years, this disciplining of property holders has intensified to the point where more and more responsibility for self-policing of risks resides with the individual insured:

> The whole idea of insurance works on the pooling of risk. . . . Those categories of the collective were very broad even fifteen years ago. . . . You'd have to have a couple of claims in a short period of time to see your premium change very much. Now it is going with the philosophy of the rest of society that you are responsible. . . . The whole concept of a pure accident is almost disappearing. There is no pure accident anymore. If you have a claim, you are partially at fault. And you need to change risk categories. . . . [This is a] move to more and more slicing and

TABLE 1 Recorded Crime, Convictions, and Cautions: England and Wales, 1976, 1986, 1996

Year	Indictable Offenses Recorded by the Police	Clearance Rate %	Indictable Convictions	Indictable Cautions
1976	2,135,700	43	415,503	97,671
1986	3,847,410	32	384,000	137,000
1996	5,036,550	26	300,600	190,800

SOURCE: Adapted from Ashworth 2001. Data derived from Criminal Statistics, England and Wales 1976, 1986, 1996.

> individualization, and more and more passing the responsibility back to the claimant. If it goes too far people will say this isn't insurance anymore. . . . As soon as I have a claim my insurance goes up. So over the next six years I pay the claim. Well heck, I can run my bank account to do that.

One might think that while the police face major limitations in detecting crime, they can be efficient in taking cases to prosecution when they do manage to apprehend a suspect. However, even when suspects are apprehended and can be prosecuted, very often they are not (Royal Commission on Criminal Justice 1993:82; McConville 1993:86; Meehan 1993). Rather, there is an effort to "define deviance down" (Moynihan 1992) by diverting cases to other institutions such as families, schools, restorative justice facilities, and so on. For example, Ashworth (2001) records "the decline of English sentencing," as shown in table 1.

While there has been an almost 250 percent increase in indictable offenses recorded by the police between 1976 and 1996, the police clearance by arrest rate has decreased considerably from 43 percent in 1976 to 32 percent in 1986 to 26 percent in 1996. During the same period the absolute number of indictable convictions decreased from 415,503 in 1976 to 384,000 in 1986 and 300,600 in 1996. On the other hand the rate of police cautions rose considerably, from 97,681 in 1976 to 137,000 in 1986 and 190,800 in 1996.

Other data presented by Ashworth (2001) indicate that in 1996, 60 percent of all male juvenile offenders and 80 percent of all female juvenile offenders were cautioned by the police rather than prosecuted. Among males eighteen to twenty years old, 35 percent were cautioned, and for females in the same age range the cautionary rate was 50 percent. Male offenders twenty-one and older were subject to cautions rather than prosecution 26 percent of the time, while females over twenty-one were cautioned 44 percent of the time. Ashworth also observes that "these are only the options available to the police; it would be wrong to overlook the various forms of diversion employed by the tax authorities, Her Majesty's Customs, local councils, and the many inspectorates (health and safety, pollution, etc.) which have the power to prosecute."

The Police as Risk Communicators

Whether dealing with crime, vehicle collisions, regulatory matters, social service, or public order, the police operate as a center of calculation (Latour 1987) for the risk-communication systems of myriad institutions. As such, police mobilization is not only a matter of intervention in the lives of individual citizens, but is also reactive to institutional demands for knowledge of risk. They are required to intersect with, and broker knowledge to and from, a full range of institutions in the risk-communication network.

In large police organizations there is a coterie of specialists who manage the vast and complex systems of risk communication. For example, the aforementioned RCMP Informatics division with six hundred full-time personnel has a highly specialized division of labor to manage its risk-communication systems. There are telecommunications engineers, information technology specialists, and information system auditors. These risk-communication operators work within the framework of rules compiled in four thick manuals that total sixteen hundred pages. A lot of attention is focused on authorizing acceptable forms. This includes detection and elimination of "bootleg forms" developed by individual officers to meet their pragmatic needs but that do not fit the system's needs. It also includes policing the classifications used and narratives produced.

At each station level there are editorial control systems in place to patrol the facts. These systems detect any interpretive leakage that has occurred in spite of the use of closed formats. We observed a station-level operation in which patrol officers' reports were initially reviewed by their supervisor for completeness and accuracy. The supervisor would also assign a "diary date," usually set for two weeks after the initial review, for reviewing the file again. At the time of the second review the supervisor could keep the file open by assigning a new diary date, or close it. When a file was closed, the supervisor "scored" it in terms of fixed-choice classifications that satisfied various users within the police organization and in external institutions. An internal report on patrol supervisors' responsibilities estimated that 70–80 percent of their time was spent checking reports.

Once a supervisor completed the scoring, the file was passed on to a "reader" for further editorial scrutiny. The reader was a full-time police officer whose sole function was to review the files once again to ensure that everything was filled out completely and accurately, and that the scoring was correct. The reader functioned only as a data checker and could not, for example, reject a file and ask for further investigation. From the reader a file would go to a data entry clerk, who would again check the completeness of the file and competence of the scoring and seek clarification of any slippage.

In selected cases there was further cleansing of the data. For example, all sexual assault, domestic violence, and major crime files were sent to the second-in-command at the station for additional scrutiny. This officer also conducted random checks on other files. A police officer described this task as one that was "concerned with how the files are taken care of. He [the second-in-command] is also concerned on the administrative side with how the file is scored because if it is not scored properly then it is going to reflect back on him at audit time."

Some of the reports reviewed by the second-in-command had to be reviewed further by form managers at the division level. In such cases a form was filled out to flag the fact that a file needed further review and data cleansing. This was designed to ensure the appearance of uniform reporting across the police organization, especially in high-profile cases. A police officer observed that in such instances, "[y]our supervisor reads your work, the sergeant checks his work, staff sergeant looks after him, the commanding officer inspects all of it. Now it goes to another group of people and they inspect it. If they find anything they send it back. You have so many people checking up on what I do on the street it makes it kind of repetitive all of the time."

In addition to this complex system for case-by-case editing and data cleansing, this police organization had various communication format auditors. There were, for example, division-level auditing teams that spent a week in each station reviewing the quality of data entry. A division-level officer involved in this process said that the main task was a random audit of files "to make sure they have all the necessary information fields they're supposed to have, compared to the computer printout"; a 5 percent margin of error was allowed. The division also had file auditors in its field-support information unit, who on a three-year cycle audited every recordkeeper in every station. They served, in effect, as supervisors of station-level coders with respect to the reliability and validity of the coders' data collection.

Of course there are still murmurings among the police that information work as the means has become an end in itself, interfering with "crime fighting" as the "real" end of police work. But in the vast majority of cases information work is all there is to it. It is both the means and the end of police work, and the reason why there is such an obsession with the production of clean data.

Police Mobilization and Knowledge Production

The police think and act in relation to the communication formats of external institutions that demand knowledge of risk. As a result, they are mobilized not in terms of consensual order, as criminal law theory would suggest, but rather in terms of the different risk logics of the institutions with which they communicate. In this respect, something only becomes actionable as police work if it fits in the risk-knowledge requirements of external institutions.

This view of police-knowledge work differs sharply from existing research on police organizations that emphasizes how the police produce knowledge for their own *internal* management purposes. Researchers have focused on how line officers do their paperwork with an eye toward "covering ass" in their dealings with their supervisors (Manning 1980; Ericson 1982, 1993; Chatterton 1991). When studies go beyond the immediate gatekeeping aspects of street-level decisionmaking, they still remain within the police institution and examine only the internal flow of knowledge (Manning 1988; Chatterton 1989; Southgate and Mirless-Black 1991). Knowledge is rarely seen as moving beyond the police institution, only into it, across it, and up it. In this police-centered vision of knowledge work, the possibility of a communication environment outside the police institution is not even imagined. Chatterton even makes the extraordinary claim that the police "have not been information driven. On the contrary they have made information police property. They have interpreted it in accordance with their own interests and within their own cultural assumptions and typifications. Information has been used to achieve rather than to set objectives" (1991:8).

The focus on police mobilization as a response to external institutional demands for knowledge of risk is also contrary to the view that police work is of "low visibility." Because of their police-centric vision and their emphasis on knowledge reproduction and distribution for internal management purposes, researchers have emphasized secrecy and low visibility in police work. Following Goldstein's (1960) seminal formulation, researchers continue to contend that "most police decisions are virtually invisible or of low visibility" and that "[s]ecrecy is emphasized . . . . information is rarely shared" (Manning 1992:357, 370; see also Geller and Morris 1992; Chatterton 1983; Reiss 1982:146). To the contrary, in the context of demands from external institutions, the police engage in numerous kinds of institutionalized *publicity* that make their work an exercise in high visibility.

As risk communicators to various institutional audiences, the police not only distribute knowledge widely but also make their own actions highly visible in producing that knowledge. High visibility is augmented by auditing; computer terminals in police cars; surveillance cameras in patrol cars, police stations and mass private property sites; and electronic filing of occurrence reports. Every new technology for the surveillance of populations is also a technology for the surveillance of the population of police. As in other knowledge-based occupations, the police worker, in the very act of producing and distributing the knowledge needed to get the job done, also produces and distributes knowledge about his or her work (Ericson and Shearing 1986; Poster 1990, 1995).

Institutions beyond Criminal Justice

The risk-communication view of policing we are advancing here obviously de-centers the criminal law and criminal justice aspects of police work. Much of the demand from other institutions is for knowledge of risk that does not relate to crime (for example, vehicle collisions, missing person, unwell person, safety education in schools). Moreover, much of the knowledge about crime is produced for institutions other than criminal justice (for example, insurance, health, education, welfare). As documented earlier, the vast majority of cases are diverted away from the criminal justice institution, even when prosecution is possible. These cases are left to be handled by other institutions within their own risk-management systems, albeit with the aid of risk knowledge communicated by the police.

At the same time the criminal justice institution itself has moved in the direction of actuarial justice (Feeley and Simon 1994). There has been a proliferation of risk-assessment technologies to decide who to select for surveillance, arrest, bail, special prosecution, penal regimes, jury duty, victims programs, and so on (Royal Commission on Criminal Justice 1993; Ericson 1994b; Ericson and Haggerty 1997; Garland 1996, 1997; O'Malley 1998). The focus in criminal justice becomes the efficient production and distribution of risk knowledge for the management of populations of victims, informants, suspects, accused, and offenders.

In this context, the law of criminal procedure can be reread as providing the coercion necessary to meet the actuarial justice system's needs for knowledge of risk. The substantial erosion of rights of suspects in recent years (Royal Commission on Criminal Justice 1993; McConville and Bridges 1994), for example, can be understood as part of the wider decline of innocence (Ericson 1994a) in risk society, whereby the surveillance system's right to knowledge gains legal as well as pragmatic preference over individual due process rights that force the system to gather evidence unaided. Compulsory DNA testing, erosion of the right to silence, and reduction in accused rights to trial election options all signify the new emphasis on risk-knowledge production and control by policing authorities in risk society.

Compliance Law Enforcement within Private Policing Systems

External institutions have their own private policing systems that are based on preventative security arrangements and administrative compliance. These systems for policing risk are much more elaborate, and have greater technological and personnel resources, than the public police (Shearing and Stenning 1983; Shearing 1992; Johnston 1992, 1997; Loader 1999). A brief consideration of the private policing systems of retail stores and of insurance companies illustrates the policing of risk in conjunction with, and beyond, the public police (Haggerty and Ericson 1999, 2000).

In the city of Oxford, England, all downtown retail stores have full-time security officers. The security officers in each store are linked to their counterparts in other stores through a radio communication system that also is connected to the local police station. These security officers spend a good part of each day watching customers on surveillance cameras, and they use the video evidence from these cameras to proceed against shoplifters. In many cases the store goods are electronically tagged to trigger an alarm at the store entrance should a shoplifter proceed that far. The private security operatives and their surveillance cameras extend to the public streets outside their stores, so that they also police the downtown public space during the hours of store opening. They do all the work of preventative security, public order policing, detection, apprehension, arrest, rights cautioning, production of evidence, and statement taking. The police only enter the picture when called upon to do so, and then only to refine the information on the offender and offense for brokerage to other institutions.

As introduced earlier, private insurance companies are a key institution of preventative security as they discipline property holders into being self-policing agents. There is no doubt that the retail security arrangements in Oxford described above are heavily influenced by insurance contract stipulations. Property insurance companies often undertake security inspections, making every potential property crime victim also a *suspect,* that is, suspected of not doing enough to reduce the risk of loss. Moreover, every actual property crime victim is also treated as an insurance *offender.* As an offender, she or he is likely to suffer one or more costly penalties on an escalating scale: higher premiums, higher deductible levels, more exclusion clauses, lower insurance limits, cancellation of the policy, and "redlining" as a bad risk to the point where no insurer can be found (Squires 1997).

Insurance fraud is typically dealt with by external compliance systems and very rarely dealt with by criminal prosecution (Ericson, Barry and Doyle 2000). There are many reasons why an insurance adjuster or investigator must tread lightly even when a fraudulent claim is suspected. First, there is often a great deal of ambiguity regarding the evidence for what is claimed. Exaggeration or soft fraud is easy to visualize but difficult to investigate and take action against. Second, in an industry where the operating philosophy is moral utilitarianism and therefore the supreme value is efficiency, it is often judged more expedient to make "nuisance payments" to claimants rather than investigate their suspected fraudulent claims. Furthermore, the loss can be absorbed in future higher premiums to the claimant and across the pool of insured persons. Third, and pervading the above considerations, is public relations. The claims process is also part of the sales process, since "all that an insurance company has to sell is its promise to pay" (Baker 1994:1401). Indeed, an insurance company may want to keep its dishonest customers because they continue to pay premiums that the company needs to invest and make profits. It is sometimes easier not to bite the hand that feeds, even if one's own hand is nibbled at from time to time.

There is an obvious tension, if not contradiction, in the compliance-oriented private policing of insurance relationships. On the one hand, as we have seen, anyone with a stake in a private property insurance relationship is contractually induced into participating in loss reduction, and penalized for failures. On the other hand a great deal of fraud and other loss through moral hazard is tolerated and even fostered in insurance relationships. As Garland (1997) observes, part of the responsibility of being *homo prudens* in risk society is to recognize which losses are not only inevitable but necessary for the smooth flow of social and economic life. Surveillance for preventive security has limits, as does law enforcement. "Precisely because crime occurs in the course of routine social and economic transactions, crime reducing intervention must seek to preserve 'normal life' and 'business as usual.' The characteristic modes of intervening involve the implantation of non-intrusive controls in the situation, or else attempts to modify the interests of the actors involved" (Garland 1997:87).

In compliance-oriented systems of risk management, such as insurance, the police are relegated to a secondary role as front-end suppliers of risk knowledge. They give insurance investigators routine and full access to police files, a legislated requirement in some insurance fields in Canada. They produce data on loss situations, and on people who create opportunities for loss, via occurrence and vehicle collision reports. Increasingly police involvement in this regard is minimized through self-reporting systems (for example, victim voice entry; self-report forms for minor vehicle collisions), or reports taken only by police clerical staff (for example, for thefts). In one large urban police organization we studied, one-quarter of complaints are recorded without even dispatching a patrol officer. As an officer from this organization explained, "People will call in the theft of an item. They know there isn't a hope in hell of finding it and they really don't have an interest in reporting it to the police, but they know they can't get their insurance claim until they do report it to the police. It's a paper exercise."

Governing through Crime

While the police can do little to control crime directly, and are primarily brokers of knowledge about crime and other risks to external institutions, they are nevertheless a central agency of government (Rose 1999). Indeed, their participation in the risk-communication systems of external institutions has made them part of those institutions and their modes of governance. Crime risk, and fear of it, has become the basis for police involvement in governance well beyond crime control itself. In addition to the governing of crime, there is governing through crime (Simon 1997). Crime risk, and fear of it, is the basis for proliferating surveillance systems in those public spaces and social institutions that the police still have jurisdiction over. Police involvement in public contact surveillance systems, public schools, watch programs, and missing persons registries are illustrative.

Census Taking

The "contact card" is the most pervasive device for police governance of populations. It is used to report police observations of people suspected of being out of place or associating with undesirables. Patrol officers are required to satisfy quotas for the submission of contact cards. The cards are sent to analysts who computerize the data and prepare and distribute profiles of suspect populations and their proper places.

Computer terminals in police vehicles permit the electronic entry of street-check information. This technological innovation has, along with increased quota expectations, encouraged greater numbers of random checks. In the eyes of police officers who have computer terminals, it has created the potential for more pervasive and systematic inspection of populations that appear out of place. As one patrol officer said:

> You can program into this machine a street check . . . whereas before I wouldn't have bothered filling out a form . . . because they were time consuming, a pain in the ass and nobody ever bothered to do anything with them. . . . What we are doing is a proactive patrol . . . go out in residential areas . . . and just write down anything suspicious. Vehicles, young fellow walking down the road at two o'clock in the morning. . . . [Computers] increase our street checks something like 700 percent. . . . [Previously] there was no way we could keep track of who was on the go. Now you do your street check, stop a specific car in a neighborhood at four o'clock in the morning and someone may find out that that night there was a specific break [burglary] or car broken into. You can go back and check this person and maybe they are responsible. The more people you know who are moving or who are on the go then the more people you are keeping track of. . . . We do the subdivision areas late at night and just kind of sneak around and park on the side of the road to see who is moving and do spot checks [on] who is driving or walking.

Another contact card system provides a means of tracing populations that reside in targeted residential areas. Inquiry forms are used to record systematic data on householders interviewed in connection with a crime or other risk in an area. In one police jurisdiction we studied, the attending officer was required to complete a form for each person in the household aged fourteen or older, which had spaces for, among other things, name, marital status, vehicle ownership, occupation and employer, name and address of ex-spouse, and number of persons living in adjacent houses (adult males, adult females, and children). The form included an admonition to the officer to "Be alert for spontaneous response." In light of the very low clearance rate in residential burglaries, police officers viewed this brand of police census taking as a tracking device for possible future use, rather than as a means of solving the crime that initiated the inquiry. As one interviewee remarked, "You have to check with neighbors on the left side and on the right and across the street. To some people that seems like a pain in the ass and you are not going to find anything, but we have found very often that you may be looking for the guy who is across the street down the road. And all of a sudden you have that in your computer."

School Programs

The police have a long history of serving as risk experts in schools. In particular they visit schools to provide instruction on traffic safety and personal security. Larger municipal police organizations usually have full-time officers dedicated to such education. Their role often extends to overseeing and evaluating school safety-patrol units.

Police education efforts in schools have broadened in recent years. Society's obsession with the risks of drugs has placed drug education on school curricula, and the police are brought in as experts. Some police organizations have full-time "drug awareness" officers who lecture in schools and elsewhere.

We studied a primary-school program staffed by four full-time police officers and a social worker who was also a police employee. The social worker was initially hired to help the police gain acceptance in the schools. The original justification of the program was the need for education about the risks of delinquent activity, especially the use of illegal drugs, but the program rapidly expanded into other areas. A person involved with the program explained the place of the educational component in relation to concerns about risk and security, exemplifying how crime is used as the basis for broader forms of governance:

> Drugs are the medium . . . but we've got programs that talk about self-esteem, problem solving, peer pressure. . . . [Drugs are] something that's in the news and in the media and all that kind of stuff, so it's a good way to catch kids' attention. . . . There's this concern in school about violence now. . . . And I predict that pretty soon the people that make the videos will pick up on that as a medium and develop some good programs to deal with it . . . [but] the underlying message is always the same . . . to get the students familiar with the officer who will be in the school. . . . The real thing that we're trying to do is to be accessible to the students and to the parents and the teachers. . . . A kid blows up . . . calm him down and get him back to the classroom. The teaching staff don't have time to do it.

"High needs" or high-risk schools were identified based on an epidemiological analysis of a whole range of population health problems such as truancy, poor nutrition, misbehavior at school, and crime. This selection of school organizations was followed by a selection, using the same criteria, of high-risk students. An official publication of the police organization was clear on this risk-management approach, stating that the program offered "outreach services to selected elementary schools . . . identifying children (primarily in grades 4, 5 and 6) who are experiencing problems, and assisting with the coordination of a multi-agency effort to help these children and their families."

High-risk children were identified by a wide range of informants. There was input from officials in health and welfare agencies, from teachers and school counselors, and from parents. Home visits were sometimes deemed necessary. The children themselves were primary informants, often relating problems that were not school-specific. A program official stressed that "students and their parents . . . can access the officer about anything they want. And they don't necessarily have to let the school know. We've got disclosures of sexual abuse, physical abuse from kids. And we've got parents coming seeking information on marriage separation, wife battering, husband battering. . . . The officers can make referrals to any community agency. . . . We advise the [school] principal that we've done that."

Members of the unit kept notes on potential high-risk children, and used a student-profile form to rate welfare history, school history, special problems, contact with other agencies, and family criminal history. The various knowledges were brought together at case conference sessions attended by the schools' police officer and staff as well as representatives of other agencies. Higher-risk students were identified and marked down for counseling by outside agencies or the school police officer. One such officer remarked that counseling was provided

> in the sense of trying to find out what the problem is. And then get the students and the family to the resource that can best deal with the problem. . . . There's some students that are more behavior problems. The student is taken out of class and actually spends some time with them [a police officer] one-on-one, playing board games. We've got some officers doing, building models with groups of kids . . . who have trouble interacting with their peers. . . . If these kids can be truly identified at the early stage, and if they can establish some sort of bond with a police officer, maybe they will think twice about the person they might be letting down if they go out and get in trouble.

The three dozen or so most risky individuals were placed in a risk-management system set up to track them throughout their school careers.

An official police statement on the program emphasized that "the officer's effectiveness is enhanced if he/she is viewed as being a member of the school staff." According to one police official, officers in the program were indeed viewed as school staff: "[officers are] part of the staff almost . . . get consulted . . . participate in the . . . school resource group . . . case conferencing . . . the problems can be academic behavior, whatever. . . . The officer might have a role to play, an equal role to play in the school. They really have worked their way into more of a, almost staff position, an extra resource. The resource just happens to wear a uniform and have a different viewpoint."

We also studied a high-school program that was staffed by twelve full-time uniformed officers and a sergeant who were stationed across the twelve largest high schools in the city. This program had many of the features of the primary-school program. There was extensive classroom instruction on crime, police, the law, driver education, bicycle safety, anger management, and suicide. In addition, the high-school police officers sought opportunities to integrate police instruction into courses in the academic curriculum. For example, a police traffic management specialist was brought into mathematics class to show how formulas and measurements were part of practical police work. In keeping with their strong sense of what counts in risk society, the program staff kept accurate records of all this activity. In a twelve-month period they recorded 812 presentations to a total of 27,009 students.

These presentations had several purposes and effects. They provided knowledge about legal institutions and processes, helped to promote the sensibility that the police are problem solvers, and stimulated new problems for them to solve. A program officer related that after recent presentations there were "now four people we've identified with suicidal problems in those classes and I helped to set straight."

The high-school officers worked to establish trusting relationships with individual students in the hope that those relationships would eventually pay off in the currency the police value most—risk-relevant knowledge. An officer described his risk-knowledge work in this way:

> I want to get involved with the new ones on a one-to-one basis so if they have a need then they'll come to me without being intimidated or scared, or [concerned] that I'm going to publicly announce what they come in to see me about. When they come in to see me I always have my window-blind down so nobody can see in. I have to give them that confidentiality when they're with me . . . there's always that stigma attached to [seeing me] . . . a student wants to see me behind [closed doors] in my office, confidential matters. I also provide that *service* to them. In fact, just this week I had one, was very startling actually. She had information on a major hydroponic operation in the city and we're dealing with that as an informant.

Crime Stoppers had a limited presence in the schools through wall posters. There was a desire by some, however, to have a full-time, student-based Crime Stoppers operation. Others argued that this approach would make the informant-centered nature of the police presence too obvious. A compromise was reached by setting up a school watch program, which one interviewee described as helping to

> make the students responsible for the security of their school. It's similar but not the same as Crime Stoppers. There's no reward for it. If there's something going on in the school that somebody sees, then they'll report it. There's going to be a box set up where they can put the information in a box, slide [us anonymous tips]. . . . So they will look after the security of the school. And then, if there's something that we can grab and run with it, that's what we'll do. We'll charge somebody or have it ground out for investigation if it's in the community.

The community policing ideal of making everyone responsible for his or her own security permeated the school program. School staff were regarded as security agents, as an embodiment of Sir Robert Peel's notion that "the police are the public and the public are the police." A school police officer said of school teachers, "They're security guards also, not just me . . . [and] I'm not just a uniform walking around here. . . . I am a staff member. We're all staff members. . . . I'm just like anybody else . . . we all deal with the same problems." This conception of security collaboration enabled the police to naturalize their role in the educational institution. A school police officer said that his ability to maintain security depended on his ability to blend into the school environment and thereby to cultivate informants: "[Cultivating informants] depends on how much visibility you have in the school, and I make a point of walking around, dropping in on classes just so they know I'm there. . . . Staff at the school I work with don't have a problem with that."

Watch Programs

Police-fostered watch programs have proliferated in myriad school, business, residential, and other public settings. These programs mobilize the inhabitants of local territories to become reflexive with respect to risks. Reflexivity is not only intended to prevent crime and capture criminals but also to help inhabitants confront their emotional responses to risk and to become responsible for governing their own territories. This sensibility is exemplified in a Block Watch brochure that says the program is designed to help people deal with their fears, as well as with crime, through intensive territorial surveillance that includes self-policing: "[Block Watch is] to deter *fear* and incidence of crime . . . through saturation . . . increase the identification and reporting of suspicious activities . . . [and] provide neighborhood cohesiveness. . . . [G]etting to know your neighbors . . . works best in low transient population communities. . . . [Block Watch requires] an observant eye for any unusual activity and common sense precautions. . . . Crime prevention is not a series of lectures but a part of daily life."

One large urban police organization we studied ensured that crime prevention, among other governmental tasks, was made part of daily life by introducing a computerized version of Block Watch. Known as the Personal Computer Community Organization Prevention System, or PCCOPS, this program is based on a computerized telephone dialing system that automatically sends out prerecorded messages to member residents. In a jurisdiction we studied, eight divisional police stations had acquired the system. In one division there were approximately thirteen thousand residents and fifteen hundred businesses in the contact databases. The program was "mapped" onto neighborhood units of about three hundred telephone numbers in each unit. The system operated four lines, each capable of making four calls at once, which allowed up to 320 three-minute calls to go out each hour.

People who sign up for the program receive messages that begin, "It's the City Police—Neighborhood Watch Computer—Dialed Alert Calling." They receive "alert calls" regarding risks such as recent criminal acts, threats posed by rabid animals, and lost children. They also receive "information calls" reminding them of their responsibility for managing their own risks. Other functions include informing people about upcoming Neighborhood Watch meetings and in some cases about inconveniences such as public works programs.

PCCOPS exemplifies community policing as risk-communications policing. A police officer told us that even though there were some cases in which the program had led to the capture of criminal suspects, that function was not central to it: "You can't evaluate its effectiveness [in crime prevention and detection]. . . . It's provided us a means of communicating with the community on a regular basis without having to go and knock on the door to do the town crier bit. We don't have the manpower to do the town crier." A local government official who had become involved in developing the program said that it was, despite appearances, "still policing . . . police and community policing community." He observed that crime prevention was the best message to initially put forward in selling the program, but that in the long term the program could be used for governance more broadly: "So I thought the best way of keeping people informed is through a computer link-up. Rather than have the police force or myself, whatever, these constant meetings, constant dropping-off of pamphlets, letters, it really is a waste of time and money and resources are limited. . . . So you sort of involve yourself in community building, at the same time as crime prevention."

The police viewed PCCOPS as a convenient tool for making some of their routine tasks easier. When involved in direct, face-to-face relations with the police, people can make annoying demands that are tangential or irrelevant to the task at hand. It is far better, the police think, to avoid face-to-face contact by relying on computer-assisted dialing systems such as PCCOPS:

> [When you go door to door] and you tell them that little Johnny or Mary from next door is missing, they're concerned but they're going to say, "Are you going to my neighbor?" And you say "Yes." [They reply] "When you tell them could you also mention that their dog is awfully noisy at night?" This happens. So you go five minutes at every house because you get twelve houses on one side of the street and you've used up an hour of your time. . . . I can record a message on the dialer and call sixty to eighty houses in that hour because they're not expecting to tell that machine about the barking dog next door, and it cascades. . . . I can't be rude. I'm there as a professional so [when] it's a two-way conversation . . . I have to because its face to face, listen to whatever you're going to say to me.

Missing Persons

As suggested by the use of PCCOPS to trace the whereabouts of "little Johnny or Mary," risk society hopes to keep track of everyone. People who go missing even temporarily are registered, and the fact that they cannot be traced is in turn communicated to a variety of institutions. The police are at the fulcrum of the missing-persons knowledge system, once again serving as key brokers of risk knowledge to other institutions, including knowledge of how to provide for one's own personal security well beyond crime control per se.

Because the vast majority of missing persons are young people, many police organizations coordinate their missing-persons systems through their youth services division. An urban police organization we looked at received approximately thirty-two hundred missing-persons reports each year, almost 85 percent of which concerned young people. It had a full-time missing-persons coordinator who, according to his supervisor, "doesn't actually go out and search for people—he coordinates the files." Indeed, apart from the rare occasion when foul play was suspected, or there was a request for information from the voluntary organization Child Find, the unit did not actually investigate disappearances.

If the initial missing-person report mentions that the person might be at a certain location, the police will on occasion check it out. Otherwise, all that happens is that a form is completed and filed. There is such a large volume of missing-person cases from social service agencies and group homes for youths that their workers are bound by an agreement with the police not to report a missing-person case until eight hours have elapsed since the disappearance. An officer involved in administering the system said that this arrangement "saves some paper headaches for us." If the missing person has a record of disappearances, the responsibility for finding and dealing with the person is returned to the reporting agency. The officer also raised another point—police reluctance in some cases to simply return missing youths to the relatives or friends who report their disappearance: "We have one very vocal parent who would like us to drag his daughter back by her toenails, but I guess my fear is that she's being sexually abused at home. And here, we, the police, dragging them back to that situation. What we'll do is recommend that social services get involved, you know, crisis unit."

In missing-persons cases the police are almost exclusively risk-knowledge brokers. They enter missing-persons data into the CPIC system; check other institutional data systems to which they have access, such as those maintained by hospitals; notify school and welfare organizations and volunteer agencies such as Child Find; and, in some cases, distribute photographs of and notices about missing persons. Impelled by a risk-management sensibility, the goal of police knowledge workers in the missing persons field is to have no more than 3 percent of the year's missing persons still missing at the end of the year. This national standard is set by the RCMP.

The RCMP maintains a Missing Children's Registry staffed by police officers, a research analyst, and statistical analysts. The heavy reliance on statistical expertise emphasizes the fact that the registry's primary tasks are indeed registration and the associated risk profiling of youths who, however temporarily, cannot be accounted for.

Table 2 shows that the vast majority (74 percent) of unaccounted for young people were runaways. Abduction by strangers was very rare indeed. Only 78 of 59,135, or 0.1 percent, of recorded cases in 1991 were a result of "stranger abduction." And it must be noted, too, that the definition of "stranger" used by the registry included close relatives (such as grandparents, aunts, and uncles) and friends who did not have legal custody of the child! The available data do not indicate how many of the seventy-eight

TABLE 2 Missing Child Registry Cases, 1991

	Cases Entered		Cases Removed	
Reason	N	%	N	%
Stranger abduction	78	0.1	64	0.1
Accident	60	0.1	34	0.1
Wander off/Lost	783	1.3	746	1.4
Parental abduction	412	0.7	326	0.6
Runaway	43,786	74.0	40,426	74.1
Unknown	11,863	20.1	10,952	20.1
Other	2,153	3.7	1,967	3.6
Total	59,135	100.0	54,515	100.0

SOURCE: Adapted from Royal Canadian Mounted Police 1991.

stranger abductions were in fact abductions by relatives or friends, but it is reasonable to assume that most fell into that category. Clearly, stranger abductions were not a substantial problem for the authorities, although they have great symbolic importance in our society (Best 1990).

The police help foster this symbolic importance because it enables them to govern through crime. For example, in addition to routinely supplying news releases to the media, the registry cooperated with the producers of *Missing Treasures*, a "child find" version of police reality television (Fishman and Cavendar 1998). This show featured reenactments of high-profile, missing-child cases and solicited public assistance in supplying knowledge relevant to those cases. A police officer involved, talking after the termination of the show, commented:

> It's been a success in that it's brought forward the information to the public. I don't know of any particular case we can point to that we found the child because of that . . . [but it helps people to] realize that things like this happen and they have to have some protection for their children . . . tips for parents . . . keep the problem of missing children there in the forefront to the public so they don't forget about it.

At the symbolic level the police unite with other institutions in promoting the education of parents, who are expected to educate their children about the problem of stranger abductions. Thus, despite its own evidence, the 1991 *Annual Report on Canada's Missing Children* stresses the need to be eternally vigilant about the risk of stranger abductions:

> [B]ecause such high profile is given to any stranger abduction, the public's perception is that this phenomenon is common in Canada. This in fact is not the case. However, it is still prudent for parents to teach their children to be "street smart" and to be aware of the dangers of our

> society. Street proofing of children is essential to preventing such tragedies. Many of Canada's police are actively involved in preventative policing and are able to provide tips on personal safety. It is important to remember that the legal definition of "stranger" is anyone who does not have custody of the child. Therefore, children who are taken by a grandparent, aunt, uncle, or friend of the family would be entered into CPIC under the category of stranger abduction.

Eternal vigilance is fostered by asking parents to include their children in special registration systems. One police organization we studied ran an "Operation Child Identification Program" in which detailed written descriptions, photographs, and fingerprints were placed on file. A brochure produced by a provincial solicitor general's office and distributed by police throughout the province urged parents to maintain their own home-based knowledge system for mapping and training their children: "Build a home information centre, which includes a map of your neighborhood and its play areas, and have your child identify where he will be at all times, and when he will return. . . . Maintain up-to-date records which include a recent photograph of your child, his height and weight, medical and dental histories, and if you wish, a video tape and fingerprint record." Parents are now also being encouraged to maintain a sample of their child's DNA for potential identification purposes.

A police officer we interviewed saw such urgings as part of the "continual reinforcement" needed to persuade parents to maintain good records. In her view, these records would be important in the event of an apparent missing-child case, because parents are usually in an "emotional state" at such times, which interferes with rational, efficient police work. In other words, families are to be like other institutions, providing data that are properly formatted and readily accessible: "They have that information just there, they can hand it to the officer, it saves a hell of a lot of time in the police officer trying to calm them down enough to ask questions so they can get the information from them—details and description. The person wants the policeman to get out right now and go out and find their kid."

Parents are not only to keep detailed records of their childrens' identities, they are also to remain perpetually reflexive with respect to risks. The aforementioned brochure stressed that the safety tips it offered "will not completely protect your child, however they will increase the level of awareness." Indeed, parents were made aware by the brochure of imagined negative consequences that lurked behind the most mundane aspects of a child's everyday life: "Avoid clothing and toys which personally display your child's name, because children are less likely to fear a stranger who knows their name . . . know all of your children's friends, their families and their phone numbers; insist that your child ask for permission to visit his friends . . . accompany your child on door-to-door activities, such as Halloween or school fund-raising."

As is suggested by the instruction to avoid labeling a child's property with his or her name lest it give dangerous strangers a way of becoming friendly with the child, many of the lessons in the brochure focused on communication. In the brochure, community policing as risk-communications policing extended into the home- and family-based education of the young. For example, children were expected to manipulate appearances and even lie in the interests of risk reduction. "When children are home alone, [they are] to tell phone callers that you are there, but you are busy, and cannot come to the phone, and that the caller should call back later." Like electronic home-security alarm systems, children were to be given a code that would help signal who were trusted insiders and who were to be excluded from contact: "[U]use a pre-selected code word with your child and those whom you may ask to give your child a ride; where necessary, change the code word with your child after it has been used for a period of time." No mention was made of the confusion that might ensue for a mother trying to remember the codes of the six children being picked up in her station wagon on the way to their Saturday morning hockey game. The parent was to know everything about the child's communications with other adults. In communications between children and adults who were not close family members, confidentiality was to be breached: "Some secrets—like surprise birthday presents—are fun, but a secret that another adult says only the two of you can know is not right—come and tell me."

The fear of child abduction has recently been extended literally to the cradle. An electronic ankle bracelet for infants, trademarked "Hugs," is being marketed to hospitals as

> a fully supervised and tamper-resistant protection system that automatically activates once secured around an infant's ankle or wrist. Staff is immediately alerted at a computer console of the newly activated tag, and can enter pertinent information such as names and medical conditions. Password authorization is needed to move infants out of the designated protection area and—if an infant is not readmitted within a predetermined time limit—an alarm will sound. An alarm also sounds if an infant with a Hugs tag is brought near an open door at the perimeter of the protected area without a password being entered. The display console will then show the identification of the infant and the exit door on a facility map. Alternatively, doors may also be fitted with magnetic

locks that are automatically activated. As well, Hugs can be configured to monitor the progress and direction of the abduction within the hospital. Weighing just 1/3 of an ounce, each ergonomically designed infant tag offers a number of other innovative features, including low-battery warning, the ability to easily interface with other devices such as CCTV cameras and paging systems and time and date stamping. (*Canadian Security* 1998)

Governing through Fear

All of these systems for governing through crime are based on governing through fear. Risk society is characterized by the marketing of (in)security. "In" or trendy security products are sold in the same way as other consumer products (Slater 1997; Loader 1999). The selling is facilitated by the reflexive awareness of insecurity that accompanies the probabilistic thinking of risk knowledge. And the more security products that are available, the more the signs of insecurity and the greater the fear. Fear ends up proving itself (Beck 1992). It is therefore understandable why some police organizations, such as the Thames Valley Police in England, now include a motto on the side of their vehicle that states their dedication to "Reducing Crime, Disorder and Fear."

NOTE

Unless indicated otherwise, the data reported in this essay derive from our research on the police and risk communication systems in Canada. This research is reported more fully in Ericson and Haggerty 1997. Earlier versions of this essay were presented by Richard Ericson at the Centre for Criminal Justice Studies, Faculty of Law, University of Leeds (Frank Dawtry Lecture); Centre for Criminological Research, Faculty of Law, Oxford University; Mannheim Centre for Criminal Justice, London School of Economics and Political Science; and the Insurance Law Center, School of Law, University of Connecticut. He thanks Adam Crawford, Roger Hood, Paul Rock, David Downes, and Tom Baker for organizing these talks, and all those present who responded critically. The authors also thank Andrew Ashworth for sharing data on trends in the criminal justice system of England and Wales, and Matthew Ericson for his observations on private policing in Oxford.

REFERENCES

Ashworth, Andrew. 2001. "The Decline of English Sentencing, and Other Stories." In *Punishment and Penal Systems in Western Countries*, ed. M. Tonry and R. Frase. New York: Oxford University Press.

Baker, Tom. 1994. "Constructing the Insurance Relationship: Sales Stories, Claims Stories, and Insurance Contract Damages." *Texas Law Review* 75:1395–1434.

Barclay, Gorden, Cynthia Tavaras, and Andrew Prout. 1995. *Information on the*

Criminal Justice System in England and Wales. London: Home Office Research and Statistics Department.

Beck, Ulrich. 1992. *Risk Society: Toward a New Modernity.* London: Sage

Best, Joel. 1990. *Threatened Children: Rhetoric and Concern About Child-Victims.* Chicago: University of Chicago Press.

Canadian Security. 1998. "The Importance of Hugs." November/December.

Chatterton, Michael. 1983. "Police Work and Assault Charges." In *Control in the Police Organization,* ed. M. Punch. Cambridge: MIT Press.

———. 1989. "Managing Paperwork." In *Police Research: Some Future Prospects,* ed. M. Weatheritt. Aldershot: Gower.

———. 1991. "Organizational Constraints on the Uses of Information Technology in Problem-Focused Area Policing." Paper read at the British Criminology Conference, July. York, England.

Clarke, Ronald, and Michael Hough. 1984. *The Effectiveness of the Police.* Home Office Research Unit. London: HMSO.

Comrie, M., and E. Kings. 1975. "Study of Urban Workloads: Final Report." London: Home Office Police Research Services Unit.

Cumming, E., I. Cumming, and L. Edell. 1965. "Policeman as Philosopher, Guide and Friend." *Social Problems* 12:276–86.

Draper, Hilary. 1978. *Private Police.* Harmondsworth: Penguin.

Ericson, Richard. 1982. *Reproducing Order: A Study of Police Patrol Work.* Toronto: University of Toronto Press.

———. 1993. *Making Crime: A Study of Detective Work.* 2d ed. Toronto: University of Toronto Press.

———. 1994a. "The Division of Expert Knowledge in Policing and Security." *British Journal of Sociology* 45:149–75.

———. 1994b. "The Royal Commission on Criminal Justice System Surveillance." In *Criminal Justice in Crisis,* ed. M. McConville and L. Bridges. Aldershot: Edward Elgar.

Ericson, Richard, and Kevin Haggerty. 1997. *Policing the Risk Society.* Toronto: University of Toronto Press; Oxford: Oxford University Press.

Ericson, Richard, and Clifford Shearing. 1986. "The Scientification of Police Work." In *The Knowledge Society: The Growing Impact of Scientific Knowledge on Social Relations,* ed. G. Böhme and N. Stehr. Dordrecht: Reidel.

Ericson, Richard, Dean Barry, and Aaron Doyle. 2000. "The Moral Hazards of Neo-Liberalism: Lessons from the Private Insurance Industry." *Economy and Society* 29:532–58.

Feeley, Malcolm, and Jonathan Simon. 1994. "Actuarial Justice: The Emerging New Criminal Law." In *The Futures of Criminology,* ed. D. Nelken. London: Sage.

Fishman, Mark, and Gray Cavender, eds., 1998. *Entertaining Crime: Television Reality Programs.* New York: Aldine de Gruyter.

Garland, David. 1996. "The Limits of the Sovereign State: Strategies of Crime Control in Contemporary Society." *British Journal of Criminology* 36:445–71.

———. 1997. "'Governmentality' and the Problem of Crime: Foucault, Criminology, Sociology." *Theoretical Criminology* 1:173–214.

Geller, William, and Norval Morris. 1992. "Relations between Federal and Local Police." In *Modern Policing*, ed. M. Tonry and N. Morris. Chicago: University of Chicago Press.

Goldstein, Joseph. 1960. "Police Discretion Not to Invoke the Criminal Process: Low Visibility Decisions in the Administration of Justice." *Yale Law Journal* 69:543–94.

Haggerty, Kevin, and Richard Ericson. 1999. "The Militarization of Policing in the Information Age." *Journal of Political and Military Sociology* 27:233–45.

———. 2000. "The Surveillant Assemblage." *British Journal of Sociology* 51:605–22.

Johnston, Lesley. 1992. *The Rebirth of Private Policing*. London: Routledge.

———. 1997. "Policing Communities of Risk." In *Policing Futures: The Police, Law Enforcement and the Twenty-First Century*, ed. P. Francis, P. Davies, and V. Jupp. Basingstoke: Macmillan.

Jorgensen, Birthe. 1981. "Transferring Trouble: The Initiation of Reactive Policing." *Canadian Journal of Criminology* 23: 257–78.

Latour, Bruno. 1987. *Science in Action*. Cambridge: Harvard University Press.

Loader, Ian. 1999. "Consumer Culture and the Commodification of Policing and Security." *Sociology* 33:373–92.

Manning, Peter. 1980. *The Narc's Game: Organizational and Informational Limits on Drug Law Enforcement*. Cambridge: MIT Press.

———. 1988. *Symbolic Communication: Signifying Calls and the Police Response*. Cambridge: MIT Press.

———. 1992. "Information Technology and the Police." In *Modern Policing*, ed. M. Tonry and N. Morris. Chicago: University of Chicago Press.

McConville, Michael. 1993. "An Error of Judgement." *Legal Action* (September).

McConville, Michael, and Lee Bridges, eds. 1994. *Criminal Justice in Crisis*. Aldershot: Edward Elgar.

McMahon, Maeve. 1992. *The Persistent Prison? Rethinking Decarceration and Penal Reform*. Toronto: University of Toronto Press.

Meehan, Albert. 1993. "Internal Police Records and the Control of Juveniles: Politics and Policing in a Suburban Town." *British Journal of Criminology* 33: 504–24.

Moynihan, Daniel. 1993. "Defining Deviance Down." *The American Scholar* 62: 17–30.

O'Malley, Pat. 1991. "Legal Networks and Domestic Security." *Studies in Law, Politics and Society* 11:171–90.

O'Malley, Pat., ed. 1998. *Crime and the Risk Society*. Aldershot: Dartmouth.

Poster, Mark. 1990. *The Mode of Information: Poststructuralism and Social Context*. Cambridge: Polity.

———. 1995. *The Second Media Age*. Cambridge: Polity.

Reiss, Albert. 1982. "Forecasting the Role of the Police and the Role of the Police in Social Forecasting." In *The Maintenance of Order in Society*, ed. R. Donelan. Ottawa: Supply and Services Canada.

———. 1987. "The Legitimacy of Intrusion into Private Spaces." In *Private Policing*, ed. C. Shearing and P. Stenning. Beverly Hills: Sage.

Rose, Nikolas. 1999. *Powers of Freedom*. Cambridge: Cambridge University Press.

Royal Canadian Mounted Police. 1991. *Annual Report on Canada's Missing Children*. Ottawa: Royal Canadian Mounted Police.

Royal Commission on Criminal Justice. 1993. *Report*. Cmnd. 2263. London: HMSO.

Shearing, Clifford. 1992. "The Relationship between Public and Private Policing." In *Modern Policing*, ed. M. Tonry and N. Morris. Chicago: University of Chicago Press.

Shearing, Clifford, and Philip Stenning. 1983. "Private Security: Implications for Social Control." *Social Problems* 30:493–506.

Simon, Jonathan. 1997. "Governing through Crime." In *The Crime Conundrum: Essays on Criminal Justice*, ed. G. Fisher and L. Friedman. Boulder: Westview.

Skogan, Wesley. 1990. *The Police and the Public in England and Wales: A British Crime Survey Report*. Home Office Research Study No. 117. London: HMSO.

Slater, Donald. 1997. *Consumer Culture and Modernity*. Cambridge: Polity Press.

Southgate, P., and C. Mirless-Black. 1991. *Traffic Policing in Changing Times*. London: HMSO.

Squires, Gregory, ed. 1997. *Insurance Redlining: Disinvestment, Reinvestment, and the Evolving Role of Financial Institutions*. Washington, D.C.: Urban Institute Press.

Stinchcombe, Arthur. 1963. "Institutions of Privacy in the Determination of Police Administrative Practice." *American Journal of Sociology* 69:150–60.

Walsh, W. 1986. "Patrol Officer Arrest Rates: A Study of the Social Organization of Police Work." *Justice Quarterly* 2:271–90.

[11] Uncertainties of Earthquakes: Absorbing Risk, Mitigation, and Infrastructure

Dangers, by being despised, grow great.
Edmond Burke, 'On the Petition of the Unitarians' (1792)

When tremendous dangers are involved, no one can be blamed for looking to his own interest.
Thucydides, *The Peloponnesion War* (c. 400 B.C.)

Life is the art of drawing sufficient conclusions from insufficient premises.
Samuel Butler, 'Lord, What Is Man?' *Note-Books* (1912)

Uncertainties of Earthquakes

The uncertainties of earthquakes pose a markedly different constellation of risk, responsibility, and response ability for the insurance industry. Fundamental conditions for insurance – ability to calculate the chances of the event occurring and the magnitude of the losses that may result – are extremely difficult to meet in underwriting earthquake coverage. The timing, location, and effects of earthquakes are unpredictable. Therefore, the only feasible approach is to try to absorb the impact of the risk.

Earthquake risk can be absorbed in two ways. First, the physical infrastructure of the built environment can be strengthened to offset property damage and, by extension, injury and death following an earthquake. Second, the insurance industry infrastructure can raise substantial capital to assist in recovery following an earthquake. The responsibility is to mitigate losses in these two ways. However, as we shall see, the construction of both a shock-resistant physical infrastructure and an insolvency-resistant insurance infrastructure entails additional uncertainties.

There are severe data limitations with respect to when and where a catastrophic earthquake will occur and the probable maximum loss (PML) that will result (Brun, Etkin, Low, Wallace, and White 1997; Munich Reinsurance 1992). Large magnitude earthquakes are rare and occur without warning, making data collection especially difficult. Canada has never had a catastrophic earthquake and, therefore, researchers must assume that data from other subduction zones are representative of, and applicable to, Canada. However, data from other zones are also very limited. Most seismic events occurred before the development of instrumentation to measure them. Moreover, the historical data available cannot be accurately translated into a specific contemporary setting. 'Therefore there is a high degree of uncertainty associated with any earthquake risk analysis' (Low 1997: 135). Wallace and White (1997: 5) observe that the unexpected earthquake in Northridge, California, in 1994 meant that 'reliance on the historical record for estimating the PML for a particular company, or the property-and-casualty industry as a whole, became obsolete.' The 1995 earthquake in Kobe, Japan, occurred along a previously unknown fault and thus was unexpected.

Even in the limited contexts where there is scientific infrastructure to measure seismic activity, the data collection process is subjective. The data necessary to establish a PML are based on human observations beyond technological instrumentation. Moreover, the technical measurements of the magnitude of an earthquake are open to competing interpretations.

> The Guttenberg-Richter Scale is the scale most commonly used to measure a seismic event. It describes the 'total energy of the seismic waves radiating outwards from an earthquake as recorded by the amplitude of ground motion traces on seismographs at a normalized distance of 100 km from the source' (Smith 1996) ... The Guttenberg-Richter scale does not include ground shaking intensity, duration, or frequency, which are necessary to infer potential damages. Accordingly, the M is usually converted in a seismic module to a Modified Mercalli Index (MMI). MMI provides a measure of seismic ground shaking intensity by assigning a numerical value to the human observations of felt ground motion and the extent of physical damage to buildings and undeveloped land. The expe-

> rienced individual will rate the intensity of an earthquake from MMI=I, not felt except by a very few under exceptionally favourable circumstances, to MMI-XII, total destruction ... Though MMI is extremely subjective, it can be argued that it is no less scientific than Guttenberg-Richter Scale measurements since seismologists can disagree on the exact rating of the magnitude of an event ... For international comparison of seismic shaking intensity, MMI is highly uncertain. However, within a given jurisdiction, MMI provides a common forum. Seismic measurement is still limited. That is:
>
> - Not all seismic parameters are confidently measurable yet, such as depth to hypocentre
> - Not all seismically active areas are equipped with instrumentation, and
> - Often, in areas that are equipped, the instruments are either not triggered, or not immediately triggered, during an event. (Low 1997: 139–40, 144)

The available data are debated by experts. Within the scientific literature there is a 'West Coast' debate about seismic activity in the Cascadia subduction zone 150 kilometres off Vancouver in the Pacific Ocean (ibid.: 129–32). One side of the debate argues subduction is occurring aseismically and may stop entirely within a century. There is no historical record of major seismic activity in this area, and at most a few moderate earthquakes will be experienced over the coming centuries. The other side of the debate contends that a similar plate to the one in the Cascadia zone was the source of the largest recorded earthquake in history, which occurred in Chile in 1960. This side also contends there was a major earthquake along the Cascadia subduction zone three centuries ago. Compression and bulging along the coastline suggest two plates are locking, building energy for another major earthquake.

Problems with data collection and interpretation have led to imaginative analytical techniques and models. Lammare and associates (1992) have devised a statistical approach that tries to overcome incomplete datasets. Attempting to 'quantify uncertainty,' they refer to their approach as the bootstrap method' (Low 1997: 144–5)!

Following the unexpected earthquakes at Northridge and Kobe, computer simulation models have become popular. However, at best 'seismic risk modelling is to be used as a diagnostic tool to aid in decision making and management of risk. Alone, it does not provide solutions' (ibid.: 126). Indeed, the available models all have fundamental problems with respect to unknowns, assumptions, uncertainties, and validation (ibid.: 157–62). As a result Wallace and White (1997: 5) ask, 'How were risk managers in the insurance industry to assess the reliability of the estimates produced by these models?'

We interviewed risk managers in both state emergency planning programs and the insurance industry about their capacity to act on expert knowledge about earthquakes. A state official responsible for emergency planning observed that unlike California, British Columbia has no surface faulting to provide some observable evidence.

> Earthquakes are potentially extremely large and they're totally unexpected in terms of an accurate prediction of when they'll occur ... Whether you're a *believer* in one in five hundred [years] catastrophic earthquake or one that occurs every twenty to thirty years and is moderately damaging ... Scientists can't even watch to see what is going on. So to quote our seismologist, he says that the next earthquake that causes damage will probably be from a fault that he doesn't even know exists and it could be under Victoria, it could be under Vancouver ... Planning is being done in the absence of experience ... Planning an earthquake ... people don't know what they're dealing with. It's essentially working off a piece of paper in your mind.

A commercial underwriter for a large and conservative insurance company said that his firm undertook its own geological survey of the Vancouver region. The region was mapped into precise zones based on MMI analysis of a Guttenberg-Richter scale 7 earthquake. The mapping was so fine-grained that in the interviewee's former high-rise residence, 'I know that my building was probably going to be pretty safe, but I was going to be able to go fishing off my balcony, because right around [the corner] was just going to disappear, because that's reclaimed land.' In his present home, 'according to our maps, my living room is in one Mercalli zone and my bedroom is in another. So who knows what is going to happen there?' When asked about the apparent precision of this mapping and his company's expense in producing it, this commercial underwriter said, 'We've got so many different experts talking about different things – there is no true answer. But – we're a security industry ... if we're too conservative, that's better than being too loose. We should *assume* there's sound evidence that there's going to be a quake in Vancouver. Now, how do we handle it?'

This interviewee expresses a common sentiment about underwriting earthquake catastrophe insurance and, indeed, insurance more generally. One has to act as if the evidence is solid in order to act at all. Underwriting, like life itself, is the art of drawing sufficient conclusions from insufficient premises. Earthquake underwriters must create a sense of objective knowledge out of their incomplete, subjective, and differently interpreted data. While science provides indispensable knowledge upon which to act, it also produces uncertainty and makes the world unstable and mutable. As Porter (1995: 7–8) observes, 'Quantitative estimates sometimes are given considerable weight when nobody defends their validity with real conviction ... Quantification is a way of making decisions without seeming to decide. Objectivity lends authority to officials who have little of their own.'

Absorbing Risk

Insurers respond to the uncertainties of earthquakes by absorbing risk in two ways. First, they participate in programs that try to make the built environment more resistant to catastrophic loss from earthquakes. Second, they try to absorb risk through their loss ratio practices. In particular, they participate in elaborate reinsurance arrangements to ensure that the enormous capital that is required to fund a catastrophic loss is available across the industry. They also underwrite earthquake insurance in creative ways in order to generate premiums for investment and, hopefully, capital accumulation that can be used to offset catastrophic loss claims.

Major efforts to address earthquake risk through physical infrastructure usually involve the state in partnership with the private sector, including the insurance industry. One of the many ways in which the state serves as the ultimate insurer (Moss 2002) is through fostering civil engineering solutions to building, bridge, and road infrastructures and to vital supply lines such as gas and water that can reduce losses in the event of a large magnitude earthquake.

The state also develops building code standards for earthquake resistance. Buildings that do not meet earthquake resistance code standards bear high costs in the event of a catastrophe. However, it is expensive to build or renovate up to code standards. It is also sometimes a guessing game as to what natural hazard building code standards one should try to meet. The city of Kobe, Japan, was built to withstand very heavy winds and storms, which requires light walls and heavy roofs. Light walls and heavy roofs are disastrous in an earthquake. When Kobe experienced an earthquake along an unknown fault line, heavy roofs collapsed, accounting for most of the property damage as well as an estimated 90 per cent of 5,470 deaths (Wallace and White 1997: 9). Another consideration is that buildings which are better at protecting people because they are constructed to collapse gradually can also increase the overall cost of structural property damage (ibid.: 10).

In California the reality of recent earthquake catastrophes encouraged the government and insurance industry to provide incentives for loss prevention. For example, 300 companies that together underwrite more than one-half of the business established the Insurance Institute for Property Loss Reduction. One project involved collaboration with city and state officials in Los Angeles to assist policyholders in retrofitting their homes for earthquake resistance (Brun et al. 1997). There is also a United States Insurance Services Office that rates the effectiveness of local enforcement of building codes so that insurers can rate properties and vary premiums according to local enforcement (ibid.).

In Canada there are no such financial incentive schemes and building code-rating systems. The industry has asked all levels of government to increase spending on making the built environment more earthquake resistant. An impetus for government expenditure was provided by a study of the Vancouver lower mainland area funded by Munich Reinsurance (1992). Following this study, a new emergency operations and communications centre was built to withstand an 8.5 magnitude earthquake on the Richter scale. The hope is that it will still be standing even if little else is. Building codes are unevenly developed, legislated, and enforced and there is 'buck passing' among levels of government and the insurance industry. '[T]he incentive for one level to minimize hazard is reduced if another level ultimately pays for that loss. One such example is building codes, which are researched and recommended nationally, legislated by the provinces, and enforced at the municipal level. If building codes are not enforced, funds for repairing avoidable damage come from private insurance companies or the federal and provincial governments' (Wallace and White 1997: 8).

The insurance industry focuses more on claims management after the fact than on prevention. In Canada the property and casualty insurance industry has established a claims emergency response plan for each province to address all major natural disasters. The plan includes a sharing of claims specialists across member companies, who in turn coordinate with emergency response officials. An important reason for this organization is the minimization of losses through exaggerated insurance claims, a common problem after catastrophes. The problem is not only with claimants themselves, but with suppliers such as building contractors who price gouge in a high-demand, low-supply situation (Baker 1994; Baker and McElrath 1997). Following Hurricane Andrew, in Florida, for example, the cost of building materials was inflated by as much as 300 per cent.

In some contexts, insurers do foster physical infrastructure measures among their policyholders. We observed an insurer's loss control specialist on an inspection of a commercial client's premises. Following his detailed inspection of the premises, he had a meeting with the chief financial officer of the company. About twenty minutes of this meeting was devoted to business interruption problems in the event of an earthquake. The chief financial officer was told that he should have a disaster control plan and that models could be supplied. He was informed that it would be wise to obtain electrical generators and make other supplementary arrangements because the municipality might be unable to supply electrical power for an extended period. He was informed of the possible need to outsource company operations to other facilities in the event of a catastrophe. Computer and data system back-ups were recommended, as were new storage racks in the warehouse that would meet earthquake-shaking standards.

Individual homeowners can also take loss prevention measures (Brun et al. 1997: 170). Structurally they can strengthen and anchor the foundation of their homes and brace walls, posts, and chimneys. Within the home they can arrange for the shutting off of utilities, brace the water heater, and secure heavy furniture, pictures, and cupboard latches. However, these measures are not requirements of the home insurance policy contract.

The primary means through which insurers absorb earthquake risk is their loss ratio practices. In particular, they focus on developing an elaborate network of reinsurance partners to absorb the catastrophic losses that might result from a substantial earthquake. We interviewed the vice-president in charge of reinsurance for a large property and casualty insurance company. He said that his company had catastrophe reinsurance at different layers with seventy reinsurers and that total coverage was $400 million, for which annual premiums totalled $12 million. The main reason for having this hefty annual premium over several decades – with only minor claims for a couple of hailstorms – was the risk of an earthquake in British Columbia. The decision about reinsurance levels was not based on expert assessments of earthquake risk. To the contrary, the expertise available is so uncertain that the company could only speculate on what might be adequate coverage for an earthquake catastrophe.

> [We have problems with] quality of data ... garbage in, garbage out ... I'm uncomfortable with this black box side where you put all your stuff in and these numbers come out and, my gosh, there's the answer! It's not real ... There [are] changes in the model as well, like year over year, which could drive out some pretty significant variations in terms of output ... We had a number that was sort of here, and, gosh, there's a new version that's come out suddenly, our number is here now. I mean if I was trying to assess your exposure based on the output of that, you'd drive yourself crazy ... Do you pick a one-hundred-year return period or two hundred and fifty or five hundred or a thousand or ten thousand, like what number do you pick? Beyond a certain point you, say, 'Well, gee, we might have to buy reinsurance for every single nickel of property value that we have out in British Columbia,' which is obviously ridiculous and not even doable ... So we have to pick a cut-off point saying, 'Here's the range of probability, we're dealing with a five-hundred-year return period or whatever,' and work to that. But that generates about $100 million [PML], and indexed for inflation [e.g, in relation to building replacement costs] $125 million or maybe $150 million. So we buy $400 million ... We know there's a whole lot we don't know about earthquake faults in British Columbia compared to California ... And even in California where they think they know a whole lot about where it is, they have Northridge which was in the area where they didn't even know they could have an earthquake. They didn't even know there was a fault there ... How could we say, 'Well, gosh, this lovely model has come up with this number and that's got to be the right number so we'll buy to that level?' We buy more than double that level because we *feel* we need to. Because there's a whole lot we don't know and we don't want to be caught in a situation. Our first obligation is to make sure we can pay our policyholders.

Similar concerns were expressed by other insurance executives we interviewed. The CEO of a large property and casualty insurance company also said that his company took a conservative approach in 'picking a number' and gambling on levels of catastrophe reinsurance. Although he concurred that the data and models used to ascertain

PML are highly problematic, he also criticized companies that choose to be less conservative in their estimates or, worse still, do not bother with data or models at all.

> [An earthquake of high magnitude is] a phantom event. We know it's going to happen. It might be five hundred years away. You know there's competing models. One model says it's going to be forthcoming, it'll be a \$200 million event [for our company] and the next one says it'll be a \$400 million event. I mean you might as well blind yourself and get dizzy before you throw the dart in terms of picking a number. There are companies out there, if there was an event tomorrow, haven't got the capacity to handle it. They're making a promise, they can't keep it ... [We use] latest science ... in favour of the more conservative. Whereas many people have only picked the model that produces the lowest results. Some aren't using any models at all, whereas we're dealing predominately with licensed reinsurers, all our reinsurers are high quality ... There's *nobody* that can stand up and say for certain that they can keep the promise because we don't know.

The generation of premium revenues for investment and capital accumulation is also crucial for loss ratios. Premium setting involves the insurer in determining 'how much coverage to offer and what premium to charge so as to make a reasonable profit while not subjecting itself to an unacceptably high chance of a catastrophic loss' (Kunreuther 2002: 4). But premium setting is extremely difficult in the case of earthquake insurance because both the chance of the event and the estimation of loss are beyond the capacity for reasonable calculations. Kunreuther et al. (1995) argue that in highly ambiguous situations such as earthquake underwriting, insurers tend to inflate premiums. They support this contention through a survey of 896 underwriters in which respondents were asked to determine premiums required to insure a factory against property damage from an earthquake. In the judgment of the researchers, respondents tended to propose inflated premiums. However, this judgment is problematic since it seems impossible establish a reasonable premium because the risk and its probable effects are so unpredictable. Furthermore, insurers typically set premiums more in relation to competitive market conditions than to fanciful data on risk.

Our interviewees made it clear that insurers underwrite and price earthquake insurance largely in terms of local markets rather than in relation to expert knowledge on PML and the possible insolvency of their company in the event of a catastrophe. An earthquake underwriter we interviewed said that his work entailed reading the market to make 'an educated guess and a bit of a hopeful bet, which is after all the fundamentals of insurance.' A state regulator we interviewed agreed that reading the market in these terms is what earthquake underwriters do. The 'expected experience' with earthquakes is always related to the 'public's willingness to accept particular premium rates. And there's always some company in the market that is willing to drive down the premiums just to maintain your client base.'

At the time of our research there was a highly competitive or 'soft' market for earthquake insurance coverage in British Columbia. Limits of coverage were increasing and premiums and deductibles were decreasing. The marketing manager of a large commercial insurance broker said in interview, 'The exposure hasn't changed, we can still have a significant earthquake ... They [insurers] want money, they want to invest that money, they want to use that money. So they're prepared to give some things to allow themselves to write business.'

For many insurers earthquake coverage is simply an extra made available with a bundle of coverages on the general commercial or home policies of their clients. If a client wants earthquake coverage, it is added largely because it is necessary to close the deal for the general policy. A CEO said in interview, 'we're not trying to sell earthquake, sometimes you have to supply some earthquake capacity to underwrite a whole account.' He said that his company was very conservative in this regard. '[I]f there's a bad one, some of those insurance companies are going to go under. And we're convinced that we will not, we'll forego business today rather than put on more earthquake capacity.' When asked about less conservative companies, he said they were driven by a greater need to generate premiums for investment in a soft market and, therefore, often included earthquake coverage as a 'loss leader ... You'll have a company that will start giving away the earthquake for free, I mean they're not even charging for it: Earthquake has gotten very cheap again and very abundant, that's mainly due to competitive pressure.'

A commercial underwriter working in this soft market concurred that earthquake coverage was being thrown in as an incentive by most insurers, often regardless of their ability to pay in the event of a catastrophe. 'They're not charging for it, they're providing full earthquake limits on their policies, they've lowered their deductibles ... [Brokers] go to any number of insurers who will give them full quake with no initial premium and low deductible, which we won't do that. But if a quake ever happens, we'll be in a position where we will financially be able to pay the claims that we will experience whereas the other insurers, I am not sure they will. So it is something that we contend with the brokers a lot.'

This underwriter's contention was that she lost commercial insurance business to competitors because they offered cheap or free earthquake insurance even if unable to pay claims. She was restricted from competing on these terms because her company was more prudent. 'Earthquake has impaired and restricted our underwriting in Vancouver. A company with our capacity could go hog wild out here. Probably even make money, even in the depressed prices of this market.'

Earthquake coverage itself is a means of generating some premium revenue for investment profits. However, the main function of earthquake coverage is to attract consumers to broader homeowner and commercial insurance packages. In the opinion of a federal government regulator of insurance company solvency, in British Columbia it is 'unusual to find 60 per cent of homeowners have actually got earthquake insurance. You know why it is? Well, gee whiz, we find that their premium rates are ridiculously low. Caution flags start to go up. If you look at it, and you find also that the way they've managed that risk is to close their eyes to it, then I don't have prudent management here. It's way too low. People wouldn't pay the kind of insurance premium that you typically should be paying.'

Another peculiarity of earthquake insurance underwriting is the lack of differentiation among policyholders in terms of the degree to which they are presumed to be exposed to risk of an earthquake. For example, in British Columbia there is a legislated contract provision in the homeowner's insurance policy that provides coverage for any damage caused by a fire following an earthquake. This provision creates a moral risk at the level of the policyholder. As articulated in interview by an insurance company's disaster planning specialist, 'If you don't have earthquake insurance and the house is hit, toss a match in it.' A solvency regulator made the same point. 'If there's an earthquake and you're still standing, you toss the match so the gas is all over the place. There's a moral hazard.' In her view the fire insurance premium should vary by earthquake risk. 'The idea that it's totally socialized by being a flat thing across a whole bunch of regions is bananas from my perspective.'

This particular provision of homeowner insurance policies makes underwriting of these basic policies difficult. Somehow underwriting should include estimates of potential loss resulting from fires after earthquakes, but such estimates are largely guesswork. Wallace and White (1997: 12) feel that the 'distribution of quake-related fire protection may be inciting insurance firms, under competitive market conditions, to underestimate further, or ignore, earthquake-related fire losses in computing prices for basic coverage ... [and] disadvantage firms that attempt to price fire damage properly.' They also note that fire coverage in the basic homeowner's policy is 'more generous and less costly' than earthquake coverage, for example, carrying a much lower deductible. As a result even those with earthquake coverage added to their homeowner's policy 'could commit arson in order to benefit from a lower fire deductible and this could greatly compound damage resulting from fire following a quake' (ibid.). In addition an insured with no earthquake shake damage coverage, but whose building was damaged by the shaking, could also be tempted to commit arson as the fire damage would be covered and it could be very difficult at the time of a major quake to determine which damage was fire and which arose from the shake.'

Some insurers have tried to address this moral risk by devising policies that they hope will escape the legislated requirement. A vice-president of one company we studied said that 85 per cent of its policyholders had earthquake coverage on their home policies, well above the industry average. The reason for this high level was that earthquake coverage was included in the basic homeowner's policy rather than as an additional coverage rider, which is the usual practice. Responsibility for not having earthquake coverage is placed on the client, who must exercise the option to remove it. However, removal also includes removal of fire following earthquake coverage, which is the pricing key. He said that his company was able to obtain lower rates from reinsurers because the fire following earthquake moral risk was dealt with in this manner.

Earthquake risk is also socialized among property and casualty insurance policyholders who live in regions of Canada where there is no earthquake risk. An earthquake underwriting specialist for an insurance company said in interview that policyholders of all lines of property and casualty insurance across Canada are unwittingly 'on the risk' of an earthquake in British Columbia. 'The quake problem has always been recognized in British Columbia, quantified in British

Columbia, not necessarily charged for in British Columbia. In essence using property fire rates, which were barely sufficient to fund for the eventuality of a quake. When you're improperly funding for a quake in British Columbia, you're in essence degrading the rates you have here and saying to Alberta risks and Manitoba risks and Ontario risks, "Well, you're funding this risk as well ..." People have been looking on a book basis and saying, "Do we have enough money to sustain a quake?"'

An insurance company solvency regulator for a state agency expressed his worries about how an earthquake in British Columbia could result in a failure to meet different types of insurance claims across the country. 'When everything is lying on the ground, broken up, who are they going to call? They can't call their private insurer because it's not there anymore! And, by the way, people are going to call them for their auto accident in Ontario. They can't call them either [laughs] 'cause they're not there anymore! Who are people going to look to? This is the idea of preferring that the private sector step up ... to these things and for individuals too.'

Mitigation

Since it is impossible to prevent an earthquake from occurring through direct intervention, the responsibility is to mitigate the effects should a 'big one' occur. As we have already seen, the risk can be absorbed through the engineering logic of earthquake resistant physical infrastructures and the economic logic of insolvency resistant insurance infrastructures. However, it is extremely difficult to make people responsible in these ways.

The uncertainties of earthquakes make people highly equivocal about investing in physical infrastructure that will mitigate loss. How does one estimate the probability of a catastrophe in the specific case of property one owns and therefore decide the level of earthquake resistant construction and at what cost? If the risk is perceived as too remote in time and specific place there is little incentive for such loss prevention measures. If the risk is perceived as too immediate, then preventive efforts may also be seen as not worth the investment. It may be preferable to walk away from the property and declare bankruptcy in the event of a catastrophe.

Compared to other types of property insurance (Ericson, Doyle, and Barry 2003: chap. 8), it is difficult to enforce loss prevention efforts as part of earthquake coverage. An official involved in emergency preparedness programs for a state agency said that effective enforcement of earthquake loss mitigation standards would only be possible if insurance was mandatory. When insurance is mandatory – for example, in the case of vehicle insurance – the state and industry can write sanctions into the insurance contract that 'responsibilize' the property holder to take preventive action. When insurance is not mandatory, an escalation of costly sanctions against a policyholder will lead her to seek an insurer with less stringent requirements or simply to drop the coverage.

Insurance companies are especially reluctant to get tough in earthquake loss prevention requirements if they are operating in a soft market. A tough approach to loss prevention in this circumstance will entail a loss of customers to competitors.

The insurance industry tries to make state agencies take more responsibility for loss prevention, but in a jurisdiction where there has never been a catastrophic earthquake, this too is difficult. Referring to a specific earthquake loss mitigation program, our emergency preparedness interviewee said, 'the people who don't like it the most are the politicians' because they are more focused on 'the priorities of the moment.' He and a second emergency preparedness official then expressed their frustration at trying to involve the public in earthquake loss prevention programs.

> *First official:* [People] haven't experienced it. You can't paint a picture that is accurate enough to convince them and even if you do there is a certain gambling aspect in every citizen.
> *Second official:* It's a large unknown ... [The public believes] they're going to have to pay for it at the end ... [in] tax dollars.
> *First official:* In recorded history in British Columbia there's never been a casualty in an earthquake.
> *Second official:* There was one dead fellow that was rowing his boat.
> *First official:* Rowing his boat, he had a heart attack. Given that, are people going to take it seriously? ... [We're not even prepared for floods] Dyking systems over there, it's in dreadful shape. It has not been maintained for years.
> *Second official:* A year ago the water was that far [hand gesture] from the top of the dyke. Everybody saw it. Did that have any effect? They said, 'It didn't go over, the dykes held.'
> *First official:* [referring to an 'emergency preparedness week' radio and

> television media blitz] We want to terrify them. [But] we've learned here that you don't try to terrify senior citizens ... They don't do anything because they're not afraid of dying today ... It doesn't take much imagination to visualize these horror scenarios, but that's not motivational ... The common man has a lot of common sense. What is the probability? Not news. No one can confirm it.

The general lack of interest in earthquake loss prevention is another reason why it may not be feasible to require it as a condition of insurance contracts. We interviewed an earthquake specialist for a multinational insurance company that specialized in commercial underwriting. He said that earthquake loss prevention requirements were not written into his company's policies. Rather, recommendations were made as part of on-site inspections by company loss control experts. He said these experts often appealed to human injury or death risks posed by inadequate prevention measures, more than to property damage, as a means of securing compliance.

A loss control inspector for the same company said in interview that if the company contractually mandated an earthquake prevention and recovery plan from a commercial client, 'we'd probably be laughed out and rightfully so because it's not ... very generic.' He said that all he could do is 'to get the thought process going ... the "what if" scenarios, "Well, what if the press goes down? ... What if your raw materials supplier in Japan can't get this?" and if we get a blank look back, we know that we could have a problem here and that's what we try and work with.'

People also ignore earthquake preparedness in the form of insurance coverage because the risk is remote in time and unspecified in place. People in earthquake-prone areas may not buy earthquake insurance because they see a catastrophe as improbable or an act of God. Even when a significant earthquake has occurred in the region they may adopt the 'gambler's fallacy' that one hazardous event means there will not be another (Petak and Anderson 1982; Palm 1990; Insurance Bureau of Canada 1995).

In a survey conducted by the Insurance Bureau of Canada (1995), most people said they would turn to insurance companies (70 per cent) rather than the state (17 per cent) in the event of an earthquake. However, many of these people did not even have earthquake insurance coverage. Indeed, 60 per cent of people interviewed had no home or tenant insurance at all, but said they would look to insurance companies for support after an earthquake, while only 23 per cent of this group said they would look to the state! Evidently their faith in the private insurance market was so great they thought it would help them even if they were not part of it. Wallace and White (1997: 13) make an understated observation that, 'These results point to the need for increased public education about risks related to natural hazards and ways of reducing vulnerability, such as insurance coverage.'

The public does respond when there is a significant earthquake elsewhere in the world, especially one that is closer to home culturally and geographically. For example, after the significant earthquakes in California in 1989 and 1994, property owners in British Columbia increased their demand for earthquake coverage. Underwriters we interviewed pointed to this tendency and said that they had to be careful under this circumstance not to use the opportunity to sell too much coverage, which would lead to unfavourable exposure. They also said that the effect is short-lived. After the initial shock demand dissipates and the market softens. An interviewee observed, 'It gets calmer and people [insurers] start giving the endorsements away ... I'll throw in earthquake for no extra fee ... same with hurricanes ... In this industry memory tends to lapse over a year or two period. Over five years, everyone forgets it.'

The cultural economy of earthquake underwriting is revealed in comparing British Columbia with Quebec. While Vancouver and Montreal have similar risks of catastrophic earthquake, only 5 per cent of homeowners in Montreal purchase earthquake insurance compared to 60 per cent of homeowners in Vancouver (Wallace and White 1997: 13). In the province of Quebec, less than 1 per cent of homeowners purchase earthquake insurance, while in British Columbia 33 per cent of homeowners purchase it (Insurance Bureau of Canada 1996: 16). Among commercial insurance policyholders 30 per cent of those in Quebec have earthquake coverage compared to 80 per cent in British Columbia (ibid.).

We interviewed an earthquake underwriting specialist for a multinational insurance company. His assessment was that Quebec 'has areas that are as bad and a few that are worse than most of Vancouver. It's just not as active a seismic zone.' He attributed the huge discrepancy in coverage between the two jurisdictions to cultural factors. In particular, he felt that the proximity of British Columbia to California led to more 'hype' in the media and attendant fear about a major earthquake. When asked why the insurance industry does not promote the risk and need for coverage in Quebec, he replied that the main barrier was negative 'public relations, because the peoples' first reaction probably would be, "Here comes the insurance industry to try and get more money out of us. They're just trying scare tactics. There really isn't an earthquake exposure and they want us to think there is."'

As we document in the following section on infrastructures, responsibility for mitigation is negotiated among state agencies and private insurance companies. For individual property holders, earthquake preparedness is viewed as a market choice rather than a socialized responsibility requiring compulsory insurance. We interviewed a state official responsible for emergency planning who stated emphatically, 'If the individual knows it is going to happen eventually, surely the individual has the responsibility to do something ... You can't expect the government to do everything. At least you have to be prepared to be on your own for 72 hours; [build] up to seismic code when you're renovating ... [or] if you build [something] new ... insure.'

The problem for the individual consumer is acquiring knowledge upon which to act. As we have seen, the insurance industry itself is aware of the uncertainty of scientific knowledge and therefore speculates. Indeed, many companies underwrite earthquake coverage knowing that they are unlikely to meet their promise to pay in the event of a catastrophe. Knowledge of this moral risk posed by insurance companies is also something about which many consumers remain ignorant. The CEO of a major property and casualty insurance company said in interview that the industry as a whole was irresponsible in keeping the consumer uninformed about both earthquake risk and the risk of companies that insure it.

> If we were forced to provide the protection as an industry that we should in behind our promise, which not everybody is doing, we are going to find that the economics of providing this stuff are a lot less [attractive]. And the consumer at some point in time should be able to say, 'Well maybe I really don't want all that coverage, or maybe I have a deductible, or maybe I could do some form of co-insurance, or maybe I don't want to buy it from this company at all because you won't be there.' The consumer can't make any of these decisions because that information isn't there. Nobody is educating them and nobody is giving them the information to be educated. And that's fundamentally wrong.

Infrastructure

The comments of this CEO indicate significant problems with the insurance infrastructure for earthquake risk. These problems coalesce around the possibility that an earthquake catastrophe might be of such magnitude that many insurance companies in Canada would become insolvent. This insolvency would ramify throughout the industry and affect policyholders in other lines of property and casualty insurance. Nevertheless insurers still underwrite earthquake risk as a means of generating extra premium dollars and selling their commercial and home insurance packages.

In this section, we begin by examining the risks to policyholders posed by insurance companies that routinely underwrite earthquake insurance despite the prospect of insolvency. We then consider how insurance companies create risks among themselves (Bohn and Hall 1999). This occurs because all property and casualty insurance companies are required to pay into the Property and Casualty Insurance Compensation Corporation [PACICC] compensation scheme for policyholders of failed companies. If several companies that underwrite earthquake insurance fail after a catastrophe, more prudent companies will have to pay substantial sums into the compensation scheme, which may cause some of them to fail as well. The reinsurance market is another source of risk. Many reinsurers are outside Canadian regulatory jurisdiction and they may have exposure of which the primary insurer is unaware. In the event of a catastrophe a reinsurer may also not be in a financial position to meet its promises. Finally, we examine state and industry surveillance efforts to manage these risks of insolvency. These efforts suffer from the same limits to knowledge, market constraints, and loss prevention problems faced by the insurers themselves. Moreover, once the state involves itself in catastrophe insurance additional uncertainties emerge.

It must be kept in mind that the situation described here pertained during our field research in the late 1990s. Changes to insurance markets, industry practices, and government regulation have taken place since then. Nevertheless, insolvencies always loom with regard to major catastrophic risks such as earthquakes (Froot 1999).

Insurance company officials and state regulators we interviewed were unanimous in declaring that the property and casualty insurance industry in Canada routinely underwrites earthquake insurance in the face of insolvency if a large magnitude earthquake occurs. A state regulator said that the only certainty is uncertainty: the consumer and her agent must put their faith in what appears to be a strong company because no one really knows what will occur and what the impact will be. 'An earthquake that is eight [on the Richter scale] or something like that, flattens every place: will every company be able to pay up? No ... When they had the big hurricane [Andrew] down in Florida, a lot of insurance companies just walked away and said, "Well, we can't pay" ... That could occur here. You look at your company, it looks pretty strong, your broker *hopes* it's strong, and at the end of the day you don't really know.'

Wallace and White (1997) provide some dramatic figures to express the enormity of the problem. If there is a large magnitude earthquake shock in the Vancouver region, the risks posed by insurance infrastructure will create economic shocks in the future. In 1994, while the PML of a large magnitude earthquake in Vancouver was between $9.7 and $12 billion, the estimated capacity of the insurance industry to cover claims was $2.3 billion (ibid.: 12). By 1997, it was estimated that a sizeable earthquake

> could now cost $30 billion, or one-third of the province's GDP. Such an event could cause an economic shock 10 times greater than the most recent recession, and less than half of this loss would be covered by insurance (IBC, 1994a). If current trends continue, the economic vulnerability of Canadians to an earthquake in British Columbia will increase ... The Canadian insurance industry is at risk ... The IBC has estimated that roughly one-quarter of companies writing property insurance in British Columbia would become insolvent following an earthquake in Vancouver (IBC 1994). Furthermore, these insolvencies would be felt throughout the Canadian insurance market, which might not be able to meet claims from other areas of the country. A contagion effect could occur if policyholders cancelled policies with companies that they felt might become insolvent, making insolvency a self-fulfilling prophecy for many firms. (Ibid.: 8, 12–13)

We interviewed an underwriter for a multinational company that sells commercial earthquake coverage in British Columbia. He said that his company took a pragmatic approach to underwriting earthquake insurance. 'Well, if I really thought we were going to have one, I wouldn't live here. We looked at this [company office] building and we decided it's going to sway and snap off on the fifteenth floor. So, we haven't moved.' He continued with his pragmatism. 'The earthquake rate is generating premium, it's going into the general pool. It's not like anyone is setting it aside [in an earthquake reserve pool]. Frankly, our company isn't.' This interviewee also readily admitted that the company's pragmatic approach was a gamble and might not pay off. 'If a major quake happens in Vancouver, it probably is going to fry the industry ... I don't know how the industry would recover from it. Are we capitalized at this moment to say, "Yep, we've got the liquid cash ready to roll?" Tough to say ... Whether we're capitalized or not has too many variables to say yes, or no.'

We also interviewed the earthquake-underwriting specialist for the same company. He made it clear that while earthquake insurance underwriting is routine, it would result in a catastrophe for the insurance industry if a significant earthquake occurs. 'A subduction quake off Vancouver Island that caused a major event in Vancouver, I believe that last figure was $34 billion in anticipated damage. Our industry cannot at its current rates sustain $34 billion in any catastrophe. You would see a number of companies liquidate, a number of companies would be bankrupt, a number of companies ... would probably have to rely on parents ... Reinsurers would be fairly hard hit.'

There is considerable variation in how companies address this threat of insolvency. More prudent companies that restrict their underwriting and have substantial reinsurance identify less prudent companies as the source of greatest risk. An earthquake underwriting specialist for a multinational company complained about smaller company 'mavericks ... who don't really seem to care about earthquake ... I say that more as a consumer who doesn't want the insurance industry to collapse due to a quake because I'm going to have claims too and I want them paid for.' The vice-president of reinsurance for another large company talked at length about the irresponsibility of many companies that was affecting his company as well as the industry as a whole. 'We're saying the insurance industry can't afford to pay for earthquake in British Columbia. There's all this promise to pay in the policies that have been issued, but we as an industry don't have the resources to pay that ... even if ... you use modelling ... and double that just in case ... For the expected loss of like $15 billion or $16 billion – after you take off deductibles and the fact that some people don't buy earthquake insurance – our industry will probably need to pay close to $10 billion. And we can't pay anywhere near that ... even with reinsurance.'

A major concern for these interviewees was their compulsory participation in PACICC, which requires still solvent companies to compensate policyholders whose insurers have become insolvent. PACICC was established primarily as a means of protecting policyholders from isolated insolvencies that arise occasionally from insurance risks and operations. At the time of our research a policyholder with an insolvent company could claim from PACICC up to 70 per cent of unearned premiums ($1,000 maximum) and $250,000 in respect of claims arising from each policy issued by the now insolvent company. These arrangements are manageable in the event of single company failures that occur from time to time. However, there are potentially catastrophic consequences if several companies collapse at once, because the claims against remaining companies will be so large that some might fail also in a house-of-cards effect. An official involved in the compensation scheme said that in the event of a large magnitude earthquake 'a lot of companies would go bankrupt ... [This] could have a house-of-cards effect back in Toronto because there's fewer healthy companies to assess the bailout, and at $250,000 a claim that can add up pretty damn quick ... Some of our members have said we should exclude any claims participation types that have to do with earthquakes. That's not our role. I don't insure types of coverages ... We protect policyholders of bankrupt insurance companies. I don't care whether it is fire or earthquake or volcanoes.'

We studied a large insurance company whose executives were very concerned about other companies that posed risks in the context of PACICC arrangements. This company was conservative in both its approach to underwriting earthquake insurance in British Columbia and its level of reinsurance to cover a catastrophic loss. It developed its own network of expertise in earthquake modelling, PML estimates, and reinsurance and shared this expertise with insurance solvency regulators for the state. The vice-president for reinsurance said that training sessions were offered to regulators as an additional way to convince them that even strong companies like his own could fail because of the risks posed in PACICC arrangements.

> Our concern is that our industry could be brought down by something like an earthquake happening or that we ourselves could be brought down ... [Under PACICC obligations we would] have to ante up for the company that went down. And we're saying that in an extreme event like an earthquake, that kind of mechanism wasn't meant to deal with that. If we have a lot of companies disappear, as we think they will, the few companies that are remaining, if they are assessed and they have to pay the losses for all

> those companies that went down, it's going to pull us down ... even though we're doing all the right things and doing everything we can to make sure we can pay.

The vice-president for distribution of the same company said that while the company did everything possible to cover its own exposure to earthquake catastrophe, it still faced the potentially catastrophic risks of other insurance companies and PACICC.

> Our exposure to earthquake is our largest single concern. And we are not actually big players in that whole market ... But one of the things that we've been really vocal about over the past few years is the extent to which the industry is prepared for a major earthquake in British Columbia. And frankly it is not. We think we are, but we think we are in a minority ... People have a right to expect to have their claims paid ... We're vulnerable because ... PACICC ... has agreed to indemnify claimants if insurance companies go under. And we think many, many insurance companies will go under if there is a major earthquake in British Columbia ... The only thing that will save us in the short run is that there's a maximum assessment that can be made against us in any one year.

The CEO of another large insurance company said in interview that he preferred not to underwrite earthquake insurance, but he was forced to do so to be competitive. Nevertheless, he restricted earthquake underwriting to the point where it was having a detrimental effect on his overall business. Competitors were underwriting earthquake insurance to gain market share, but in a catastrophe his company would have to pay for his competitor's irresponsibility through PACICC.

> Richmond-Delta – which all the theorists say will disappear like jelly in the ocean – if I restrict my writings on what otherwise looks like a good piece of business, I lose. And then if somebody else doesn't restrict but they don't have the where-with-all when the event takes place to do it [cover the claims] and I have to contribute to PACICC as part of the industry – and I will – I basically pay twice rather than once ... And I just got myself on the board of PACICC because I've had no luck at resolving this issue going at it one way. I'm about to go at it another way ... We've actually curtailed our business – of *any* business in certain areas – so that the amount of exposure we're taking is manageable with the resources we've got. That gives you

problems in the marketplace and, in the short term, as long as that event hasn't happened, I'm losing money, falsely, but losing.

Concern about PACICC was not limited to large companies watching small companies steal business from them through irresponsible underwriting. Some small companies were also concerned that their better lines of property and casualty business were jeopardized by other companies that decided to gamble on earthquakes. The CEO of a company that specialized in a vehicle insurance niche market outside British Columbia complained vehemently about how his company was jeopardized by others who speculated on earthquakes in British Columbia.

In many cases, insurance companies will not have sufficient reinsurance to cover them ... For example, the [name] Insurance Company is out there with a minimal amount of capital, writing a lot of business in British Columbia. Now if they happened to become insolvent because of an earthquake and they had $2 or $3 billion in losses that they couldn't cover, then suddenly the rest of the industry would have to cover that. And then if we had a share in proportion to our premium rates in the country and we had to take $3 billion of capital out of the insurance industry, a number of other insurance companies would suddenly become insolvent as well. As they become insolvent, then all of their policyholders would be into PACICC as well ... a chain reaction until the final few would also go broke ... A situation like that would be very detrimental to Canada itself. Because you destroy the insurance industry here, how could everyone driving a car, owning a house, industry, they're all dependent upon insurance. You can't expose the insurance industry to such a disaster through a fund that was set up with a totally different intention.

The primary underwriters of earthquake insurance face similar problems in relation to reinsurers. Most earthquake risk is laid off with reinsurance companies, some of whom may also gamble irresponsibly and become insolvent in the event of a catastrophe. If insolvencies occur, other reinsurance partners have to cover the losses and a house-of-cards effect results. An earthquake-underwriting expert for a multinational company explained in interview that

if you have any given reinsurer on too many of those buildings, there is where your real problem lies. Because an earthquake [is] ... going to pierce those reinsurance dollars very quickly ... If you had a reinsurer who was

> not cognizant of earthquake exposures, they could run hog wild in a market like this. Where competition is fierce and rates are low, they could gobble up business by simply undercutting all the competition ... tending to pick up the lower layers of the excess, where all the money is. So they're going to be the first reinsurer burned, they're going to be the first reinsurer to lose all of their funds, they're going to be the first reinsurer to go bankrupt. That is going to start a chain reaction where other reinsurers have to start dropping down because that's the nature of reinsurance: if you can't collect from one, the ones above will drop down. And what you've done there is taken somebody who had put themselves higher up for a reason, collected less money in return, all of a sudden dropping down to pay a layer they did not expect to pay so, in essence, shifting the burden where it wasn't expected to be shifted.

Both the institution of privacy and the multinational dimensions of the reinsurance business mean that neither a primary insurer nor the solvency regulator in its country of origin can obtain full disclosure regarding the risks posed by reinsurance pacts. An earthquake-underwriting specialist for a multinational insurance company we studied said that solvency regulators for the state are very disadvantaged in accessing relevant information about reinsurers. As a consequence regulators rely on the primary insurers to assess insolvency risks in the reinsurance relationship. He said that his company bound reinsurance in the United States and, therefore, Canadian regulators had no direct jurisdiction over them.

> So they have to shift certain onus to us because they can't go after the reinsurers, they can't even find out who we're using in some cases ... They haven't got time to call all 300 companies [we use] ... wherever they may be – France, England, United States – and find out every treaty reinsurer and then in turn investigate them ... So to a degree they do shift the onus onto us and make us responsible for reporting who is there and some details about them ... Red flag system, if they saw particular reinsurers popping up ... or unknown reinsurers popping up again and again ... [or a reinsurer is driving] business down, down, down in terms of price and up in terms of exposure.

This interviewee said his company was so well capitalized and so well endowed with its own expertise internationally that it handled its natural catastrophe exposures in Canada, including earthquake risk, largely outside of reinsurance arrangements. A significant reason for this approach was the company's belief that reinsurers pose substantial risks. '[Our PML is] calculated pretty much outside of reinsurance ... reinsurers may have exposure out there of which we're not aware either, so we can't necessarily count on them.'

We interviewed an underwriter for a multinational company that underwrites earthquake insurance in both British Columbia and California. She said the surveillance and regulatory regime in California was stricter and more intrusive, whereas in British Columbia she was allowed to underwrite earthquake insurance at whatever price would attract business in a soft market. The company's California office had just been fined $1 million

> for deviating too much from the EPA's rating that we have on our system, whereas I've got files that are 20 per cent of what the low end of the range is because that's the market and you either write it or you don't. Whereas in the States they get fined for that kind of stuff. So from my standpoint I'm happy, just leave the regulators out of it, let the competitive market environment detail what the best thing is for that client. If the client can get $12 grand [premium from a competitor] and we're going to have to charge them $16 or $20 grand, but the [regulator's] range is telling me I have to do $30 or $40 grand, well who is that benefiting? Just because I put in some filed rates [with the regulator]? I'm a big believer in free enterprise. Stay out of our way, just let us do our thing.

Some of the insurers underwriting earthquakes in British Columbia met on a regular basis to discuss their underwriting practices and use moral suasion with each other. They circulated a list of each company's practices, such as policy conditions (e.g., deductibles) and specific geographic areas that should not be underwritten. However, this effort at collective self-regulation did not include all companies, in particular, those seen as posing the greatest risks of insolvency. One member of the group said that the joint declaration of reasonable deductible levels, excluded areas, and so on was at least a signal to others about their degrees of irresponsibility.

The responsibility of an individual company for self-regulation varied by the capital it could access to gamble on earthquakes. For example, interviewees told us that the time-line standards an individual company chose to estimate PML varied by its practical underwriting capacity and access to capital rather than scientific assessment or prudence with respect to solvency. The vice-president for reinsurance of a more conservative company complained that the solvency regulator only required models based on a 250–year projection. He said that the regulator's response was that 'there's a lot of companies that perhaps can't make that 250 level first, so let's get everybody there and then look at the next step.'

The Office of the Superintendent of Financial Institutions (OSFI) established a task force in 1995 to address earthquake insurance issues and problems. The main impetus for the task force was the insurance industry's desire to increase the involvement of OSFI because companies were experiencing too many problems trying to regulate each other. A solvency regulator described the situation as 'a bit unusual' and motivated by the fact that 'they don't like somebody getting an advantage in any way if they can help it ... some feeling that people were not pricing for this risk appropriately.' An industry association official concurred. She said that the industry was pressing the state by arguing that all three levels of government were also exposed to the risk of irresponsible underwriters. 'So what we're saying is, if the insurance industry for whatever reason is unable to meet its obligations, then the government is going to be on the hook. So better you talk to us now so that we can together ensure the viability of this product and of the insurance companies to respond, than to wait and find out after the fact.'

A state solvency regulator said that his agency was especially keen to avoid having the Government of Canada become the deep pocket following an earthquake catastrophe. He referred to the Florida hurricane catastrophe risk, where state involvement in the insurance constellation creates a significant moral risk at the level of the insured. 'You virtually have people who double and triple the size of their houses ... And you know that every five years they're going to get wiped out but they couldn't give a hoot. And private coverage has gone way down ... They think governments have deep pockets and there's no pricing mechanism for pricing it properly.'

Another state solvency regulator said that it is imperative to emphasize that governments are not the ultimate insurer of earthquake risks. The way to reinforce this is to emphasize continually an individual choice and responsibility model. Each insurance company is responsible for underwriting earthquake risk prudently and the key to doing so is to make individual policyholders pay differentially for whatever risks they face.

> Do something. Don't sit around and pontificate about it ... that doesn't advance us at all ... The government should not be the bearer of costs of earthquakes. I mean if people want to live in Richmond [a suburb of Vancouver], which is a huge earthquake risk area, that is one of the costs of living in Richmond, which should be reflected in their choice of living there, to be one of the economic signals to perhaps move people out of there ... The premiums will be higher in Richmond ... And people can make choices, rather than having the taxpayer in Penticton, who has no earthquake risks, footing the bill for the guy who wants to live in Richmond.

In 1994, it was estimated that a catastrophic earthquake in British Columbia could require $12 billion in federal assistance, not counting compensation to policyholders whose insurers become insolvent (Wallace 1997: 200). Two state officials responsible for catastrophe emergency programs said in interview that their responsibility was to spread risks among individuals and institutions, including moral risks. In the process, the state should not contribute to moral risk itself by giving the impression that it is the ultimate deep pocket in the event of a catastrophe. However, this is largely a smoke and mirrors dance, where 'insurance' is to be provided by private industry and 'disaster relief' is at the discretion of government after the fact.

> *First official:* [We seek] a way of spreading the responsibility for a potential risk throughout society ... an individual and a corporate responsibility to manage that risk financially by insurance ... And the government's disaster assistance plan is based on that premise. It is not available for insurable risks ... [which are judged] largely on the advice of, and in conjunction with, the insurance industry itself.
> *Second official:* That's not to say that immediately following a disaster earthquake, the government changes its mind – which is not stated policy of course ... We don't plan on it. And we certainly don't advise people not to get insurance because that might happen.
> *First official:* Government policy is that disaster assistance is not provided for reasonably and readily insurable risks ... It's moral hazard in that aspect. But disaster financial assistance isn't insurance anyway. It's relief ... If you had a government policy, and enumerate in that policy that indeed assistance in this instance would be available, then indeed you are ... undercutting the rationale for buying insurance and for assigning a degree of responsibility that indeed government feels is appropriate for individuals

> and corporations to manage their own risks ... [It would be] political death to say no [to disaster relief] in most circumstances of course, but it would be financially irresponsible for government in effect to write a blank cheque.

The state experiences particular difficulty in displacing responsibility for earthquake risk management because the threat is so remote. It is especially problematic to govern at a distance when the danger is at a distance. A state regulator of insurance company insolvency said in interview that the remoteness of the possibility of a catastrophic earthquake and the fact that there has never been one in Canada makes it politically impossible to make insurance compulsory. Agreeing with this assessment, one of his colleagues said that the remoteness of a possible earthquake catastrophe also means that no one is happy about giving up much of their capital in long-term planning for it. Just like the insured who is reluctant to pay substantial earthquake insurance premiums, insurance companies themselves have difficulty thinking that they should be reserving substantial capital for something that is modelled to occur centuries into the future. This regulator said that he has to convince insurance companies that 'once every 500 years you might have a huge claim, but in between you're going to be collecting some premiums. Hold it guys, it isn't your money yet! Five hundred years from now you might need it!'

In contrast to the Canadian situation, jurisdictions that have experienced a major earthquake actively involve the state in insurance markets. For example, in California, since 1985, insurers have been legally required to provide earthquake coverage to anyone who has a homeowner's policy with them. Following the Northridge earthquake in 1994, about 90 per cent of insurers severely restricted the sale of new homeowners' policies or stopped selling them altogether. In 1996, the State of California stepped in with an earthquake-specific insurance company, the California Earthquake Authority. The California Earthquake Authority offers earthquake coverage to homeowners in collaboration with private sector primary insurers and reinsurers (Kleindorfer and Kunreuther 1999: 153).

In Canada, the federal solvency regulator is not in a position to govern insurance company practices more directly. It cannot gain sufficient access to knowledge of company practices in solvency risk management. Moreover, most of the knowledge it does obtain must be kept confidential for fear of undermining public confidence in vulnerable individual companies. Any actions which upset the regulator's compliance relationship with companies are likely to further restrict access to knowledge. A regulator said in interview that all his agency could do was articulate standards in a best practices guideline, require insurance company managers to report regularly on compliance with the guideline, and hope that managers themselves are able to govern their own earthquake risk loss ratio practices effectively. The 'responsibilization' of managers includes having them 'demonstrate that you have appropriate reinsurance coverage, and/or capital and/or reserves, dedicated reserves, to meet the 250-year-return period event ... What we can do is check that the company management is going through the right kind of processes, that their data is being captured in the right kind of ways, some of these kinds of things, so we can have more *faith* in the estimates that they're developing ... This involves some reliance on the fact that appointed actuaries, auditors and boards, directors, and their committees are doing what they're supposed to be doing under the Insurance Companies Act.'

In the mid-1990s the property and casualty insurance industry pressured Canadian governments for special tax considerations on money earmarked for earthquake catastrophe management (Brun et al. 1997: 172; see generally Bradford and Logue 1999). The proposals were made in the context of awareness that the industry itself would face a catastrophe following a large magnitude earthquake. The industry requested: 1) relief from paying income tax on earthquake insurance premium income; 2) segregated investments on capital reserved for earthquake-related claims and tax exemption on those investments; 3) a credit facility from the British Columbia and Quebec governments for an interim period of twenty-four years in order to build sufficient reserves; and 4) more government spending on earthquake-resistant physical infrastructure, including tax incentives to encourage individuals to invest in this form of absorbing risk.

The federal government initially resisted the tax concessions requested, especially the tax exemption on reserve investments. We interviewed a federal cabinet minister who strongly opposed either tax exemption or tax deferral because it would deprive the government of assets it might need for disaster relief. He argued that the government is in effect the main 'insurer' of such catastrophic loss, a fact made all the more evident by the admission of some insurance companies that they did not have assets to cover an earthquake catastrophe. He also said that this admission raised serious questions about why these companies were even selling earthquake insurance. He was adamant that the government not give insurance companies the institutional equivalent of the Registered Retirement Savings Plan scheme for their long-term corporate benefit.

On the other hand, federal solvency regulators we interviewed were in favour of tax concessions. One said in interview, 'As a regulator I would like to see very low taxes, so I can get as much capital and surplus in the companies as I possibly can. Taxes draw down capital, and surplus pulls back earnings, so our objectives and Revenue Canada's objectives are a tad different here.' A colleague emphasized that private insurance arrangements for catastrophes help to absorb if not dissipate risks to the economy. Part of the calculus may be tax-based support, but this element intersects with everything from what pricing is reasonable for consumers to the ways in which international reinsurance markets can absorb risks. The regulatory objective is the most liberal regime possible to reduce the extent to which the state 'insures' through disaster relief.

> [We examine whether] better private arrangements for catastrophes are advantageous, and that therefore the state ought to offer some kind of guarantee for contingency funds as a potentially cheaper way of sharing that risk around in a societal sense than being on the hook for the disaster relief ... The safety and soundness of the institutions we regulate is only a small part of the considerations that are part of that determination ... Suppose that we say there is no ultimate back-stop contingency underwritten by government ... Suppose that we tighten up the rules on how much you can write without adequately funding it, reserving against it ... or adequately pricing it ... The response is going to be essentially some combination of less insurance, or higher prices for that insurance company, to consumers. And in that, we can through those kinds of techniques make sure that there's not a catastrophe in the insurance industry by virtue of insurance companies having written business that is fundamentally unsound business. The cost of that will be shifting more of the cost of the earthquake onto private sector participants: From a pure risk sharing point of view, is it more efficient to share these risks within Canada, with governments being part of the sharing, or is it more efficient to share those risks around the world, through the international insurance market? ... It's better risk diversification to share those risks internationally, and in fact you'll end up with an overall cheaper product ... because the likelihood of separate events that can be negatively correlated in Canada

is probably a hell of a lot lower than it is having those trends of separate events negatively correlated around the world that you might share risks across.

In 1998 the federal government initiated some tax concessions to help the private insurance industry build reserves to meet earthquake catastrophe claims. We interviewed two officials responsible for provincial-level emergency planning and relief programs. They saw these concessions as simply the latest move in the ongoing negotiation of earthquake insurance infrastructure between the insurance industry and the state.

First official: [Before the soft market the industry was] making earthquake insurance so high that nobody got it, as a way of blackmailing the government. They tend to talk in worst case terms, [to] say this could bankrupt the industry if we don't do this. The fact is they haven't had an earthquake that comes close to bankrupting the industry, and now [with the tax concessions] they can save up for it, the answer is in their hands, provided that the earthquake doesn't happen for the next fifty years. If it does happen then they're bankrupt, and if it doesn't then they're not. But that's what insurance is about.
Second official: Well, that's what the claim is about. There's a lot of poker playing going on there.
First official: But insurance is a gamble.
Second official: Or, as they say, 'risk management' [laughs].
First official: Another model is catastrophe bonds. It's like reverse insurance. If there is no disaster your return is greater. If there does happen to be one and they have to use funds or spend the bonds, you are out of luck.
Second official: It can be looked at as a form of lottery. It's a voluntary tax. If you're lucky, you'll make money.

Tax concessions that allow insurance companies to build reserves for earthquake-related claims were granted in exchange for more stringent auditing and reporting requirements. Among the risks being scrutinized in this more stringent regime is the moral one that some companies might be falsely claiming tax exemptions for earthquake reserves absent earthquake exposure. In the words of an earthquake underwriting specialist for a multinational company, there is a mandatory requirement to report 'actual earthquake exposure ... to ensure that insurers who have no earthquake exposure aren't tucking away earthquake dollars and protecting them from income tax and things like that.'

Conclusion

In many respects, no one in the earthquake insurance relationship is fulfilling their responsibilities to mitigate the potential for catastrophic losses. Individuals are reluctant to take action to improve the earthquake-resistant features of their built environment. They are also reluctant to pay earthquake insurance premiums, except temporarily when a significant earthquake in a culturally close jurisdiction gives them cause for concern, or when the earthquake coverage is cheap or simply given away in a bundle of property and casualty insurance coverage. Insurers have little capacity within their insurance contract incentives or powers of moral suasion to lead policyholders to improve their physical infrastructures for risk absorption. They also appear to have little capacity to persuade each other about the need for greater responsibility in gambling on earthquakes. The state ends up as the ultimate risk manager (Moss 2002), both through spearheading the strengthening of the physical infrastructure and by being left on the hook for insurers' inability to meet promises to pay. Indeed, based on the evidence presented in this chapter, in the event of a major earthquake the state may be left with an economic shock as great as the physical shock to the built environment and those who inhabit it. While state officials bravely espouse a liberal view that it is up to individuals to make market choices about how they want to absorb earthquake risk, and up to the insurance industry to help them mitigate it responsibly, they know that this model is precarious. In efforts to construct a shock-resistant physical infrastructure and an insolvency-resistant insurance infrastructure, uncertainties proliferate.

211a References

References

Baker, T. 1994. 'Constructing the Insurance Relationship: Sales Stories, Claims Stories, and Insurance Contract Damages.' *Texas Law Review* 72: 1395–1434

Baker, T., and K. McElrath. 1997. 'Insurance Claims Discrimination.' In G. Squires, ed., *Insurance Redlining: Disinvestment, Reinvestment, and the Evolving Role of Financial Institutions,* 144–56. Washington: Urban Institute Press

Bohn, J., and B. Hall. 1999. 'The Moral Hazard of Insuring the Insurers.' In K. Froot, ed., *The Financing of Catastrophe Risk,* 363–89. Chicago: University of Chicago Press

Bradford, D., and K. Logue. 1999. 'The Influence of Income Tax Rules on Insurance Reserves.' In K. Froot, ed., *The Financing of Catastrophe Risk,* 275–306. Chicago: University of Chicago Press

Brun, S., D. Etkin, D. Low, L. Wallace, and R. White. 1997. *Coping with Natural Disasters in Canada: Scientific, Government and Insurance Industry Perspectives.* Toronto: Institute for Environmental Studies, University of Toronto

Ericson, R., A. Doyle, and D. Barry. 2003. *Insurance as Governance.* Toronto: University of Toronto Press

Froot, K., ed. 1999. *The Financing of Catastrophe Risk.* Chicago: University of Chicago Press

Insurance Bureau of Canada. 1995. *Public Opinion Environment.* Toronto: Insurance Bureau of Canada

Insurance Corporation of British Columbia. 1996. *Motor Vehicle Insurance in British Columbia at the Cross Roads: Vol. 1: The Case for Change.* Report prepared by KPMG, Exactor Insurance Services Inc., Eikler Partners Ltd. (19 December)

Kleindorfer, P., and H. Kunreuther. 1999. 'Challenges Facing the Insurance Industry in Managing Catastrophic Risks.' In K. Froot, ed., *The Financing of Catastrophe Risk,* 149–94. Chicago: University of Chicago Press

Kunreuther, H. 2002. 'The Role of Insurance in Managing Extreme Events: Implications for Terrorism Coverage.' Draft manuscript

Kunreuther, H., J. Meszaros, R. Hogarth, and M. Sprania. 1995. 'Ambiguity and Underwriter Decision Processes.' *Journal of Economic Behavior and Organization* 26: 337–52

Lammare, M., B. Townshend, and H. Shah. 1992. 'Application of the Bootstrap Method to Quantify Uncertainty in Seismic Hazard Estimates.' *Bulletin of the Seismological Society of America* 82: 104–19

Low, D. 1997. 'Seismic Risk Models.' In S. Brun et al., *Coping with Natural Hazards in Canada: Scientific, Government and Insurance Industry Perspectives,* 121–64. Toronto: Institute for Environmental Studies, University of Toronto

Moss, D. 2002. *When All Else Fails: Government as the Ultimate Risk Manager.* Cambridge: Harvard University Press

Munich Reinsurance Company of Canada. 1992. *Earthquake Economic Impact Study: A Study of the Economic Impact of a Severe Earthquake in the Lower Mainland of British Columbia.* Toronto: Munich Reinsurance Company of Canada

Palm, R. 1990. *Natural Hazards: An Integrative Framework for Research and Planning.* Baltimore: Johns Hopkins University Press

Petak, W., and A. Anderson. 1982. *Natural Hazard Risk Assessment and Public Policy: Anticipating the Unexpected.* New York: Springer–Verlag

Porter, T. 1995. *Trust in Numbers: The Pursuit of Objectivity in Science and Public Life.* Princeton: Princeton University Press

Wallace, L., and R. White. 1997. 'The Impact of Natural Hazards in Canada: Scientific, Government and Industry Perspectives,' 5–14. Toronto: Institute for Environmental Studies, University of Toronto

[12]
National Security

Terrorism and the Politics of Uncertainty

Terrorism *is* the politics of uncertainty. For example, Jihadist terrorism targets the values, science, technology, and law of Western risk societies, seeking to transform them into uncertain societies. Terrorists are in the business of uncertainty, playing on randomness to keep whole populations in fear, anticipation, and disestablishment. They underscore the potential ungovernability of modern societies, how those with little power can work cheaply and efficiently against powerful institutions to destroy.

Terrorists stage destructive events that ensure they will live on in the "vast metaphorical spectator spaces" of mass media (Taylor 2004: 170). These events strike at the Western liberal valorization of life at all costs and an orderly death. They do so by making death unpredictable, irrational, and highly symbolic (Bayatrizi 2005). Terrorists transcend life as order, security, prosperity, and freedom by glorifying a different symbolic state: a destiny, a cause, a pride, a sacrifice (Baudrillard 2003: 68).

Suicide bombers construct the Western obsession with uncertainty and fear of death as weakness and even cowardice, juxtaposed to their fearless embracing of death (Reuter 2004: 15). Often supported by family and community, theirs is a spiritual mission in which martyrdom and the afterlife rise above any desire to survive. The spiritual instructional manual for the 9/11 attack on the World Trade Center informed participants, "You will notice that the plane will stop, then will start to fly again. This is the hour in which you will meet God." The al-Qaeda ideology of destruction, while rooted in the Islamic tradition, ignites followers from different nations and backgrounds. To the extent an al-Qaeda network exists, it is mainly in the form of dispatching its own loyalists to scenes of local conflict where natives are converted to the view that their struggle is part of a global clash of civilizations. "Thus, injustices perpetuated in Chechnya or on the West Bank can stir up hatred within Morocco and Saudi Arabia, and unintentionally provide aid and comfort to opportunists who stoke the flames of righteous anger everywhere" (Reuter 2004: 18). This disparate nature of al-Qaeda has led Burke (2004) to conclude that it is more an ideology than an organization. There was an al-Qaeda infrastructure in Afghanistan, but it has been destroyed and many of bin-Laden's associates are on the run or have been detained or killed. However, the ideology remains strong and is spreading well beyond any link to bin-Laden or his immediate associates. Indeed bin-Laden has become part of the ideology, in the sense that his role model is used to advance the "Jihadi International" cause.

While rich with myths and symbols that make it seem highly irrational in the context of Western liberal conceptions of life and death, the bin-Laden model is highly rational. Indeed the myths and symbols are a crucial part of the rationality, mobilizing adherents to strategic action that one CIA analyst views as exhibiting "brilliance, eloquence, sanity, religious sincerity, [and] astute tactical skills" (Scheuer 2004).

The rationality includes methods and targets of attacks that provide poignant reminders of the limits of scientific and technological efforts at risk management. Many attacks, most spectacularly 9/11, involve the use of science and technology against itself. Science and technology simply rewards the suicidal will. All attacks expose the limits of risk assessment and management in conventional terms of frequency and severity

(Ericson and Doyle 2004b). Frequency is extremely difficult to ascertain for a given target. Terrorism is intentional catastrophe, and the same target can be struck repeatedly or not at all. Severity is also extremely difficult to estimate. Moreover, the consequences of a terrorist attack are assumed to be so severe that terrorism by definition is a risk beyond price.

The rationality also includes methods and targets of attack that provide poignant reminders of the limits of law in risk assessment and management. The new asymmetries of power between nation-states in conflict with non-nation-state actors blur the boundaries between war and peace, and with them the laws of war and domestic law enforcement. There is a new sense of permanent war and absence of peace requiring new laws of both war and domestic peacekeeping. The deterrent capacity of the legal power to punish is destroyed because terrorists express a desire to die. The relationship between law, power, and the state is radically reconfigured as an integral part of terrorism as intentional catastrophe.

> [Terrorists] annihilate the entire logic of power, since no credible threat can be made against someone who has no desire to survive. All of our notions of security and our civilization have been based on this unspoken assumption, which we heretofore have believed to be self-evident. For example, consider that for airport security checks, up until now, the only precaution thought necessary was the matching of every piece of luggage with an on-board passenger, since, as everyone knew, no one would think of blowing themselves up in midair. Or so we thought. The presumption of individual self-interest and fear of death underlies the function of the market economy and the power of the state: suicide bombers cancel these out. Deterrence, punishment, and retaliation all become meaningless when faced with an aggressor who will impose the utmost penalty for himself at the very moment of his victory. (Reuter 2004: 3)

Terrorism makes precautionary logic obvious. Following 9/11, political speech in the USA took a dramatic turn aimed at making precautionary logic part of everyday life. President Bush hit home in various sound-bites the need to preempt the terrorist threat "before it fully materializes." His then National Security Advisor, Condoleezza Rice, declared that extraordinary police and military mobilization against terrorism is necessary before the "smoking gun becomes a mushroom cloud" (Janus 2004: 577–8).

Investigations of the failure to prevent the events of 9/11 focused on the problems of bureaucracy, communication, and tunnel vision in the FBI, CIA, and other security agencies, and stressed the need to exercise the catastrophic imagination as a crucial ingredient of future security. The 9/11 Commission Report (Kean and Hamilton 2004: 339) said the 9/11 attacks reflected security agencies' failure of "imagination – the lack of organizational capacity to imagine such an attack." Ironically, it recommended efforts to bureaucratize imagination: "It is therefore crucial to find a way of routinizing, even bureaucratizing, the exercise of imagination" (ibid.: 334). While a bureaucratized imagination seems paradoxical, what is being recommended is the embedding of precautionary logic in the security systems of organizations. In all of their planning, strategies, and practices, security agents are to imagine the Leviathan of the biblical social imaginary, a sea monster intent on leaving tsunami-like destruction in its wake.

Precautionary logic has become central to the US politics of uncertainty, feeding into and fed by other features of its political culture. There is a concerted effort to conflate the need for precaution at home with precautionary strikes against terrorism abroad. This conflation was a key feature of Bush's strategy in the 2004 presidential election, continuing the post-9/11 campaign to simultaneously terrorize the American population into the precautionary logic of homeland security, and populations in Iraq and elsewhere in the Middle East through preemptive attacks.

This conflation of security at home with aggression abroad is effected through the view that the United States is at war with terrorists however defined. The USA has long used "war on" metaphors to identify suitable enemies and justify extreme security measures against them: "the war on crime," "the war on drugs," even "the war on poverty" when welfarism had a glimmer of hope in the American political culture of the 1960s. "The war on terrorism" in some respects encapsulates all of these "war on" campaigns because it is not only directed at foreign enemies and global security, but also at enemies within, blurring into precautionary approaches to domestic crime, drugs, welfare fraud, and anything else signifying moral degeneracy (see chapter 5; Barak 2005).

Agamben (2005) links the pervasiveness of "war on" metaphors in American culture to the fact that the sovereign power of the president is based in declared emergency linked to a state of war.

> [O]ver the course of the twentieth century the metaphor of war becomes an integral part of the presidential political vocabulary whenever decisions considered to be of vital importance are being imposed. Thus, in 1933, Franklin D. Roosevelt was able to assume extraordinary powers to cope with the Great Depression by presenting his actions as those of a commander during a military campaign . . . President Bush's decision to refer to himself constantly as the "Commander in Chief of the Army" after September 11, 2001, must be considered in the context of this presidential claim to sovereign powers in everyday emergency situations. If, as we have seen, the assumption of this title entails a direct reference to the state of exception, then Bush is attempting to produce a situation in which emergency becomes the rule, and the very distinction between peace and war (and between foreign and civil war) becomes impossible. (ibid.: 21–2)

Richard Clarke, a former member of the US Security Council, even argues that al-Qaeda is a "phantom enemy" manufactured through the precautionary logic of instrumental politicians: "those with the darkest imaginations become the most powerful" (Clarke 2004). Raban (2005: 22) observes there is now "a world of chronic blur, full of slippery words that mean something different from what they meant before September 2001." It is the blur of a war on everything, envisaged by US military officials long before 9/11:

> In broad terms, fourth generation warfare [involving a nation-state in conflict with a non-state actor] seems to be widely dispersed and largely undefined; the distinction will be blurred to the vanishing point. It will be nonlinear, possibly to the point of having no defineable battlefields or fronts. The distinction between "civilian" and "military" may disappear. Actions will occur concurrently throughout all participants' depth, including their society as a cultural, not just a physical, entity. Major military facilities, such as airfields, fixed communications sites, and large headquarters will become rarities because of their vulnerability; the same may be true of civilian equivalents, such as seats of government, power plants, and industrial sites (including knowledge as well as manufacturing industries). Success will depend heavily on effectiveness in joint operations as lines between responsibility and mission become very blurred. (Lind et al. 1989: 22–6)

Fundamentalist religiosity is also integral to precautionary logic in American political culture and the war on everything that flows from it. Radical political conservatism is entwined with a religious ethos powered by disgust with all manner of moral degeneracy believed to characterize Western societies. In this respect at least there is an affinity with militant Islamism. As Moyers (2005) observes, the religious right has become a powerful force in US electoral politics. Before the 2004 elections, 186 members of Congress were backed by the religious right, a number that has increased since the election. In the Senate, 45 members are similarly backed.

The religious right also has an enormous mass media infrastructure to ensure a strong presence in public culture, including approximately 1,600 Christian radio stations and 250 Christian television stations. There are also thousands of assembly halls in which church as theater is performed to live audiences. The *Toronto Star* church theater critic, Tom Harper, attended a one-day conference at a Baptist church in

Florida on the theme, "Left Behind: A Conference on Biblical Prophecy about End Times" (ibid.). He described conference speeches as full of "venom and dangerous ignorance" about a range of suitable enemies, including Islam as "a Satanic religion" and Muslims who intend "to impose their religion on all of us." A "final" war was said to be inevitable, but believers in the church's "Rapture" do not have to worry because sometime in the next four decades they will be swept to heaven. In this rapturous mindset, there is no need to worry about myriad sources of catastrophic loss or even where oil supplies will come from beyond the next four decades. The apocalypse was foretold in the Bible and believers will rise above it all, just as the terrorists of 9/11 imagined they would take a second flight that day to meet their God.

Counter-law I: Laws Against Law

Counter-law flourishes in this political culture of precautionary logic and war on everything. As Robert Cheaney (2004) wrote in "The sleeper scenario: terrorism-support laws and the demands of prevention," there is an imagined need to develop enabling legal regimes to aid in the search for malicious demons everywhere. "[T]he overriding priority of the Department [of Justice] since 9/11 is to prevent attacks before they occur using all available tools . . . [these tools will produce] significant internal incentive [for security officials] to expand their capacity for prevention" (ibid.: 578).

Following 9/11, the US government moved swiftly to enact counter-law. The primary move was the enactment of the USA Patriot Act – The Uniting and Strengthening of America by Providing Appropriate Tools Required to Intercept and Obstruct Terrorism Act 2001 (Pub. L. No. 107–56, 115 Stat 272) – codified in various sections of the United States Code.

The USA Patriot Act erases established principles, standards, and procedures of criminal law in the name of national security. It places no limit on presidential authority to criminalize those deemed "unlawful enemy combatants," including

US citizens. "Unlawful enemy combatants" is a dangerous offender-like status that criminalizes suspects for imagined future harm they might cause rather than past crime. People can be assigned this status on the basis of categorical suspicion: the wrong face in the wrong place at the wrong time. There is also suspicion by association: someone is suspected because they know someone who is suspected. Otherwise legitimate acts of non-violent political dissent may also be constituted as dangerous. The president is sovereign, the sole power for the real hard decisions that escape the law even as they carry the legal imprint of the USA Patriot Act.

Unlawful enemy combatants can be held without specific charges and for an indefinite period. At the beginning of 2005, only 4 out of 549 prisoners held for two to three years at the Guantánamo Bay detention camp had been charged with a specific offense. The designation of enemy combatant is made at hearings held by military Combatant Status Review Tribunals (CSRT). The suspect is not allowed a lawyer, only a personal military representative who is a military officer without legal training and obliged to serve his superiors who run the CSRT. Witnesses may be called, but only as screened by the military and said to be available. Stafford Smith (2005: 44) observes that the CSRT process "is just another form of interrogation . . . They've been interrogating these guys for two to three years, and now they send someone in who they say is your Personal Rep, and he gets to ask you more questions, and then he goes back and reports to the other side." At the beginning of 2005, there had been CSRT hearings for 440 suspects and 439 were deemed unlawful enemy combatants subject to indefinite detention.

Unlawful enemy combatants are subject to extreme interrogation tactics, including torture. While initial revelations of torture in the mass media suggested that it occurred in isolated cases involving aberrant security operatives – more dangerous offenders – it is now clear that torture was carefully planned as an integral component of the counter-law infrastructure. Greenberg and Dratel (2005) have published over 1,000 pages of legal memoranda documenting how the US government argued away laws and conventions against torture. In spite of its enormous expenditure on sophisticated surveillance technology and networks, the US government did not have adequate intelligence on Jihadist terrorism. Information extracted through torture of captured terrorist suspects was to be the answer to the information deficit. The best legal minds in the Justice Department and Defense Department were mobilized in a manner akin to how corporate lawyers help their clients overcome legal obstacles to the interests they wish to pursue (see chapter 4). Dratel (2005: xxii) refers to this as "the 'corporatization' of government lawyering: a wholly result-oriented system in which policy makers start with an objective and work backward, in the process enlisting the aid of intelligent and well-credentialed lawyers who, for whatever reason – the attractions of power, careerism, ideology, or just plain bad judgment – all too willingly failed to act as a constitutional or moral compass that could brake their client's descent into unconscionable behavior constituting torture by any definition, legal or colloquial."

The legal memoranda show how the US government internalized the view that the Third Geneva Convention rules on who is a soldier, spy, terrorist, or innocent, and how the issue is to be decided by a competent tribunal, was not applicable to what they planned. Against the advice of Secretary of State Powell and the long history of US policy and practice in this area, the White House proceeded to legitimate torture. In a memorandum to President Bush, White House Counsel Alberto Gonzales argued:

> "[T]he nature of the new war [on terrorism] places a high premium on . . . the ability to quickly obtain information from captured terrorists and their sponsors in order to avoid further atrocities". . . He said this "new paradigm renders obsolete Geneva's strict limitations on questioning of enemy prisoners" and made other Geneva provisions "quaint" . . . Seven months later Assistant Attorney General Jay S. Bybee hardened the "constitutionally dubious" argument into a flat assertion of presidential immunity from legal restraints on torture. In a memorandum

to White House Counsel Gonzales, Bybee said that in a war like the one against terror, "the information gained from interrogations may prevent future attacks by foreign enemies. Any effort to apply [the criminal law against torture] in a manner that interferes with the President's direction of such core war matters as the detention and interrogation of enemy combatants thus would be unconstitutional." The argument got further elaboration in a memorandum of March 6, 2003 . . . from an ad hoc group of government lawyers to Secretary of Defense Donald Rumsfeld . . . "Congress may no more regulate the President's ability to detain and interrogate enemy combatants," it argued, "than it may regulate his ability to direct troop movements on the battlefield." So presidential power overrode the International Convention Against Torture, to which the United States is a party, and the Congressional statute enforcing the convention. (Lewis 2005: xv)

Donald Gregg, a former national security adviser to the US government, subsequently wrote an article in the *New York Times* in which he made it clear that torture of enemy combatants is a product of this counter-law rather than of a few bad apples in the military. In his view, the legal memoranda "cleared the way for the horrors that have been revealed in Iraq, Afghanistan and Guantánamo and make a mockery of the administration's assertions that a few misguided enlisted personnel perpetuated the vile abuse of prisoners" (cited by Lewis 2005: xvi).

The legal memoranda document not only the desire to abrogate the Geneva Convention, but also strategies to place detainees beyond the reach of any court of law, and to absolve security operatives implementing the policies of liability for war crimes (Dratel 2005). The Guantánamo Bay detention camp location was chosen not only as a secure site, but also because it could be purported to be outside the jurisdiction of US courts and perhaps any other courts. Various legal analyses were undertaken "to give the policy architects and those who implemented it the benefit of the doubt on issues of intent and criminal responsibility while at the same time eagerly denying such accommodations to those at whom the policies were directed. Such piecemeal application of rights and the law is directly contrary to our principles: equal application of the law, equal justice for all, and a refusal to discriminate based on status, including nationality or religion" (ibid.: xxi).

Some aspects of this law against law have considerable support in prominent legal and academic circles (e.g., Dershowitz 2002; Ignatieff 2004; Posner 2004). For example, Posner (2004) invokes law and economics language to argue that "marginal costs" of civil liberties have increased significantly since 9/11, and that there is a need to formulate a new threshold in cost–benefit tradeoffs that preempts "Johnny-one-note civil libertarians uttering fallacious slogans" with their "bromides about free speech" and obsession over "coercive interrogation." Posner prefers the "war on" metaphors of American political culture as a way to instill precautionary logic and justify laws against law.

> It has been a commonplace since Thomas Hobbes wrote *Leviathan* that trading independence for security can be a profitable swap . . . In wartime we tolerate all sorts of curtailments of our normal liberties . . . conscription, censorship, disinformation, intrusive surveillance, or suspension of habeas corpus. A lawyer must say that this is because war is a legal status that authorizes such curtailments. But to a realist it is not war as such, but danger to the unusual degree associated with war, that justifies the curtailments. The headlong rush of science and technology has brought us to the point at which a handful of terrorists may be more dangerous than an enemy nation because the terrorists (unlike an enemy nation) may be undeterrable, may have both the desire and the ability to cause a global catastrophe, and may be able to conceal not only their plans and their whereabouts but their very existence from the world's intelligence services. (ibid.: 216, 230)

Posner's will includes legalized surveillance and restriction on a wide range of people in everyday life. For example, he feels scientists should be legally subjected to surveillance and enforceable standards of preventive security in order to preempt the threat that they will become the accomplices of bio-terrorists, unwittingly or otherwise. University students from suspect countries need to be subject to enhanced security screening. One-half of all foreign students return home, and "it is doubtful that all those who [do so have] . . . by virtue of their sojourn in the United States, become inoculated against rabid anti-Americanism" (ibid.: 232).

The USA Patriot Act includes unprecedented powers of surveillance. Based on the premise that malicious demons might be sleeping anywhere, law enforcers are given sweeping access to private spaces, places, and communication networks. In this legislation, the old model of resourceful police intelligence is replaced by one of universal suspicion that spells the end of innocence: everyone is suspect and treated as such to a degree; everyone is on a continuum of risk.

There is a legalization of access to communication and database infrastructures that might yield signs of suspicious activity, for example those of telephone companies, Internet Service Providers (ISPs), libraries, retailers (e.g., book stores, travel agencies, car dealers), and schools (e.g., under a "foreign student monitoring program"). Restrictions are eased regarding court orders and warrants to search for information. For example, court orders pertaining to telephone communications are extended to cover email and Internet communications, and to cover the entire country rather than only the judicial district in which the order is issued, which was the previous practice. ISPs are given incentives to provide access to information about their customers even without a court order. Incentives include holding them immune from legal liability if they provide such access in "good faith" with government, and offering them compensation for costs associated with their assistance.

The USA Patriot Act also provides for the widening of surveillance powers under the Foreign Intelligence Surveillance Act. For example, there is a widening of the duration of court orders, the scope of access to private sector business records, access to email, and "roving surveillance" schemes. The much laxer legal standards of the Foreign Intelligence Surveillance Act regarding physical searches, wiretaps, and access to private sector databases are extended to criminal investigations as long as domestic law enforcers can argue that there is an element of foreign intelligence gathering in their investigations.

While using the USA Patriot Act and related legislation to legalize its access to the spaces, places, and communications of other entities, the US government has simultaneously tried to draw the veil of administrative decency over its own operations. For example, in signing a November 2002 bill related to federal law enforcement activities, President Bush attached a statement regarding reporting obligations laid down by Congress in which he asserted his presidential authority "to withhold information 'the disclosure of which could impair foreign relations, the national security, the deliberative processes of the Executive, or the performance of the Executive's constitutional duties,' as defined in each case by the President" (Whitaker 2006: 153–54). There is growing recognition that this asymmetry of knowledge and power violates US First Amendment constitutional rights of free speech and access to information (Janus 2004: 579). Total information awareness is for some and not others.

This national security regime of law against law is designed to cast the net as widely as possible, identify suitable enemies, not worry about false positive identifications, drop any pretense of due process of law, and effect summary justice through incapacitation, torture, and elimination. It ignores *actus reus*, the legal principle that criminalization must be based on a specified criminal act. Indeed, there is not even a pretense of what might be termed *probabilis reus*: criminalization on the basis of actuarial knowledge of risk. There is only the law against law principle of *finus reus*: when criminalization appears necessary for national security, no other justification is needed and established legal principles are preempted, finished (Brodeur 1981; Brodeur and Leman-Langlois 2006).

In the aftermath of 9/11, the US government used a variety of other legislative maneuvers to circumvent normal legal process. While most laws against law were designed to ferret out and criminalize terrorists, there was also swift counter-law action to protect selective aspects of the economy. For example, extraordinary steps were taken to protect the airline industry, which was already in difficulty before 9/11. In addition to liabilities for the four airplanes destroyed and lives lost in 9/11, the industry suffered an immediate decrease in passenger traffic. The Air Transportation Safety and System Stabilization Act (ATSSSA), passed by Congress within twelve days of 9/11, provided a number of temporary financial measures to bail out and stabilize the industry: $5 billion direct compensation; $10 billion loan guarantees for both 9/11 costs and any subsequent terrorist attack; a $100 million liability cap on future terrorist attack claims; discretionary reimbursement of airline insurance premium increases; discretionary reinsurance protection; and an interim insurance program (Campbell 2002; Standard and Poor's 2002: 4).

The most extraordinary provision of the ATSSSA was the Victims' Compensation Fund (VCF). This provision was designed to compensate victims of 9/11 in a direct and timely manner, as an alternative to the tort liability system. Anyone who suffered personal injury in the terrorist attacks of 9/11, or beneficiaries of those who experienced wrongful death, could apply to the VCF. Since the claim was payable by the US Treasury, the VCF was not really a "fund" or insurance but simply a contribution to disaster relief. The VCF payment was reduced by collateral sources available to the claimant, such as life and health insurance, pension benefits, and specified charitable donations the victim received from the Liberty Fund or similar sources.

If the victim or beneficiary opted for the VCF, they were required to relinquish any right to sue through the tort liability system. As such, the VCF arrangement was consistent with the many other laws against law following 9/11 that short-circuited legal process or avoided it altogether. The events of 9/11 precipitated *the* mass tort of all time, and the

VCF provided an alternative that would preempt the extraordinary legal, time, and psychic costs of litigation. The fact that if litigated, all cases would be assigned to one court, the Southern District of New York, ensured a crippling backlog of cases. Indeed, cases from the 1993 terrorist attack on the World Trade Center were still pending in this court when the 2001 attack occurred!

The VCF was the "purest" no-fault statute ever adopted in the United States. The statute was drafted by leading representatives of the plaintiffs' bar, a group that would benefit enormously from litigation. The plaintiffs' bar cooperated in the VCF process because it felt it had no choice but to do so. Indeed, it not only helped to develop the VCF alternative to the tort system, but also offered free legal services to victims and their families as a gesture of solidarity.

On one view the VCF was "an unprecedented social welfare relief program" (Campbell 2002: 211). It was the first direct obligation federal bill since Medicare 36 years earlier, social security being the only other direct obligation provision in US history. The official in charge of the program called it an "Unprecedented expression of compassion on the part of the American people to the victims and their families . . . designed to bring some measure of financial relief to those most devastated by the events of September 11 . . . [and] an example of how Americans rally around the less fortunate" (ibid.: 15–16).

The VCF was also an example of how Americans rally around their less fortunate industries, providing a form of socialism for business enterprise. The VCF was a crucial ingredient in efforts to bail out the airline industry, as signified by the fact that it was included in the ATSSSA. The ATSSSA capped airline liability for 9/11 to their insurance coverage at the time. In effect, the VCF provided a federal immunity to commercial entities (airlines) for state-based tort claims, dispossessing the states of legal jurisdiction. In the legal opinion of some, the fact that taking the VCF option preempted the victim's right to sue also made it unconstitutional.

Many other strategic uses of law have developed in the ongoing "war on terror" campaign. For example, Welch (2002, 2005) reveals how the US Justice Department initially charges some terrorist suspects with immigration infractions under civil law in order to circumvent the due process standards of criminal law that might be invoked by defense attorneys if there were criminal proceedings. Indeed, under US immigration law, unlike criminal law, those arrested are not entitled to legal aid attorneys and many are thereby immediately rendered defenseless.

Counter-law II: Surveillant Assemblages

As we have already documented, laws against law help to support the surveillant assemblages of national security. However, these assemblages are based on additional foundations. Existing technologies are reconfigured and new technologies are invented to facilitate surveillance. Similarly, existing organizational arrangements are reconfigured and new organizations created to enhance surveillance and visibility. These technological and organizational transformations in turn mobilize both private sector entities and individual citizens as an integral part of the national security surveillant assemblages.

The technological infrastructures for surveillance have greatly expanded in the name of national security (Levi and Wall 2004; Amoore and De Goede 2005; Bennett 2005). Caught up in the marketing of (in)security following 9/11, organizations bought into an array of surveillance technologies aimed at monitoring people and lethal weapons. According to the publisher of the new *Homeland Defense Journal*, "The Sept. 11 attacks will be the biggest catalyst for US technological innovation since the Soviets launched their Sputnik Satellite in 1957, spurring the competing US space program" (Krane 2002: D16). In the year following 9/11, technology companies opened sales offices in Washington and staffed them with retired military and security officials. The big players included Microsoft, IBM, Dell Computers, and Oracle Corporation, which proposed a national identity card and database. Smaller firms also saw the opportunity for expansion. For example, "Visage Technology Inc., a small Massachusetts company that makes drivers' licenses, used a post-Sept. 11 investment of $25 million to purchase a biometrics firm, open an office with a view of the US Capitol and recruit John Gannon, a former deputy director for intelligence at the CIA, as a board member. The company hopes to sell face recognition kiosks to government" (ibid.).

There is of course a long history of developing the latest technologies of surveillance and identification in the name of national security. For example, J. Edgar Hoover gained control of the fingerprinting system as part of establishing the FBI as a domestic surveillance agency in the 1920s (Cole 2001: 246–7). Hoover's dream of total information awareness "saw universal fingerprinting as the key to a national web of individualized surveillance, under his personal control" (ibid.). While his dream was never fully realized, Hoover did manage to develop the largest fingerprint file in the world through the requirement of the Alien Registration Act (1940) that all immigrants and other "aliens" be fingerprinted. "Hoover returned fingerprinting to its origins, as a mechanism for state monitoring and surveillance of citizens, especially those deemed foreign, politically radical, or otherwise dangerous" (ibid.).

The key difference in the contemporary era is the capacity to combine different surveillance technologies into a surveillant assemblage, yielding new forms of knowledge and control. A single surveillance technology such as a CCTV camera is usually a mile wide but only an inch deep because it does not in itself provide detailed knowledge about the person whose behavior is being momentarily captured and made visible. However, when combined with other technologies – for example, combining digitized CCTV systems with computer databases – depth and intensity of surveillance are achieved. In particular, new computer-based systems of data matching and data mining create new patterns of human traces – a person's "data double" (Haggerty and Ericson 2000) – that can identify them as a particular type of person, suspicious or otherwise. Many surveillant assemblages that were originally developed in commercial contexts to market segment consumers are also models and sources for population data potentially useful in national security contexts (Amoore and De Goede 2005; Turow 2006; Gandy 2006). For example, insurers use data matching and data mining systems to identify "prospects as suspects" (Ericson, Doyle, and Barry 2003: chap. 7) – insurance applicants they should not insure – as well as those who are suspected of making fraudulent insurance claims (ibid.: chap. 9). The technological infrastructures and algorithmic models used in this commercial context of identifying suspects have applications to any effort to identify suspicious behavior.

The new surveillant assemblages of national security post-9/11 seek both breadth and depth. Breadth is to be achieved through CCTV systems that aim to protect key urban venues in ways similar to the systems that proliferated in the UK in the wake of IRA terrorism. For example, "[a]ided by a federal grant of $5.1 million, the city of Chicago is spending $8.6 million on a system of smart video cameras, equipped with software that will raise the alarm when the cameras spot people loitering, wandering in circles, hanging around outside public buildings, or stopping their cars on the shoulders of highways" (Raban 2005: 25). The aim is to ensure that "Anyone walking in public [is] to be almost constantly watched" (*New York Times*, September 21, 2004). Depth is signified by the very name of the FBI's CARNIVORE "super search engine which, when installed on Internet service providers, is capable of trolling through email traffic and flagging communications of interest to the agency based on the identities of senders and receivers, keyword recognition, and so forth" (Whitaker 2006: 143). Breadth and depth are achieved through surveillant assemblages that cast nets for all manner of possible threats to homeland security, hoping to land big fish as well as the small fry.

> The Department of Homeland Security is the co-sponsor, with the FBI and the Justice Department, of Operation Predator, intended to track down pedophiles via their use of the Internet – presumably because pedophiles, whose civil liberties are held in high esteem by almost nobody, are indeed guinea pigs for a more sweeping exercise in cyberspying that might net terrorists . . . our e-mails, shared files, and visits to suspect Internet sites are obviously more likely to identify us as al-Qaedist than any tendency we may exhibit to wander in circles in front of tall buildings. When FBI director Robert Mueller announced that Operation Predator "sends a clear message that the digital environment will not offer sanctuary to those pedophiles who lurk in peer-to-peer networks. We will identify you. We will bring you to justice," it seems improbable, given the DHS's involvement in the scheme, that he had pedophiles only, or mainly, in mind. (Raban 2005: 25; see also Janus 2004)

While electronic surveillance technologies have the breadth to traverse organizational boundaries and the depth to make visible previously unknown spaces and population profiles, they do not do so on their own. Organizational change occurs in conjunction with technological change, and the transition is not straightforward.

The US government created the Department of Homeland Security as an umbrella organization for bringing closer together a number of different security-related organizations, including the FBI and CIA. This organizational change is a means of trying to break down divisions between different government agencies that have worked semi-autonomously and at times in competition and conflict with each other. It also serves to advance the conflation of war abroad and war on threats to domestic security at home, including but not limited to the war on terrorism. Furthermore, it seeks to break down barriers that separate databases in different government agencies, in order to bring together information from counterintelligence investigations of foreign threats and ordinary domestic criminal law enforcement. The view is that borderless threats require borderless law enforcement across organizational entities nationally and internationally, and across categories of citizens and non-citizens.

The US government imagines a global surveillance state. This was symbolized in the Total Information Awareness (TIA) Program logo of an eye at the apex of a pyramid scanning the globe, accompanied by the slogan *Scientia ist potentia*, knowledge is power. The TIA program was housed in the Defense Advance Research Projects Agency (DARPA) and headed by Vice Admiral John Poindexter, infamously known for his involvement in the Iran Contra affair. DARPA's TIA plans for omniscience met with resistance across the political spectrum on the grounds that they signified the end of privacy. The TIA began to backtrack on its more ambitious claims; however, further concern was raised when Poindexter proposed a terrorism risk catastrophe bond market in which investors would speculate on future terrorist activity and profit if a catastrophe did not occur within the period during which the bond was held. The hope was that this futures market in terrorism would extend surveillance capacity because investors would demand better data to predict terrorism futures, and these data could in turn be used in the national security effort. For many, including then Deputy Defense Secretary Donald Rumsfeld, this proposal was the final indicator that the TIA program had become a political liability. Poindexter was dismissed and the program was terminated.

As Whitaker (2006) observes, the termination of the formal TIA program did not in any way stop other TIA-like initiatives. For example, DARPA also created Lifelog, "which seeks to amass every conceivable bit of information that can be gathered from every source (including audiovisual sensors and biomedical monitors) about an individual's life, and download it all into a vast, searchable database" (ibid.: 158–9). In the spring of 2003, the FBI and CIA jointly created the Terrorist Threat Integration Center to integrate information from all available foreign and domestic sources for possible signs of terrorism.

The effort to connect the surveillance infrastructures of national security and domestic security has led to an organizational and operational blurring between them (see also chapter 5). For example, in at least 75 cases identified by the Foreign Intelligence Surveillance Act review court, the FBI was said to have misled the court in its justifications for electronic surveillance (Whitaker 2006). In particular, the FBI justified electronic surveillance applications in the name of foreign threats to national security but used intelligence gathered for bringing charges in domestic criminal cases. The US Justice Department appealed this decision to the new Foreign Intelligence Surveillance Court of Review, and this court concluded that amendments to FISA under the USA Patriot Act permit such criminal prosecutions as long as the surveillance also has a significant foreign intelligence purpose. Attorney General John Ashcroft declared that this was a new legal permit for criminal investigators and intelligence agents to collaborate, and announced plans to intensify covert surveillance operators through designated intelligence prosecutors in each federal court district as well as a new intelligence warrant unit in the FBI. Ashcroft later "revealed that he had personally authorized secret electronic surveillance and physical searches without immediate court oversight in 170 'emergency' cases since the 9/11 attacks – more than triple the emergency searches authorized by other attorneys general over the past 20 years (Schmidt 2003)" (Whitaker 2006: 151).

There was a simultaneous effort to break down barriers to surveillance between government and private sector organizations, and among private sector organizations themselves. This effort was based on the view that Little Brother collaboration will yield more than the sum of its parts, a Big Brother surveillance infrastructure of total information awareness. The process began with the 9/11 investigation itself, which relied heavily on the data doubles of suspects in credit card, telephone, and air miles databases. It continued with an expansion of enabling regulations and technologies for surveillance in a wide range of private sector contexts. New air transportation information systems and screening procedures were developed to track the movement of people and goods

(Brodeur and Leman-Langlois 2006). Money trail surveillance by financial institutions, already in place regarding the drug trade and other forms of organized crime, was enhanced. With the aid of the USA Patriot Act provisions, financial institutions are enlisted in the government's money trail surveillance program on threat of severe sanction, including seizure of assets, for failure to cooperate. Many other fields of business enterprise have been enlisted, for example in creating surveillant assemblages that might identify financiers of terrorist activity or purveyors of nuclear, biological, and chemical materials.

On a different level, there is an effort to mobilize entire industries because of their key role at the foundation of surveillance infrastructures. One such industry is private security, which, because of its special legal access to private spaces on behalf of property owners, has a unique position as front-line "eyes and ears" in the national security effort.

Private security was a fast-growing and substantial part of the US economy prior to 9/11. One estimate of private security spending in the United States during the 1990s is $40 billion annually, with almost half devoted to private police staff and the remainder to preventive security technologies (Anderson 1999). The Organization of Economic Cooperation and Development (OECD) projected that private security would expand considerably following 9/11, with possible effects on economic growth and productivity: "A doubling of private security might reduce the level of potential output by 0.6 per cent after five years and the level of private sector productivity by 0.8 per cent" (2002: 136). The New York City Comptroller reported that, in 2001, over 1 percent of all workers in New York City were security guards. He observed that in the four years following the 1993 World Trade Center (WTC) bombing, there was a 22 percent increase in spending on private security guards. Assuming the same level of growth over four years following 9/11, the additional cost would be about $1 billion. The Comptroller also noted that some of this post-9/11 increase in private security would be driven by contract stipulations of the insurance industry.

"Security-related spending, however, is a cost that may be seen as an investment because it helps to narrow the future property/casualty [insurance] premium between NYC and other cities" (Thompson 2002: 22).

Joh (2004) documents the role of private security operatives in various contexts of terrorism-related security. For example, Disney World in Florida has an 800-member security force attuned to the post-9/11 environment. On the eve of the invasion of Iraq, the Federal Aviation Authority granted Disney World, as well as Disneyland in California, a no-fly zone as a precautionary measure. In an ethnographic study of policing in a large commercial complex in Manhattan, Joh found ongoing relations between city police and private security operatives regarding terrorism-related security threats.

At the same time private security operatives are sometimes viewed as a source of threat because of their intimate knowledge of, and access to, critical infrastructures, and the fact that they are often ill-trained, poorly equipped, inadequately regulated, and at the margins of the labor market. Private security operatives are said to be in need of intensified surveillance even as they are embraced as essential to surveillance infrastructures.

As indicated in the statement above by the New York City Comptroller, the private insurance industry is also a key player in the development of surveillance infrastructures. It has unique capacities to govern other organizations through contracts which define the meaning of terrorism and specify the security measures the insured must put in place to help preempt terrorism.

In the insurance world there is a marketplace of definitions of terrorism, open to negotiation depending on how insurers wish to participate in a specific terrorism risk with specific clients. For example, a reinsurance company I studied (Ericson and Doyle 2004a: chapter 5) created a very broad definition of terrorism as an opening position with which to negotiate contracts with primary insurers and in turn their clients. An executive involved in these negotiations said that, "we might throw out these words, then someone else might throw out another set of words to define terrorism, and we work through it . . . Everybody usually has a different point of view on things, which are guided maybe by corporate risk appetites and such." A colleague added, "There are as many terrorist exclusions in the marketplace as there are ceding companies. So at last count I think we were above 250 [companies]. So there's probably 250 some-odd wordings for terrorism exclusion in the current marketplace." He stated that the final definition of terrorism settled on for a given insurance contract depends on the other terms of the contract. "There's a lot of negotiation that goes back and forth with the companies depending upon our participation in the program, limits offered, attachment points, whatever, where we may come off some of those [definitions that exclude specific aspects of terrorism] objectives . . . Sub-limits are one of the ways to obviously reduce your exposures, to reduce your limits, then maybe we can give a little bit on the wording."

Insurance contracts also place terrorism-related preventive security requirements on the insured, with the capacity for detailed, on-site inspections for compliance. A senior executive of a reinsurance company explained to me how 9/11 changed the commercial risk underwriting environment in this regard.

> It's impacted our whole underwriting process, where, before we renew reinsurance contracts, we ask for a lot more information from our clients . . . Stuff that before nobody would care to find out or ask about. Now it's being asked by the reinsurer, and in turn the insurance company needs to find out from the insured and make sure that information is kept up to date . . . You are also dealing with a very "live" [hard] market. This [9/11] came at the end of a very soft market. Typically in a soft market people don't dare ask a lot of questions, the client goes somewhere else . . . [T]he market started turning before 9/11 – 9/11 really pushed it up in a much more dramatic fashion. Now it's OK to ask ten, twenty, thirty questions before you renew your account, and get that information.

Another reinsurance executive said that his company was questioning ceding insurers about their clients' preventive security arrangements with respect to terrorism. This new vigilance was exercised in relation to all commercial reinsurance under consideration, but intensified if the buildings involved were deemed symbolic targets of terrorism.

> One of the first questions we ask our underwriters toward their clients is, "What do your clients do about the terrorism exposure?" . . . There's things you can do on an underwriting basis, on a loss prevention basis . . . to avoid a terrorist act. For example, you own a building and you have a security guard at the entrance, that will prevent a lot of unwanted people from wandering around the building. The WTC, the top door to the roof had been locked for some reason. A good loss control person, had he or she done a review, would have noticed the door probably should not have been locked, lives would have been saved . . . We have developed a number of detailed questionnaires . . . [regarding] accessibility, security, after-event evacuation procedures, those types of things.. . . And this target-class list . . . main targets of terrorism, many of those [questionnaires] have to do with security . . . precautions that are taken. We're just trying to limit the accessibility of these targets to outsiders, to people that we don't want in there. Inside concerns, how are you monitoring the inside of your plant?

In direct underwriting situations, some insurers send loss control engineers to field sites with detailed questionnaires addressing terrorism-related security arrangements. This assessment is used to decide whether terrorism coverage should be excluded entirely, or included at particular sublimits and prices. Agreed levels of surveillance personnel and technologies are negotiated in this process.

Insurance company executives I interviewed offered various examples of increased vigilance about commercial operations. A reinsurance company executive used the example of a trucking company and said that before 9/11 the drivers' licenses may have been checked annually for authenticity but now "we may come up with a recommendation that if you want us to reinsure your business, we want you to *insist* on having drivers' records checked on a quarterly basis. Because there is turnover and you never know who is going to drive a truck on a particular day. So in those cases, we would make a proactive check that they do so, and we would come back and follow up . . . We can certainly get off that business, or break the contract, if we don't like what we see." Another interviewee illustrated the point with "the courier company that couriers packages, or a small airlines company, I wouldn't necessarily exclude terrorism but I would ask questions. 'What have you done since 9/11 to increase your security? Do you check what's in the packages before they board the plane? How are your pilots trained? How do you screen people?' "

There is no doubt that business enterprise became more vigilant after 9/11. In a survey of chief executive officers asking them to identify "post 9/11 precautions," the following were mentioned most frequently: review of disaster plan (90 percent), background checks on contractors (51 percent), background checks on employees (39 percent), limiting staff on a single flight (36 percent), and considering alternative office space (35 percent) (Insurance Information Institute www.iii.org.25, April 2002). Organizations were urged to examine building infrastructures regarding their physical security features. With visions of the *Titanic* as *the* infallible technology that failed, it was pointed out that the WTC had been touted as "collapse proof." Those contemplating future high-rise construction were implored to take note of total loss risks, while those responsible for existing buildings were asked to address remedial measures that might reduce such risks. On a mundane level, advice flowed on the need for target hardening. "For instance, installing a film across windows can reduce the risk of injuries from flying glass. By putting a barrier around a building, a company can keep potentially dangerous cars and trucks away" (Green 2002).

The US government has also sought mobilization of all citizens in the national security surveillance effort. This mobilization is spearheaded by the US Department of Homeland Security (DHS) and its partner, The America Prepared Campaign, Inc. (APC) (www.ready.gov; www.americaprepared.org).

DHS has published a 200-page manual for citizens entitled, *Are You Ready? An In-Depth Guide to Citizen Preparedness*. This manual covers preventive measures and recovery plans regarding a wide range of catastrophic risks, including terrorism. In the section on terrorism, a photograph of the smoldering remnants of the WTC is placed in the center of a long definition and description of terrorism. This material makes it clear that terrorism refers to a very broad range of criminal activity and that the response to terrorism inevitably entails more criminalization.

> Recent technological advances and ongoing international political unrest are components of the increased risk to national security . . . Terrorism is the use of force or violence against persons or property in violation of the criminal laws of the United States for purposes of intimidation, coercion or ransom. Terrorists often use threats to:
>
> - Create fear among the public
> - Try to convince citizens that their government is powerless to prevent terrorism
> - Get immediate publicity for their causes
>
> Acts of terrorism include threats of terrorism; assassinations; kidnappings; hijackings; bomb scares and bombings; cyber attacks (computer-based); and the use of chemical, biological, nuclear and radiological weapons.
>
> High-risk targets for acts of terrorism include military and civilian government facilities, international airports, large cities, and high-profile landmarks. Terrorists might also target large public gatherings, water and food supplies, utilities, and corporate centers. Further, terrorists are capable of spreading fear by sending explosives or chemical or biological agents through the mail. (DHS 2004: 145. 148)

With targets as vague as "large cities," "large public gatherings," "water and food supplies," and "corporate centers," the citizen must be ready for the malicious demon of terrorism in all places at all times. The whole world is to be watched as if one is always in an airport security environment. Thus, *Are You Ready?* recommends adoption of precautionary logic at home, work, and play. For example, there is the admonition to "Take precautions when traveling. Be aware of conspicuous or unusual behavior. Do not accept packages from strangers. Do not leave luggage unattended. You should promptly report unusual behavior, suspicious or unattended packages, and strange devices to the police or security personnel" (ibid.: 148). The minutiae include 14 signs of what might make parcels suspicious.

- Are unexpected or from someone unfamiliar to you
- Have no return address, or have one that can't be verified as legitimate
- Are marked with restrictive endorsements such as "Personal," "Confidential," or "Do not x-ray"
- Have protruding wires or aluminum foil, strange odors, or stains
- Show a city or state in the postmark that doesn't match the return address
- Are of unusual weight given their size, or are lopsided or oddly shaped
- Are marked with threatening language
- Have inappropriate or unusual labeling
- Have excessive postage or packaging material, such as masking tape and string
- Have misspellings of common words
- Are addressed to someone no longer with your organization or are otherwise outdated
- Have incorrect titles or titles without a name
- Are not addressed to a specific person
- Have hand-written or poorly typed addresses

DHS has developed a Security Advisory System to mobilize citizens into precautionary activity. Treating the uncertainty of terrorism as if it is a risk, five threat levels are identified: severe, high, elevated, guarded, low (figure 2.1). "Risk includes both the probability of an attack occurring and its potential gravity. Threat conditions may be assigned for the entire nation, or they may be set for a particular geographic area or industrial sector. At each threat condition, government entities and the private sector, including businesses and schools, would implement a corresponding set of 'protective measures' to further reduce vulnerability or increase response capability during a period of heightened alert" (ibid.: 174).

As indicated in figure 2.1, citizens are to become more suspicious and vigilant at each threat level. Even when the alchemists of risk in the DHS give the green light to go about business normally because there is a low risk, normality includes joining community surveillance organizations such as Citizens Corps, Volunteers in Police Service, and Neighborhood Watch, and taking courses in emergency preparedness. This is because "There is always a risk of terrorist threat. Each threat condition assigns a level of alert appropriate to the increasing level of terrorist attacks" (ibid.).

The DHS and APC collaborate with a wide range of organizations in business enterprise, mass media, education, and communities to mobilize citizens as agents of surveillance. APC declares on its website that it "is an all-out drive to galvanize Americans to prepare themselves and their families." Skepticism, cynicism, and resistance among citizens is to be overcome through communication strategies that make people appreciate that knowledge is power, and that safety measures with respect to terrorism can be normalized in the same way as countless other such measures in everyday life (cf. Hunt 2003).

APC's website observes that citizens have an inclination to be dubious about the threat, given past US government efforts to spend trillions of dollars of citizens' money on the elusive pursuit of malicious demons. However, the war on terrorism is different because in this case the enemy is real.

Severe Risk

Complete all recommended actions at lower levels.
Listen to local emergency management officials.
Stay tuned to TV or radio for current information/instructions.
Be prepared to shelter or evacuate, as instructed.
Expect traffic delays and restrictions.
Provide volunteer services only as requested.
Contact your school/business to determine status of work day.

High Risk

Complete recommended steps at lower levels.
Exercise caution when traveling, pay attention to travel advisories.
Review your family emergency plan and make sure all family members know what to do.
Be Patient. Expect some delays, baggage searches and restrictions at public buildings.
Check on neighbors or others that might need assistance in an emergency.

Elevated Risk

Complete recommended steps at levels green and blue.
Ensure disaster supplies are stocked and ready.
Check telephone numbers in family emergency plan and update as necessary.
Develop alternate routes to/from work or school and practice them.
Continue to be alert for suspicious activity and report it to authorities.

Guarded Risk

Complete recommended steps at level green.
Review stored disaster supplies and replace items that are outdated.
Be alert to suspicious activity and report it to proper authorities.

Low Risk

Develop a family emergency plan. Share it with family and friends, and practice the plan.
Visit www.Ready.gov for help creating a plan.
Create an "Emergency Supply Kit" for your household.
Be informed. Visit www.Ready.gov or obtain a copy of "Preparing Makes Sense, Get Ready Now" by calling 1-800-BE-READY.
Know where to shelter and how to turn off utilities (power, gas, water) to your home.
Examine volunteer opportunities in your community, such as Citizens Corps, Volunteers in Police Service, Neighborhood Watch or others, and donate your time.
Consider completing an American Red Cross first aid or CPR course, or Community Emergency Response Team (CERT) course.

Figure 2.1 *Citizen guidance on the Homeland Security Advisory System*
Source: Adapted from Department of Homeland Security (2004: 175)

> Unlike the catastrophe of a nuclear war and the fruitless Cold War civil defense campaigns that accompanied that threat – *the consequences of certain kinds of terrorist attacks can be significantly mitigated if fear and panic are replaced by knowledgeable preparation* . . . A citizen education and preparedness campaign in the September 12th Era is not an abstract, feel good program. It will lessen psychic and economic damage. *And it will save lives. It is a real line of defense . . . Everything the Campaign does will have to overcome the obstacles of complacency, cynicism and ridicule.* Those behind the campaign know that they cannot fully avoid these reactions. They intend to face them head on by engaging the best creative and research minds in the country to craft messages that will break through. The Campaign must convey urgency, without fear. It must galvanize, not terrify.

APC Communications try to normalize precautionary measures with respect to terrorism as no different than what is already taken for granted in other safety environments, such as having smoke detectors in the home and wearing a seatbelt while driving. "Similar to the approach used by the seat belt and recycling campaigns of recent years, the objective of all America Prepared Communications is to build awareness of preparedness as a philosophy, to encourage Americans to integrate thinking about preparedness into their everyday lives, and to provide specific information and direction about actions to take to achieve peace of mind."

One APC ad campaign appeals to consumer identities. Each ad features a particular consumer item in a household closet or cabinet that has been consumed in excess: shoes, lipstick, compact disks, neckties. The picture of excessive consumption is overlain with "But Do You Have A [naming a security item]? READY.GOV. You have the things that make you happy. Get the things that make you prepared. Get a kit. Brought to you by The America Prepared Campaign Inc." One such ad is shown in illustration 2.1. The message is that overspent Americans (Schor 1998) should get their priorities right and redirect more of their disposable income to security

Illustration 2.1 *Advertisement: But Do You Have a Whistle? Reproduced by permission of Allison Phinney, Verified Identity Pass, Inc.*

products. This act is depicted as both good sense and good citizenship.

DHS and APC also operate through key institutions to galvanize citizens in the war on terror. One such institution is schools, which are seen as both vulnerable to terrorism and a site for mobilization of precaution against terrorist activity. For example, APC developed a Standard and Poor's-like rating of the 20 largest school districts in the US on their preparedness for a terrorist attack or other emergency. The school districts were graded as best, good, needs improvement, and failing, with the results published in a 70-page document and on the APC website. This shaming exercise was aimed at redirecting resources away from other education system expenditures and toward security products. While the chair of the APC states that one should not blame the victim – impoverished school districts that have already lost out through cutbacks and other neo-liberal government security spending priorities – he then proceeds to do precisely that. "Those who are failing should be embarrassed into improving. Indeed although there are no villains here, if the overall conclusions of the 9/11 Commission are to be taken seriously, we should hope that those responsible for schools that should be doing more will be embarrassed out of claiming a lack of resources or other priorities as excuses for not acting." Indeed it is especially embarrassing to be publicly scolded for not doing enough to protect the safety of children, even if it is at the expense of their education.

Another initiative used school children to mobilize their parents in the war on terror. Children were enlisted as "deputies" to recruit their parents for an educational visit to www.ready.gov, purchase of an emergency kit, and completion of a family communication plan in the event of an emergency. Two competitions were held, one for the school with the greatest number of parents enlisted in absolute terms, and one for the school with the greatest number of parents enlisted in proportionate or ratio terms, taking into account the school size. The prize in each case was $10,000 for the school library fund and having DHS Secretary Tom Ridge as school principal for a day.

DHS also mobilizes citizens through the newly created umbrella of Citizens Corps. Citizens Corps seeks to coordinate myriad surveillance and emergency response organizations already in place: police volunteers, Neighborhood Watch, Fire Corps, medical reserve corps, Senior Corps, AmeriCorps, Learn and Serve America, emergency response teams, and many others. "The mission of Citizen Corps is to harness the power of every individual through *education, training and volunteer service* to make communities safer, stronger and better prepared to respond to the threats of terrorism, crime, public health issues, and disasters of all kinds." This mission requires "*Personal responsibility*. Developing a household preparedness plan and disaster supplies kits, observing home health and safety practices, implementing disaster mitigation measures, and participating in crime prevention and reporting." As of March 2005, DHS claimed to have established 55 state and territory Citizen Corps Councils and 1,608 county, local, and tribal Citizen Corps Councils serving 189 million people, two-thirds of the US population.

There are many other accounts of community organizations forming around terrorism as a national security threat. For example, operating under the motto, "Watching America with Pride, Not Prejudice," and using the acronym CAT eyes, the Community Anti-Terrorism Training Institute formed as an "anti-terrorist citizen informant program [and is] being adapted by local police departments throughout the East Coast and parts of the Midwest" (Takei 2003). Commenting upon this development, Whitaker (2006: 159–60) observes that "The program's founder ambitiously envisions an eventual 100 million informers, a ratio of watchers to watched of about one to two, as compared with the East German *stasi* ratio of one to eight."

As indicated by the above "mission" and "personal responsibility" statements of Citizen Corps, DHS and APC initiatives are not limited to terrorism as a national security threat. Rather, they address myriad domestic security threats and problems, a point that is taken up in more detail in chapter 5. DHS and APC websites and published materials make it clear that while terrorism is the primary spur to intensified homeland security, there are many other threats to homeland security: bullying, child abuse, drunk driving, Internet-based threats, television-based threats, rape, substance abuse, tobacco abuse, and family communication breakdown, to name a few. "Governing through terrorism" (cf. Simon 1997, 2006; Ferguson 2005; Altheide 2006; Welch 2006) mobilizes citizens against the uncertainties of many other "terrors" in everyday life.

The Two Leviathans

Jihadist terrorism is a real threat. National security efforts to address this threat produce myths. These myths in turn constitute new realities of crime, risk, and uncertainty.

The war on terror perpetuates myths that seem more associated with the Leviathan of the biblical social imaginary. First, there is a belief that the Jihadist Leviathan is a fearless demon bent on death and destruction. Its power to create tsunami-like waves of devastation is underpinned by imaginary networks that are global in their reach. Second, the entire terrorist movement can be toppled if only the heads of its mastermind monsters can be decapitated. During the 2004 presidential election debates on television, even the Democratic Party candidate John Kerry was scripted to repeat at many junctures, "We will *kill* the terrorists. We will *kill* the terrorists. We will *kill* the terrorists." Third, there is a need for preemptive war abroad in the name of preventing attacks at home. National security cannot be separated from global security. Fourth, there is a new doctrine of *parens patriae* regarding homeland security: citizens are children in need of constant protection from danger, precautionary moral lessons, and surveillance.

These myths of the war on terror constitute new realities. There is the reality of counter-law I, laws against law, which undermine the principles, standards, and procedures of democratic legal institutions that have been foundational to the enactment of the liberal social imaginary. There is the reality of counter-law II, surveillant assemblages that not only counteract democratic legal institutions but also substitute a new basis for governing that is patently undemocratic in its mobilization of categorical suspicion, suspicion by association, discrimination, decreased privacy, and exclusion.

Happily there has been some democratic resistance. There are mounting court cases and some legal decisions freeing some terrorist suspects and placing some limits on laws against law (Janus 2004: 579). There was successful resistance to the original Total Information Awareness initiatives (Whitaker 2006). But the war on terror continues to use both forms of counter-law more or less unabated, to the point where the USA begins to resemble the Leviathan of the biblical social imaginary more than the Leviathan of the liberal social imaginary (Ferguson 2005). Indeed, given US aspirations to be a global Leviathan, its myths of terror – malicious demons, leaders to be decapitated, wars to be fought abroad in the name of security at home, and the need for *parens patriae* – extend around the world, accompanied by the new realities of counter-laws I and II.

As we have already seen, the national security regime of counter-law reaches into other fields of security provision and in turn draws upon them. In the USA and elsewhere, precautionary logic and its embodiment in the two forms of counter-law were well entrenched in other fields of security long before 9/11. At the same time, these other fields of security have taken on new forms in the wake of 9/11.

71a

References

Agamben, G. (2005) *State of Exception.* University of Chicago Press, Chicago.

Altheide, D. (2006) *Terrorism and the Politics of Fear.* Altamira Press, Blue Ridge Summit, PA.

Amoore, L. and De Goede, M. (2005) Government, risk and dataveillance in the war on terror. *Crime, Law and Social Change* 43, 149–73.

Anderson, D. (1999) The aggregate burden of crime. *Journal of Law and Economics* 42, 611–42.

Barak, G. (2005) A reciprocal approach to peacemaking criminology: between adversarialism and mutualism. *Theoretical Criminology* 9, 131–52.

Baudrillard, J. (2003) *The Spirit of Terrorism and other Essays.* Verso, London.

Bayatrizi, Z. (2005) *Death Sentences: The Modem Ordering of Mortality.* Ph.D. thesis, Department of Anthropology and Sociology, University of British Columbia.

Bennett, C. (2005) What happens when you book an airline ticket? The collecting and processing of passenger data post-9/11. In: Zureik, E. and Salter, M. (eds.) *Global Surveillance and Policing: Borders, Security, Identity.* Cullompton, Willan, pp. 113–38.

Brodeur, J.-P. (1981) Legitimizing police deviance. In: Shearing, C. (ed.) *Organizational Police Deviance.* Butterworths, Toronto, pp. 127–60.

Brodeur, J.-P. and Leman-Langlois, S. (2006) Surveillance fiction or high policing. In: Haggerty, K. and Ericson, R. (eds.) *The New Politics of Surveillance and Visibility.* University of Toronto Press, Toronto, pp. 171–98.

Campbell, R. (2002) America acts: the swift legislative response to the September 11 th attack on America. Paper to the conference, Liability and Insurance after September 11th, Insurance Law Center, University of Connecticut School of Law, 21–22 March.

Canadian Broadcasting Corporation (1998) *In Security.* Witness Program Video, CBC, Toronto.

Cheaney, R. (2004) The sleeper scenario: terrorism-support laws and the demands of prevention. *Harvard Review on Legislation* 42, 1–90.

Clarke, R. (2004) *Against All Enemies: Inside America's War on Terror.* Free Press, New York.

71b

Cole, S. (2001) *Suspect Identities: A History of Fingerprinting and Criminal Identification.* Harvard University Press, Cambridge, MA.

Department of Homeland Security (2004) *Are You Ready? An Indepth Guide to Citizen Preparedness.* Federal Emergency Management Agency, Jessup, MD.

Dershowitz, A. (2002) *Why Terrorism Works: Understanding the Threat, Responding to the Challenge.* Yale University Press, New Haven, CT.

Dratel, L. (2005) The legal narrative. In: Greenberg, K. and Dratel, J. (eds.) *The Torture Papers: The Road* to *Abu Ghraib.* Cambridge University Press, Cambridge, pp. xxi–xxiii.

Ericson, R. and Doyle, A. (2004a) *Uncertain Business: Risk, Insurance and the Limits of Knowledge.* University of Toronto Press, Toronto.

Ericson, R. and Doyle, A. (2004b) Catastrophe risk, insurance and terrorism. *Economy and Society* 33,135–173.

Ericson, R., Doyle, A., and Barry, D. (2003) *Insurance as Governance.* University of Toronto Press, Toronto.

Ferguson, N. (2005) *Colossus: The Rise and Fall of the American Empire.* Penguin, New York.

Gandy, O. (2006) Data mining, surveillance and discrimination in the post-9/11 environment. In: Haggerty, K. and Ericson, R. (eds.) *The New Politics of Surveillance and Visibility.* University of Toronto Press, Toronto, pp. 363–84.

Green, M. (2002) Cat models look to predict losses from future attacks. *Best Wire,* 29 August.

Greenberg, K. and Dratel, J. (eds.) (2005) *The Torture Papers: The Road to Abu Ghraib.* Cambridge University Press, Cambridge.

Haggerty, K. and Ericson, R. (2000) The surveillant assemblage.
British Journal of Sociology 51, 605–22.

Hunt, A. (2003) Risk and moralization in everyday life. In: Ericson, R. and Doyle, A. (eds.) *Risk and Morality.* University of Toronto Press, Toronto, pp. 165–92.

Ignatieff, M. (2004) *The Lesser Evil: Political Ethics in an Age of Terror.* Princeton University Press, Princeton, NJ.

Janus, E. (2004) The preventive state, terrorists and sexual predators: countering the threat of a new outsider jurisprudence. *Criminal Law Bulletin* 40, 576–98.

Joh, E. (2004) The paradox of private policing. *The Journal of Criminal Law and Criminology* 95, 49–131.

Kean, T. and Hamilton, L. (2004) *The 9/11Report: The National Commission on Terrorist Attacks Upon the United States.* St. Martin's Press, New York.

71c

Krane, J. (2002) Terrorism worries bring big business: pitch the product the right way and "you'd be amazed at what you sell." *Toronto Star,* 29 August.

Levi, M. and Wall, D. (2004) Technologies, security and privacy in the post-9/11 European information society. *Journal of Law and Society* 31, 194–220.

Lewis, A. (2005) Introduction. In: Greenberg, K. and Dratel, J. (eds.) *The Torture Papers: The Road to Abu Ghraib.* Cambridge University Press, Cambridge, pp. xiii–xvi.

Lind, E. et al. (1989) The changing face of war: into the fourth generation. *Marine Corps Gazette* (October), 22–6.

Moyers, B. (2005) Welcome to doomsday. *New York Review of Books* 52(5), 8, 10.

Organization of Economic Cooperation and Development. (2002) Economic consequences of terrorism. *OECD Economic Outlook* 71, 117–40.

Posner, M. (2004) *Catastrophe: Risk and Response.* Oxford University Press, New York.

Raban, J. (2005) The truth about terrorism. *New York Review of Books* 52(1), 22–6.

Reuter, C. (2004) *My Life* is *a Weapon: A Modem History of Suicide Bombing.* Princeton University Press, Princeton, NJ.

Scheuer, M. (2004) *Imperial Hubris: Why the West* is *Losing the War on Terror.* Brassey's, Dulles, VA.

Schmidt, R. (2003) U.S. expands clandestine surveillance operations. *Los Angeles Times,* March 5.

Schor, P. (1998) *The Overspent American: Upscaling, Downsizing and the New Consumer.* Basic Books, New York.

Simon, J. (1997) Governing through crime. In: Fisher, G. and Friedman, L. (eds.) *The Crime Conundrum: Essays on Criminal Justice.* Westview, Boulder, CO, pp. 171–90.

Stafford Smith, C, (2005) Representing "the enemy": human rights and the war on terror. *Criminal Justice Matters* 58, 44–7.

Standard and Poor's. (2002) Terrorism insurance coverage remains in doubt. *Standard and Poor's Insurance,* 15 April.

Takei, C. (2003) Building a nation of snoops. *Boston Globe,* May 14.

Taylor, C. (2004) *Modern Social Imaginaries.* Duke University Press, Durham.

Thompson, Jr., W. (2002) *One Year Later: The Fiscal Impact of 9/11 on New York City.* Comptroller of the City of New York, New York.

Turow, J. (2006) Cracking the code: advertisers, anxiety and surveillance in the digital age. In: Haggerty, K. and Ericson, R. (eds.) *The New Politics of Surveillance and Visibility.* University of Toronto Press, Toronto, pp. 279–307.

71d

Welch, M. (2002) *Detained: Immigration Laws and the Expanding I.N.S. Jail Complex.* Temple University Press, Philadelphia.
Welch, M. (2005) *Ironies of Imprisonment.* Sage, Thousand Oaks, CA.
Welch, M. (2006, forthcoming) Seeking a safer society: America's anxiety in the war on terror. *Security Journal.*
Whitaker, R. (2006) A Faustian bargain? America and the dream of total information awareness. In: Haggerty, K. and Ericson, R. (eds.) *The New Politics of Surveillance and Visibility.* University of Toronto Press, Toronto, pp. 141–70.

Name Index

Agamben, G. 323
Altheide, D. 177, 178, 185, 187, 191, 192, 194, 208, 353
Amoore, L. 334, 336
Anderson, A. 299
Anderson, D. 340
Arcuri, A. 131
Arnott, R. 227
Ashcroft, J. 339
Ashworth, A. 261
Atkinson, A. 244

Baker, T. 226, 227, 229, 241–2, 291
Baldwin, J. 131, 142–3
Barak, G. 323
Baranek, P. xi, xiii, xvi, xvii, 175, 180, 184–6, 188, 191, 193, 196, 198–9, 202–3, 208–14
Barclay, G. 258
Barnard, C. 70
Barry, D. x, xviii, 267, 297, 336
Barthes, R. 181
Bates, A. 182
Baudrillard, J. 319
Beck, U. 240, 242, 244, 280
Becker, H. 41, 43
Bell, D. 208
Bennett, C. 334
Best, J. 277
Biderman, A. 83
Bittner, E. 70, 85
Black, D. 83, 97, 117
Bohn, J. 302
Bok, S. 161
Bordua, D. 53
Bormann, E. 216
Bottomley, A. 83, 118
Bottoms, A.E. 131, 137
Bradford, D. 313
Brandt, R. 162
Brannigan, A. 190
Bridges, L. 265
Brodeur, J.-P. 166, 331, 340
Brun, S. 236, 286, 290–91, 313
Bush, George 322, 323, 327

Cain, M. 70, 77, 78, 85
Campbell, R. 332–3
Carriere, K. xix, 191
Castles, M. 239
Cavendar, G. 277
Cayley, D. 184, 213
Chan, J. xi, xiii, xvi, xvii, 175, 180, 184–6, 188, 191, 193, 196, 198–9, 202–3, 208–14
Chappell, D. 84
Chatterton, M. 264
Cheaney, R. 325
Chibnall, S. 157, 158, 159, 198, 210
Christie, N. 83, 105
Clarke, D. 198
Clarke, M. 231–2
Clarke, R. 257, 323
Clifford, J. 215
Cobb, B. 77
Cohen, S. 212
Cohn, Ellen G. ix
Cole, S. 335
Coleman, J. 105, 118
Comrie, M. 258
Cox, S. 77
Cousineau, D. 130
Crisell, A. 178, 180–86, 190–91, 195–6
Cumming, E. 83, 258

Dandeker, C. 223
De Goede M. 334, 336
Derrig, R. 228
Dershowitz, A. 329
Ditton, J. 117, 118, 119, 217, 231
Dornstein, K. 229
Downes, D. 86, 280
Doyle, A. x, xi, xii, xiii, xiv, xviii, 267, 297, 321, 341
Draper, R. 193, 258
Dratel, L. 327
Drechsel, R. 210

Duffy, J. 217
Dussuyer, I. 193
Dworkin, R. 190

Edell, L. 258
Eliot, T.S. 191
Elliott, P. 192, 195, 213, 215
Ennis, P. 83, 84
Epstein, E. 184, 191, 194, 195, 196
Ericson, M. 280
Ericson, Richard V. x, xi, xii, xiii, xiv, xv, xvi, xvii, xviii, xix, 49, 64, 66, 69, 79, 83, 105, 107, 112, 118, 156, 157, 158, 162, 163, 169, 174, 180, 184, 186, 188, 191, 193, 196, 198–9, 202–3, 208–9, 211–14, 216, 217, 222–3, 229, 239, 243–4, 257–8, 264–6, 297, 321, 336, 341
Etkin, D. 286

Farrington, David P. ix
Feeley, M. 265
Ferguson, N. 353–4
Fijnaut, C. 157
Fishman, M. 157, 159, 167, 198, 209, 212, 277
Fiske, J. 180–81, 183–4, 186, 190–91
Foot, D. 241
Foucault, M. 79
Froot, K. 302
Fuller, L. 215

Gandy, O. 216, 223, 336
Gannon, J. 335
Garland, D. xii, xiii, 240, 242, 265, 267
Geertz, C. 190, 215, 216
Geller, W. 264
Giddens, A. xi, 155, 161, 227–8, 241 *passim*, 243, 227–8, 241, 243
Gillian, L. 182
Gitlin, T. 181, 191, 210
Goffman, E. xi, 41, 42, 46, 155, 157, 161, 180, 182, 183, 185, 212
Golding, P. 194, 210
Goldstein, J. 264
Gonzales, A. 327
Gowri, A. 223, 241–2, 244
Green, J. 242
Green, M. 344
Greenwood, P. 59, 65–6, 106, 112
Grosman, B. 74

Hackett, R. 210, 211
Hacking, I. 208, 216, 244
Haggerty, K. xi, xii, xv, 216, 222, 223, 239, 243, 265, 266, 336
Hall, B. 302
Hall, S. xvii
Hamilton, J. 197
Hamilton, L. 322
Harper, T. 324
Hartley, J. 173, 180, 184, 186, 189, 191, 212
Heimer, C. 226
Hollaran, J. 213
Hoover, J.E. 335
Hough, M. 257
Hudson, J. 85
Hunt, A. 347

Ignatieff, M. 329

Janus, E. 322, 331, 337, 354
Joh, E. 341
Johnston, L. 266
Jorgensen, B. 83, 257

Karrane, K. 215
Kean, T. 322
Kermode, F. 215
Kerry, J. 353
Kings, E. 258
Kitsuse, J. 217
Knorr-Centina, K. 215
Kokis, R. 103
Kramer, M. 215
Krane, J. 334
Kunreuther, H. 293

Lammare, M. 287
Latour, B. 239, 262
Lee, J. 74
Leman-Langlois, S. 331, 340
Lemert, E. 46, 53
Leon, J. 84
Levi, M. 334
Levy, M. 181, 213
Lindbeck, A. 227
Loader, I. x, 244, 266, 280
Lofland, J. 41, 42, 44, 47, 48
Logue, K. 313
Low, D. 286–7
Luhmann, N. 208

Lyman, S. 162, 192

McCabe, S. 118
McClean, J.D. 131, 137
McConville, M. 131, 142–3, 261, 265
McElrath, K. 291
McMahon, M. 157, 258
McQueen, R. 233, 235
Mann, E. 74
Manning, P. 8, 55, 99, 171, 257, 264
Marcus, G. 215
Marsland, D. 227
Matza, D. 43, 44, 45
Meehan, A. 261
Meyer, J. 83
Meyrowitz, J. 157, 178, 180, 183–4, 187, 188, 192, 193, 195, 196, 201, 208, 213
Midgley, M. 191
Mirless-Black, C. 264
Mistzal, B. 208
Monaco, J. 179, 183, 187, 190
Morris, N. 264
Morrison, W. 77
Moss, D. 289, 316
Moylan, J. 77
Moyers, B. 324
Moynihan, D. 261
Mueller, R. 337
Muir, W. 70
Mulkay, M. 190, 213
Murdock, G. 194, 210, 213, 215

Nardulli, P. 143
Nietzsche, F. 215

O'Malley, P. 222, 239, 241–2, 244, 260, 265
Orcutt, J. 212

Palm, R. 299
Paulu, B. 182
Pearson, G. 212
Pepinsky, H. 97
Petek, W. 299
Pietropaolo, D. 184, 215
Poindexter, J. 338
Polstein, R. 127
Porter, T. 289
Posner, M. 329
Poster, M. 265
Postman, N. 184, 186, 193, 201
Prout, A. 258
Punch, M. 161, 169
Putnam, H. 190, 191

Raban, J. 323, 336, 337
Ramsay, J. 74
Rayher, J. 241
Reichman, N. 226
Reiner, R. 157
Reiss, A. 70, 77, 84, 97, 161, 258, 264
Reuter, C. 319–20
Robinson, J. 181, 213
Rock, P. 42, 53, 159, 161, 244, 280
Rose, N. 239, 242–3, 268
Roshier, B. 199
Rubington, E. 42, 43, 44
Rubinstein, J. 74, 77–8, 99, 166
Rumsfeld, D. 338
Runciman, W.G. 189
Ryle, G. 190

Sanders, W. 106, 112
Scheppele, K. 215
Scheuer, M. 320
Schiller, D. 193, 217
Schlesinger, P. 185, 188, 194, 198, 202, 209, 210, 215
Schor, P. 349
Schur, E. 43
Scott, M. 162, 191
Seaton, J. 193, 198
Shearing, C. 84, 174, 216, 265, 266
Sheptycki, J. 244
Sherizen, S. 217
Sherman, L. 77
Simon, J. 353
Silverman, D. 112
Simms, N. 215
Simon, J. 223, 240, 265, 268
Skogan, W. 106, 118, 257
Skolnick, J. 66, 77
Slater, D. 216, 238, 280
Smith, A. 196, 197, 201
Southgate, P. 264
Sparks, R. 83, 84, 105, 117, 118
Squires, G. 267
Staples, W. 240
Stehr, N. xii
Stenning, P. 266
Stenson, K. 244

Stiglitz, J. 227
Stinchcombe, A. 258
Strange, S. 222
Sullivan, T. 243, 244
Sutcliffe, F. 118

Takei, C. 352
Tavaras, C. 258
Taylor, C. 319
Taylor, I. 171
Thompson, J. 208
Thompson, W. 341
Tuchman, G. 168, 196, 202
Tumber, H. 213
Turner, B. 212
Turow, J. 216, 217, 238, 336

Van Maanen, J. 164
Van Outrive, L. 157
Varhinger, H. 215
Verdun-Jones, S. 130
Voumvakis, S. 163, 212

Wagner-Pacifici, R. 191
Wall, D. 334
Wallace, L. 286, 288, 290, 297, 300, 303, 311
Walsh, W. 258
Webster, F. 217
Weinberg, M. 42, 43, 44
Welch, M. 334, 353
West, M. 244
Westley, W. 77
Wheeler, G. 159, 162, 167, 198
White, R. 286, 288, 290, 297, 300, 303
Whitaker, R. 331, 336, 338–9, 352, 354
Williams, C. 77
Williams, R. 186
Wilson, O. 66, 70
Wood, D. xi
Worzel, R. 243

Yagoda, B. 215

Zelizer, V. 241–2
Zhao, Y. 210, 211

For Product Safety Concerns and Information please contact our EU representative GPSR@taylorandfrancis.com
Taylor & Francis Verlag GmbH, Kaufingerstraße 24, 80331 München, Germany

www.ingramcontent.com/pod-product-compliance
Ingram Content Group UK Ltd.
Pitfield, Milton Keynes, MK11 3LW, UK
UKHW050800180926
475701UK00008B/1163
* 9 7 8 1 1 3 8 3 7 8 6 9 8 *